WEB OF HATE

WEB OF HATE

Inside Canada's Far Right Network

WARREN KINSELLA

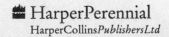
HarperPerennial
HarperCollins*Publishers*Ltd

To Suzanne,
with love

Photograph of Kelly Lyle courtesy of Harvey Kane.
Photograph of Bill Harcus and Brett Hayes courtesy of Harvey Kane.
Photograph of Nationalist Party of Canada courtesy of Bernie Farber.

First published in hardcover by HarperCollins Publishers Ltd: 1994
First HarperPerennial edition: 1995

Canadian Cataloguing in Publication Data

Kinsella, Warren, 1960-
    Web of hate : inside Canada's far right network

1st HarperPerennial ed.
Includes index.
ISBN 0-00-638051-4

1. White supremacy movements – Canada.   2. Fascism – Canada.
3. Racism – Canada.   4. Canada – Race relations.   I. Title.

FC104.K55 1995   305.8'00971   C94-932395-0
F1035.AIK5 1995

---

95 96 97 98 99 ❖ HC 10 9 8 7 6 5 4 3 2 1

Printed and bound in the United States

Contents

THANKS

Dozens of people over the years have assisted me as I probed Canada's organized hate groups. It is not an exaggeration to state that some of them have risked their lives to do so. Many of those who assisted me are listed below. Others, for reasons that will shortly become obvious, I cannot name here.

Before I thank anyone, however, I would like to emphasize one important point: this book is the product of my own observations, and is reflective of my own opinions. It does not represent anyone else's point of view—or any government's point of view—in any way whatsoever.

In British Columbia, I have been greatly assisted by Alan Dutton and others at the Canadian Anti-Racism Education and Research Society; David Lethbridge and his Salmon Arm Coalition Against Racism; Michael Peters; and journalist Terry Gould. Special thanks also go out to my West Coast research team: David Plewes, Lisa Cordasco and James Villeneuve.

In Alberta, where I first encountered organized hate in March 1980,

I have been befriended and assisted by many, including: my former city editor at *The Calgary Herald*, Dave Pommer; filmmaker Larry Ryckman; Calgary lawyer Hal Joffe; University of Calgary professor David Bercuson; and Edmonton lawyer Tom Engel. Deserving of special mention are Keith Rutherford, who has continued to battle racism after a brutal attack by neo-Nazi skinheads; Harvey Kane, who has placed himself in danger's way many times to provide me with much of the information found in this book; Gillian Steward, my managing editor at *The Calgary Herald*, who gave me the latitude I needed to make my first investigation into the Aryan Nations in 1986; and my award-winning photographer pal at the *Herald*, Larry MacDougal, who tells me that I aged him by a year with every venture we made into neo-Nazi territory.

In Saskatchewan, I have been helped by Connie Sampson at *The Prince Albert Daily Herald*, who has done outstanding work on the activities of provincial Aryan Nations leader Carney Milton Nerland, as well as Peter J. Gilmer at the Saskatchewan Coalition Against Racism.

In Manitoba, I was greatly assisted by Helmut Loewen of the Manitoba Coalition Against Racism; Joanne Faryon at *The Winnipeg Sun*; and Winnipeg police officers Doug Zaporzan and Conrad Gislason. Special mention goes to University of Manitoba professor Peter St. John and his family, for their kindness and hospitality—and to my friend at *The Winnipeg Free Press*, Dan Lett, who assisted me on one memorable "Nazi hunt" in March 1993.

In Ontario, many people have helped to make *Web of Hate* a reality. At the Canadian Jewish Congress, I have been assisted by Manuel Prutschi; at the B'nai Brith, I received the help of Karen Mock, Warren Bass and Lorne Shipman. Others who have helped include Avvy Go at the Chinese Canadian National Council and Tony Davy at the Black Business and Professional Association. Journalists who have taken time to keep me on the right path include Catherine Allman; Derek Raymaker; Charlie Greenwell; Stevie Cameron and Kirk Makin at *The Globe and Mail;* Julian Sher and his book *White Hoods;* Scot Magnish at *The Ottawa Sun;* Howard Goldenthal at "the fifth estate"; many of my students at Carleton University's School of Journalism; Jonathan Ferguson at *The Toronto Star;* plus Jane Taber, Ian MacLeod and Peter Hum at *The Ottawa Citizen.* Others who have helped me are Charles Mojsej at the Canadian Human Rights Commission; Stan Farber; Malcolm Lester; policy analyst Dan Hayward; and University of Guelph professor Stan Barrett, who contributed greatly to my understanding of this issue with his 1987 book, *Is God a Racist?*

At my "day job," I am indebted to the people who always made sure I was aware of developments in this area: Suzanne Dompierre, Roméo LeBlanc, Marc Laframboise, Frank Schiller, Joan Lajeunesse, Scott Shepherd, Bruce Hartley, Phil Goodwin and Randy McCauley. Thanks also go to David Dingwall and Jean Chrétien, who always encouraged me to pursue my interest in this subject. Special mention goes to three extraordinarily brave men who have never let me down, and who have become great friends along the way: Ian Kagedan at the B'nai Brith, who always returns my unending phone calls; Detective Dan Dunlop, whose Anti-Hate Unit at the Ottawa Police Force has become a model for the rest of Canada; and Bernie Farber, who has given me his time, his support and even a bed to sleep on.

In Quebec, I have been assisted by Martin Thériault at the Canadian Centre on Racism and Prejudice, and Jack Silverstone at the Canadian Jewish Congress.

In the Maritimes, thanks go to my friend Brian Tobin, Charlie Perry at *The Times-Transcript* in Moncton and various people at the Canadian Jewish Congress.

In the United States, I have received the wise counsel of Irwin Suall at the Anti-Defamation League. Also helpful were former Silent Brotherhood member Tom Martinez; journalist Kevin Flynn; FBI agent Wayne Manis; and Leonard Zeskind at the Centre for Democratic Renewal.

Most of all, however, I thank Phyllis Bruce for taking a chance on me; Helen Heller, my agent, and the person who urged me to write this book; my parents, who brought me up to fight intolerance, wherever it exists; and my wife, Suzanne, who sacrificed the most to make

Web of Hate a reality. Suzanne's love, patience and advice kept me going through some difficult times.

Thank you, all.

W.K.

WEB OF HATE

1
A DEADLY WEB

They are known as anti-Semites, or white supremacists, or neo-Nazis, or racial separatists, or Identity Christians, or Klansmen, or Creators, or Dualists, or Odinists, or any one of a score of other names. They come together to form groups with names like Aryan Nations, Heritage Front, Northern Hammerskins, Canadian Liberty Net or Church of the Creator. Their organizations come and go, but they—the men and women who hate—mostly do not. Year after year, from one end of Canada to the other, they persist. In small towns and big cities, on school grounds and in Armed Forces barracks, they defiantly cling to the tenets of hate, and they organize. They pass out leaflets at street-corners, they paint swastikas on synagogue walls, they burn crosses at night rallies, they set up hate lines, they deny the Holocaust. Some of them beat people up; some of them kill people.

In recent years, many Canadians have come to realize that the purveyors of hate are a tenacious lot, possessing ample resources and a fierce commitment to the ideology of bigotry. In a startlingly short time, the haters have moved from three-paragraph news items tucked behind the Classifieds to chilling front-page stories detailing assaults, threats and murders. Along with the cross-burnings and neo-Nazi rallies that have routinely taken place in every region of Canada since 1990, there have been other examples of the growing web of hate: assaults on non-whites and gays in suburban Vancouver by white supremacist skinheads; an attack by neo-Nazis on a retired Edmonton broadcaster that left him blind in one eye; the killing of an aboriginal man by a far right leader in Prince Albert; beatings and bombing plots by a Ku Klux Klan cell in Winnipeg; riots provoked by white supremacist groups in Toronto and Ottawa; the killings of two Montreal men by the teenage members of a homophobic neo-Nazi group; racially motivated battles in schoolyards in Moncton and Halifax and across the Atlantic provinces. The list is a long one.

More disturbing, perhaps, is that white supremacists and neo-Nazis are being found—with increasing frequency—in institutions that many had believed to be free from such contamination. In the summer of 1993, Canadians learned that about two dozen members of the elite Canadian Airborne Regiment were associated with far right groups. And that fall, during a federal election campaign, the Reform Party was confronted with evidence that some of its candidates had more than a passing acquaintance with anti-Semitism and white supremacy. Some weeks before he was expelled from the party, for example, York Centre candidate John Beck told one Toronto newspaper: "If an immigrant comes into Canada and gets a job for $150,000, he is taking jobs away from us . . . the Gentile people, the white people." (And another startling revelation came in August 1994, when Canadians learned that a leader of the neo-Nazi Heritage Front had been a paid informant of the Canadian Security Intelligence Service (CSIS). This was quickly followed by media reports that the Heritage Front informant, Grant Bristow, had "spied" on the CBC, the Canadian Jewish Congress and the Reform Party.)

These, of course, are the manifestations of hate that make their way into newspapers and television broadcasts. But there are many other examples, ones with which most Canadians are familiar: racist pamphlets left behind on a seat on a bus; anti-Jewish or anti-minority slogans spray-painted on the walls of buildings; snide references about immigrants and refugees by politicians who themselves are the descendants of immigrants and refugees. These are the incidents that generally go unreported by the news media, but are no less hurtful to their intended targets.

When confronted by the growing web of hate, it is the inclination of many Canadians—too many—to avert their eyes and cross to the other side of the street. Unaware, and in some cases uncaring, they persist in the belief that it is too dangerous to turn back the rising tide of hate and that it is too dangerous to get involved. But the simple fact is that, whether we like it or not, we *are* involved. The haters are here, and they are not going to go away.

In March of 1980, when I was 19 years old and a member of a Calgary punk rock band known as the Hot Nasties, I encountered organized racism for the first time.

On St. Patrick's Day, the Hot Nasties opened a concert for the popular British punk band 999. The concert took place at MacEwan Hall at the University of Calgary and drew a few hundred punkers from across southern Alberta. In punk circles, rock-star attitudes are frowned upon, and the line between performer and audience is often blurred, if not non-existent. So, when the Hot Nasties finished our short set, we climbed off the stage and into the crowd. We started to dance around with our pals.

About ten minutes into 999's performance, as dozens of punkers were slam-dancing and pogoing with wild abandon, I spotted a lot of movement about 30 feet away, to the left of the stage. I squinted through the maze of sweaty bodies and saw what appeared to be a group of men making salutes. Fascist salutes.

I turned to Alan Macdonald, lead singer of the Sturgeons, another Calgary punk band, and Ras Pierre Schenk, the Hot Nasties' guitarist. "Hey, are those guys over there actually making Nazi salutes?" I asked them.

Schenk and Macdonald looked where I was pointing. "I don't think so," Macdonald said. "Why would someone be doing something like that?"

Unconvinced, I pushed my way through the crowd, with Schenk not far behind. As I got closer, I could not, as the saying goes, believe my eyes. A group of large, muscular young men were, in fact, making Nazi salutes in the general direction of the stage. One of them, a stocky fellow with cropped blond hair, was wearing a T-shirt bearing the words "DROWN THE BOAT PEOPLE." In high school and first-year university, I had read about the Holocaust, and I knew a little about the Ku Klux Klan. But this was my first encounter with an overt and apparently organized display of racism, and it left me stunned. I became very angry.

I stepped up to the T-shirt. "I think you should stop doing that," I yelled over the wail of a 999 song.

He turned on me. "Who the fuck are you?"

"Doesn't matter who I am," I said. "But you should stop doing that right now."

"Fuck *you*," he said, moving closer, "you fucking *Jew*."

"I'm not Jewish, I'm Catholic and I'm Irish," I said. "And you should stop."

In an instant, an impressive brawl had broken out, involving me, Schenk, the neo-Nazis and members of various Calgary punk rock bands. Like most fights, it was difficult to know who is winning it when one is in the middle of it. But before long, the T-shirt and his friends had retreated from the hall, bloody, bruised and beaten. We patted ourselves on the back and continued to dance.

Following 999's last encore, our gang swung through the doors of MacEwan Hall, ready for a few beers. We stopped when we spotted the young fascists near the stairs, dabbing at their wounds. A few feet away, a group of university security officers was watching us closely; there would be no more fighting tonight. After a few curses were exchanged our group made its way towards the front doors. As we did so, the big Nazi in the T-shirt pointed at me.

"We'll be back," he said.

*

The man in the T-shirt was right. In the intervening years, as Canada's racist right has become increasingly visible, and increasingly violent, I believe that it has grown to become a significant social problem. There are many people who would dispute this conclusion, of course, but it can be fairly noted that those same people are usually heterosexual, white and not Jewish. After nearly a decade of research in organized hate, I have learned one thing above all else. I have learned that people's perspective on the problem of organized racism dramatically changes the first time they spot a swastika painted on their place of worship, or wake up to find a cross burning on the front lawn.

Since that disturbing night in March 1980, I have spent many hours attempting to answer the many difficult questions that surround this troubling phenomenon: *Who* are the men and women who make up Canada's hate movement? *What* threat do they pose to mainstream Canadian society, if any? *Where* are they found? *Why* are they growing stronger? *Web of Hate* is an attempt to answer these and other questions. Though it will not answer every question it raises, it is my hope that it will present the outlines of an issue that is as troublesome as it is frightening.

Fear, after all, is what these groups and individuals are all about. And, just as Canada's neo-Nazis and white supremacists work to frighten those they vilify—the non-whites, the disabled, the gays, the Jews, the "race-mixers"—it is also my intention, frankly, to shake up everyone who reads this book. I believe that in order for Canadians to be confronted with, and respond to, the reality of organized hate, they must see it the way its victims see it. They must see it close up, so close that they cannot ignore it.

There are many far right individuals and groups in Canada worthy of further examination—there are approximately 40 groups—but it would be impossible to deal with all of them in a single book. Throughout *Web of Hate*, therefore, I am primarily concerned with the most extreme elements of the various neo-Nazi and white supremacist groups—that is, those who advocate the use of violence or non-democratic means against the established order, sometimes known as the radical right—simply because these are the ones we need to be concerned about first. I will also profile several men who, while denouncing neo-Nazi and white supremacist groups, have become closely associated with those very groups. (For the sake of clarity, I have defined groups as "neo-Nazi" when they embrace traditional National Socialist ideology, in particular, anti-Semitism; "white supremacist" organizations are those whose immediate concern is race, and who have little or no interest in what is described as "the Jewish question." Individual members of groups, of course, may embrace both concerns.)

For approximately seven years now, I have been collecting information on Canada's racist right. For an equal length of time, I have been conducting interviews with the men and women who are leaders in Canada's hate movement—Jim Keegstra, Ernst Zundel, Wolfgang Droege, Terry Long, Malcolm Ross and many others. I have attended meetings of neo-Nazi groups in every part of Canada; I have witnessed cross-burnings; I have pored through their hate propaganda. At the same time, I have discussed this frightening social problem in hundreds of encounters with police officers, journalists, social workers, lawyers and human rights activists. With few exceptions, all agree: the problem is getting worse.

In the minds of the many editors I have argued with about this issue, organized hate is the province of tabloid television hosts and ethnic newspapers and not worthy of serious journalists. For others, organized hate is not significant because hooded Klansmen are not marching down city streets in great numbers, or because neo-Nazis have been unsuccessful in securing a majority in Parliament. With respect, they are wrong. Racism is growing in Canada.

Whenever I am asked to speak or write about organized hate groups, one question inevitably comes up. Why have I—a white, married, middle-class Gentile—devoted so much time to such a disturbing topic? To my great surprise, even minority activists have asked me this question, and it is one that still makes me a little angry, although I suppose I should be used to it by now. The implication is that the only people who *should* be concerned about hate are the victims of it. Racism should concern all fair-minded Canadians who care about the values upon which our society is based. We must continually safeguard those values and, as others have noted before me, we must never forget the lessons of history.

It is my hope that *Web of Hate* will introduce some of the key men and women who make up Canada's neo-Nazi and white supremacist groups, and their beliefs—however abhorrent you may find them. And it is equally my hope that you will see how their definition of "victim" changes all the time.

Anybody, in fact, can be one.

2

CANADA'S WESTERN KLAN

On Christmas Eve in 1865, six young men met in the law offices of Thomas M. Jones in Pulaski, Tennessee, for a few laughs. Before the evening was over, they would conceive, somewhat inadvertently, the beginnings of the modern white supremacist movement in America.

Gen. Robert E. Lee had surrendered a scant nine months earlier, and the young men—all of them former Confederate soldiers—were bored. Present on that fateful night were Calvin E. Jones, John B. Kennedy, Frank O.M. Cord, John C. Lester, Richard R. Reed and James R. Crowe. The six gathered around the fireplace in Jones's office, talking about the war. They were restless.

Like many Southerners, Messrs. Jones, Kennedy, Cord, Lester, Reed and Crowe were also a little angry. The economy of the South, from the plantations to the cities, had been shattered by the Civil War. There was widespread hunger and poverty; families had been torn apart. Moreover, the Union's hated Reconstruction policy seemed to have been specifically designed to humiliate the South and its bourbon aristocracy. And, perhaps worst of all, the North's occupation army still roamed Dixie, reminding every Confederate soldier of the extent of Lee's defeat.

Pulaski was a small town, 75 miles south of Nashville, and the last watering hole before the Alabama state line. It was named after a Polish hero of the American War of Independence. In 1865, only a few hundred people lived in Pulaski, and, for six energetic young men who had recently traded in their Confederate uniforms, there was very little to do. To alleviate their boredom, the six men decided that Christmas Eve to form a social club. It would be a secret society, but one primarily dedicated to the pursuit of good times.

The following week, the group's members met again to discuss their club, which one man wanted to call the Merry Six. Richard Reed, who had studied a little Greek, suggested calling the group Kuklos, which roughly translated means circle. John Kennedy, a former captain, added the designation "clan." After further discussion, much of it lubricated by liberal amounts of whiskey, the group settled on Ku Klux Klan. The name stuck.

Growing increasingly amused, the men started assigning various titles to positions within the Ku Klux Klan—all of them calculated to sound as ridiculous as possible. The head of the group was to be the Grand Cyclops. Second-in-command would be the Grand Magi; the Grand Turk would recruit members, and the Grand Scribe would act as secretary. Members would be called Ghouls. Their purpose, one founder later wrote, was "to have fun, make mischief and play pranks on the public." A few days later, the six pulled sheets over themselves, placed grotesque homemade masks on their faces—masks topped by pointed hats—and, with their identities protected, jumped on their horses and galloped through the streets of Pulaski. They caused quite a stir.

For the first year, the Ku Klux Klan was, by all accounts, a harmless fraternal organization that devoted most of its time to dreaming up elaborate hazing rituals and amusing pranks. But by late 1866, the Ku Klux Klan had grown to include cells from towns around Pulaski, and it had largely abandoned its founders' original fun-loving intent. The emancipation of slaves both infuriated and frightened the Klansmen. Dressed in white sheets, the Klan's horsemen started to roam the backroads at night, terrorizing blacks and Northern "carpetbaggers" with threats, beatings and, ultimately, lynchings. (The Klan was not alone in its advocacy of white supremacy; no less than Louisiana's Democrats resolved that "we hold this to be a Government of White People, made and to be perpetuated for the exclusive benefit of the White Race, and that the people of African descent cannot be considered citizens of the United States." Virtually every other Southern state enacted similar statutes.)

When Congress passed the Reconstruction Acts in early 1867— laws that abolished the Confederate state governments, divided up the South into military districts and gave civil rights to blacks—the Ku Klux Klan was whipped into a frenzy and membership in the secretive group boomed. In April 1867, Klansmen from several Southern states travelled to Nashville for their first convention, where they passed a resolution stating that their main objective was the "maintenance of the supremacy of the White Race in this Republic." They also pledged to oppose "social and political equality for Negroes and Congressional advocates of harsh Reconstruction measures." The Klansmen elected their first leader, ex-Confederate general and slave trader Nathan Bedford Forrest.

Forrest was an effective leader. Like a white supremacist missionary, he travelled throughout the South, quietly signing up new members and spreading the Klan gospel. By 1868, he could reliably claim 550,000 members across the Southern states. Simultaneously, reports of Klan-led church-burnings, shootings, hangings, torture, whippings and mutilations grew more frequent. An 1871 congressional committee, for instance, was told that "murders of Negroes [by the Klan] are so common as to render it impossible to keep accurate accounts of them." In 1868, the committee was told, more than 2,000 Florida blacks had been killed by the Klan, which tellingly referred to itself as the Invisible Empire, in less than a month.

Historical accounts of this troubled period in U.S. history are instructive. But the writings of an actual Ku Klux Klan "historian" are testament to the truly hateful nature of the Klan, past and present. The author is Louis Ray Beam, Jr., one-time Grand Dragon of the Texas chapter of the Knights of the Ku Klux Klan, and a Vietnam veteran. Widely revered in modern neo-Nazi and white supremacist circles, Beam is a close associate of many Canadian racist leaders and he is regarded as an expert in Klan lore, or klancraft. For that reason, Beam was invited by the Canadian Aryan Nations leader to testify at a 1991 Alberta Human Rights Commission Board of Inquiry into a cross-burning. (The board concluded its deliberations before Beam could be heard.) In his notorious 1983 book, *Essays of a Klansman*, Beam provides a twisted account of the Southerners' response to the Reconstruction Acts:

> Backing the negroes were the scalawags, local whites who often as draft dodgers had avoided service in the Confederate Army or, worse, who had fought with the North to destroy the Constitution. Allied with the scalawags were the carpetbaggers, unscrupulous adventurers from the lower classes of the Northern society as well as Semitic Jews, who descended on the South like a plague of locusts. A tripartite relationship of thievery, criminality and oppression was soon formed between negroes, scalawags and carpetbaggers. Backing this unholy alliance were the bayonets of the Union Army. . . .
>
> For the occupied South, to paraphrase Rudyard Kipling, time would be counted from the date "that the Saxons began to hate." Out of this darkness that was the Reconstruction appeared the white-hooded and robed men of the Ku Klux Klan. Like Cavalier Knights from King Arthur's Round Table, they rode forth to right the wrongs of oppression and defend the helpless widows and children of the dead Confederate soldiers. With a vengeance that only God-fearing men can exact, the Klan burst forth upon the Southland like first rays of the morning sun. A purifying, cleansing purge proceeded that preserved the South from total destruction and prevented its people from being entirely subjected.

By January 1869, with the Ku Klux Klan coming under increasing congressional scrutiny—and Reconstruction state governments acting against it—Forrest ordered the Invisible Empire disbanded. Although Klan-sponsored terrorism continued unabated for a year, the Ku Klux Klan had largely collapsed as an organized force by early 1870. In 1871, Congress passed a tough anti-Klan law, in which night-riding and the wearing of masks were prohibited, and hundreds of Klansmen were arrested. At this point, the Forrest-era Klan completely fell apart.

It would remain dormant until the fall of 1915, when the Ku Klux Klan was reincarnated through the efforts of William (Doc) Joseph Simmons. Alabama-born, Doc Simmons was a veteran of the Spanish-American War as well as a Methodist minister and failed medical student. He was a fiery and effective stump speaker. On October 15, 1915, Simmons rented a bus for 34 like-minded residents of Georgia; in the countryside outside Atlanta, he led the group in a cross-burning. The Ku Klux Klan was back in business.

Simmons had rebuilt the Invisible Empire for one purpose: money. Initially, he benefited from renewed interest in the Klan thanks to D.W. Griffith's pro-Klan film epic, *Birth of a Nation*. But after five years, he had not achieved the degree of support he had hoped for. This all changed, however, in 1920, the year Doc Simmons met two talented young publicists, Edward Y. Clarke and Elizabeth Tyler. Clarke and Tyler's company, the Southern Publicity Association, had previously represented the Salvation Army and the Red Cross, with modest results. But when Clarke and Tyler hooked up with Simmons in the summer of 1920, the trio soon experienced commercial success well beyond their collective imagination. Membership in the Ku Klux Klan soared—and so did revenues. For every $10 Klan initiation fee, Simmons, Clarke and Tyler received $8. The rest was shared with staff organizers, called kleagles. Targeting blacks, Jews, Orientals and, particularly, Catholics in its propaganda, the new Ku Klux Klan was a hit. In 15 months, Clarke and Tyler poured more than $200,000 into Klan coffers. Significantly, Doc Simmons's Klan started to attract an unprecedented degree of interest in the North, where anti-immigrant sentiment was widespread because of a worsening economy. By 1923, up to 6 million men and women were Klansmen in the United States; three former presidents were even reported to be associated with the Klan: Warren Harding, Woodrow Wilson and Harry S. Truman.

It was only a matter of time before the Invisible Empire would slip across the border into Canada. In late September 1921, both the *Montreal Daily Star* and the *Standard* revealed the formation of a Montreal branch of what the *Star* called "the famous Ku Klux Klan." Within months, cross burnings and Klan activity were being reported in and around Toronto, Hamilton, Ottawa, Sault Ste. Marie, Welland, London and even Niagara Falls. In late 1922 in Oka, Quebec—a town that would later acquire a reputation for intolerance towards Natives—the rest house at the Gentlemen of St. Sulpice was burned to the ground by Klansmen. Eight other Catholic institutions were set ablaze by the Klan in the final months of 1922.

Then, as 1922 was drawing to a close, the Ku Klux Klan burst onto the scene in western Canada with a single dramatic and horrifying act: the burning of St. Boniface College, a Catholic institution, in Winnipeg. The arson had been preceded by a written warning from the Klan.

Ten students were killed in the St. Boniface fire. When asked about the murders, Doc Simmons denied responsibility, stating, "The Ku Klux Klan is [not in] any way responsible for incendiary fires in Canada or elsewhere."

In the 70-odd years since it made its first appearance in Canada, the Ku Klux Klan has enjoyed varying degrees of success in different regions of the country, from the Atlantic provinces to British Columbia. But apart for one brief period in the early 1980s, the Klan has always found the most fertile ground west of the Lakehead.

This may be because Canadian westerners, like American Southerners, have never particularly felt close to the locus of power. Or, it may be the result of resentment towards Roman Catholic French Canadians, whom westerners traditionally feel have been the primary—or sole—beneficiaries of Confederation. Or, perhaps, it may be the outcome of the anti-establishment "frontier" mentality that persists in the rural west. Whatever the reason, the Klan's strength in western Canada cannot be denied. At the height of its powers in Saskatchewan alone, it could boast of the allegiance of nearly 40,000 members. In June 1929, the Klan joined with that province's Conservatives to dislodge the Liberal Party's 24-year grip on power. In its day, it was a formidable force.

Following the fatal fire at St. Boniface College, it is perhaps encouraging that the Klan did not achieve a great many victories in Manitoba. In the summer of 1924, there was a visit to Winnipeg by Oklahoma Klansman James R. Bellamy, who warned that Canada was "being overrun with undesirable sects and beliefs." Despite Bellamy's hopes, the Manitoba Klan remained literally and figuratively invisible until precisely four years later. Then, in June 1928, one Daniel C. Carlyle made an appearance at a downtown Winnipeg dance hall. The former streetcar operator railed against "the scum of papist Europe" and Jews, whom he termed "slavemasters throttling the throats of white persons to enrich themselves." About 150 men and women attended Carlyle's meeting. After a number of newspaper exposés—and the resulting public outcry—Carlyle apologetically slipped from the scene. He reappeared years later in Saskatchewan as a campaigner for leftwinger Tommy Douglas's successful 1935 bid for federal office.

In British Columbia, the Ku Klux Klan improved only marginally on its poor showing in Manitoba. It did, however, come to public notice rather early. In November 1921, calls for new members started to appear in B.C. newspapers; pamphlets produced by the Canadian Knights and Ladies of the Ku Klux Klan in Vancouver declared that the KKK stood for "Canada for Canadians, Anglo-Saxons for Anglo-Saxonism, White race for White race." An office called the Executive Chambers of the Imperial Palace of the Invisible Empire was established in West Vancouver. The Vancouver-based group made a dramatic bid for rural membership in the November 17, 1922, edition of the Cranbrook *Courier*, in which it ran the following advertisement:

KU KLUX KLAN!

Applications for Membership in the Cranbrook Klan No. 229 will be received by the undersigned during his two-day stay in Cranbrook, B.C., December 8th and 9th, when Klan No. 229 will be organized.

ALL APPLICATIONS MUST BE IN WRITING

All applicants must be British subjects, between the ages of 21 and 40 and must be qualified horsemen possessing the necessary skill and daring to uphold law and order at all costs.

H. MONCROFT, CHIEF KLANSMAN, CANADIAN DIVISION

No one had ever heard of H. Moncroft before, but one thing was certain about the American Klansman: no one would ever hear of him again. The Canadian Knights and Ladies of the Ku Klux Klan fell apart. British Columbia's aspiring Klansmen were therefore obliged to bide their time, until the fall of 1925, when three Oregon Klan organizers appeared on the scene.

The group's leader was Louisiana resident Luther I. Powell, a clever bigot who had turned the Ku Klux Klan into a formidable force in the Pacific Northwest of the United States. He hoped to do the same in B.C. Said one of his kleagles about the provincial Klan's objectives: "We don't go for lynching or taking the law into our own hands. We are bound by oath to conform to the lawful and constitutional authorities. We stand for the supremacy of the White race, the exclusion of Orientals, the elimination of dope, and are after political grafters." The B.C. Klan eagerly devoted its energies to mining the province's apparently endless seam of anti-Oriental sentiment. But the provincial government had beaten them to it, with a variety of viciously racist laws, among them the Chinese Immigration Act of 1885, which eventually placed a head tax of $500 on every Chinese immigrant. After returning to Washington State to attend to business, Powell was denied re-entry by immigration officials. Once again, the Klan faded away.

It did, however, meet with a certain degree of prosperity in

Alberta. In April 1923, *The Calgary Herald* reported that Roman Catholic churches in the city had received arson threats from a previously unheard-of Klan chapter. As was—and is—so often typical of police officials confronted with revelations about far right activity, the Calgary chief of police dismissed these and other threats, calling them the work of "a crank." But John James Moloney, for one, was no crank. Born a Roman Catholic in Hamilton, Ontario, in February 1897, Moloney had served as an altar boy under the direction of Father Charles E. Coughlin, who would go on to infamy as one of the most powerful anti-Semites in the history of the United States. As a young man, Moloney broke with the church after being fired from a lay missionary position. By August 1922, he had converted to Presbyterianism and was giving fiery anti-papist speeches. The youthful polemicist set his sights on Alberta's untapped market of white supremacists in the mid- to late-1920s. The Klan was headquartered in Edmonton, where Moloney wrote anti-papist tirades and assiduously built alliances with Orangemen throughout the province, signing up thousands of Klansmen in dozens of towns from Camrose to Wetaskiwin to Ponoka. Cross-burnings were reported across the province, as were beatings in Red Deer, and even a tarring and feathering of a Lacombe black-skinned blacksmith who was believed to have fraternized with a white woman.

Moloney's newspaper, *The Liberator*, boasted a circulation of 250,000. In it, he asserted that the pope—and Quebec's Catholic Church—were conspiring to achieve "total domination" of Canada. He also berated politicians who were "catering to Rome" and Liberal MPs who were trying to "solidify the foreign vote." He circulated copies of the infamous anti-Semitic hoax document that had been produced by the Russian czar's secret police, "The Protocols of the Learned Elders of Zion." With the assistance of the Orange Order of Alberta, Moloney also petitioned against the "promiscuous use of French on the radio." He burned crosses at Edmonton racetracks and assisted in union-busting efforts at the Crowsnest Pass.

Politically, Moloney also enjoyed good fortune. In volume one of his autobiography, the appropriately titled *Story of My Life*, he took credit for electing Daniel K. Knott as mayor of Edmonton by informing the electorate that the incumbent, Liberal Party supporter Maj. Jim Douglas, was a "Papist sympathizer" who was behind "a plot of a Jesuitic nature to bring our city under the police leadership of a Roman Catholic colonel." United Farmers of Alberta Premier J.E. Brownlee was strangely tolerant of the Ku Klux Klan, giving it a provincial charter. His minister of agriculture, George Hoadley, stated that the Klan's objectives were "along Dominion lines."

The triumphs were not long-lived. By 1933, Moloney and his Alberta Klan were being buffeted by a score of prosecutions and lawsuits. For some Klansmen, charges of theft, criminal libel and fraud led to jail terms. In 1935, Moloney slunk out of the province, his Alberta Ku Klux Klan a memory for all but two or three hundred members who would meet for occasional barbecues.

For much of the 1920s and 1930s, Manitoba, Alberta and British Columbia were all plagued by Invisible Empire infestations. But none of those provinces, even taken together, could hope to equal the Ku Klux Klan's unprecedented conquest of Saskatchewan. From the late 1920s to the early 1930s, the province's Klan was an awesome force. It toppled a government; it established more than a hundred chapters across the province; and it signed up close to 40,000 members—the single most populous white supremacist organization in Canada's history. A number of theories exist about why Saskatchewan's Klan was so tremendously powerful. Julian Sher, author of *White Hoods: Canada's Ku Klux Klan*, notes that the Klan was used by "a Conservative party hungry for power," thereby enhancing both its legitimacy and its longevity. Martin Robin, the author of *Shades of Right: Nativist and Fascist Politics in Canada, 1920–1940*, the best book produced on Canada's Ku Klux Klan, writes: "The Ku Klux Klan did not invent prejudice in Saskatchewan. It was already there in abundance, rooted in groups and processes—economic, social and political—perceived as threatening to the status and power of native, Anglo-Saxon, Protestant Saskatchewanians."

Although people in Saskatchewan may have been ready to be culti-vated by a few shrewd Ku Klux Klan manipulators, the harvest did not come until comparatively late. In November 1926, three Indiana men, former South Bend Exalted Cyclops Hugh Finley (Pat) Emmons, Klan organizer Lewis A. Scott and Scott's son, Harold, joined forces to establish the Saskatchewan Realm of the Invisible Empire of the Knights of the Ku Klux Klan. Emmons was a drinker, a gambler and even a snitch (after a power struggle with another Klan leader earlier in 1926, Emmons had revealed a few Klan secrets to a U.S. senate committee). But he was selected by the Scotts because of his formida-ble reputation as a tub-thumping, barn-burning white supremacist salesman. Not long before Christmas 1926, Emmons and the two Scotts braved the elements and made their way towards Regina, where they set up shop at a local hotel. They were, as Martin Robin puts it, "a trio of Hoosier hucksters."

The trio wasted no time. They printed up a pamphlet titled "Why I Intend To become A Klan Member," and they placed advertisements in newspapers alerting locals to Klan organizational meetings. Within a very short period, the Saskatchewan Ku Klux Klan had struck it rich. Emmons and the Scotts claimed that 40,000 $10 memberships were sold, earning the recruits hate propaganda as well as the details of secret passwords. When one considers that Saskatchewan's population at the time was 750,000, this was an impressive turnout. Documents in Saskatchewan's provincial archives reveal that in the tiny village of Woodrow, for example, 153 residents were members of the Klan out of a population of 218. In its publications, the Klan took aim at the large number of immigrants then flooding into Saskatchewan, people it called "non-preferred Continentals [who were] conniving to Balkanize" Canada. "Many, if not most" of the immigrants were Roman Catholics, the Klan darkly noted. Liberal amounts of anti-crime rhetoric were thrown in for good measure. As messages go, it was simple-minded and slanderous, but in Saskatchewan, it sold.

At well-attended rallies held in every corner of the province, Emmons described the Ku Klux Klan as "the greatest Christian, benevolent fraternal organization in the world today" and he occasionally described himself as a Canadian from "south of Toronto." In one May 1927 speech, he declared that the Invisible Empire favored "one Language—English—from coast to coast" and warned that any "Jap, Negro or Chinaman" who threatened the business interests of "white Canadians" would be driven out. This sort of white supremacist ultra-Protestantism played well with Saskatchewanians. One Moose Jaw "Konklave," on June 7, 1927, drew nearly 10,000 Saskatchewan Klansmen, some of them arriving from Regina on Canadian Pacific Railway cars.

To tend to the growing empire, Emmons set up an office in Regina and hired experienced staff. He also offered honoraria of up to $25 to ministers who agreed to speak at Klan rallies; many did. When asked what the key to his phenomenal success was, Emmons later recalled: "We sent people 'antis.' Whatever we found that they could be taught to hate and fear, we fed them. We were out to get the dollars and we got them."

By late 1927, however, Saskatchewan Klansmen were starting to ask where, precisely, their membership dollars were going. Sensing, correctly, that the boom was about to be lowered on their Klan scam, Emmons and the two Scotts slipped out of Saskatchewan in October, only ten months after their arrival. The Scotts repaired to Australia with some $500,000 plundered from Klan coffers, while Emmons made his way to Florida with what he said was "only" $20,000. Emmons was later indicted in Saskatchewan for theft, and, surprisingly, agreed to return for his trial. Even more surprising was his eventual acquittal; he proved to the court's satisfaction that the Toronto-based Imperial Palace of the Canadian Klan had given him permission to keep virtually every cent he collected.

Alarmed by the scandal and the fallout it would have on Ku Klux Klan fortunes, the group's Toronto leaders hurriedly dispatched veteran Klan organizer "Doctor" J.H. Hawkins to Saskatchewan to fill the void left by Emmons and the Scotts. Reportedly an optometrist by profession, Hawkins was also a mesmerizing speaker, and he easily recouped what had been lost in the dark days of the Emmons/Scott scandal. He did so with fervid appeals to the baser instincts. In one July 1928 speech in Saskatoon, for instance, the Virginia-born Hawkins told his audience: "Let us see that the slag and scum that refuse to assimilate and become 100 per cent Canadian is skimmed off and thrown away."

Hawkins's anti-Catholic wheat belt crusade was also bolstered by the presence of the unchallenged king of anti-papism, John J. Moloney, who travelled from Alberta to Saskatchewan in early 1928. Like a white supremacist tag-team, Hawkins and Moloney together pushed the prejudices of Sakatchewanians to new heights. The Klan's powers seemed almost limitless.

By 1928, the Ku Klux Klan could boast of the allegiance of no fewer than eight mayors, 11 village clerks, seven reeves, 12 secretary-treasurers and 37 councillors. Chiefs of police, ministers, World War I vets, doctors, teachers, justices of the peace, lawyers and scores of Orangemen were also part of the Saskatchewan Klan's political power base. It could even count on the occasional support of no less than R.B. Bennett, the federal Conservative leader and future prime minis-ter. Favored targets were separate Catholic schools and French lan-guage training (which was virtually non-existent in any event). In Gravelbourg, a school district where Catholics were in the majority, Klan propagandists alleged that the Union Jack was being removed from classrooms only to be replaced by crucifixes and other detested symbols of papism. A prosecution of anti-Catholic ratepayers who had refused to tender their assessment—swayed by the Klan agitprop—was dismissed by two justices of the peace, Klansmen both.

But Hawkins and Moloney had an even larger and more powerful target in Saskatchewan: Liberal Premier James G. Gardiner.

Although Gardiner's Liberals maintained a healthy majority in the provincial legislature, the premier was worried about the Klan rallies and the Klan-inspired court cases. In a letter to Prime Minister William Lyon Mackenzie King dated August 23, 1927, Gardiner wrote: "There has been organized in the Province of Saskatchewan a Ku Klux Klan . . . some of the organizers have come to the West from Ontario. It would appear, from their general activities in the Province, that the main object of the organization is to spread propaganda which will be of benefit to the opponents of the Government, both Provincial and Federal, at the time of the next election." Gardiner was not indulging in overstatement. By the time of the January 1928 Throne Speech debate, the Liberal premier was engaged in a full-bore battle with the Ku Klux Klan and its chosen ballot-box proxies, the Progressives and the Conservatives. The Klan's main object, Gardiner told the legislature on January 30, "is to play upon the prejudices of the people . . . We in Canada have never found it necessary to get proper enforcement of law and order by having an organization parade about the country wearing hoods over their heads so that people do not know who they are. Any man who has not the backbone and courage to stand in the open has no place in British institutions of government."

Gardiner continued his crusade against the Saskatchewan Klan for much of 1928 and 1929, marshalling sworn affidavits and statistics to support his argument. He was met, every step of the way, by Klansmen and crypto-Klansmen who could smell power. At an election rally in the town of Davidson, for example, powerful Klan barrister J.F. Bryant was joined onstage by a confident young Prince Albert lawyer who railed against French language instruction; the lawyer's name was John G. Diefenbaker. Sure that Saskatchewanians would reject bigotry, Gardiner called an election for June 1929 and was beaten. For the first time since Saskatchewan had become a province, in 1905, the Liberals lost their control of the legislature. The Grits dropped from 52 to 26 seats, while the Conservatives shot from four to 24. With the assistance of the Progressives, the Conservative leader, Dr. J.T.M. Anderson, formed a minority government.

As Anderson dutifully enacted a series of anti-French measures, his confidants, particularly John J. Moloney, merrily torched crosses, and revelled in their new power. From inauspicious beginnings only three years earlier, Moloney and Hawkins had built a Ku Klux Klan that could claim thousands of members and dozens of chapters in every corner of the province. And, most significant of all, Moloney and his hooded gang could claim, with justification, to have brought a government to its knees. For Saskatchewan's Ku Klux Klan, it was a very good time.

Almost six decades later, and hundreds of miles west, the Imperial Wizard of the Invisible Empire Association of Alberta, Knights of the Ku Klux Klan, pauses to reflect on the good old days, when John J. Moloney and his legion of night riders inspired fear and respect across Alberta and Saskatchewan. "In 1927," says the Klansman, "the Grand Master of the Orange Order asked Ku Klux Klan organizers from the United States to come here, to Alberta, to organize the Klan. Mr. John Moloney eventually ended up leading a Klan organization here, and he incorporated the Klan officially in September 1932. That lasted until 1950. When I moved here in 1965, I joined the Oddfellows Fraternal Order and the Klan as well."

He pauses. "The Klan was still in existence then, in a very minor way. It was viewed as a very Protestant organization here, because the organization in the 1930s, and even before that, got its members from the Orange Order. In fact, I still view the Klan as being a white fraternity, basically. There are provisions in the Klan's charter where people [belonging to minority groups] may join as registered supporters. I can't say that has ever happened, but if a number of people who want to join who are neither Christian nor white . . ." He trails off, saying nothing for ten full seconds. "Then I think that the natural developments should take their course."

Meet Teàrlach Barra Eoin Ros Dunsford Mac a'Phearsoin, professional herbalist, registered minister of the National Spiritist Church, maligned Ku Klux Klan leader, convicted criminal and modern heir to the legacy of John J. Moloney.

Mac a'Phearsoin is one of Canada's more elusive white supremacist leaders; he very rarely grants interview requests. When he is finally pressured into attending one, in a small room in a deserted building in northeast Calgary, he comes armed with a tape recorder and a dozen or so strangely worded letters testifying to his good character. In person, he is somewhat shy, shielding his eyes behind a tinted pair of prescription glasses; he favors suits, and his beard is kept neatly trimmed. He does not drink or smoke. When asked a question he does not like, he flips through sheafs of documents covered with his spidery handwriting, hoping to change the subject, or he launches into an obscure dissertation about Moloney or the true history of the Invisible Empire. He is clearly defensive about his beloved Klan, repeatedly insisting—as so many other far right leaders do—that it is not anti-Semitic or white supremacist but merely "a white Christian fraternal organization." To buttress the point, he even produces his résumé, which states, among other things, that he "assists the Alberta Human Rights Commission with regards to matters of concern to the Alberta Jewish community."

Born Ivan Ross Macpherson on August 8, 1948, in Charlottetown, P.E.I., the future Klan leader was abandoned by his parents. He was later adopted by a childless couple, Evelyn and Charles Dunsford, who named their new son Barry. Barry Dunsford spent much of his childhood on the island, where he distinguished himself as a rather odd youth, with an interest in the occult, séances and bagpiping. At the age of 12, he acquired an interest in the Ku Klux Klan from an uncle who had been a member some years earlier, in Seattle. The uncle urged him to read about the Klan's history. He did so, and was soon seen embracing a decidedly conservative outlook on the world. He eschewed long hair, for example, because it was "an outward symbol of the acceptance of drugs." At the age of 17, and after he secured a certificate (honors) in typing at Union Commercial College in Charlottetown, the neatly barbered Barry Dunsford and his parents travelled west, to Calgary.

By the spring of 1972, Mac a'Phearsoin—who by now had adopted the Celtic form of his birth name to emphasize his Scottish origin—had started to organize with the help of four other white supremacists, one of them his mother. After perusing provincial records, Mac a'Phearsoin had learned, to his surprise, that there was no existing claim to ownership over the Ku Klux Klan appellation or its various insignia. In May 1972, he and his colleagues promptly registered the Confederate Klans of Alberta as a society under the provincial Societies Act. In its charter, the group declared that one of its objectives was "to attempt to preserve, by legal means, chiefly through public educational propaganda and mutual fraternity, the traditions and ideals of the Celtic and Anglo-Saxon races, or more generally, the traditions and ideals of the white races." There were five members: three in Calgary and two in Banff. (Mac a'Phearsoin was fond of Banff and its environs, occasionally driving there with some of his friends to consume a few tabs of LSD.) Mac a'Phearsoin was named Imperial Wizard of the Confederate Klans of Alberta and declared himself a foe of communism, abortion and drug abuse. After receiving a few death threats, he purchased a .22-calibre revolver for $51 from a gunsmith in Okotoks.

In the spring of 1972, Mac a'Phearsoin claimed and was given copyright over a number of Ku Klux Klan symbols by the federal copyright office in Ottawa. Among the insignia registered that year were "unpublished artistic works" such as "Klansman on Horse" and the infamous "Triple K" symbol, often seen stitched on Klan robes, the "Blood Drop" symbol and "Midnight Mystery." Over the coming decade, Mac a'Phearsoin would attempt to license or sell rights to the Ku Klux Klan insignia to a variety of neo-Nazi groups, including the Canadian branch of the Aryan Nations. (The Aryan Nations was for many years the most virulently anti-Semitic group in Canada, and one of the most violence-prone.) In February 1986, he successfully sold rights to his symbols to South Carolina Grand Dragon Robert Echols Scoggin. For $5,000 (U.S.), Scoggin was given U.S. rights to five Klan symbols for a 50-year period. Like members of the Aryan Nations, Scoggin was an energetic hate-monger: in February 1966, an overwhelming majority of the U.S. House of Representatives had found Scoggin and six other Klan leaders in contempt of Congress for refusing to turn over Ku Klux Klan records to the Committee on Un-American Activities. Scoggin received a fine and a year in prison.

"I have known Dr. Teàrlach Mac a'Phearsoin for many years," Scoggin said in 1982, "and know him to be a loyal Klansman and

Imperial Wizard of the Ku Klux Klan . . . No true Klansperson has hate for anyone because of race, creed or color. Pride of race does not mean prejudice."

By August 1972, Mac a'Phearsoin was claiming there were 11 klaverns across the province, five in Calgary, four in Edmonton, one in Red Deer and one in Lethbridge. Members, he said, numbered up to 325 Albertans, some of them drawn to the Klan by newspaper advertisements. Alberta Attorney-General Merv Leitch told reporters at the time that the RCMP had investigated Mac a'Phearsoin's group and had come away unconcerned about the potential threat posed by the embryonic Confederate Klans. No attempt would be made to decertify the group, Leitch said, because the Klansmen were entitled to registration, "no matter how repugnant one might find their objectives." In September 1972, the Confederate Klansmen declared their support for the Progressive Conservatives in the federal election.

Then, in September 1974, the Confederate Klans of Alberta suffered a blow from which it never recovered: Teàrlach Dunsford Mac a'Phearsoin killed a man. A non-white man.

The Mexican, Elias Acuilar Ramirez, was 21 when Mac a'Phearsoin brought him home to his parents' place on Centre Street in Calgary. The two had met earlier that summer in Santa Rosa, Ramirez's home town; they quickly became close friends. After a brief discussion, Mac a'Phearsoin's parents agreed to take Ramirez into their home. The Dunsfords said they would provide him with room, board, clothes and a small salary—although what services Ramirez would perform was never made clear.

Just before 11:00 o'clock on September 12, 1974, and three days after the arrival of Martinez, the Dunsfords were in their beds, sound asleep. Mac a'Phearsoin and Ramirez, meanwhile, were down in the Dunsfords' basement, in the Klan leader's bedroom. On the walls, Confederate flags, Klan certificates and Civil War lithographs had been tacked up. Knotted ropes hung from the ceiling. Scattered here and there was correspondence from Ku Klux Klan leaders from across North America.

At precisely 11 p.m., a single shot rang out. Evelyn Dunsford jumped out of bed and ran down the stairs. She found her son in the hallway, the $51 revolver in his hands. He was crying. "My God," Mac a'Phearsoin wailed, "it can't be, it can't be." His mother peered into his bedroom, where she saw Martinez's body sprawled on the bed. His trousers were pulled down and his penis was exposed. There was a single bullet hole in the Mexican's chest, two inches below a tattooed peace symbol.

Mac a'Phearsoin appeared to be in a trance, mumbling to himself. His mother hugged him, then went upstairs to call the police.

That night, Det. Loren J. Shields was working traffic detail in a uniform car. Shortly past 11:00, his car and another received a call about the shooting on Centre Street. The officers sped to the nondescript home, where they were met at the door by Mac a'Phearsoin. He was wearing a nightgown and he was weeping uncontrollably. "He's dead," Mac a'Phearsoin told Shields. "He's been shot."

"Where is the person who has been shot?" Shields asked.

Sobbing, Mac a'Phearsoin led the police officers downstairs. The Dunsfords hovered in a doorway, blinking in the light; they did not appear to understand what was going on, Shields would later recall. At the door to his bedroom, Mac a'Phearsoin pointed at the body of Ramirez. Shields checked the body for a pulse; there was none.

"Where is the weapon?" he asked. Mac a'Phearsoin led him to an adjoining room, where the revolver had been placed on a chair, under a Confederate flag. "We were arguing," Mac a'Phearsoin said, crying. "The gun went off. I think he's dead. Help me, please, dear God, I think I've shot him."

To Shields and his police colleagues, there appeared to be little doubt that Mac a'Phearsoin had, in fact, shot Ramirez. Shields placed the Klan leader under arrest, then led him outside to his cruiser. Mac a'Phearsoin did not resist. He was charged with criminal negligence causing death. His parents posted bail.

Many years later, Loren Shields is asked whether Calgary police found it significant that the Imperial Wizard of the Confederate Klans of Alberta had shot and killed a non-white. Says Shields: "We didn't discuss the Klan. We didn't really question him in regard to that. There was always some speculation as to what the real motivation was, but we never established a motive for it to be murder. You could speculate all you wanted. It could have been a homosexual thing, or it could have been a situation where he didn't like Mexicans. No one knew."

Nor, apparently, did anyone care. At his trial, held in December 1975, Mac a'Phearsoin was defended by A. Webster Macdonald, Sr., a colorful local lawyer who is listed as a reference on Mac a'Phearsoin's résumé. Evelyn Dunsford was called to give evidence about what she recalled of the death of Ramirez, whom she called "that poor boy." Mac a'Phearsoin's mother revealed that her son had been hospitalized before the shooting "for nerves a few times" and that he had been on medication on the night of Ramirez's death. "He could never hurt anything," Evelyn said. "He could never shoot anything. He couldn't even hook a fish or run over a gopher with his car."

Another witness, 26-year-old L.E. Burwell of Calgary, a one-time friend of Mac a'Phearsoin's, told the packed courtroom that he had warned the Klansman about the dangers of carrying a loaded revolver. Mac a'Phearsoin insisted on keeping it nearby, he said, because he was afraid of a possible attack by an anti-Klan activist. Burwell said his relationship with Mac a'Phearsoin ended when the Klansman "made a pass at me." When called to the stand himself, Mac a'Phearsoin stated that Ramirez had asked to see the revolver that evening. He claimed that Ramirez told him the loaded revolver could be "unloaded" by pulling back the hammer.

After a three-day trial, the Confederate Klans leader was fined $1,500 for criminal negligence causing death and $500 for dangerous use of a firearm without lawful excuse. "During this trial, we have heard much about the Ku Klux Klan," said Court of Queen's Bench Justice W.K. Moore, "but the operations of the Klan are irrelevant to this case."

In passing sentence, Moore told the court: "The accused's not turning away when he was loading the revolver showed a reckless disregard for the safety of Ramirez. The accused knew the gun was loaded.

He is an intelligent person and knew he was holding a lethal weapon."

The shooting and the resulting trial were the beginning of the end for the Confederate Klans of Alberta. In July 1975, the group was dissolved by the provincial government. But Alberta had not heard the last of Teàrlach Dunsford Mac a'Phearsoin.

"Crosses Burn at Red Deer," the newspaper headlines screamed. It was mid-August 1980, and the Klan, after a five-year silence, was back.

Late on a Sunday night, two cross shapes—one 15 feet long, the other 20—were left blazing in the lawns of two families in a quiet Red Deer neighborhood. Someone had splashed gasoline on the lawns while the families slept, then set them on fire. One of the families was Japanese; the other was Pakistani. The lawn-burnings had been preceded by another such event in Red Deer, in June, at the bungalow home of an East Indian. Tracked down by reporters, Teàrlach Mac a'Phearsoin, now leader of the newly minted Invisible Empire Association of Alberta, insisted that the incidents had "nothing to do with our members . . . I'm 99 per cent sure it was none of our 26 members in Red Deer that did this. In fact we condemn it. It was either a Nazi group out of Toronto, or some crazy local people." Despite his claim, though, Mac a'Phearsoin would later admit that he had warned the RCMP about the planned attacks seven days before they took place.

Two weeks after he condemned the Red Deer attacks, Mac a'Phearsoin and his followers had a change of heart. They decided to hold another cross-burning in the same city. "To clear up any misconceptions about the Klan," Mac a'Phearsoin declared, a Ku Klux Klan initiation ceremony would be held in a Red Deer park in October. About 25 people, half of them from Saskatchewan, would be inducted into the Invisible Empire in a ceremony presided over by South Carolina Grand Dragon Robert Scoggin. But the City of Red Deer fought back. Within hours, Mayor Ken Curle declared that a cross-burning would violate local open fire bylaws. "Burning crosses goes well beyond burning leaves," said Curle.

The cross-burning ceremony did not take place, but Teàrlach Mac a'Phearsoin had reincarnated himself. After five years, it appeared that the unfortunate little September 1974 incident involving carelessness with a firearm was now safely behind him. In February 1980, Mac a'Phearsoin and a group of like-minded white supremacists registered the Invisible Empire Association of Alberta, Knights of the Ku Klux Klan, under the province's Societies Act. In its three-page application, the Invisible Empire Association stated that it would fight for "racial and religious integrity . . . all members of this society will be required to marry within their own religious affiliation and racial colour." It also stated that it would work to "preserve the rituals, paraphernalia and symbols of the original Ku Klux Klan of the 1860s as headed by Gen. Nathan Bedford Forrest of Tennessee and as revived in 1915 by Col. the Reverend William Joseph Simmons of Georgia." Its head-quarters would be based in Calgary.

For much of the early 1980s, Mac a'Phearsoin busied himself with his consulting firm, Kardec Business Consultants, his National Spiritist Church, and with attempts to license the rights to his Ku Klux Klan symbols. According to police sources, he also acted as a paid police informant. Whenever a neo-Nazi criminal event was about to take place, Mac a'Phearsoin would somehow acquire knowledge about it; he would then offer to sell information to the police or the minority communities affected. In late December 1981, for example, he met with two Calgary Jewish leaders to "warn" them about a possible attack on Shaarei Tzedec Synagogue in the south-west part of the city. Sometime during the evening of January 8, 1982, the letters "KKK" were spray-painted on the doors of the House of Israel building, behind the synagogue.

In an interview, Mac a'Phearsoin claims, without cracking a smile, that the true Ku Klux Klan is a "fraternal" organization that is not interested in discriminating against anybody. But when asked if he would permit a Jew to join the Klan, he pauses, then says: "If they proved to me they were not trying to set up some sort of cell, and that they joined to support the Klan. One has to keep some sort of control, you know, otherwise there is always somebody ready to try and seize control of your organization." Pressed on the subject of race relations, Mac a'Phearsoin demurs, saying, "The Klan believes that intermarriage between the races should be abolished. With regard to marriage, I would not perform a marriage between two people of different color." But he insists he is not a racist.

In 1984, Mac a'Phearsoin's efforts to reap profit from his insider's knowledge of the Canadian far right moved into a new, more sinister, phase. Late in that year, he secretly entered into negotiations with a number of leading Alberta anti-Semites to establish a "racialist" radio station. One of these people was Jim Keegstra.

Keegstra was by then well-known to many Albertans, as he was to Mac a'Phearsoin, as the province's most infamous Jew hater. In the many years since it became public knowledge that the Eckville, Alberta, high-school principal was teaching students that Jews were "money thugs" and "gutter rats," he has consistently denied any involvement in any known anti-Semitic or white supremacist organization, likening himself to a one-man crusade. Asked about his links to the Ku Klux Klan in an interview, he says, "I know none of those people. I wasn't one of those people." But outside the confines of his social studies classroom at Eckville High School, Keegstra was, some say, an enthusiastic supporter of the Ku Klux Klan. (He is also known to be a frequenter of the Canadian Aryan Nations headquarters in Caroline, Alberta; eyewitnesses have often spotted him there with other far right types. But Keegstra refuses to discuss those relationships as well.)

In 1972, the year that Mac a'Phearsoin and Keegstra first met, the Eckville resident had been teaching for 11 years. Along with his wife, Lorraine, and their four children, the Alberta-born Keegstra had been a resident of Eckville since 1968. Initially, he taught only industrial arts and automobile maintenance—in 1954, he had obtained his auto mechanic's ticket at the Southern Alberta Institute of Technology, in Calgary—but soon he was teaching about history. A committed follower of Social Credit founder and avowed anti-Semite Maj. C.H.

Douglas, Keegstra had faithfully digested most of Douglas's rantings about the Jewish conspiracy before he had completed high school at Rocky Mountain House. By the time he reached adulthood, Jim Keegstra was a confirmed bigot. And the best evidence of the bigotry Keegstra passed on to his students at Eckville High School is contained in the essays the teenagers wrote themselves.

One boy, Richard Denis, penned an essay titled "The World Menace Since 1776," in which he stated: "In this essay I will show you how the virus of this disease [of Communism and Socialism] consists of one kind of people. The Jews since 1776 have financed and supported the spread of Communism. . . . This essay shows how the Jews are conspiring to take over the world. And when they do they will set up a New World Order under a one world government. In my opinion this must come to a dead halt. We must get rid of every Jew in existence so we may live in peace and freedom." Keegstra gave Richard Denis a grade of 65 per cent for his essay. Another student, Gwen Matthews, wrote that during the French Revolution, Jews created "the Feast of Reason: they carried aloft a number of prostitutes. They would strip her and lay her on the altar. Then they killed an innocent girl, and poured blood on the hooker. Then they cooked the girl and ate her."

By 1982, the year that Gwen Matthews graduated, Keegstra was starting to face a battery of complaints about his teachings from horrified parents. But he was not to be fired until January 1983. Later that month, he was charged with willfully promoting hatred against an identifiable group, the Jewish people.

Ten years before the Eckville controversy, however, and ten years before Jim Keegstra's name became a household word, the teacher and the Klansman met. Keegstra is fuzzy about the details of his encounter with the Knights of the Ku Klux Klan Imperial Wizard—saying only he "may have" met with him—but Mac a'Phearsoin is not. Says Mac a'Phearsoin: "I knew of Jim Keegstra's beliefs, because he approached me in 1972, along with some other people, with the object of purchasing my copyrights on the Klan, which had been registered a short time before that in Ottawa. At the time, I didn't know a great deal about him, except that he was connected with the Canadian League of Rights." The negotiations were unsuccessful, and the rights to the Ku Klux Klan symbols remained in Mac a'Phearsoin's hands.

Adds Mac a'Phearsoin: "I knew his beliefs, and I knew he was connected with Nazism, because of the people who had come with him." Mac a'Phearsoin will not name the other "people," but sources say they included Keegstra enthusiasts in the yet-to-be-formed Christian Defence League, such as Tom Erhart, a self-professed "Aryan," and a Calgary man who published material stating that there is an active worldwide conspiracy of "international, money-lending, Babylonian Talmud-believing, Satan-worshipping Zionist 'Jews'." While Keegstra will not confirm the meeting with the Klan leader, neither will he deny it. When asked what he thinks of Mac a'Phearsoin, Keegstra laughs. "That weirdo?" he says, and laughs again.

In late 1984, Mac a'Phearsoin and Keegstra met again. This time, the planned venture was a radio station, called Radio Free Alberta. The station would be based in Drumheller, a town about an hour's drive northeast of Calgary. Also involved in the venture was Erhart, who at the time was a vice-president of the national Social Credit Party. Erhart, a longtime associate of Keegstra, had incorporated Radio Free Alberta some time before. Says Mac a'Phearsoin: "I met with Mr. Keegstra and Mr. Erhart, who explained that the station would be used to promote their views and similar views. Views of people like Mr. Keegstra and the Aryan Nations. And that Jews, for instance, couldn't be on the station to express their viewpoints."

Under the contract signed between Erhart and Mac a'Phearsoin dated February 14, 1985, Radio Free Alberta agreed to pay Kardec Consultants $6,000 to set up the radio station, doing everything from printing letterhead to preparing the Canadian Radio-Television and Telecommunications Commission (CRTC) licence application. Business cards were made, carrying Erhart's home telephone number and the legend "Eternal vigilance is the price of freedom." The station would primarily broadcast religious programming. Says Mac a'Phearsoin: "I had no objection, of course—and would have no objection—to Keegstra or anyone else expressing their viewpoints. So long as those people who might be attacked would have an opportunity to retaliate."

Like so many other Mac a'Phearsoin ventures, Radio Free Alberta never got off the ground. And for the Imperial Wizard of Alberta's Invisible Empire Association, things went from bad to worse. In 1988, Mac a'Phearsoin was charged with gross indecency, following a complaint by a mentally disabled teenager. The boy told police that Mac a'Phearsoin drove him to a deserted field outside of Calgary and instructed him to engage in mutual masturbation. (In November, Mac a'Phearsoin was convicted and fined $1,000.)

Then, in June of that same year, following a period in which Mac a'Phearsoin had watched, disconsolate, as the Church of Jesus Christ Christian, the religious wing of the Aryan Nations, grabbed all the hate-monger headlines, the Alberta Ku Klux Klan was dealt a final, fatal blow. Late in the evening of Friday, June 3, 1988, two members of Mac a'Phearsoin's Calgary klavern were arrested by Calgary police.

The arrests were the culmination of a week-long investigation by 20 members of the Calgary Police Service and the RCMP into the Invisible Empire Association's Knights of the Ku Klux Klan. Charged with conspiracy to commit murder and conspiracy to commit property damage or serious injury by use of an explosive were two men: 19-year-old Robert Wilhelm Hamilton and 29-year-old Timothy David Heggen. The plan had been to blow up the Calgary Jewish Centre along with Jewish businessman Harold Milavsky, chairman of Trizec Corporation, an international real estate conglomerate.

Hamilton and Heggen had been members of Mac a'Phearsoin's Klan for most of the spring of 1988. Heggen was a simple, slow-witted man who had been a recluse for most of his adult life. He lived in the southeast Calgary basement of the home of his adoptive father, a retired 74-year-old farmer from Staveley; when he told the elder Heggen that he had joined the Ku Klux Klan and showed him a photograph of Mac a'Phearsoin, his father dismissed it all as a joke. Usually unemployed and living off an inheritance left to him by his mother, Heggen had toiled briefly at the Post Office and Union Carbide. He was drawn into the Ku Klux Klan after he became alarmed about the growing number of immigrants in Canada. Hamilton, meanwhile, was a much more enthusiastic Klansman, having joined the group in February 1988 as what Mac a'Phearsoin called "a registered supporter." He lived in a grimy stucco walk-up at the edge of downtown Calgary. In May, Hamilton led seven other hooded Klansmen in an anti-abortion protest outside Calgary City Hall; at the demonstration, he called himself an Imperial Kleagle and darkly hinted that the Alberta Klan was about to embark upon "a new beginning." The next month, Hamilton told one undercover officer that he wanted to kill "as many Jews as possible" with the Calgary Jewish Centre attack.

In an interview two years before the bomb plot came to light, Mac a'Phearsoin claimed that the true Ku Klux Klan was neither anti-Semitic nor white supremacist. He said: "Many, many groups, and in fact many Nazi groups, have used the name Ku Klux Klan as a front to perpetrate all sorts of things. It was used by anti-Semitic people especially during the 1930s and the late 1920s. What it became, I dis-agree with. And I would like to see it returned to what the original intention for it was. People have used [the Ku Klux Klan name] wrongly, in violation of the original four oaths of the Klan. And terror-ism certainly isn't one of them."

But according to the Court of Queen's Bench judge who presided over the case, and according to the lawyers who defended Hamilton and Heggen and the Crown attorney who prosecuted them, this sort of claim was pure and unadulterated bilge. The mastermind of the bomb-and-assassination plot was none other than Teàrlach Dunsford Mac a'Phearsoin. In May 1988, the Imperial Wizard hatched the whole scheme. For pure malice, Mac a'Phearsoin persuaded the two Klansmen to also bomb a blue Chrysler belonging to the wife of a well-known Calgary pharmacist. The woman was targeted simply because Mac a'Phearsoin was piqued that the woman had outbid him during negotiations for the purchase of the car. Once he had convinced Hamilton and Heggen to do the dirty work, Mac a'Phearsoin fell back on old habits: he started writing to Crown prosecutors, Calgary lawyers and members of the Jewish community.

In his letters, Mac a'Phearsoin stated that he knew of a plot against the Jewish community and demanded $200,000 (U.S.) in exchange for the relevant facts. One of the letters, dated June 4, was sent to Harvey Kane, executive director of the Jewish Defence League of Calgary; alarmed by what he read, Kane immediately contacted the Calgary police. He was told that the police were aware of the matter and were dealing with it: a number of undercover officers had been assigned to check out Mac a'Phearsoin's claims.

Unaware that they had been double-crossed by their putative leader, Hamilton and Heggen started to make inquiries about where a large quantity of explosives could be purchased. By happy coincidence, a man describing himself as a bomb expert came forward to help out. The man was an undercover police officer.

At sunset on Friday, June 3, Hamilton and Heggen travelled to Heritage Park, a tourist attraction featuring vintage trains and actors wearing period costumes on the shores of Glenmore Reservoir, in the city's well-to-do southwest end. At the appointed time, Hamilton and Heggen moved to a boat jetty and waited as a vessel headed towards shore. Shortly after the undercover officer arrived in a rubber dinghy, and shortly after Hamilton and Heggen had removed the bombs—clever 75-pound fakes packed with batteries, lights and sand—two dozen police swept down and arrested them. In Heggen's car, police found pamphlets blaming the Palestine Liberation Organization for the bombings. Mac a'Phearsoin's hope, apparently, had been to provoke a confrontation between the Arab community and whites, thereby increasing membership in his Klan, at $100 per. (When reporters confronted Mac a'Phearsoin, he claimed that he did not know Hamilton and Heggen. Later, he stated that he had known them, adding that he had kicked them out of the Invisible Empire Association after the pair allegedly met with an Aryan Nations leader.)

Incredibly, Mac a'Phearsoin was not charged. But at Hamilton and Heggen's trial, which took place in Calgary in February 1989, Court of Queen's Bench Justice Allen Sulatycky made clear that the Imperial Wizard should have been. The judge said Mac a'Phearsoin appeared to have masterminded the plot and, accordingly, was Calgary's Number One hatemonger. "In their immature naiveté, [Hamilton and Heggen] were victimized by a man who should face, and would face if he were charged with this offence, a penalty approaching the maximum." The maximum penalty was 14 years' imprisonment.

After plea-bargain negotiations between the Crown and defence counsel, Hamilton and Heggen pleaded guilty to lesser charges. There would be no lengthy trial. Each Klansman received a five-year sentence for possessing explosives with an intent to damage property. Mac a'Phearsoin was not in court to hear what Sulatycky had to say about him.

As a Ku Klux Klan leader, Teàrlach Dunsford Mac a'Phearsoin was finished. His luck had finally run out. Following the bomb-plot trial, Mac a'Phearsoin quietly wound up the Invisible Empire Association of Alberta, Knights of the Ku Klux Klan, delisted his telephone number and moved out of his Highland Park home. He lived under an assumed name in Edmonton, where he published a magazine about herbalism. In 1994, he was again jailed for sexual assault on a young male.

Driving north of Winnipeg, on Highway 7, one passes a few local landmarks, among them Stony Mountain Penitentiary, Bristol Aerospace and Ducks Unlimited. In time, one reaches the little town of Stonewall, incorporated 1908. At Dan Dee's Restaurant—"Elvis Eats Here"—one turns south again for about five minutes, until the sign announcing Grassmere Church Road looms up on one side. Turn right. Past a historical marker announcing the one-time site of Tecumseh School No. 34, hidden behind the trees there is a grouping of barns and modest white houses, low to the ground. The sign out front reads "HARCUS FARMS."

On the driveway, shovelling snow onto the gravel so it will melt in the bright late-March sun, Bob Harcus watches an uninvited guest approach. His wife, Jean, looks on from the house, through a shut-tered blind. Harcus is wearing a trucker's cap and a frown. Around his mouth and his eyes, he looks a lot like his infamous son, Bill.

After a pronounced silence, Harcus explains that his son no longer lives at home. "We've been through quite a bit here," he says, glanc-ing back at the house. "My son has separated himself from all of that now. It's one of those things. People make mistakes, eh? He realizes that now.

"I don't think he realized what he was getting himself into."

Did Bob Harcus tell his son to get out of the Ku Klux Klan?

"Oh, certainly," he says. He looks down. "I gave him advice to get out of it. We disagreed with many of his views, a lot of his views. And he had to leave home because of it. He was bent on being part of this organization, and we just didn't agree with it. It caused havoc with our younger kids." He looks uncomfortable. He seems unable to pronounce the words "Ku Klux Klan." After a minute, he says: "We suffered ourselves from it, as a family.

"We've lived here all of our lives, our family. It was tough on us, and it was tough on the community too. We've had nothing negative said to us by the community, here. They were all very good. But it was tough on the older people to see that sort of thing happening. They didn't know how to handle it."

The Harcus family has lived in Stonewall since 1937, running their pig farm, selling some grain, minding their business. Bill was Bob and Jean Harcus's first child. He spent all of his young life in Stonewall. He attended high school there, where he received counselling from at least three mental health professionals for his frequent expressions of intolerance and anger. For a time, he dabbled in Satanism with a group active in the Stonewall area, indulging in such pastimes as grave dese-cration. Later, he studied graphic arts at Red River Community College, which he enjoyed; while there, he also took a couple of com-puter courses. Harcus is a talented artist, but it troubled some that he seemed to devote most of his time to detailed sketches of Adolf Hitler and Canadian neo-Nazi leaders.

On Sundays, his Satanism days behind him, Bill Harcus attended New Life Baptist Church in Stonewall, where, as a teenager, he first heard about an unusual new faith catching fire in conservative rural communities across Canada and the United States: Christian Identity. Followers of Christian Identity believe that Anglo-Saxons are the true biblical Israelites and that Jews are the literal spawn of Satan, that non-whites have no souls and that Adolf Hitler was Elijah the Prophet. Christian Identity also holds that non-whites are "mud people," lacking souls. "We have to save the white race," Harcus would later remark, "or we will have no more Christianity. That's why we need an organization that can let us be revolutionary."

Intrigued by Identity, young Bill Harcus enrolled in private Bible study classes in nearby St. James. Every Wednesday night, for two or three hours, passages from the King James Version were read and interpreted literally. The group numbered about a dozen every week, and each participant brought his or her own Bible. Within a short time, Harcus was a devout follower of the tenets of the Christian Identity faith. Within an equally short time, he was rubbing elbows with some of the most violent neo-Nazi extremists in Canada and the United States.

He attended the Christian Identity classes for at least three years, and was given a certificate attesting to his diligence. But he was no missionary. "I am a Christian and I attend a Christian Identity Bible study," he wrote to one Nazi pal in December 1990. "I don't force it on others in the movement, though. That only turns people off the idea."

In 1988, at the age of 17, Harcus frequently left Stonewall to travel to Winnipeg, where he hung out with a group that jokingly called itself CROW—Canadian Rowdies on Welfare. Harcus shaved off his hair and adopted the skinhead look, Doc Marten boots, nylon bomber jacket, clip-on suspenders. He was, by then, a committed white supremacist, distributing neo-Nazi pamphlets he'd obtained from Klan groups in the United States. No one far right group occupied his time; rather, he belonged to many groups. One night, when he was passing out "white power" leaflets at an unlicensed rock gig, Harcus was approached by a huge tattooed teenager named Brett Hayes. The two hit it off. Hayes, a 19-year-old who sported a Mohawk haircut and described himself as a former "nazi punk," says Harcus "got me into this stuff [white supremacy]." He says the two became "very close friends."

Hayes has since claimed to have rejected white supremacy. He is now a resident of Calgary and leader of that city's Skinheads Against Racial Prejudice (SHARP) chapter. Hayes recalls that, in 1988 and 1989, Harcus and others would often meet at a McDonald's on Portage Avenue in Winnipeg. A typical evening would see skinheads getting drunk at The Albert, a local watering hole, and then "fag-bashing" on the Legislature grounds. Recalls Hayes: "We'd bash their heads into the ground. We wanted to kill them." For good measure, Harcus carried a large folding Buck knife and which he kept for what he called "slashing." Occasionally, the group would borrow Bob Harcus's truck, and load it up with cement blocks. The skinheads would then drive around Winnipeg at night. When they spotted a Native passed out by the side of the road, they would grab one of the cement blocks and drop it on him.

In April 1988, they celebrated Adolf Hitler's birthday with a drinking party, scrawling "DEATH TO THE JEWS" on city mailboxes. On another occasion, in May 1988, just before dark, Harcus and Hayes and a few other skins trooped to the Winnipeg Jewish Community Centre, on Hargrave Street. There, Harcus and Hayes unfurled a full-size Nazi battle flag. While the pair held up the flag and laughed—and while passers-by looked on in disbelief—another skinhead took their photograph. Asked why the group felt it necessary to raise the swastika in front of a facility frequented by Jews, Hayes says: "Well, at the time, it was just for fun. We didn't like that building at all. We just thought it would be neat to do that, right in front. It was open, and people were watching from inside."

Hayes is asked again to explain the significance of the flag-waving. What did it signify? After reflecting, Hayes says: "To rid Canada of the Jews, by any means necessary."

Including killing? Including murder?

"Sure," Hayes says, unfazed. "Sure."

Hayes recalls that Harcus was magnanimous with his friends and followers. On one occasion, when the leg of Hayes's pit-bull was broken, Harcus gave him money to pay for the veterinarian. Other skinheads, such as the Aryan Resistance Movement's Mike Parmiter, tell similar stories about Harcus's generosity. In exchange, Harcus got what every neo-Nazi leader wants: disenfranchised young men who were prepared to listen to and fight for the white supremacist message. Asked later about his ability to attract converts to the white power cause, Harcus shrugs. "The more well versed we are [in white supremacist lore], the more able we are to attract more people."

In 1988, Harcus moved from Stonewall to Winnipeg, his conversion to anti-Semitism and white supremacy complete. For a time, Harcus and Hayes roomed together. Often, the pair would throw parties where neo-Nazi skins would give stiff-arm fascist salutes, listen to the latest offering by British skinhead band Skrewdriver (Hayes's favorite) and drink themselves into oblivion. Hayes boasts that he and Harcus were the undisputed leaders of Winnipeg's growing neo-Nazi skinhead movement. Says Hayes: "Me and Harcus, we had it totally under control in Winnipeg. Nobody would bother us. Nobody would bother us at all."

In this same period, Harcus was looking for a group to which he could devote his considerable racist energies. Just as others browse through shopping malls, Harcus flitted through a labyrinth of North American neo-Nazi and white supremacist organizations, sampling their wares. He spent his evenings, for example, writing letters and busily networking with Nazi skinheads across North America. Two of the many groups he contacted were Detroit's Northern Hammerskins and the SS Action Group in Dearborn, Michigan. The Hammerskins are loosely affiliated with the ultra-violent Confederate Hammerskins in Dallas; Northern Hammerskin chapters would be established across Canada by early 1994, following the collapse of the Heritage Front and, earlier, the Aryan Nations. The SS Action Group was founded in 1979 and publishes a periodical called *Aryans Awake!*, which states: "We wish to wipe out Zionism and every Jew who supports it throughout the world." In 1988, the year Harcus contacted the SS Action Group, two dozen members of the organization clashed with 200 anti-racist demonstrators outside the Federal Building in Ann Arbor, Michigan.

In the fall of 1990, Harcus travelled to Detroit to meet with leaders of both the Northern Hammerskins and the SS Action Group. "I had a good time there," Harcus told one friend in a letter written on his own letterhead, replete with swastika. On the same trip, Harcus went to Milwaukee, where he met with Donald V. Clerkin of the Euro-American Alliance. The Euro-American Alliance was founded by Clerkin in 1976 as a "nationalist front" to do battle with "our Jewish and colored enemies." For Harcus, the friendship with Clerkin would later prove to be as profitable as it was strategic.

Harcus contacted Canadian racist groups as well. In late 1989, he corresponded with Donald Clarke Andrews, leader of the Nationalist Party of Canada. Andrews, who had formed his group in 1978, sought to establish what he called a "constitutional racist state" where non-whites and Jews would be excluded. Andrews had previously led the neo-Nazi Western Guard, in Toronto. He was notable for his closeness to the Libyan government, which had given him funding to print hate literature, and to recruit dozens of skinheads in the Toronto area. However, by 1989, the year that Harcus contacted him, Andrews's Nationalist Party was in decline and losing members to the newly formed Heritage Front—some of whose leaders later treated Andrews to a humiliating beating. Through Andrews, Harcus met his next roommate, Dennis Godin, a Winnipeg neo-Nazi skinhead.

In a handwritten note to "Comrade Godin" on Nationalist Party letterhead, Andrews encouraged Godin to meet with Harcus, whom he called "a skinhead racist member": "Drop him a line. He seems positive and intelligent. Let's set up a network for mutual cooperation." In his own October 18, 1989, letter to Godin, Harcus wrote: "Don Andrews personally told me that you were a member of the Nationalist Party of

Canada also. I've got a small group of guys who are members as well. I was interested if we could maybe meet sometime and discuss our common political beliefs. I've been putting up NPC calling cards along Portage Avenue and other areas—maybe you've noticed. I am especially interested in organizing a political cell in which we can combine our efforts towards the development of the Constitutional Racist State."

In December 1989, Harcus moved into Godin's Winnipeg apartment. The two became close friends and, according to Godin, lovers. In a 1992 newspaper interview, Godin stated that the two men started a homosexual relationship about four months after Harcus moved in. The physical relationship was eventually ended by Harcus, Godin said: "As he became more influenced by reading this literature—racist literature—by speaking to others of like mind, by corresponding with other white supremacists, he became more convinced that what he was doing was incorrect."

By late 1989, Harcus was edging away from skinhead-style neo-Nazism as well. At the age of 18, the young neo-Nazi had loftier ambitions. He wanted to do more than get drunk and go on periodic queer-bashings. His chosen vehicle was, for an Identity Christian, an unusual one: the Ku Klux Klan.

Whereas most Christian Identity followers have traditionally joined the Church of Jesus Christ Christian Aryan Nations, Harcus was different. He was also, it seems, clever: the Ku Klux Klan had not been truly active in Manitoba since the late 1920s. Harcus reasoned, correctly, that a new Klan formed by him would whip up a massive controversy in his home province.

While living with Godin, Harcus made one of his first contacts with one of the many Klans in the United States. Using the pseudonym Bill McBride, Harcus wrote to the Missouri Knights of the Ku Klux Klan, a group that was made up of more than a few Identity Christians, for information on initiating Klan activity in Manitoba.

In February 1990, Godin and Harcus collaborated on a pro-Nazi magazine they titled *Maximum National Socialism*. The publication, primarily distributed outside Manitoba to the likes of the Euro-American

Alliance and the Missouri KKK, takes issue with Jews, gays and non-whites. The cover features a Harcus ink drawing of a crowd giving fascist salutes; above their heads, a banner is held aloft, bearing the pro-Nazi Celtic cross symbol. "We felt forced to put out this publication," Harcus and Godin write, "because we had to speak out against the moral and spiritual garbage that is around us all today." The editorial continues: "Crime, family breakdown, drugs, sexual perversion, and deranged forms of lifestyles surround us at this time. Why? These repulsive topics exist in our community because [of] the influence of alien cultures . . . these aliens cannot appreciate the uniqueness and beauty of the white race. SEND THOSE ALIENS BACK TO THE MUDSWAMPS FROM WHICH THEY CRAWLED."

The magazine goes on to enthusiastically libel homosexuals and what it calls "SHARP boot fags." Somewhat ironically, on the subject of homosexuality Harcus and Godin are most vicious, opining that gays deserve to die from AIDS. The pair also lionize Jim Keegstra, Toronto anti-Semitic publisher Ernst Zundel and former Western Guard activist John Ross Taylor as "Canadians who display love for their own kind." The magazine concludes with a listing of the names and addresses of a dozen neo-Nazi groups, among them the SS Action Group, the Aryan Nations, the Euro-American Alliance and a St. Catharines, Ontario, skinhead group called Stride for Pride.

In April 1990, Harcus returned to his parents' farm in Stonewall. By that time, he had made up his mind to cast his lot with the Invisible Empire. According to Godin, who has since renounced his neo-Nazi beliefs, Harcus—now sporting a fuller head of hair and cowboy-style clothing—threw himself into recruiting members for his Manitoba chapter of the Knights of the Ku Klux Klan. In Stonewall, Harcus worked at Mid-West Pet Supply, a pet food factory, and saved up enough money to purchase a set of official Klan robes. After a few fractious months living with his parents, Harcus returned to Winnipeg, where he rented an apartment at 1625 Notre Dame Avenue, in a run-down industrial area known to locals as Weston. The two-storey apartment building was across the street from abandoned railway yards, and the Manitoba Labatt's plant. Amid the odor of cooking oil and mildewed carpets, Harcus lived on the top floor, in Number 5. "The place smells like Pakis were sacrificing a dog in my apartment," Harcus would remark. He applied for a permit to purchase a Chinese-made semi-automatic assault rifle for "self-defence," but police turned down the request.

The apartment was crammed to the rafters with pro-Nazi leaflets, tapes and books, as well as silk screening materials for Harcus's white supremacist T-shirt designs. One popular design featured a muscular Viking above the words "ARYAN WARRIOR." Another depicted Ku Klux Klan night riders, astride their horses. And another one carried the words "NINE OUT OF TEN NIGGERS HAVE AIDS."

It was in this apartment that Bill Harcus would build his organization into a formidable force. It was here that the modern Manitoba Knights of the Ku Klux Klan was born. "The Klan is the most traditional of the white supremacy groups," Harcus later told supporters. "But as long as there is a white man, there will be a Klan."

At about the same time that Harcus was moving into his new headquarters, the Winnipeg police department was growing increasingly concerned about the neophyte Klansman and his friends. Through diligence and hard work, Harcus had succeeded in recruiting at least 30 committed members to the Manitoba Klan. Two cells were in Winnipeg; another was based in Gimli, a town north of the capital, near Lake Winnipeg. All of the cells were controlled by Harcus and two other men, Theron Skryba and Joseph Lockhart. This was no fly-by-night Klan; it was active and vocal. Hate propaganda appeared with increasing frequency across the city; non-whites were being beaten in bias attacks; there were rumors that the Klansmen were building caches of illegal arms; and, by early 1991, the group was running a 24-hour telephone hate line out of Harcus's apartment.

The phone line was busy at all hours, and the messages were uniformly vile. (Another phone line was hooked up in the apartment, but that one was for Harcus's personal use.) The messages typically ran about a minute in length. Most often, they dealt with immigration, homosexuality and the international Jewish banking conspiracy. Harcus, who recorded the messages himself, was careful to ensure that his words did not run afoul of Canada's anti-hate laws. But he walked very close to the line. On May 9, 1991, for example, his message dealt with race relations: "We hold that it is obligatory for the negro race and all other colored races in Canada to recognize that they are living in the land of the white race by courtesy of the white race. And the white race cannot and will not be expected to surrender to any other race."

On May 23, he discussed the Klan itself: "The Klan is simply a movement for white people of the highest standards of Western Christian civilization." On June 20, Jews: "This nation is being destroyed by the gutters and gleaners [sic] for nothing but phoney pieces of printed bank notes . . . Now is the time to rise up and say 'Hell no' to these parasitical maggots." On July 10, the coming race war: "If you feel you have what it takes to settle this war, write us or leave a message at the sound of the tone. We are the Invisible Empire!" On July 24, the Manitoba Klan's rebirth: "The crosses are being raised throughout this nation and will once again signal a fiery crusade and a beacon of hope and deliverance." On August 23, the farming crisis: "Here in Manitoba we see the plight and tragedy of 7,000 farmers losing everything they have to the banks and the federal government. Yet it is the same parasitical, Satanic system that has endless reams of money to give to the Third World immigrants, affirmative action, foreign aid . . ."

And on November 20, Harcus ranted at length about well-publicized efforts by the Manitoba Human Rights Commission to shut down his hate line: "They can cut this line, they can revile, slander or persecute us with their controlled media and witch-hunts. They can pass their useless laws with their shyster lawyers and their inquiries. But they will never crush this nationwide, worldwide growing resistance and spirit of revival to deliver our kindred people from the treacherous tentacles of the Satanic One World Order."

In November 1990, the police concluded they could ignore Harcus no longer. Harcus's Klan would be infiltrated and evidence would be collected to put it out of business for good. Following months of preparation, undercover officers Sgt. Doug Zaporzan and Sgt. Shirley Ann Hooker were assigned to the case and given false names. They were to pose as boyfriend and girlfriend. In October 1991, Zaporzan rented a room at the Canadiana Hotel, where he would live throughout the investigation. On October 29, Hooker was introduced to Harcus in Zaporzan's room. For the next few weeks, Zaporzan, Hooker and Harcus would spend a lot of time together.

The trio shared a few laughs about the need for Harcus to find a girlfriend, and about an impaired driving charge the Manitoba Klan's Grand Dragon was facing. Then Hooker told Harcus she used to sell computers. Harcus started peppering her with questions. He wanted to know how printed material could be transferred across the U.S.–Canada border by modem, thereby avoiding the country's prohibitions against trafficking in hate. Harcus encouraged Hooker to call his hate line, and she did so. She listened to a message about the Canadian leader of the Aryan Nations. "That's really good," Hooker told Harcus. "I like that." He was pleased.

On October 30, the group met again, and this time Theron Skryba was in attendance. Skryba, then 24, was a stocky Aryan poster boy, complete with the requisite blond hair and blue eyes. To make ends meet, he delivered papers for a local tabloid, *The Winnipeg Sun*. (Ironically, it was two talented investigative reporters at the *Sun*, Joanne Faryon and Dawna Dingwall, who uncovered much of the Manitoba Klan's activities in 1992.)

On the night they met him, Skryba was wearing a Ku Klux Klan blood-drop T-shirt under his jacket. Along with Skryba's girlfriend and two other white supremacists, the group rendezvoused at the Royal Fork Restaurant. As they walked to their table, Harcus spotted an Indian man playing piano.

"Oh, look," he said, loud enough for half the restaurant to hear, "I see we have the piano wog tonight." As the group sat down at their table, Harcus gestured at one of the waitresses. "Bad enough we have the piano wog," he said. "Now we have these Mexicans serving us."

After the buffet, Skryba leaned in to the table and started to talk about guns. As Zaporzan and Hooker would soon learn, it was a favorite subject of the Manitoba Klansmen. Skryba told the newcomers that he was seeking a clip for his automatic rifle. "Automatic is the only way to go," Skryba said, "because when shit happens, you have to be prepared."

The group nodded at his assessment. "We need to bring in more guns from the States. They are a lot cheaper down there, and the Americans aren't afraid to make a deal," said Skryba. "You don't even need a permit. All you have to do is make a cash deal outside the store. It's easy."

Eyeing Hooker and Zaporzan, Skryba said the Manitoba Klan needed "a border connection. It would make things easy."

Hooker stirred. "It would be like cross-border shopping."

Skryba grinned, trying to look tough. "Yeah, we'll send you down to the States to shop, all right."

Later, Harcus, Zaporzan and Hooker drove down Portage Avenue towards Downs Motor Inn, stopping so that Zaporzan could put gas in his truck. While the sergeant was outside filling up, Harcus spotted a new mini-van cruise by. It was filled with Natives. He exploded with rage. "Bunch of boggans," he said. "So poor, yeah. Right. Our tax dollars are paying for that. And I can't even afford to own a vehicle. That's our government for you. They do everything for the Indians. Give them anything they want as soon as they whine. That's our democratic system. It makes me sick."

Hooker nodded. "Yeah. The government gives them a lot."

"These Indians cry about how poor they are, yet they come to the city and drink and gamble all their money away. . . . They don't appreciate nothing. They destroy everything."

Later, when Harcus was back at his apartment, Zaporzan and Hooker detailed the evening's events in their notepads. Discussions they were not privy to, meanwhile, were being captured by electronic bugging devices the police had placed in Harcus's apartment.

The trio got together again on November 5, when they drove up to

Stony Mountain Penitentiary in Zaporzan's truck. Harcus was eager to visit Carney Milton Nerland, leader of Saskatchewan's Church of Jesus Christ Christian Aryan Nations, and Zaporzan was eager to provide the transportation. Zaporzan and Hooker picked up Harcus near his apartment at around noon. Playing dumb, Hooker asked Harcus who Nerland was. Harcus scowled at her. "He is one of the great Klansmen," Harcus said.

"What's he in jail for?" Hooker asked.

"He shot some Indian," Harcus sniffed. "The Indian was trying to break into his place. He was just trying to protect his property."

At Stony Mountain, Zaporzan and Hooker waited in the truck while Harcus visited with Nerland. When Harcus returned, some 30 minutes later, he was downcast. He explained: "Carney is in solitary 24 hours a day. Indians are putting glass in his fucking food, and he's pissing blood. When he sends his clothes to the cleaners, they come back shredded. They're trying to break him. . . ."

Zaporzan grunted. "*Will* they break him?"

"No," Harcus said. "No way. He's a real man. He's given everything for the cause. He's a real hero." He paused. "Jigaboos are allowed open visits and he's not. He told me there's a price on his head. Five tins of tobacco and $10,000 on the street."

As the trio headed back to Winnipeg, Harcus was silent. Finally he spoke. "Carney Milton Nerland is a fucking political prisoner."

In the ensuing weeks, the extent of Bill Harcus's operations became disturbingly clear to undercover officers Doug Zaporzan and Shirley Ann Hooker. According to evidence later presented in court, Harcus was attempting to set up a computerized white power "bulletin board" in Manitoba with the assistance of Louis Beam, Jr., the former Texas Grand Dragon; he was planning to establish a Manitoba-based Christian Identity cell called the Aryan Separatist Church; he had retained a woman at the Continental Hotel to sew Ku Klux Klan robes for his members; he was teaching his members how to build homemade bombs; contrary to Corrections Canada regulations, he was smuggling hate literature to Carney Nerland and other prisoners at Stony Mountain prison; he was stockpiling weapons, including a .38 calibre handgun he kept hidden on his parents' Stonewall property; he was circulating a U.S.-produced "hit list" of "race traitors," prominent Jews and minority activists who had been targeted for assassination; he was even hoping to blow up what he called "a Jewish law office" in Winnipeg. Some of the plans—the hit list and the law office bombing in particular—had apparently not gone much beyond a few drunken discussions at Invisible Empire social gatherings. But in most other respects, Bill Harcus and his Manitoba Klan were enjoying a surprising degree of success.

Most significant to the Winnipeg police was the fact that Harcus and his group were producing and circulating thousands of copies of hate tracts, including the infamous 1981 Aryan Nations pamphlet, "The Death of the White Race." The ten-year-old hate sheet featured a photo of a black man and a white woman hugging above the cut-line "THE ULTIMATE ABOMINATION." Calling upon Aryans to fight what it called the "alien invasion of North America," the pamphlet read: "Whiteman, think. Your children will be outnumbered fifty to one by colored people, who have been inflamed to hatred of our people by the Jewsmedia. Nature's laws are as impartial as they are harsh. Love your own kind, fight for your own kind or perish." Winnipeg's police department considered that sort of language perilously close to advocating genocide, an activity prohibited by the Criminal Code.

By the end of November, with Winnipeg in the grip of Grey Cup fever, Harcus's natural state of paranoia had dissipated. He appeared to have complete confidence in Zaporzan and Hooker. By that time, Harcus was asking Hooker to lead a Klan cell for women; Zaporzan, meanwhile, was trusted enough to ferry hate propaganda to and from Harcus's apartment. On November 20, Zaporzan and Hooker picked up the Klan leader at his apartment. As he got into Zaporzan's truck, Harcus handed the police sergeant a bag full of newly printed Manitoba Knights of the Ku Klux Klan cards. "I've got about 2,000 more back in the apartment," he said, "and I've got a lot more on order. They're coming in from Montreal."

The conversation turned to music. Hooker asked Harcus, a country music aficionado, whether he planned to attend a show by a popular country group, Highway 101. "How did you hear they were coming to town?" Harcus asked.

"Don't you listen to the radio?" Hooker asked. "They're getting all these big acts in before the Grey Cup."

Harcus grimaced. "Yeah, the Nigger Cup," he said. After driving down Main Street, Harcus told Zaporzan to stop. He jumped out to pick up a bag full of hate propaganda from a Klansman who lived on Poplar Avenue. In the plastic bag were copies of Louis Beam's *Essays of a Klansman*; *The Spokesman*, a Klan newspaper; and a variety of anti-Semitic publications with titles like *Jew Watch*. Also in the bag were a few prerecorded tapes of speeches by Canadian racist leaders.

The group's next meeting was December 2 at the apartment on Notre Dame Avenue. As Zaporzan and Hooker sat in his cluttered living room, Harcus showed off his satin Grand Dragon robe, as well as a newly pressed Nazi uniform. There was talk about selling Klansmen's robes to Alain Roy, leader of one of the biggest Canadian Ku Klux Klan cells in Montreal. Conversation turned to bombings, as it often did with Harcus. The Klan leader discussed his desire to blow up the stands at a Winnipeg athletic event, like the Grey Cup. "But I guess you'd kill a lot of innocent people," Harcus said, then laughed.

"Have you got that book on explosives yet, Bill?" Zaporzan asked.

"No," he said. "Not yet. Theron has another book of mine on bombs. And I've got another member who has this book on poisoning people and use of police band radios and stuff like that. Are you interested in those?"

"Oh, yeah," Zaporzan said. After more small talk, he and Hooker left. The next day would be the threesome's first hate propaganda drive.

At noon on December 3, the two police officers picked up Harcus at his home. He was out front, wearing a black trucker's cap with the word "Convoy" stitched on the front. Climbing into the cab of the truck, Harcus said he didn't favor his Hank Williams, Jr., cap any more because the Winnipeg Police Department had surveillance photos of him wearing that one.

The trio headed towards a local shopping mall while Harcus started leafing through a bag of hate propaganda. Today's leaflet, he said, would be the Aryan Nations' "Death of the White Race" effort. Zaporzan and Hooker asked him if they could get into "legal trouble" for distributing the material. Harcus laughed. "If they prosecute, they will prosecute me only. And it will be a 50-buck fine, tops. Then I'll get a Legal Aid lawyer and drag it through court. So don't worry," he said. "Just be careful—don't flog them all in one place or work in some kind of a pattern. Be unpredictable."

A few minutes later, Zaporzan pulled into the parking lot at Garden City Shopping Centre and cruised towards the entrance to Sears. Harcus told Zaporzan and Hooker to "randomly distribute" the leaflets among the many cars parked in the lot. Hooker looked uncertain. "It's okay to do it here?" she asked.

"Yes," Harcus said.

"We won't get in shit or anything, will we?"

Harcus frowned at Hooker. "Well, if you're worried about that, then let's not do it," he said petulantly. After an awkward moment passed, Hooker told Harcus she wanted to go ahead, so Zaporzan parked and the trio got out of the truck. Harcus told Zaporzan and Hooker to place the folded leaflet under the windshield wiper on the driver's side. "And don't pick yuppie vehicles," he told them. "Put them on the poor slob trucks."

Their task completed, the group piled into the truck and sped away. They drove to Humpty's Family Restaurant on Oak Point Highway for burgers and conversation.

"So what do you think of your first literature drive?" Harcus said.

Hooker smiled. "I enjoyed it," she said. "But at first I was scared."

"Don't worry," Harcus said, stuffing french fries in his mouth, "we didn't do anything illegal."

*

Unfortunately for William James Harcus, the Winnipeg Police Department thought otherwise. The production and distribution of the "Death of the White Race" leaflet, police concluded, was contrary to section 318 of the Criminal Code of Canada. That section reads that "everyone who advocates or promotes genocide is guilty of an indictable offence and liable to imprisonment for a term not exceeding five years." In the code, "genocide" is defined as "acts committed with intent to destroy in whole or part any identifiable group."

On Wednesday, December 18, 1991—two weeks after Harcus's "literature drive" at the Garden City Shopping Centre—the Manitoba Grand Dragon's apartment was raided by police. Harcus was arrested at about 9:00 p.m. at the St. Vital Shopping Centre, as he was placing yet more hate sheets on parked cars. A few hours later, he was charged with advocating genocide. Armed with search and arrest warrants, police swept into five other residences across Winnipeg. Also arrested, at his Manitoba Avenue home, was Theron Skryba.

On Thursday afternoon, Harcus appeared in court for a bail hearing. He was granted a release on the condition that he post a $3,000 surety, surrender his passport and report to police every week until his next court appearance. But Harcus could not post bail, and he apparently could not persuade his family to help out. He remained behind bars at the Winnipeg Remand Centre.

That same day, police staged a dramatic press conference where they announced the arrests of Harcus and Skryba. They displayed to reporters hate propaganda, high-powered rifles and Nazi memorabilia. Simultaneously, the Manitoba Telephone System shut down Harcus's Klan hate line. Inspector Conrad Gislason, the shrewd police veteran who led the 13-month investigation, told the packed room that the Manitoba Klansmen were "intelligent, well schooled and well trained in the activities of the Klan." Up to 20 police officers had worked on the case, Gislason said, adding that more than a few had risked their lives to work undercover in the Ku Klux Klan. (Klansman Joseph Edward Lockhart was later charged with mischief for erasing and replacing a telephone answering machine message at the Coalition Against Homophobic Violence in Winnipeg.) From across Canada, anti-racist groups praised the city's police department for its speed and efficiency.

After finally posting bail, Harcus went into hiding. He returned to the law courts building in Winnipeg on January 9, 1992, with Theron Skryba. The two swaggered into court and past a battery of news photographers. Harcus was sporting a new look: cowboy hat, mustache, and a mouth jammed full of chewing tobacco. He was the Urban Racist Cowboy. The Klansmen's cases were remanded until February 13. Initially, Harcus and Skryba were represented by a local criminal defence lawyer. But then, in late March, the pair made what was perhaps their smartest move in months: they retained Douglas Christie to represent them.

Douglas Hewson Christie, Jr., is a Victoria, B.C., lawyer who has achieved notoriety by defending the likes of Jim Keegstra, Ernst Zundel and other far right newsmakers. Because he does not work for free, rumors circulated as to who was footing the legal bill. Christie refused to say. But Milwaukee's Donald Clerkin, head of the Euro-American Alliance and a Harcus enthusiast for two years, said he planned to raise funds among white supremacist and neo-Nazi groups as soon as possible. Harcus's networking with U.S. extremist groups was paying dividends.

Harcus and Skryba entered not-guilty pleas. Their trial was set for the last week in June. By that time, Christie would be representing Lockhart as well.

As the trial opened in a crowded Provincial Court on June 22, Doug Zaporzan was the first officer to be called by the Crown to the witness stand. As Harcus, wearing a button-down dress shirt and slacks, sat in the courtroom taking notes and occasionally referring to a well-worn Bible, Zaporzan recounted the December 3 literature drive at the Garden City Shopping Centre parking lot. Under intense cross-examination, Christie persuaded Zaporzan to admit that there had been some drinking while the undercover operation was under way. But Zaporzan, unruffled, insisted that his recollection of events was never impaired by alcohol.

The court next heard from an expert on hate crime from the Atlanta-based Center for Democratic Renewal and Education. While the expert was grilled by Christie, the three defendants grinned and laughed at his testimony. On June 26, the owner of the print shop where the "Death of the White Race" leaflet was produced was called to testify; Zaporzan also returned briefly to the stand. To accommodate conflicts in the lawyers' schedules, the trial was adjourned until the first week of September, when Shirley Hooker was called to the stand.

Throughout the first few days of the case, many police officers were uncomfortable. They felt that the Crown Attorneys prosecuting the case, Assistant Deputy Justice Minister Stu Whitley and his assistant, John Barr, appeared to be too dismissive of the legal arguments Doug Christie was raising.

For the prosecution, the debut of Sgt. Shirley Ann Hooker marked the beginning of the end. Throughout Hooker's testimony, the undercover officer made continual reference to her notes, which she said she had written following each encounter with Harcus. But Hooker's notes bore an uncanny similarity to transcripts made of conversations picked up by electronic eavesdropping devices. "I want you to ask yourself whether it is humanly possible to remember [a] conversation in minute detail without listening to the tapes?" Christie demanded, clearly insinuating that there had been evidence of tampering. Hooker insisted that she actually had the ability to make word-for-word notes of a 38-minute conversation without making recourse to the tape transcripts. But Christie—and, increasingly, Provincial Court Judge Wesley Swail—didn't believe her.

Suddenly—after insisting for two days that her note-taking had all been done from memory—Hooker changed her story. She admitted that she had made use of the surveillance tapes after all. Seven of the 62 conversations Hooker had recorded in her notepad were based upon the tapes, she said. When confronted with the evidence, Hooker said: "I do not believe I lied. I made a mistake . . . I did not wish at any time to mislead the court. I believe in the Bible. I'm a religious person."

It was all over. At first, Stu Whitley said he was prepared to continue, notwithstanding Christie's call for a mistrial. But at day's end, Whitley was saying, "The Crown needs time to consider our position." Over the Labor Day weekend, half a dozen Manitoba Justice Department officials pored over transcripts and tried to think of a way to keep the case alive. But they couldn't. The Crown, one senior police officer later said in an interview, had "grossly underestimated Doug Christie's abilities—by light years, as a matter of fact."

On Tuesday, September 8, a stone-faced Whitley returned to court to read a prepared statement before Swail and the court. "The evidence in this case has taken a startling turn," Whitley said, in what was perhaps the Manitoba legal community's understatement of the year. "While it may be there was no intention to mislead the court, no one can safely say that has not occurred."

The charges against Harcus, Skryba and Lockhart were stayed, and an internal review started to examine the way the Winnipeg Police Department had handled the case. Mobbed by reporters on his way back to Stonewall, Harcus would only say, "It's unjust what they did to me." He then walked off.

Reached at his parents' home many months afterwards, Harcus refuses to grant an interview request. "You'll just slander me like the rest of them," he says before slamming down the phone.

Bill Harcus's father stands in the driveway to his farm, squinting into the middle distance. He muses for a moment.

He has just been asked whether his son made a mistake. Bob Harcus is impassive as he considers the question. Finally, he speaks. "I don't think, really, it was a big issue. There was political pressure put on it by the media and the police. You know what the media can do. He was, uh, the scapegoat, as far as I was concerned."

It is suggested that Bill Harcus was much more than a scapegoat. It is suggested that he was, at the tender age of 21, one of the most

capable leaders the modern Ku Klux Klan has ever seen in western
Canada. His father shrugs at this. "There wasn't that much to lead,
really," he says. "Like I say, it was all blown out of proportion."

With the exception of men like Teàrlach Dunsford Mac a'Phearsoin
and Bill Harcus, the Ku Klux Klan has not been successful, lately, in
attracting many new recruits in Canada's western provinces. Other
groups, such as the Northern Hammerskins, the Aryan Nations and the
Heritage Front, easily surpass the various Klan cells in both membership and visibility. But the Ku Klux Klan remains the grandfather of
most modern white supremacist groups in this country.

It is worth noting that many of Canada's modern racist leaders—
most notably Wolfgang Droege of the Heritage Front—got their start
in the Ku Klux Klan. Through it, they have been able to build friend-
ships and alliances that have lasted decades. Using the lessons they
learned while members of the Invisible Empire, they have been able
to establish highly successful racist groups. They have learned from
the Klan's history, and built upon it.

Like many other aspects of Canadian life, it is also worth noting
that the Ku Klux Klan is essentially an American phenomenon
that, for a time in the early part of this century, generated much
excitement in Canada. Part of the reason for its early successes
here was the presence of American leaders who knew how to organize. And part of the reason for its current decline has to do with
the American influence: even white supremacists and neo-Nazis, it
seems, are occasionally nationalistic.

As a result, Canadian racist leaders have continued to search for a
uniquely "Canadian" version of the white supremacist Klan models
developed in the United States. While their successes in developing
such a version have been few and far between, the message left by the
failed prosecution of Bill Harcus—and by Teàrlach Mac a'Phearsoin's
apparent escape from justice—is that the men and women of the Ku
Klux Klan should never be dismissed lightly. They are dedicated to
their cause and, without much doubt, they will one day be back.

3

DIAL 88 FOR HEIL HITLER

It is a rainy evening in November 1992, and the boys are getting together for their regular Thursday meeting at the Croatian Centre on Commercial Drive in Vancouver. There is not a large turnout tonight—only seven men. They chat while the one named Ernie Britskie fetches coffee.

When a writer drops by to listen and take a few notes, one of the men stands up and tells Britskie he is displeased. "Ernie, you shouldn't have invited this guy," the man says, gathering his things. "You will regret it. You'll see." The man storms out.

Ernie Britskie, a retired carpenter, gives a little smile and encourages the boys to start the meeting. They do so.

The meeting's chairman is a man known only as Joe. As he reads from dispatches from headquarters in Washington, D.C., Ernie Britskie leans against a counter, sipping his coffee, saying nothing. Britskie is a large man, with big hands and an impressive nose. When he speaks, which is not often, his deep-set eyes appear to radiate compassion for all of the world.

Britskie is one of the unofficial leaders of Vancouver's resident hate movement. Over a decade or so of involvement in the far right, Britskie has formed links with a startling variety of neo-Nazi, Klan, white supremacist and Christian Identity groups. For a time, he led a front organization named the Freedom Coalition. Every Monday night, members of the Freedom Coalition would meet in the basement of Britskie's tiny green bungalow at 4159 Nanaimo Street. There, members of the Aryan Nations, the Ku Klux Klan, the British/European Immigration Aid Foundation (BEAF), the Canadian League of Rights, the B.C. Association for the Preservation of Canadian Values and the violent skinhead group known as the Aryan Resistance Movement (ARM) would gather to chat about the Jew problem, the nigger problem, the Paki problem. The smokers would sit in the laundry room, while the non-smokers would crowd onto battered couches in the den. The Freedom Coalition fell apart in May 1989, Britskie recalls ruefully, when a writer from *Vancouver* magazine, posing as a supporter, gathered enough inside information to write an exposé.

Like mainstream B.C. politics, the province's burgeoning hate movement is strikingly different from the national norm. Here, coalitions are formed and broken overnight; no one hate group maintains a grip on power for any lengthy period. Members hop from one organization to the next with nary a backward glance. Ernie Britskie is like this: from the anti-immigrant movement to the Aryan Nations to the Freedom Coalition, Britskie has seemingly done it all. This year, he is the de facto leader of the local chapter of Lyndon LaRouche's bizarre anti-Semitic cult headquartered in Virginia. Next year, he will probably be leading something else.

Chairman Joe, who looks not a little unlike Les Nesman, the newsreader on the television sitcom "WKRP in Cincinnati," is reading from a letter from Lyndon LaRouche himself, whom the men call Lyn. Joe talks about the fire at Windsor Castle (LaRouche followers detest the monarchy), and how the Reichmann brothers got their start, then says: "Christian nations are being destroyed." His listeners nod in solemn unison. One of the group, a squat little man, is conscientiously taking notes, scribbling with the stub of a pencil on a cash register receipt roll. His eyeglasses are taped together at the bridge.

For the most part, it is unusual to find many LaRouchites active in Canada. The LaRouche movement, after all, is largely a U.S. phenomenon, with only a few pockets of support north of the 49th parallel. But, as it is in so many things, British Columbia is an exception.

The Lyndon LaRouche anti-Jewish empire is run from Loudon County, Virginia, a Washington suburb. It oversees an international web of front companies, political groups, campaign committees and bogus scientific institutes. The 74-year-old LaRouche, who at one time had been an avowed Trotskyite, formed his anti-Semitic, monarchy-hating alliance in 1972. Within time, he had made contacts with a number of neo-Nazi groups and individuals, including the anti-Semitic Liberty Lobby and American Nazi Party veteran Roy Frankhauser. In his official publications, *New Solidarity* and the *Executive Intelligence Review*, both of which Ernie Britskie is selling tonight, at cost, LaRouche has stated that Zionism "is the state of selective psychosis through which [the monarchy] manipulates most of the international Jewry" and that Adolf Hitler had assumed power with the backing of certain Jewish financial interests. LaRouche, who ran for President of the United States in 1980, 1984 and 1988, is now behind bars, serving a 15-year sentence for tax fraud, racketeering and other crimes. His imprisonment has contributed to a steep decline in his empire's fortunes but he continues to proselytize.

After the meeting breaks up, Britskie chats with the eastern writer who has come to visit him. Britskie is friendly but guarded. Asked if he knows British Holocaust denier David Irving—who has just completed a speaking tour through British Columbia, before being summarily deported by Canadian immigration officials—Britskie smiles. "Oh yes, I know David. He's a great guy. They haven't shut him up yet."

He smiles again. "They haven't shut me up yet, either."

Britskie tells his guest that he should speak with "some of the younger guys." He says: "I'm just an old guy. I'm on my way out, what with old age and all. You should really speak with some of the youngsters, like Tony or Greg. And have you talked to the Salmon Arm folks?"

Britskie is referring to Tony McAleer, head of the Canadian Liberty Net, Greg James of the Aryan Resistance Movement, and Eileen Pressler's Council on Public Affairs (CPA) in Salmon Arm, B.C. "I'd like to," says the guest. "But how do I reach them?"

Britskie smiles. "Let me take care of it."

Ernie Britskie is true to his word. Within a day or two, the elusive Greg James is on the line.

James, born in 1971 in Vancouver, is the skinhead boss behind the ultra-violent and revitalized Aryan Resistance Movement (ARM). He is a member of the white supremacist rock band, Odin's Law, and has lately been seen organizing on behalf of the Northern Hammerskins, distributing pro-Nazi stickers in schoolyards. He is also a "Fifth Era" hatemonger, meaning he has abandoned all hopes of securing change through manipulation of the news media. Instead, he believes only violent fascist revolution will achieve his goals. He is a secretive fellow, with cropped blond hair, a stocky frame, a shy manner and a thin voice, but Ernie Britskie has somehow persuaded him to talk. A racist tattoo can be found on the top of his head. At the end of this particular day, James has spent a number of hours recruiting members at school grounds in Surrey and North Delta. He is tired; preaching the neo-Nazi gospel to children is apparently hard work.

ARM had previously been based in Vancouver, James explains, but he decided to move the group's headquarters to the suburb of Surrey in 1992 to take advantage of the boom in interest in racist ideology among teenagers. His success in recruiting young people prompted a December 1992 investigation by alarmed members of the Surrey School Board.

"Times change, and we have to change, too," James says. "We are gearing ourselves a lot more to young people. And it's paying off.

It's not just skinheads, either. We're getting replies from all over the place to our literature."

ARM's Nazi "literature," as James calls it, is among the most venomous in the country. When ARM was based in Mission, B.C., in the late 1980s, for example, it published posters that became nationally renowned for their viciousness. "FIGHT TERROR WITH TER-ROR," one poster reads, above a drawing of an SS soldier in uniform. "We do not wish for law and order, for law and order means the continued existence of this rotten, rip-off, Capitalist Jew System. We wish for anarchy and chaos which will enable us to attack the System while the Big Brother Pigs are trying to keep the pieces from falling apart." Another poster, which depicts four skinheads standing around a peace activist who has been lynched and castrated, reads: "SMASH COMMUNISM WITH SOME GOOD OLD-FASHIONED JUSTICE! Are you going to let Canada become a defenceless nation governed by spineless wimps and heterophobic, disease-ridden perverts? Canada's forefathers would be spinning in their graves if they could witness Canada's castrated society, infested with hordes of creatures of indistinguishable racial origin. . . . Are we going to let the Socialist-Communist mobs march in our streets or are we going to deal with the problem and HANG RED SCUM!"

When it was in Mission—a town about 80 miles east of Vancouver, in the province's Bible Belt—and run by 25-year-old Aryan Nations skinhead Scott Graham, ARM attempted to recruit members through advertisements in editions of *Buy and Sell*, or posters plastered on construction sites in downtown Vancouver. Respondents, and there were not many, were sent copies of the nameless semi-monthly ARM bulletin. ARM's logo was emblazoned on its cover: a sword-bearing eagle super-imposed on a large swastika. Inside the crudely typed bulletin, Graham and his members ranted about "non-white vermin," the "Jewsmedia," and a well-known Canadian doctor who performs abortions.

Elsewhere, members are offered free legal advice on how to keep out of trouble: "I would like to remind supporters engaging in litera-ture distributions not to enter private property when engaging in a 'hate' campaign. Remember it's completely legal to distribute our literature. As long as you stay off private property, the police cannot seize your literature. REMEMBER IF THE POLICE ASK YOU ANY QUESTIONS, YOU ARE NOT REQUIRED TO TELL THEM ANYTHING, SO KEEP YOUR MOUTH SHUT. Loose lips sink ships."

The Aryan Resistance Movement was formed by Scott Graham and Tony McAleer, or, as he then called himself, Tony McLean, in 1987. Back then, it had about a dozen skinhead members in and around Mission, with about an equal number in Vancouver. ARM took its name from neo-Nazi "martyr" Robert Jay Mathews, leader of the Aryan Nations terrorist offshoot called the Silent Brotherhood. Before he was killed in a shoot-out with FBI agents in Washington State in 1984, Mathews sometimes referred to his secretive pro-Nazi terrorist cell as the Aryan Resistance Movement. Through the years, other groups have adopted the same name. In the United States, some neo-Nazi prison inmates have called themselves the Aryan Resistance Movement. This shadowy group publishes a hate sheet called *Whitefire*, and it encourages its members to work within the prison system and "not break ZOG [Zionist Occupation Government] rules and regulations" to hasten their release and return to racist activity. In the October 1986 newsletter of (now deceased) Klan and Aryan Nations leader Robert Miles, the U.S.-based ARM is said to have "an outstanding network of communications in prisons across the nation."

The Canadian Aryan Resistance Movement, which is primarily made up of skinheads, also can claim a formidable national network, although it does little work with inmates. It has boasted of chapters in Whitby, Niagara Falls, St. Catharines, Kitchener, London and Mississauga in Ontario; Victoria, White Rock, Mission, Surrey and Vancouver in British Columbia; Halifax, Nova Scotia; St. Foy, Quebec; and even a group of sympathizers in Detroit. It has a sister organization, called Women for Aryan Unity, which has detailed its raison d'être in ARM's own publications: "We are not another division in an already-divided movement! One of our foremost main goals is to bring people together. We are here to work with our males, not against them. . . . We include the word "unity" in our name as we feel there is an extreme lack of it in today's white society."

For much of 1989 and 1990, Scott Graham's ARM distributed hate propaganda at streetcorners in downtown Vancouver. ARM skins wore swastika tattoos, ARM bomber jackets that read "WHITE POWER CANADA" and SS symbols cut into their hair. They made contacts with Tom Metzger's White Aryan Resistance in California as well as Terry Long's Canadian Aryan Nations chapter in Caroline, Alberta. For fun, they busied themselves with burning crosses or dropping off pamphlets at the homes of mixed-race couples stating that "MONGREL-IZATION IS RACIAL TREASON."

In 1989, the second year of ARM's existence, the group's formal publication was upgraded after an infusion of funds. None of the group's members will say where they obtained these funds. But the FBI possesses sworn affidavits showing that ARM sought funding from Libyan government officials based in Washington, D.C., in 1988. It is not known if the group ever received any money from Mu'ammar Qadhafi's regime—one early member, McAleer, denies it—but the Libyans have funded other Canadian neo-Nazi groups, among them the Toronto-based Nationalist Party of Canada.

ARM's publication was called *The Spokesman*. It was a hate magazine that featured clippings from the mainstream media as well as the pro-Nazi press. "There is the lack of an appropriate movement in Canada geared not only to white adults of all occupations, but to our youth," one issue reads. "There has been a massive response to our mailings from skinheads . . . white working-class youth who are pissed off at the decaying cesspool our society has become, and want to do something about it."

Following a brief surge in activity in 1989, Graham's group appeared to be losing members as well as momentum in 1990. In that same year, Greg James, who had been a member of the Aryan Resistance Movement for only a few months, says he took over ARM and moved it to Surrey. With German roots on his father's side, James says he was drawn to ARM when he picked up a copy of *The Spokesman*. "We consider ourselves now to be an education group and an umbrella group," says James. "We have Christian Identity members, National Socialist members, what have you. We are non-religious. That doesn't mean we are anti-religion. It's just that, for us, race comes before religion."

One of the more active B.C. hate groups with which ARM is closely associated is the Canadian Liberty Net, led by former ARM member and founder Tony McAleer. McAleer—who used the pseudonym Tony McLean while associated with the Aryan Resistance Movement but now favors the false name Derek J. Peterson—is, at the tender age of 26, a veteran in British Columbia's hate circles. A jowly man with close-cropped hair and an engaging manner, McAleer was born in England. More precisely, he proudly declares, he was born on the same day in August 1967 that American Nazi Party leader George Lincoln Rockwell was gunned down by one of his aides in an Arlington, Virginia, laundromat. "The very same day," McAleer says, as if he were the reincarnation of Rockwell.

As a youth, McAleer recalls, he was attracted to racist ideology. "I've always had leanings this way," he says. "But I wasn't politically active." That changed in 1982, when he spent some time in his English birthplace. Although he did not associate with the National Front, the British Movement or any of the other English pro-Nazi groups, McAleer started to socialize with skinheads. Most of them, he noted, were already neo-Nazis.

By the time he returned to Canada in 1984, McAleer was a committed racist skinhead himself. During the day, he worked at a pest control company. In the evenings, he talked to friends about an idea he believed would revolutionize Canada's far right. After his unsatisfying experience with the Aryan Resistance Movement, McAleer—who has visited the Aryan Nations compound in Hayden Lake, Idaho, many times—wanted to do something dramatic. He decided to set up his own hate line network. McAleer was inspired in this undertaking by Louis Beam, the Aryan Nations' "Ambassador-at-Large" and the former Texas Grand Dragon of the KKK. In the early

1980s, Beam established the Aryan Nations Liberty Net in the United States. The computerized system provided users with an array of services, including a national computer bulletin board, an electronic mail service, a listing of "Aryan Patriot Groups," and a system that assigned points for assassination of various enemies of the white nationalist movement.

McAleer lacked the funds necessary to create a network on the scale of the version developed by Louis Ray Beam. But, using the false name Derek J. Peterson, he secured a new phone number from B.C.Tel in October 1991, which would initially be operated out of his West 36th Avenue apartment in Vancouver. It was there that he lived with his common-law wife and two children. (Later, the phone company would be given a post office box number as a billing address. The Liberty Net shared the post office box with the Aryan Resistance Movement; Tony McAleer and Greg James are close friends.) For $350, he purchased a software package called Big Mouth. Says McAleer: "All I needed was a lot of hard-drive space, and I had that. It didn't cost all that much. But it cost me $10,000 to buy a decent computer."

McAleer's Canadian Liberty Net was, and remains, the most sophisticated of the dozen-odd neo-Nazi telephone hate lines in existence in this country. In April 1992, callers were greeted with a message telling them that they had reached the Canadian Liberty Net, "Canada's computer-operated voice message centre to promote cultural and racial awareness amongst white people. If you are offended or upset by the free expression of European cultural and racial awareness, press 6 on your touch-tone phone and do not attempt to enter the Canadian Liberty Net. For those of you who wish to hear our messages, press 1 on your touch-tone phone to learn about how to use the system or press 88 to go to the main menu." (The choice of the number 88 was not accidental. The eighth letter of the alphabet is H. North American neo-Nazis often sign off telephone calls with the words "eighty-eight"—which refers to the letters "HH," the movement's short form for "Heil Hitler.")

After pressing 88, one hears: "Welcome to the main menu. Please note any message and/or editorial comment found in this system are those of the contributor or box holder and do not necessarily reflect the opinions or the intentions of Canadian Liberty Net. Now press 1 for the Leadership Forum, press 2 for a Lesson in History or press 3 for Miscellaneous Messages, or you can press 5 to leave a message. Please note once you leave your message you will be disconnected."

Press 1, and the machine responds: "This is the Leader's Forum. Press 1 for Canada, 2 for the U.S. and 3 for international."

Press 1 again, with this result: "Press 1 to hear from Janice Long, the wife of Aryan Nations leader Terry Long. Press 3 to hear from Ernst Zundel, or press 4 to hear from the Heritage Front."

The system was unlike anything the hate movement had ever seen before in Canada, and it was extremely popular. By early 1992, McAleer's computer was logging hundreds of daily phone calls from committed racists and curiosity-seekers. Some of the calls were coming from great distances—in a few cases, as far away as the United Kingdom.

In February 1992, the Canadian Jewish Congress was alerted to the existence of the messages. Congress approached Aziz Khaki of B.C.'s Committee for Racial Justice and the Canadian Human Rights Commission, which has fought many legal battles with hate groups in the West. The next month, the CHRC sought an injunction in the Federal Court of Canada to shut down the Canadian Liberty Net. At first, federal authorities were confused by the Derek J. Peterson ruse. "I used Derek Peterson on the phone records, but they were looking for somebody who never existed," says McAleer, laughing. "That was just a smokescreen."

It was a smokescreen that did not fool many people for very long. By mid-March, the Federal Court had issued the requested restraining order, and Tony McAleer had retained lawyer Doug Christie. Reached by *The Toronto Star*, Christie said at the time that the injunction was pushing Canada "far into the realm of thought police." He added that his client—whom he refused to name—was considering setting up a "Canadian Liberty Net in Exile" from somewhere in the United States.

In April 1992, following the Federal Court decision, the Liberty Net carried this message: "You have reached the Canadian Liberty Net broadcasting from the Soviet Socialist People's Republic of Canada. The Federal Court injunction is still in effect and so we can provide only a limited and sanitized update. The new U.S. phone line has been ordered but there is a wait for installation. We should be up and running by May 4. . . . We still need your financial support for the upcoming legal battle. We have retained Doug Christie to represent the Liberty Net against the Human Wrongs Tribunal."

Within a matter of days, McAleer had re-established the network in the border town of Bellingham, Washington. Callers to the old Vancouver number were given the new one in Bellingham, which McAleer indeed called the Canadian Liberty Net in Exile. The new opening message stated: "Hello and welcome to the Canadian Liberty Net line for May 28th. You may be wondering what the new number is for the Liberty Net and if that's what you called for, you won't be disappointed. There may be a few problems with the system at the moment, but we'll be working out those bugs over the next little while. Please be patient. You know that we can now say what we want without officious criticism and sanction, so please enjoy our extensive list of new messages. Please enjoy our refreshing Liberty Net."

But McAleer was wrong. He could not, as he had apparently been advised, say what he wanted "without officious criticism and sanction." By the end of June, Human Rights Commission lawyers were back in court, seeking an order that McAleer and his group were in contempt of court. In July, Federal Court judge Max Teitelbaum issued a 15-page judgment that raked McAleer over the judicial coals. "I believe that the breach of the injunction order warrants a most serious penalty in order to ensure that this type of behavior does not continue," Teitelbaum wrote. He ordered McAleer to appear before a Federal Court judge to receive sentencing for contempt.

In August, the Federal Court sentenced McAleer to two months' imprisonment and handed him a $2,500 fine. Outraged, Christie boycotted a separate human rights tribunal hearing that been called to investigate complaints against the hate line. Wishing the tribunal's members "a real good day," Christie stormed out. In the hallway outside, he told reporters: "I can't proceed without instructions. My client's in jail, while the very issue of whether he should be in jail is being tried. . . . That's 1984. That's double-speak. That's Catch-22. It makes me think I'm living in Wonderland here."

But once he had served his jail time, Tony McAleer was back on the street, unfazed and unconcerned by his legal ordeal. "I'm going to keep at it," he says in the tiny apartment he lives in with his wife and son. "Definitely. They haven't shut me down. Next, I'm working on a hate computer bulletin board, like Louis Beam's. The possibilities are endless. My software is even capable of telemarketing. I can spend all night calling people."

It is noted that McAleer, who is now without a job and living on Unemployment Insurance, is heavily in debt and contemplating more. He is asked if he has paid off all of his legal bills. "Well, I still owe Christie money, but I've paid off most of it," he says, then pauses. "We have held some fund-raisers. I'm getting a lot of support from the older, right-wing conservative crowd."

Part of that "crowd," McAleer acknowledges, are the men and women who make up the Council on Public Affairs, a hate group based in a small town in the B.C. Interior, between Kamloops and Revelstoke on the Trans-Canada Highway. The Canadian Liberty Net has placed large fund-raising display ads in the CPA's official organ, *The Council on Public Affairs Digest*. Other advertisers include Christie's Canadian Free Speech League, David Irving's supporters in B.C., and Jud Cyllorn's white supremacist Procult Institute in Vancouver.

Formed in 1985 by Eileen Pressler, the council is headquartered in the couple's tidy home on the shores of Shuswap Lake. Pressler and her husband, Claus, have lived in the Okanagan since the early 1970s. Eileen Pressler is a cosmetologist and a former Social Credit government appointee to the Thompson-Okanagan Alcohol and Drug Review Committee. She is the driving force behind the CPA. Her husband, meanwhile, runs the local Pharmasave store. Among other things, Eileen Pressler, who says she is "in the research and publishing business," is a prodigious writer of letters to the editor. In one letter sent in November 1992 to the editor of *The Ottawa Sun*, for example, Pressler rips into critics of crypto-Nazi David Irving, writing: "Canadians are tired of the double standard and hypocrisy practised by our so-called journalists who are nothing more than intellectual prostitutes in allowing their lives and their craft to be the property of rich men."

In the council's "Statement of Objectives," the language Pressler employs is a good deal less blunt. "Council on Public Affairs and its members are dedicated to the preservation of freedom and justice in Canada and the defence of our Christian heritage," the statement reads. "We are a research, education and publishing organization . . . [and] we uphold the following principles and ideals: To promote loyalty to God, family and country; To defend our inalienable rights and Christian heritage; To oppose all government policies which actively promote and encourage the tyranny of a One World Government."

But, in the case of the Council on Public Affairs, all is not as it seems. On May 1, 1992, Bernie Simpson, an MLA from Vancouver, revealed to his fellow legislators that "Eileen Pressler is behind . . . the Liberty Net." Simpson continued: "At this very moment, a hate conference is being planned in the Interior by Ms. Eileen Pressler. I've just been informed that last night, during their planning session, there was a riot in Salmon Arm at which children were injured." Simpson noted that the planning session was attended by Ron Gostick, founder of the Canadian League of Rights and editor of publications such as *The Canadian Intelligence Service* and *On Target*. Scheduled to appear at the later three-day conference in Penticton, B.C., were convicted anti-Semite Jim Keegstra; anti-Jewish New Brunswick author Malcolm Ross; David Irving; Doug Christie; and "Reverend" Everett Sileven, a Christian Identity activist from Texas with links to the Posse Comitatus, a violent U.S. anti-tax group. It would be one of the largest far right events ever held in B.C.

Simpson's description of the confrontation in Salmon Arm the previous evening was not far off the mark. The planning meeting had taken place on the evening of April 30, at the Salmon Arm Community Centre. At one point, some of the more than 150 protestors present surrounded the half dozen CPA members who had gathered for the meeting. One of the neo-Nazis, 85-year-old Leonard Saunders, the *CPA Digest* assistant editor and former director of the Okanagan and District branch of the Christian Defence League, slapped a teenage girl in the face after he was surrounded by a group of demonstrators. When Okanagan University-College professor David Lethbridge and his group spotted Claus Pressler and his son videotaping them from a nearby car, the protest organizer lost his cool. Lethbridge pulled down his pants and mooned the pair. Asked about the incident a few minutes later, Lethbridge said: "The people who came into this town are filthy fucking fascists, and they deserve to be yelled at and screamed at. They were not mishandled and they were not in any way hurt or abused."

Months later, at a meeting in Vancouver, David Lethbridge is somewhat more reluctant. Sounding sheepish about his protest that went awry, he says the CLR's planning meeting was scuttled. But Lethbridge admits that his own actions were widely criticized in the Salmon Arm area. That aside, he says he is not about to give up his anti-racist activity. There is far too much racism in Salmon Arm, he says. "There have been cross-burnings up and down the Okanagan Valley we live in," says the Montreal native. "It's been happening for years now."

According to Lethbridge, Eileen Pressler has been one of the leading forces in rural British Columbia's nascent hate movement. He is right: since the late 1980s, when Pressler operated a card shop in the Centenoka Park Mall (where she openly distributed anti-Semitic and white supremacist pamphlets), Salmon Arm has become a centre for far right activity in the province. Through the offices of the Council on Public Affairs or another organization whose Salmon Arm chapter she leads, the B.C. Free Speech League, Pressler has distributed anti-Jewish tracts such as *The Protocols for World Conquest*; she has visited South Africa twice to support apartheid; she has organized B.C. tours by representatives of the Canadian League of Rights; and she has frequently played host to the likes of Keegstra, Ross, Irving and Ernst Zundel.

"How does [CPA] have the kind of clout needed to invite people like Ernst Zundel and have them show up?" Lethbridge asks. "I mean, we are just a small town in the Interior of B.C.!" He pauses.

"This stuff is just getting out of hand. I mean, Eileen Pressler just lives two blocks away from me. You can well imagine what that is like." Lethbridge laughs. "Of course, everybody in Salmon Arm lives two blocks away from me."

Jud Cyllorn calls himself "a chubby Presbyterian Scot." But he is also, by his own admission, an unapologetic white supremacist and racist.

Sitting in his large ground-level office on Water Street in Vancouver's Gastown, Cyllorn is talking in his chirpy tenor. Most often, he does not require a question, or a remark, or anything else. With very little prompting—and with no apparent intake of breath—Cyllorn will pronounce endlessly on his theories concerning race, religion and culture. Wearing a starched white dress shirt, a carefully knotted tie with a regimental design and a pair of creaseless polyester pants, Cyllorn leans forward in his chair, talking to his two guests, his eyes as round as proverbial saucers.

"The government of Canada has said everybody can have race pride except for me," he says. "So they will encourage race pride by blacks and browns and yellows and anyone in between, but as soon as any white person . . . okay, as soon as any chubby Presbyterian Scot exercises any degree of race pride, I'm called a racist. It's a means of controlling the white people. That's what it is."

Jud Cyllorn, self-confessed racist, is not particularly notable because he is a racist. In British Columbia, there are plenty of those. He is not significant because he printed up a few thousand copies of a 492-page glossy white supremacist manual called *Stop Apologizing* and mailed them to provincial and federal MPs. Lots of racists write books. Nor is it especially remarkable that Cyllorn and a few others have formed a hate group called the Procult Institute, or, as it is sometimes known, the Protestant Culture Institute. Racists, inside and outside B.C., form hate groups all the time.

No: Jud Cyllorn is notable because, for more than a little while, he served as a close aide to William Vander Zalm, a man who was once the premier of British Columbia. In July 1986, for example, the year Vander Zalm finished first in the race to become B.C. Social Credit Party leader, Cyllorn was a member of the future premier's inner circle. During the leadership race, Cyllorn, an elected Vander Zalm delegate and full-time campaign worker, sat in on strategy meetings with top Vander Zalm aides, helping to spin lines, develop speeches and choose campaign colors.

By 1988, Cyllorn could be seen advising Vander Zalm on issues as diverse as law enforcement, international finance and immigration. In some instances, he was to be paid for his advice. On June 30, 1988, for example, the manager of administration in the Premier's Office sent Cyllorn a letter of agreement between the Province of British Columbia and the portly racist's company, Trans-Atlantic Capital Services. In exchange for $1,500 of taxpayers' money, Cyllorn would provide Vander Zalm with "a strategic outline identifying key issues that the province should address with respect to its role in world financial markets [and] the ramifications of recent events such as the 1987 stock market crash." Cyllorn had apparently been asked to employ his skills as an expert in numerology—a pseudo-science favored by fortunetellers and other dime-store hucksters—to predict British Columbia's economic future.

The "strategic outline" was never delivered, first, because Jud Cyllorn considered the offered amount too small—"an insult to my intelligence," he told a reporter from *The Vancouver Province*—and, second, because when the provincial legislature's press gallery got wind of it, Cyllorn's presence on the provincial payroll unleased a massive front-page controversy. "Magic Man Has Zalm's Number," screamed one *Province* headline; "B.C. Premier Consulted Numerologist During Leadership Bid," sniffed *The Globe and Mail*. Vander Zalm did not make matters easier for himself when he said Cyllorn had been contracted to provide an "entrepreneurial immigration study. So I think the letter may have gone out with a view to seeking what the details of such a study would be, and that's the extent of that." Why Vander Zalm considered it more politically palatable that a white supremacist had been hired to prepare a study on immigration was never fully explained.

When the scandal surrounding Vander Zalm's relationship with Cyllorn did not appear to be dissipating, the premier's most senior aide, Principal Secretary David Poole, cancelled the contract. Vander Zalm refused to answer any further questions about Cyllorn, saying he did not take numerology or Jud Cyllorn very seriously: "I don't believe in that garbage and I wouldn't listen to him." But Cyllorn says Vander Zalm had already been listening to him for quite some time—every Sunday morning since 1984, in fact. And, as B.C. journalists Gary Mason and Keith Baldrey revealed in their 1989 book *Fantasyland: Inside the Reign of Bill Vander Zalm*, the B.C. premier and his principal secretary dined with Cyllorn at Vancouver's posh Union Club in late June 1988, just before the letter of agreement was made public. There, Mason and Baldrey wrote, Vander Zalm, Poole and Cyllorn "discussed some of Cyllorn's ideas, including his economic theories."

To learn about Jud Cyllorn's "ideas," one does not need to take him out for dinner at the Union Club. If one is prepared to offer Cyllorn a willing ear—and if one is prepared to do so for a number of hours—he will cheerfully disgorge volumes of racist and anti-Semitic theory, free of charge. A sampling: the Jews "are one of the invisible forces running this country, and half of it is run out of New York, not Washington, not even Canada"; Native culture, which he is writing a book about, largely consists of human sacrifices, slavery and "throwing live babies on fires"; the federal government's policy of multiculturalism "is a political means of controlling whites"; Christianity was "crushed" when former prime minister Pierre Trudeau permitted "all the non-Christians from non-industrial, non-democratic societies to show up. . . . That was the road to ruin in Canada." Where did Jud Cyllorn get these novel "ideas"?

Jud Cyllorn was born with the name James Arthur Killoran in Edmonton in 1951. His father, John, was a licensed pipe fitter who had been a member of the Royal Rifles of Canada and a prisoner of war in Hong Kong from 1941 until 1945. His mother, Janis, was a full-time mother to James, his younger brother, Joe, and his older sister, Janis. By the time the three Killoran children had reached school age, the family had relocated to Sarnia. There, James attended elementary school and, in due course, St. Clair Secondary. He was not a scholastic achiever, but friends and family recall that he had a certain flair for organization—for example, helping to lead his class to great successes in bottle-drive contests. Here, James began in the Young Progressive Conservatives and, says his brother, Joe, "he really blossomed."

Jud Cyllorn has fond memories of his youthful days in Sarnia. He recalls: "I had a very spoiled stereotypical life . . . I was a very, very lucky kid. I was hyperactive: I had an abundance of energy beyond compare." He was not one for organized sports (he claims to have been scouted by the Montreal Expos, though his brother says this is false), but he took lots of long walks with his father, talking about "ideas." In 1972, after graduating from high school, Cyllorn travelled across Lake Huron to study at the University of Michigan. He took criminology and busied himself with what he calls "competitive public speaking." Ever the Conservative, James became involved in the Young Republicans. In 1973, he recalls, he was given the opportunity to meet President Richard Nixon. "I shook his hand. But I didn't speak with him." More than two decades later, he still sounds disappointed.

James did not complete his degree in criminology. For five years, even his family did not know where he was. He says he travelled a lot, and they believe him. Cyllorn is somewhat defensive about this period in his life: "I know some fairly wealthy people, okay? People who are directors of nationally chartered banks in Canada and the United

States, okay? I got into the back door, meeting the who's who of international finance. I spent months in Amsterdam, Rotterdam and northern England, just absolutely being a very good boy and taking notes and going to a few meetings and watching, you know, thousand-metric-ton gold deals going down. I learned who the real people are."

Learning exactly who Cyllorn was consorting with in this period of his life, and how a university drop-out with a few courses in criminology was able to hang out with millionaires and "the real people" all over Europe, is difficult. He does not like to discuss trivia. He prefers to discuss his ideas.

By the late 1970s, Cyllorn was back in Edmonton. There, he was spending a lot of time on his latest interest: Kabalarian numerology. A pseudo-science based on numbers and their "vibrations," it was founded in Vancouver in 1926 by an English typographer named Alfred J. Parker. Central to Kabalarian numerology is one's name and birthdate. Each person's name carries with it a certain numeric significance, and with each number, a certain future. To change one's future, one need only change one's name. So James Killoran changed his name to Jud Cyllorn. Cyllorn will not say why he did so. Brother Joe Killoran is uncomfortable about the subject, saying it still upsets his family. "It was his business," says Killoran. "He had been away from home for quite some time, and it was his decision, I guess." He pauses. "He's different from a lot of people."

On that point, Joe Killoran will not get a lot of argument. In 1979, Jud Cyllorn was providing ample evidence that he was indeed strikingly different from most of his fellow Canadians. In that year, Cyllorn attended a public meeting in Edmonton, where immigration policies were being discussed. He vehemently attacked the policy, an *Edmonton Journal* story notes, charging that non-whites lack the Christian work ethic, exploit Canadian social programs and shoplift a lot. These are views he continues to hold.

Before the dawning of the new decade, Cyllorn had moved to Vancouver, a failed marriage behind him. (He will not discuss the divorce.) For a time, he worked as a salesman, peddling ads for a rival to the Yellow Pages. The firm was investigated for fraud, and Cyllorn was charged, pleading guilty in 1982. On his appointed day in court, Cyllorn got into a fist fight with a deputy sheriff and was charged with common assault. Found guilty on that and the fraud charge, he received a fine and probation.

In 1984, Cyllorn again reincarnated himself, this time as a financial consultant. Claiming that he had "lost so much money" on the ill-fated Vancouver Stock Exchange, he launched an unofficial probe into the crash of several stocks over a period of several months. Always one for a quick quip or a snappy slogan, he called his investigation Van-Scam.

Around this same time, Cyllorn—now running a precious metals exchange out of an office at the Hotel Vancouver—claims he was spending a not inconsiderable amount of time with future B.C. premier Bill Vander Zalm. The two were in frequent contact in 1982 and 1983, he says. (Vander Zalm has not denied the association, noting that Cyllorn was an active Social Crediter.) "I learned to read numbers quite well, and I became Bill Vander Zalm's fortuneteller . . . I told Vander Zalm that [former B.C. premier] Bill Bennett was going to quit, and he did. So I told Vander Zalm to take education. There's going to be a teachers' strike, I told him. Don't go for anything else." He pauses, waiting for some praise about his prescience. When none comes, he presses on. "He was on the news every day for 365 consecutive days. Him and the teachers."

The implication, of course, is that Bill Vander Zalm—whom Cyllorn now dismisses in unflattering terms—owed all of his political successes to him. As a policy adviser to Vander Zalm, Cyllorn urged the colorful premier to take a number of radical steps. "I wanted B.C. to take over its own immigration system," says Cyllorn. "So that made me a racist. I wanted to repatriate B.C.'s own constitution. But they didn't want me—a racist—to have any say in that at all."

Embittered, he moved away from political life in 1989 and devoted himself almost exclusively to his many business interests—and to writing *Stop Apologizing*. In time, he had written more than 200,000 pages of notes.

That 1990 book remains the most detailed summation of Cyllorn's white supremacy publicly available to date. At first glance, it is an impressive piece of work, filled with dozens of detailed graphs and color photographs sandwiched between hundreds upon hundreds of pages of text. The book contains Cyllorn's dissertations on racism, culture, refugee policy, constitutional law, taxation, economic policy, the media, a provincial constabulary, democracy and hatemongering, among other topics. Looking at it, one would concede that it is far more professional-looking than anything ever churned out by the ham-fisted Nazi printers at Ernst Zundel's Samisdat Publishing in Toronto, or perhaps even the well-funded anti-Semites at the Institute for Historical Review in the United States. Cyllorn says he invested 10 years of his life and $200,000 of his savings in producing *Stop Apologizing*. More than 2,400 free copies were sent out, to every member of Parliament, every provincial politician, 200 major Canadian businesses and even what Cyllorn calls "the Canadian Jewish Council." (No such group exists.)

Stop Apologizing is what a great many people would regard as a hateful book. But, then, Cyllorn would probably laugh at anyone who would say so. As *Stop Apologizing*'s title makes clear, he is not the least bit contrite about his anti-Semitism and white supremacy. On the contrary, he seems proud of his intolerance.

When *Stop Apologizing* was distributed to legislators across the country, it understandably upset many people. In November 1991, in the House of Commons, New Democrat Nelson Riis and Liberal Ron MacDonald asked Minister of Justice Kim Campbell to consider laying hate promotion charges against Jud Cyllorn. Campbell told the House she had not read *Stop Apologizing*, and suggested that MacDonald and Riis take up their complaint with Ontario's attorney-general. When reminded that the federal government could rescind Cyllorn's mailing privileges for distributing hate, Campbell said she was "happy to take that comment under advisement and refer it to the appropriate ministers."

There is no evidence, however, that she ever did so. After reading a copy of *Stop Apologizing*, the British Columbia Organization to Fight Racism called on the province's attorney-general to lay charges, while the Urban Alliance on Race Relations, in London, Ontario, called for a federal Justice Department probe into who financed the publication. Jud Cyllorn and his Procult Institute, meanwhile, continued to churn out hate propaganda with impunity. One yet-to-be distributed book, *A Letter to Mark*, is a lengthy diatribe about the international Jewish conspiracy.

All of these books are written, edited and distributed out of the institute's well-appointed headquarters on Water Street in downtown Vancouver, not far from a number of upscale gift and clothing shops. Stepping down from street level, visitors are greeted by a large poster with the words STOP APOLOGIZING superimposed on a large stop sign. At the receptionist's desk—which on this day is abandoned—there is a computer. On the computer's screen, there are detailed instructions on how to prepare an explosive device. On nearby bookshelves, there are books with titles like *High Speed Math*, *Canadian Constitutional Law* and *The Magic Power of Witchcraft*. There are four offices at the Procult Institute, the largest belonging to Cyllorn. Off to one side, there are a photocopying room and a small kitchen. In the large central area, there are a lectern, stage and 150 chairs. Cyllorn says the Procult Institute uses the space for "intellectual workshops" with far right leaders.

One such ultra-rightist "intellectual" is British Holocaust denier David Irving. On his last tour through Canada, in November 1992, Cyllorn was one of about a dozen B.C. white supremacists and anti-Semites who joined forces to sponsor Irving, whom Cyllorn calls a "criminologist of research [which] history only produces every so often." Earlier in the fall, federal officials had warned the self-described "moderate fascist" to keep out of Canada, but Irving had ignored the warning. Despite the protests of Cyllorn and others, Irving was put on a plane back to his home in London in mid-November.

As Jud Cyllorn sits in his office, talking about David Irving, race relations and the Procult Institute—what he calls "our own little intellectual think tank"—the Water Street steam clock gives a hollow whistle every 15 minutes. Cyllorn declines to discuss how he is able to maintain such high-priced offices in downtown Vancouver. He notes only that he has many well-to-do supporters. One of those supporters—present on this day at the institute—is Humphrey Killam, son of a wealthy B.C. family. "I've got lots of volunteers," says Cyllorn. "We're still at a philosophical stage. But we're developing into a more political force."

In the fall of 1992, Jud Cyllorn and virtually every single fascist, Klansman, Jew hater and Hitler freak in British Columbia and beyond came together to form a formidable political force. They were hell-bent, they said, on stopping the constitutional reform package called the Charlottetown Accord. Along with Cyllorn—who ran an officially registered "no" committee out of the Procult Institute's office—many others associated with the province's far right were active in the anti-Charlottetown movement. Among them were lawyer Doug Christie and Salmon Arm's Council on Public Affairs. The Canadian neo-Nazis opposed the deal because they believed that a "no" victory would lead to greater disunity and economic chaos. From there, they reasoned, it would be easier to gather support for their racist agenda. For similar reasons, Canadian racists have been traditionally supportive of secessionist movements, whether in Quebec or the west.

Cyllorn says he opposed the Charlottetown deal because it gave too much control over immigration to Quebec. Quebec, remarked Cyllorn at the time of the constitutional referendum, wants to "bring in more Third World immigrants than we can absorb—and you know what Third World immigrants represent in terms of job skills. Does that make me racist for saying that?"

It does, but it is probably not worth wasting the breath on Jud Cyllorn to tell him so. Instead, it is better simply to let him talk and talk and talk, providing along the way ample evidence that he is, in fact, a dyed-in-the-wool hatemonger, and one who was a close adviser to a man who ran the province of British Columbia, at that.

Jud Cyllorn pauses for a moment, smiling at the sound of his own voice. "I've got nothing to hide, you know," he says. "I'm not afraid. And I don't respect the system. When you get someone with my brains who doesn't respect the system, watch out."

4

COUNSEL FOR THE DAMNED

Forty feet below the walls covered with Brazilian woods, 30 feet removed from the disinterested gazes of nine ermine-clad justices, ten feet away from a circle of professional anti-Semites, the moon-faced barrister stands at the lectern, speaking in a reassured, resonant baritone. Through a combination of circumstance and conviction, he has come to the highest court in the land to argue a point of principle on behalf of his clients. Every so often, the barrister looks up from his notes to fix his pale blue eyes on the nine judges before him.

He is a tall man, with thinning dark hair, and a tight, humorless mouth. When he speaks, he invokes all of the appropriate lawyerly turns of phrase, calling a particular judge "Your lordship" or one of the many counsel present "my friend." Like all of the other 17 lawyers sitting in assembly, fat Montblanc pens hovering over note-books, he is wearing a long black robe and starchy white barrister's collar. Like all of the others, his attention is focussed upon the issue at hand: namely, freedom of speech, and what limits, if any, should be placed on it.

But the barrister named Douglas Hewson Christie, Jr., is not like any of the other lawyers present. He is, in the journalistic code favored by some of the dozen or so reporters in attendance, "the controversial Victoria lawyer Doug Christie." He is, in the view of the headline writers at *Canadian Lawyer* magazine, "Counsel for the Damned." He is, to those who make up the Discipline Committee of the Law Society of Upper Canada, a barrister who has "made common cause with a small, lunatic, anti-Semitic fringe element in our society."

It is Monday, December 4, 1989. Outside the Supreme Court of Canada, a bitter wind is sweeping along Wellington Street. As Christie makes his closing arguments, some of Canada's small, anti-Semitic fringe element nod approvingly, oblivious to just about everything else. They watch him intently, their dark eyes shining with reverence and awe. He is their savior, this pale man from Victoria; he is their St. George, come to slay the twin-headed dragon of International Communism and Zionism. In the front row, wife Lorraine at his side, there is one of Christie's clients and a party to the Supreme Court appeal: Eckville, Alberta, high-school teacher Jim Keegstra. A few rows back, in a dark, ill-fitting jacket, there is the former leader of Toronto's neo-Nazi Western Guard, John Ross Taylor. He, too, is one of Christie's clients and an appellant in the hearing. Scattered here and there throughout the spectators' benches are other admirers of Christie: Jew haters, white supremacists and conspiracy theorists.

"My premise and solemn suggestion to this court is to recognize that attacks upon constitutional rights in a free society are always better answered by debate, refutation, discussion and ridicule," Christie intones. "No one could suggest that ridicule has not been effective against my client, Mr. Keegstra. He has lost his job, he has lost his reputation in the community through many statements which, if he had the time and the money, he could probably sue for. He is a man who has suffered for his beliefs."

Christie notes that beliefs and ideas such as those advanced by his clients must be permitted to compete with other ideas. They should not be the subject of prosecutions before judges and juries, he says.

Glancing up to see what effect his words are having on the nine justices, he reminds the Supreme Court that, in the United States of America, all ideas are protected by the constitution. All ideas, he intones, "no matter how pernicious."

Webster's Dictionary defines *pernicious* as "very destructive or injurious," and to the likes of the Canadian Jewish Congress *pernicious* is a word that can be applied, with little difficulty, to many of Doug Christie's clients. "To me," says Bernie Farber, one of Canada's leading experts on hate groups and a senior official at the Jewish Congress, "evil ideas can lead to evil actions. And there's no question that the ideas we have seen from people like Ernst Zundel and Jim Keegstra are more than just pernicious. They are evil. They are soul-destroying and society-destroying."

Through the years, Christie has represented a startling number of neo-Nazi and white supremacist personages. Along with Jim Keegstra and John Ross Taylor, there has been Toronto pro-Nazi publisher Zundel; the leaders of the Manitoba Ku Klux Klan; the far right Canadian Free Speech League; New Brunswick anti Semitic teacher Malcolm Ross; Imre Finta, the first man to be charged under the war crimes section of the Criminal Code; Tony McAleer, the operator of the white supremacist telephone hate line service called the Canadian Liberty Net; and a handful of other like-minded Canadians who cluster at the margins of civilization. After a lengthy investigation, the Law Society of Upper Canada determined in February 1993 that Christie shared many of the views of his unusual clientele; asked about that, Christie is dismissive. He does not give interviews any more, he says: "Every time I make that mistake, I regret it. Every time I succumb to the seduction of the media, the result is never fair or neutral."

He is one of the best-known lawyers in Canada, having represented more headline-grabbing clients in a single year than most lawyers could hope to represent in a hundred lifetimes. But Christie has left few tracks in his 48 years. He guards his secrets well.

It is known that he was born to Doug and Norma Christie in Winnipeg in April 1946. Douglas Jr. was the eldest of three children:

there was Doug; a brother, Neil; and a sister, Jane. Christie's father was a Royal Canadian Air Force veteran. During World War Two, from 1941 to 1943 the elder Christie had acted as an air gunner for missions over enemy territory. "[My father] was instructed to fly in aircraft over Germany and bomb such cities as Hamburg and others," Christie once remarked. "And the destruction of civilian populations, according to [Canada's war crimes legislation], is a war crime. What was he doing? And why won't he be prosecuted?"

It is not every son who offers up his own father as rhetorical victim to win a legal argument, but then Douglas H. Christie, Jr., is not every son. As a boy, he served in the Air Cadets, which his father says he loved. He attended school in the Charleswood area of Winnipeg, but he was not a stellar student. "He was pretty average, I guess," says the father of the famous son. "I would say that he was inquisitive. If he thought he was right, he wouldn't hesitate to express himself. And quite often he was wrong." The father laughs. "Often he was wrong, as we all are."

Like every father and son, the two Doug Christies discussed appropriate career paths. Early on, at about the age of 12, young Doug thought it would be nice to be a farmer. The Christie clan were of Irish descent, but none of them knew a great deal about agriculture. "No, we weren't farmers," says the older Doug Christie. "But we knew an awful lot of farmers in southern Manitoba. We were always visiting farmers."

Doug Christie, Jr., decided he would try the law, but if that didn't work, he would become a farmer. It was a logical choice, he said some years later. "I had best become a lawyer since I could still become a farmer. But if I became a farmer, I could not become a lawyer."

In 1963, Doug Christie, Jr., enrolled at the University of Manitoba, where he pursued a general arts degree. His father took care of the first year's tuition, but after that, Doug Jr. paid his own way. A longtime friend says Christie was a loner in school, keeping to himself, reading a lot. He took courses in history and politics. In the fall of 1964, while Doug was still in school, his father moved to Cochrane, Alberta, a small town a few miles northwest of Calgary. There, he took up a position with the Excise Tax division at Customs and Excise Canada. In the spring of 1965, the rest of the family joined him in Cochrane. Doug Jr., however, remained in Winnipeg to complete his university studies.

In 1965, there was another change. Having been brought up as a Presbyterian, Doug Christie abruptly converted to Roman Catholicism. "He made the switch when he was at the University of Manitoba," his father says. He is asked what prompted his son to embrace a new religion. He declines to answer, saying: "Let's just leave it at that, okay?"

Christie graduated with better-than-average marks in 1967. In that same year, he moved to Vancouver to attend the University of British Columbia's law school. He decided to attend UBC, his father says, because he believed the best law faculty in the country was to be found there. Says a Victoria lawyer who knows Christie well: "He was a bit of a maverick at law school. A loner. After he graduated in 1970, he had a tough time in his articling year. But he made it through." Christie's father agrees: "He just started up in his own office in Victoria and he never looked back. Anything and everything that came along, he took it."

Christie's first decade as a lawyer was unremarkable. Like all sole practitioners, he could not afford to be picky. About a third of his cases involved Legal Aid criminal defence work; another third was made up of civil litigation, most of it personal injury suits; the remainder was a mix of real estate transactions, incorporations and the like. By all accounts, Christie was devoted to his legal practice, spending days at a desk in a box-like office in Victoria near the courthouse and nights in a bachelor apartment downtown. He was also devoted to his faith: he reportedly attended Mass every day at St. Andrew's Cathedral and he was often seen helping homeless people find food or shelter. "I do what I do out of the love of God and the service of my fellow man," Christie would later tell a Winnipeg journalist. "It's not for money. Money is not the secret of happiness."

But Christie did not turn away money when it was offered to him. Nor did he work for free. By 1980, Christie had retained the services of a part-time secretary, Irene Johnson. She has remained with Christie ever since.

Opinions on Christie's legal ability in court vary wildly. Journalists who have seen him in action say he sometimes seems disorganized and ill prepared for cases. But at least one lawyer who knows Christie, and does not consider him a friend, concedes that the controversial lawyer is a good litigator. "I agree that examination-in-chief is a weak area for him. He never manages to glean enough information from his clients when they are on the stand," says this man. "But in cross-examination, he can be devastating. And in summary [of argument], he can be quite persuasive. He thinks well on his feet."

Christie's many critics like to believe that he is an incompetent, that he is unsuccessful. They point, for example, to what they say is the lawyer's only office: a sad-looking parking lot attendant's shack, stuck in the middle of a lot a few feet north of the courthouse building. The tiny stucco structure is boarded up, with a single shuttered door that has been vandalized more than once. But sources say that this is a front. "That's sort of an office he uses sometimes," says one man. "Basically that's his downtown office, just for the sake of convenience. It's very close to the courthouse. His real office is located at his residence."

Christie's home is found on a 30-acre wooded waterfront property on Townsend Street, near Elk Lake in Saanich, north of Victoria. There, Christie and his wife and two children keep company with a few goats and geese. Christie bought the property in the early 1980s, when the main house was unfinished. He completed the construction work himself. "He's quite handy," says a friend. When not preparing for a case, he busies himself with chopping wood and menial chores.

But after a time, Doug Christie grew bored. "He's a good lawyer as far as he goes," says one supporter. "But in the early eighties, he was seriously considering giving up the law and getting into politics. And he almost did." In 1980, after a decade of representing shoplifters, impaired drivers and the like, Christie was restless. He wanted political fame and fortune. But he had a problem: in 1980, the Reform

Party did not yet exist. Christie's views—anti-metric, anti-bilingual, anti-immigration—placed the Victoria lawyer firmly outside the political mainstream. There was no party extant that shared his perspective on the Canadian body politic. His solution to this dilemma was uniquely Doug Christie: he dreamt up his own party. Alarmed by what he called "Big Brotherism," bilingualism, the metric system and "the demise of the Union Jack," Christie founded the Western Canada Concept (WCC).

His timing could not have been better. In February 1980, the federal Progressive Conservative government of Albertan Joe Clark was soundly defeated by Pierre Trudeau's Quebec-dominated Liberal Party. The Liberals, however, could not claim one elected representative west of Winnipeg. Within a short time, expressions of western alienation were at a historic high, and otherwise respectable citizens were musing aloud about quitting Confederation. Into this controversy eagerly stepped the likes of Doug Christie and Elmer Knutson.

A self-made millionaire from Torquay, Saskatchewan, who made his fortune selling tractor parts, Knutson had lived in Alberta since 1962. He led a group called the Western Federation Association, or, as it came to be known, West Fed. Although Knutson's group did not actively promote separatism, it argued that Manitoba, Saskatchewan, Alberta and British Columbia retained the right, under the 1931 Statute of Westminster, to form a separate nation.

Christie's collection of malcontents, on the other hand, did actively promote separatism, citing discriminatory freight rates, protective tariffs, oil pricing policy, taxation without representation and the usual canards about immigration and bilingualism. At first, Christie called the Victoria-based group the Western National Association. Later it became known as the Western Canada Concept.

The Concept, as locals called it, did not achieve very many dramatic political successes in the spring and summer of 1980. Christie, a patient man, bided his time. He travelled from one small town to the next, preaching the value of a separate western nation. He spoke to smallish groups and gained a few converts.

One young woman who was a committed western separatist was Keltie Zubko, a pretty 25-year-old high-school graduate from Edmonton. Zubko was attracted to the secessionist ideal, but she was more attracted, it seems, to handsome young Doug Christie. The two became romantically involved. Zubko later moved to Victoria and started assisting Christie with his legal practice and his growing western separatist movement. In time, she would become his common-law wife; in 1992, after the birth of a son and a daughter, the two married.

In October 1980, following the collapse of the federal-provincial constitutional conference, the Liberal government announced its intention to unilaterally repatriate the Constitution from Britain. Later that month, it also announced its plans to legislate the National Energy Program. The NEP was ostensibly designed to achieve three goals: energy security; greater Canadian ownership in the oil industry; and a reduction in profit for petroleum companies. But in Alberta and Saskatchewan, the NEP became the most despised federal initiative in decades and contributed to a decade-long decline in Liberal electoral fortunes west of Ontario.

Separatist movements, which had been achieving only modest gains, overnight became the most powerful political forces in the west. The NEP, which induced thousands of layoffs in the petroleum industry, boosted western separatist fortunes well beyond the wildest imaginings of Doug Christie and Elmer Knutson. In November, West Fed and the Western Canada Concept joined forces to sponsor rallies at the Jubilee auditoriums in Edmonton and Calgary. On November 20, almost 3,000 Edmonton residents—lawyers, doctors, cab drivers and oil-rig workers—packed the city's Jubilee to hear Christie thunder about a new western nation "struggling to be free." Christie railed against the Liberal government's constitutional and energy policies and called for a series of referenda on the question of separation from Canada. Former Alberta Liberal Party leader Nick Taylor, who was present at both the Edmonton and Calgary rallies, later recalled that "the floor was shaking that night." Hundreds chanted: "Free the West! Free the West!" The western separatist juggernaut seemed unstoppable.

But in just a few weeks, Christie and Knutson's uneasy alliance was losing ground. In part, this was because of an outbreak of pro-Canada sentiment. The separatist option was roundly criticized by popular Alberta premier Peter Lougheed; Alberta NDP leader Grant Notley started a much-publicized "pro-Canada" tour; and citizens' groups, among them a collection of Calgary punk rock bands calling themselves Rock Against Western Separatism, came together to push back the secessionist tide. By early December, another well-advertised separatist meeting at the Jubilee Auditorium in Calgary drew fewer than 1,200 people.

In addition, the separatist movement was weakened by the inability of Christie and Knutson to unite their two parties. Christie's organization was disrupted by internal feuding over the separatism issue; Knutson's, meanwhile, disintegrated, only to return as the anti-French Confederation of Regions Party in 1983. But West Fed and the WCC were also hurt by another development: the western separatist movement had become a point of confluence for a number of muddied streams. Soon, scores of anti-Semites, white supremacists and crypto-fascists were crawling out of the shadows to join up. Among those who were drawn to Christie's group in the early days were Jim Keegstra, future Canadian Aryan Nations leader Terry Long and Ku Klux Klan enthusiasts from across the west. Through a meeting at a WCC rally, Keegstra would later become Christie's client. Long, meanwhile, would go on to carry the Concept banner in the central Alberta riding of Lacombe in the 1982 provincial election.

By the time the Western Canada Concept had collapsed in the early 1980s, a disillusioned Christie had retreated to his acreage on Vancouver Island. (He now remains leader of the WCC's British Columbia branch alone and says he exercises no control over the WCC in other provinces. In the interim, he has run in two federal elections as an independent—in 1984, in the northern Alberta riding of Pembina, finishing fourth; and in 1988 in his home riding of Saanich, winning only 172 of the 66,000 votes available.) Says a Victoria colleague who knows Christie well: "When he got into western separatism, he hadn't thought much about Holocaust denial and so on. He kind of drifted into it with the defence of those people. I think it was difficult defending those people, because you can't defend them and refute their beliefs. [In the early 1980s] I don't think he had made up his mind. But he knew anybody who went up against the Jews would be targeted."

In June 1984, Doug Christie became counsel to one of the more notable of "those people," Jim Keegstra. In January 1983, after he was formally charged with willfully promoting hatred against Jews, Keegstra—possessing only meagre resources—had briefly considered making use of a court-appointed lawyer. But believing that all government agencies were the willing tools of the international Jewish conspiracy, Keegstra rejected that option. Instead, he telephoned Christie in Victoria. After a brief conversation, the lawyer agreed to take on the case. But he would not work for free. Keegstra told Christie about the Christian Defence League and its president, Terry Long. The CDL and Long were busily raising money for a defence fund, Keegstra said, noting that there were even plans to place pro-Keegstra advertisements in every one of Alberta's 108 weekly newspapers.

To represent Keegstra, Christie, who was registered to practise law only in British Columbia, needed to secure permission from the Law Society of Alberta. That done, he and Keltie Zubko moved to Red Deer to prepare for Keegstra's preliminary hearing. They boarded at the homes of Keegstra supporters. On June 4, the first day of the hearing, Keegstra and a phalanx of supporters showed up wearing buttons that read "FREEDOM OF SPEECH." They pushed their way past a group of reporters and Jewish demonstrators and took up positions in the new 60-seat courtroom, where they would remain with their hero for the next two weeks. (This group was fiercely loyal to Keegstra, rarely missing any of his court appearances in the days ahead.)

Normally, preliminary hearings are conducted with bans on publicity. But Christie insisted that the hearing be held in public. Puzzled, Crown Attorney Bruce Fraser and Provincial Court judge Douglas Crowe agreed to Christie's request.

Jim Keegstra's preliminary hearing should have taken no more than a few days. But Christie's cross-examination of the ten Crown witnesses—most of them former Keegstra students—turned the hearing into an endurance test. With each young witness, Christie attempted to find inconsistencies between their oral testimony and what they had written in their school notebooks many years before. Sometimes, Christie's sarcasm and persistence led to outbursts of anger; on other occasions, it reduced the Eckville graduates to tears. A few times, Crowe warned Christie to stop interrupting witnesses and to dispense with his courtroom theatrics.

One spectator who was more impressed by Christie's courtroom manner was Toronto pro-Nazi publisher Ernst Zundel. Accompanied by a video editor and a technician at the Red Deer hearing, Zundel was there to show his support for Keegstra. When he saw Doug Christie in action, he liked what he saw. "He was a tough, principled and learned attorney," Zundel recalled.

In the end, however, Christie's toughness and principles did not matter much. He lost, and Keegstra was committed for trial. But Christie, who had previously rejected a publicity ban, immediately complained that his client had been victimized by unfair media coverage. Armed with that and a few other technical arguments, Christie stormed into the Alberta Court of Queen's Bench to argue that the law under which Keegstra had been charged was unconstitutional. In a 51-page judgment handed down by Justice Frank Quigley in November 1984, each of Christie's arguments, constitutional and otherwise, was rejected. The trial would go ahead as planned in April 1985.

But Jim Keegstra was no longer Doug Christie's sole high-profile client. Zundel retained Christie in September 1984 to defend him on a charge that he had spread false news about the Holocaust. The basis of the complaint against Zundel, which was laid by a private citizen, was found in a Holocaust-denying pamphlet called "Did Six Million Really Die?" Zundel had been printing and distributing the pamphlet out of his downtown Toronto home for many years.

In November 1984, Christie obtained permission from the Law

Society of Upper Canada to represent Zundel in the Ontario trial. That same month, he and Zubko flew to Toronto at Zundel's expense. They were accompanied by the man who would act as Christie's bodyguard for many of his future high-profile criminal cases, Edgar Foth, a one-time member of the Silent Brotherhood.

Foth, like all members of the neo-Nazi terrorist organization, was an energetic supporter of both Keegstra and Zundel. And, despite Keegstra and Zundel's frequent claims to the contrary, the anti-Semitic pair were well connected to other members of North America's underground racist network. For example, Daniel Bauer—a Silent Brotherhood member who served prison time for his role in the far right group's conspiracy—says he and other violent American neo-Nazis travelled to Alberta on at least three occasions to meet with Zundel and Keegstra in the summer of 1984.

"I visited Zundel up in Alberta," says Bauer. "Keegstra, too. Keegstra is a very dedicated man. I made a point of meeting the men who seemed worthy. And they both seemed committed to our cause. There's all kinds of men who talk their talk. But Keegstra and Zundel were men who made commitments. And now they seem to be accounting for them."

Zundel's accounting started on the bitterly cold morning of January 7, 1985, at the city's downtown County Courthouse. Accompanied by Zubko, Foth, Zundel and a dozen Ontario supporters wearing hard-hats, Christie waded into a group of Jewish Defence League members. One JDL member took a swing at the lawyer, narrowly missing his impressive jawline. Shaken, Christie complained about the incident to County Court Judge Hugh Locke, stating, "I've never seen people beaten on the steps of a courthouse like that with absolute impunity before." Later, police arrested four JDL members; the presiding judge also issued a restraining order against further JDL demonstrations.

During the trial, which spanned eight weeks, Christie, Zubko and Foth stayed at Zundel's fortified Carlton Street home. Here, witnesses were prepared for trial. Among the witnesses were the likes of Dr. Gary Botting, a playwright and former Red Deer College instructor who was fired after assigning the Holocaust-denying book *Hoax of the Twentieth Century* to his students; Robert Faurisson, a professor at the University of Lyons convicted of racial defamation by a Paris court in June 1981 (and who headed Zundel's research team); and Doug Collins, a B.C. weekly newspaper columnist and revisionist who labelled the Canadian Jewish Congress "hatemongers" and later called the movie "Schindler's List" by another name—"Swindler's List." Each night during the trial, print and television coverage was reviewed by Zundel and Christie in a basement room. Christie would then deliver what was called a "mission-accomplished" statement to the two dozen "Zundelites" in attendance. Later, there would be group singalongs around the piano—beer-hall putsch style—and toasts to Christie's legal acumen.

Zundel's trial wound to a close in late February, after Zundel gave evidence in his own defence. As the stocky little National Socialist ambled back to his seat in the prisoner's dock, Doug Christie stood to give his final summation. It took five hours. Pointing at his client, Christie told the jury: "There are a lot of people who would like to see their enemies right there. If we start down that road, there will be no stopping those politicians who want to put their opponents right there. And don't think they can't find the power. There are pressure groups today who have the power." He paused and pointed again at Zundel. "Just ask him."

He continued: "For the sake of freedom, I ask you never to forget what is at stake here. The accused stands in the place of anyone who desires to speak their mind. Even if you don't agree with him, you must take it as a sacred responsibility not to allow the suppression of some-one's honest belief. . . . You 12 people have more power in your hands for good or evil than any 12 people I ever met. When you are finished with your deliberations, in all probability this country will never quite be the same. A clear answer of the innocence of my client will put an end to a process that could lead to the destruction of all society."

In his own charge to the jury, Justice Locke made clear that he was not impressed by Christie's statement. "Canada," Locke told the jury, "will be the same no matter which way you rule."

On March 1, the jury returned with a verdict of guilty on the charge that Ernst Zundel spread false news about the Holocaust when he published and distributed "Did Six Million Really Die?" On March 25, Locke sentenced Zundel to 15 months' imprisonment and three years' probation. He was forbidden to write or speak about the Holocaust during that time. And he would be deported to his birthplace, Germany, when his prison sentence was completed.

Immediately after the sentencing, Christie, Zubko and Foth jetted to Red Deer for the opening of Keegstra's trial, on April 9. The trial got under way with Crown Attorney Bruce Fraser calling a parade of witnesses—most of them former Keegstra students—to testify, just as they had done in the preliminary hearing. In each case, Fraser would ask the students to detail their time in Keegstra's classroom, then introduce their notebooks and essays as exhibits. In cross-examination, Christie, with a more restrained tone than he had exhibited in Zundel's trial, attempted to highlight inconsistencies or contradictions. Whenever possible, he encouraged sympathetic students to depict Keegstra in a positive light.

Christie showed a particular flair for attacking witnesses who did not support his theory of the case. And he appeared to be doing well until 22-year-old former student Kelly Cordon was called to the stand by the Crown. Cordon, a thin young man who did not lose his composure easily, was more than a match for Christie's vaunted cross-examination skills.

"Did he encourage you to think for yourself?" Christie asked Cordon.

"I'd have to say no to that," Cordon said. "When it came time to write a test or an essay, it had to be supporting the [Jewish] conspiracy theory."

Christie tried different approaches to elicit something positive from Cordon. But it did not work. Frustrated, he asked Cordon whether Keegstra espoused Christian principles.

"Yes," Cordon said reluctantly, adding, "Then again, he would turn around and there would be all this hatred in our notes."

"Wasn't he just criticizing wicked deeds?" Christie asked, sounding hopeful.

"It didn't always come out that clearly in his class," Cordon said. "I'm telling you that it implied hate to me."

Frustrated, Christie launched an ad hominem attack on the young man, alleging that Cordon disliked Keegstra because the former Eckville mayor had ruled against Cordon's father during a dispute over a sewer right-of-way.

Cordon was deadpan. "I don't see what my father has got to do with my social studies class," he said.

Christie looked like a lawyer who had let a witness get the best of him—which, of course, he was. "I'm not suggesting you're trying to deceive anybody," Christie mumbled. "I'm suggesting your notes don't record what was said at the time."

Cordon gazed at Christie. "My notes are accurate. And I see hate on every page."

After 32 days, the Crown rested its case, and a tired-looking Christie started to present his defence. As expected, he first moved for dismissal of the action on the grounds that none of the witnesses had disclosed any evidence that Keegstra had promoted hatred. He lost. The next day, May 24, Christie called five character witnesses who had worked with the accused as teachers in Eckville. All of them painted a favorable picture of Jim Keegstra. Christie's sixth witness was Gary Botting's wife, Heather, a sociocultural anthropologist with an interest in the occult. Christie wanted Heather Botting to testify about how Keegstra arrived at one of his key beliefs, namely, that Jews were descendants of Khazars, and not true Jews at all. After a legal wrangle about Botting's bona fides as an expert witness, she was permitted to testify. Then, Christie called Keegstra himself to the stand.

Keegstra, in short, was a good witness: he was not given to extravagant statements and he generally kept his cool. He did nothing to rebut the impression that he hated organized Judaism, but he gave his evidence in such a way that it was clear to all present that he really did believe the things he had taught his social studies students. For 26 days, he recounted his views about an international Jewish conspiracy intent upon the destruction of the monarchy, Christianity and the West. In cross-examination, Keegstra maintained his composure, but it became rapidly evident that he and Crown Attorney Bruce Fraser had little time for each other. As Fraser approached the witness box for his first go at the accused, Keegstra turned to Court of Queen's Bench Justice John MacKenzie and asked: "Who does this gentleman who is about to cross-examine me represent?"

MacKenzie looked annoyed. "This gentleman represents the Crown, as you know, Mr. Keegstra," the judge said. Some of Keegstra's followers laughed at that one. They knew Fraser represented the forces of international Jewry and, therefore, Satanism.

Fraser began by noting that Keegstra had referred to himself as a historian. Did the former high-school teacher have a degree in history?

"I do not," Keegstra said. "Don't forget, to be a teacher you don't have to have those."

"I'm not interested in anything you have to tell me except to answer my questions," Fraser growled. His eyes flashing behind his tinted glasses, Keegstra kept silent. Thereafter, he obediently answered each of Fraser's questions in his soft rural drawl. Jews are "very anti-Christian," he testified; they were, he agreed, "extremely detestable"; and, for good measure, there was a need to "get rid of Jews with Christian thinking." Throughout his time on the stand, Keegstra did not give anything away—but he did little to contradict the Crown's case against him. After a cursory 20-minute re-examination, Christie announced that the defence would rest.

For the next three days, Christie gave the jury his version of the trial and the evidence. As he had done in the Zundel trial, he told the jurors that the very foundations of freedom depended upon a not-guilty verdict. If Keegstra was found guilty, Christie said, "fear will grow and silence will grow and people will be more and more suspicious about what they say and who they say it to." And, just as he had done in the Zundel trial, Christie pointed an accusing finger at anonymous government forces that had conspired against his client. "They just want to shut [Keegstra] up and they want you to help them do it," Christie intoned. "It is a new McCarthyism of the Left."

In his own summation, Fraser ripped into Christie, calling his arguments "willful blindness," among other things. In particular, Fraser hammered away at Christie's assertion that the jury were being called upon to do no less than rewrite the Constitution. His argument that the jury's verdict would revolutionize Canada's constitutional protection for freedom of speech was outrageously false, Fraser said. "Defence counsel knows this," the Crown attorney said, clearly furious. "He tried to mislead you. Freedom of speech is not an issue for you to consider. I can't state that strongly enough. Your decision will have no effect on your children, as you were told. It will have no effect on anyone but the accused. This is simply a scare tactic."

After 30 hours of deliberation, the jury reached their verdict. It was read by the jury's foreman, Dwight Arthur, a 26-year-old graphic artist from Red Deer: guilty as charged. Jim Keegstra said nothing; his wife, Lorraine, wept. In the sentencing hearing that followed, MacKenzie rejected Fraser's request for the maximum prison sentence of two years. Instead, Keegstra would be fined $5,000. (To everyone's astonishment, Dwight Arthur approached Christian Defence League member Jim Green and offered to help raise the $5,000. Said Arthur: "If they establish a fund to help pay the fine, I will be contributing to it." Keegstra, he said, had been "furthering God's work.")

Even if he had wanted to, Doug Christie's efforts on behalf of Jim Keegstra and Ernst Zundel meant there would be no turning back for the Victoria lawyer. After 1985, he became known across Canada as the lawyer who defended neo-Nazis and white supremacists. His father, a World War Two veteran, will not say that he is pleased about his son's willingness to represent such people. But he will not condemn him, either. Says the elder Christie: "It doesn't matter who they are. They have to have defence counsel, and everyone is allowed their right to their own opinion. The [anti-Semites] all sought him out, and the cases were interesting. . . . The cases fitted in with his own principles. He didn't think [Keegstra, Zundel et al.] were guilty."

Doug Christie, of course, will not answer any questions about his feelings towards Jews. He is too clever, and too cautious, to openly embrace the sort of hatemongering of which his infamous clients are so fond. Neither is it enough to simply note that he has represented Keegstra, Zundel, Aryan Nations "ambassador" John Ross Taylor, the Grand Wizard of the Manitoba Ku Klux Klan, the Canadian Free Speech League, Malcolm Ross, Imre Finta, Silent Brotherhood member Edgar Foth and the Canadian Liberty Net. Instead, it is necessary to look at some of the few clues Doug Christie has left in his wake. There are not many, but they say something about him.

One intriguing clue came at Imre Finta's trial in May 1990. Finta is an elderly Toronto man who had the distinction of being the first person to be charged under Canada's new crimes against humanity laws. At that trial, one of the many revisionists in attendance was a peculiar Texan lawyer named Kirk D. Lyons. During breaks in the proceedings, Christie and Lyons would chat. Says one of the men who testified on Zundel's behalf, and has had a falling-out with his lawyer, "Lyons was monitoring the trial. He was there, all right."

Kirk Lyons's presence was significant, because he is the best-known defender of anti-Semites and white supremacists in the United States. In 1988, Lyons defended notorious Aryan Nations activist Louis Beam in a seditious conspiracy trial in Arkansas, and won. In the same year, he defended Posse Comitatus founder James Wickstrom in Pennsylvania on weapons charges, and lost. In 1989, he founded the Patriots' Defense Foundation, a fascist non-profit legal fund that helped neo-Nazis in trouble with the law and led a skinhead security team at an Aryan Nations march in Pulaski, Tennessee. In 1990, he represented a number of Ku Klux Klansmen who had been dismissed from the U.S. air force. The following year, he took on the defence of an Aryan Nations member charged in a conspiracy to blow up gay bars in Seattle.

In December 1991, Lyons's group moved to North Carolina, folded the Patriots' Defense Foundation and formed a shadowy new pro-Nazi group, CAUSE (an acronym for Canada, Australia, United States, South Africa and Europe). "The new organization," Lyons wrote in his newsletter, *The Balance*, "is a public interest legal assistance foundation which seeks to protect the vital rights of political activists and spokesmen who advocate the ideology that the above regions should remain predominantly Christian, Anglo-Saxon or European-derived nations, with all that proposition entails in terms of cultural, social and religious norms." Lyons, for his part, calls Christie a CAUSE "associate."

Another clue during his address to the jury at the Finta trial came when Christie said the anti–war crimes laws were part of "the most convoluted, diabolical piece of legislation that I have ever had to argue about. It has no moral justification, it has no logical sense, it has no legal merit and it has no factual basis." He continued: "Those people who came here for malice towards Imre Finta after 45 years are expressing vengeance against a man who represented to them a system they didn't like. . . . Vengeance has a bad habit of being a circle. And in one book it said that if you sow the wind, you reap the whirlwind, and people who pursue vengeance often find it comes around and hits them later." Finally, he distinguished between "eyewitnesses who were of Jewish origin, most of whom affirmed before giving evidence, and jurors who swore on the Bible upon taking their oath."

After Christie's address and an eight-month trial the jury acquitted Finta on all charges, which included unlawful confinement, robbery, kidnapping and manslaughter of Hungarian Jews in May and June of 1944. The Crown appealed to Ontario's Court of Appeal, which affirmed Christie's victory. But along the way, the appeal judges expressed their strong disapproval of Christie's litigation style, calling his jury address "clumsy," "improper" and "inappropriate in the extreme." The Crown, for one, noted that, by making a distinction between the way some Jews and Gentiles swear oaths, Christie was "appealing to religious prejudice."

A final clue about Doug Christie's position on Jews also came during the Finta trial. At a fund-raising rally for the 77-year-old Hungarian on March 29, 1990, Christie gave a speech in the Broadview Avenue Latvian Hall in Toronto. Unbeknownst to Christie or anyone else present, the speech was taped by a law student who worked for the lawyer representing the Holocaust Remembrance Association. In his lengthy address, Christie said: "This is war. A war without violence, but a war even more insidious than a violent war. With a violent war you can see the enemy. You can hear their guns. You can see their injuries. In this war, we don't see the enemy. They shoot their silent media bullets into the hearts of the matter, and they willingly turn on those like us who speak out."

Christie related to his audience how Jewish children often came to the trial "for theatre or entertainment." Said Christie: "If you want to notice what is really going on, you have got to be there in courtroom 403. You see, we have Jewish classes coming in for theatre or entertainment, but I haven't seen too many people I could recognize as non-Jewish. . . . They are all there, it seems to me, to see vengeance. That's really what it's about."

Are these comments trial evidence of anti-Jewish bias? In an unprecedented February 1993 investigation into Christie's conduct at the Zundel and Finta prosecutions, the discipline committee of the Law Society of Upper Canada decided the answer to that question was an unambiguous yes. Christie's comments, said the committee, were "anti-Semitic." He had "made common cause," it ruled, with anti-Semitic "lunatics."

"We know," the committee's 38-page report concluded, "who Mr. Christie is. In the depths of his imagery he has not lied."

5

THE RELIGION OF HATE

It is a few minutes past 11:00 a.m. on Sunday, March 8, 1992, in Hayden Lake, Idaho, and Pastor Richard Girnt Butler, the head of the Church of Jesus Christ Christian Aryan Nations, is speaking to his flock about what he calls Aryan Canada.

"You know," Butler says in his deep nasal voice, thickened by a lifetime of Pall Malls, "you know, some of those things walking around Aryan Canada, disgracing that beautiful land, wearing that dirty, filthy rag on top of their heads, which is a symbol, is it not?"

Butler is talking about the yarmulka worn by Jews. Jews are one of Butler's favorite subjects. In a widely circulated pamphlet penned by the pastor a decade earlier, Jews are described as "the adversary of our race and God." Like all members of the Aryan Nations, Butler believes that Jews were the murderers of Jesus Christ, the authors of international communism, the manipulators of the press and the banking system and, most significantly, the direct descendants of the biblical Cain, who had been fathered by the Devil. The Jews, ipso facto, are the spawn of Satan. In Pastor Richard Butler's view, the Jews have a lot to answer for. And on this cold winter day, they are being called to account for a Canadian Human Rights Commission inquiry into a September 1990 Nazi rally on a remote farm near Provost, Alberta.

"[The Jews] won't wear the Mounties' police cap when they become Mounties in this multicultural filth. They wear this filthy rag on their heads. But a white man can't wear the cross, the Ku Klux Klan symbol or the blood drop, or display the swastika on a private farm, miles away from any town, where the seven complainants who had seen part of it had to look at it through field glasses from far away, to watch this small group of white men come together for love of their own kind." Butler pauses, waggling a tobacco-stained finger in the air. The Aryan Nations leader closes his heavy-lidded eyes for a moment. "I believe that the real men of Canada are going to come together in rafts. Their countenance is going to show an anger. They are going to turn red in the face, they are going to get gloriously, furiously unhappy."

In the one hundred or so folding chairs facing Butler, no more than two dozen parishioners sit listening to the Aryan Nations leader. Some of them nod approvingly at Butler's cryptic reference to Canadian men turning "red in the face"; as Identity Christians, they know that only Aryans can blush or display "blood in the face." Some of the parishioners, however, look bored; in far right circles, Richard Butler is noted for many things, but excellence in public speaking is not one of them. One or two of the churchgoers gaze around the room, waiting for Butler to finish.

The chapel of the Church of Jesus Christ Christian is panelled in waxed knotty pine, with a few crosses dotting the walls here and there. At the back of the large room, above the lectern, is Butler's pride and joy: a nine-foot-square stained-glass window featuring the Aryan Nations symbol. Whenever reporters drop by for a chat, Butler always insists that his photograph be taken below the window, in profile. With his eyes steely and his jaw locked in what he hoped was Aryan determination, Butler has posed for hundreds of such photographs over the years. The Aryan Nations symbol depicts a crowned sword intersected by an elongated letter N, all framed by a blue shield. Emanating out of the shield, towards the corners of the window, are white and blue shafts of light on a blood-red background. From a certain angle, the logo looks like a stylized swastika; to Aryan Nations members, however, it is much more. In his booklet *The Aryan Warrior*, Butler devotes two entire pages to the scriptural origins of each aspect of the symbol, which, he writes, evokes "the Word of God, a Racial Symbol, Seven Points of Spiritual Perfection, the Beginning and Ending of the Message to a Race."

Butler is a large man, standing six feet plus and weighing in at 180 pounds. His face is distinguished by an impressively large nose; his head is topped by thinning hair going grey at the sides. As is his wont, he is wearing a navy blazer purchased, like all of the Aryan Nations uniforms, at JC Penney. On the upper left sleeve, near his shoulder, his wife, Betty, has stitched an Aryan Nations patch.

On this day, Butler's large wooden lectern is framed by the Confederate and U.S. flags. Under another flag—the Texas One Star, a gift from that state's former Grand Dragon of the Knights of the Ku Klux Klan, the much-feared Louis Beam, Jr.—there is a small altar. On it, between two vases filled with plastic flowers, is a large upright sword with three swastikas carved into the hilt.

At the far side of the chapel, facing Butler, is the entrance to Aryan Hall, which serves as both the Church of Jesus Christ Christian's meeting place and dining room. Butler can see, hanging above the hall, a few of the 12 flags representing the "Aryan Nations," among them Canada, Great Britain, South Africa and the United States. Tacked to one wall, beneath the Canadian Maple Leaf, is a large Nazi Party flag. One of Butler's prized possessions, the flag was liberated from Munich near the end of World War Two by a member of the Princess Patricia's Canadian Light Infantry. The serviceman passed it on to a member of the Ku Klux Klan, who then gave the flag to Butler as a gift.

Butler is wrapping up his 45-minute sermon, which a church member at the back is dutifully recording. Cassette-tape recordings of each of Butler's sermons are later sold to Aryan Nations members for $4.50, postage and handling not included. The Aryan Cassette Service, as it is called, is a surprisingly big generator of income for the church.

"I'm going to tell you this, folks," Butler said, and his audience stirred, knowing that soon they would be able to leave. "It's not going to be an easy battle. We're not going to win it from sitting in arm-chairs. But we do have a duty to do, to the best of our ability. Let not the blood be upon our heads, but let it be upon our enemies' heads.

"So shake the dust off your feet, for we have one job: we have to inform. And when we inform we have to recruit. Thus is going to be formed the Army of Jesus the Christ, a great white army, with many crowns on his head, upon whose side is written the King of kings, the Lord of lords. You are the kings He is King of. Throw not your crowns into the dust for the Jew. Retain them forever and ever, for thine is the power and the kingdom for ever and ever. Amen."

After a few hymns, Butler's parishioners shake the old man's hand, then shuffle off into the bright Idaho winter. It was a good ser-mon, Pastor, they say. If one were to ask those present at the 11:00 a.m. service—or the service held every Wednesday night at 7:30—all would say that Pastor Richard Girnt Butler is a nice fellow who could not hurt a fly. One of his Canadian followers, Alberta resident Terry Long, would even privately admit that Butler does not exercise as much leadership as he used to. In truth, Butler does not look like much to be worried about: he is a shy man, with a deferential man-ner, and a habit of closing his eyes for extended periods when engaged in conversation. He insists that he abhors violence.

But if one were to ask someone down the road at the FBI office in nearby Coeur d'Alene, they would say Richard G. Butler is one of the undisputed leaders of the growing international neo-Nazi movement. They would say he has flooded the United States, Canada and Europe with some of the most vile hate propaganda extant. They would say he single-handedly built a Nazi umbrella group that for many years brought together warring neo-Nazi and

Klan factions in a single, unified far-right force; the Church of Jesus Christ Christian would be its religious arm, while the Aryan Nations would be its secular arm.

And, finally, they would say that he is the spiritual grandfather of the Aryan Nations offshoot known as the Silent Brotherhood, the group they believe is the most powerful domestic terrorist threat the United States has faced in its more than 200 years of history.

Born in February 1918 in a small town in Colorado, not far from Denver, Richard Girnt Butler was schooled in racial theory long before he was even permitted to vote—or, for that matter, ride a bicycle. His father, a machinist named Clarence Butler, taught young Richard that communism was Jewish and that Jews controlled the banking system. These bankers, he was told, were funding the Bolsheviks in Russia. Within a short time, Richard Butler, age 11, had turned into a pint-sized anti-Semitic, anti-Communist dynamo, reading as much as he could about the coming race war between the Christian white majority and the Jew-led miscegenating Communist hordes.

When he was 13, Butler's family left Colorado for the Promised Land of California, as so many other Americans did during the Great Depression years. In California, the Butlers did well. After completing high school, Butler pursued studies in aeronautical engineering at Los Angeles City College. While there, he worked part-time for a company that built the B-11 bomber. The company, Consolidated Vultee Air Craft, sent Butler, then in his early twenties, to work on commercial and military air maintenance contracts in Africa. In 1941, the company transferred him to India to work on fighter planes belonging to the Royal Indian Air Force. It was in India, oddly enough, that Butler first encountered Aryan racial theory. According to Church of Jesus Christ Christian lore, Butler studied the Rig-Veda and learned of the legendary conquest of parts of India in 1500 B.C. by blond-haired, blue-eyed Europeans called Aryans. He developed an appreciation for the virtues of India's rigid and brutal caste system, and he started to speculate about how such a system could be applied in the United States. In 1946, he returned to California to marry his girlfriend Betty.

Butler's official biography states that he was "returning from wartime activities," but the supreme Aryan warrior never wore a military uniform, before or after 1946. Like David Duke and many other far right leaders, Butler likes to brag about military experience that he does not have. Upon his return to the U.S., Butler told Betty that he was worried. The U.S. had changed in his absence, he said. He later recalled that he was "deeply troubled concerning the future from the things I had observed first-hand overseas, and events resulting from governmental edicts that seemed to be always contrary to the best interests of the nation and of the white race in particular." During the televised anti-Communist purges by the Senate sub-committee led by Joseph McCarthy, Butler was an ardent fan of the headline-grabbing Wisconsin politician.

The late 1950s saw Butler becoming a father, to a girl, Cindy. Those years also saw him moving ever-further to the far right; during this period, he says he was communicating regularly with another McCarthy fan, George Lincoln Rockwell, founder and leader of the Virginia-based American Nazi Party. By 1962, Butler had become the leader of something called the California Committee to Combat Communism, a group he later said was part of his continuing effort "to arouse attention of friends, acquaintances, members of fraternal organizations and business associates to action concerning the threat of Jewish Communism." Among other things, the Committee worked to drive Communists out of the teaching profession through boycotts and public demonstrations.

Travelling around the Los Angeles area in the early 1960s, delivering speeches about the grave threat posed by left-leaning high-school gym teachers, Butler one day met retired colonel William Potter Gale. Gale told Butler he had supervised Philippine guerrilla operations for Gen. Douglas MacArthur during the war. Gale left the armed forces in 1950 and, like Butler, toiled in California's booming aircraft industry. He later started his own securities brokerage firm.

When he took Butler aside that night in 1962, Gale had already run unsuccessfully for governor of California on an anti-Jewish, pro-segregationist platform. In 1960, he formed the California Rangers, a white supremacist paramilitary organization. The group shared members and information with the Church of Jesus Christ Christian, a Hollywood-based congregation to which Gale belonged. The Rangers, the California attorney-general wrote in a 1965 report, had completely taken over the Signal Hill American Legion Post outside Los Angeles and turned it into "a front." It was the Signal Hill Post legionnaires that Butler was addressing when he met Gale.

Gale told Butler he had liked what the anti-Communist activist had to say and that he wanted him to meet the leader of the Church of Jesus Christ Christian, Dr. Wesley Swift. Swift was a one-time Methodist minister and well-known Southern California bigot with a penchant for genocide. A rabid anti-Semite and anti-Catholic, Swift had been preaching what he called the Christian Identity gospel since about 1946. He had been at the margins of society for many decades, as a member first of the Ku Klux Klan and then of the anti-Jewish Christian Nationalist Crusade. A Presbyterian by birth, Butler was not a particularly religious man. He was reluctant to go to Swift's church, but when he heard that Swift had been an early inspiration for George Lincoln Rockwell, he changed his mind. Heading out on a fateful Sunday morning, Richard and Betty Butler found Swift's headquarters at an unlikely spot—the seedy corner of Hollywood and Vine. Perched on a narrow pew, the Butlers listened carefully to what Swift had to say: he spoke a lot about who were the true Israelites, and the Aryan "nations."

Wesley Swift tapped Richard Butler's soul on that day and turned the aeronautical engineer into an unabashed neo-Nazi. Within a short time, he was a man obsessed. Richard Butler became an ardent Identity Christian.

The origins of the Christian Identity movement, as it has manifested itself in Canada and the United States, can be traced back to late eighteenth-century England. One of the earliest exponents of the pseudo-religion was Richard Brothers, who declared that he would be revealed to be "the Nephew of the Almighty" in November 1795. His creed was called British Israel or, sometimes, Anglo-Israel. Brothers's basic belief—which was to be refined in the coming decades by a small group of followers, one of whom was a bishop in the Church of England—was that western Europeans were God's chosen people, having descended from the ten lost tribes of Israel. They alone were the true Covenant People. The Jews, Brothers held, were neither true Israelites nor chosen.

The British Israel torch was ultimately passed to another Englishman, Edward Hine, who in 1871 published and sold a quarter million copies of a book, *Identification of the British Nation with Lost Israel*. Hine, who interpreted the King James version of the Old Testament literally, wrote that the ten lost tribes had wandered westward, to Britain and its former colonies, Canada and the United States. Ample proof was found, for example, in the word British, which Hine and his followers asserted was derived from the Hebraic word *berit-ish*, or man of the covenant. The Jews, on the other hand, were descendants of a tribe of Mongolian-Turkish Khazars from southern Russia. (The Kingdom of Khazaria, as Alan Davies notes in *Anti-Semitism in Canada*, existed between the Black and Caspian seas, north of the Caucasus Mountains, between A.D. 700 and 1300. In the eighth century, Khazarian king Bulan adopted Judaism as the state religion. He did so for political reasons; it was a means of maintaining his neutrality between the warring Christian and Muslim nations nearby. Khazaria thus became a haven for Jews. And, many reputable scholars believe, it did, in a sense, become a lost "tribe," the place of origin for non-Sephardic Jews.)

To the likes of Edward Hine, however, the Khazars' footsteps in the sands of time could also be followed back, with very little difficulty, to Cain. Cain's father was Satan, so the Jews—or the two tribes making up the House of Judah—were the literal children of the Devil. To them would accrue all of the Biblical curses threatened in the prophecies of the Old Testament.

Even today, at places like the British Israel World Federation book-store in a strip mall in Vancouver, where hundreds of British Israel texts are stacked alongside dusty Nazi and white supremacist pamphlets, books like *Migrations of Israel* explain Hine's view of history in remarkably similar terms: "In truth, there can be no denial of the fact that the Anglo-Saxon, Celtic, Germanic, Scandinavian and related peo-ples are indeed the descendants of the ancient Israelites. Down through countless centuries, and across the face of Asia and Europe, our forefa-thers trekked to the new promised land to fulfil the numerous prophe-cies of scripture." One of these prophecies was that the Jews, or the House of Judah, would be exterminated by God on Judgment Day.

In the 1870s, copies of Hine's best-seller were brought to the United States by enthusiasts living in Ontario, New York and Michigan. As had been the case in England, British Israel greatly excited North American anti-Semites and white supremacists. It provided them with theological justification for their bigotry. Canadian British Israelites, most of whom were rabid monarchists, swallowed the counterfeit reli-gion more or less whole. (They still maintain puny congregations in Toronto and Vancouver, boasting no more than about 1,200 active members.) And in the United States, within a very short time, Hine's book was breeding further variations on Richard Brothers's century-old absurdity. One such variation, to be preached by Dr. Wesley Swift in Southern California, was Christian Identity.

Identity took British Israelism one step further. Identity adherents were not merely content to wait for God to lay waste to the House of Judah. Swift and his Identity followers were impatient: they wanted to hasten the process and kill off all the Jews themselves. Considering the men who made up Swift's circle of friends, this should have come as no surprise. His comrades-in-arms included some of the most prominent fascists in the United States during the 1950s and 1960s: Dr. Bertram Comparet, a pro-Nazi lawyer who represented violent extremist organizations; and Rev. Gerald L.K. Smith, one of George Lincoln Rockwell's early inspirations, Swift's leader and perhaps the best stump speaker the North American racist right has ever produced.

With God on his side, Swift did not shrink from fiery public declarations about the coming Armageddon: "All Jews," he preached, "must be destroyed." And: "I prophesy that before November 1953, there will not be a Jew in the United States, and by that I mean a Jew that will be able to walk or talk." Non-whites, Swift preached, were "mud people" without souls, who were fit only to toil as slaves to Aryans. From 1946 until his death, Swift proclaimed that Jews were responsible for international communism, the two world wars, the U.S. Federal Reserve banking system, homosexuality, abortion, race-mixing, One World Government, Freemasonry, the United Nations and fluoridation.

In his booklet "Was Jesus Christ A Jew?" (his answer, not surprisingly, was no), Swift writes that there can be no fence-sitting in the days ahead: "Take your choice: Christ or the Jews, Christianity or Jewry, the Kingdom of Yahweh or world government that leads down to socialist and communist slavery. [The Jews'] dream has been the things they have financed not only throughout the ages, but from the time of Karl Marx to the revolutions of our time. The Kingdom of Yahweh has brought knowledge and blessing to the ends of the Earth. You are the 'have' nations of the world, the Christian nations of Yahweh's Kingdom, and are blessed by every covenant promise which he made to them."

A diabetic, Swift died, sightless, in a Mexican hospital in 1970, refusing to be treated by American doctors, whom he said were all Jewish anyway. The leadership of the Church of Jesus Christ Christian then fell to his disciple Richard Girnt Butler, who for seven years had served ably as national director of Swift's Christian Defense League. (The group appears to be unrelated to the CDL that sprang up in Louisiana in 1977, or the Canadian version, which was established in Alberta in 1983.) At the time, Butler was a senior manufacturing engineer at Lockheed Aircraft in Palmdale, California, and the coinventor of a process for rapid repair of tubeless tires. By then fairly well off, he chose to give up what was probably a lucrative career to, as he put it, "devote my full energy and time to my greatest and all-consuming desire, serving God and nation."

Richard Butler served God and nation to the best of his abilities, but by 1973 it was clear that parishioners were drifting away in droves from his Church of Jesus Christ Christian. He was no Wesley Swift orator; his public speaking lacked both originality and spark. Reluctantly, Butler discussed the dwindling attendance with his wife and a few of his followers. They concluded that they should all—the Butlers and about a dozen church members—move to a part of the United States that was beyond the corrupting influences of non-whites, Jews and urban society. So, in April 1973, Richard and Betty Butler purchased 19.6 acres of rural land just outside Hayden Lake, Idaho. The Butlers, who had previously vacationed in the area, had found a new home for the Church of Jesus Christ Christian.

The Aryan Nations compound in Northern Idaho is 115 miles south of the Canadian border and seven miles outside Hayden Lake. It is to be found in a quiet, out-of-the-way part of the Idaho panhandle, where the nearest black or Jew is in Coeur d'Alene and the nearest FBI agent is just as far. Before the trouble started in 1978, a few hundred well-to-do cottagers, among them one or two Hollywood stars, used to while away tranquil summers on the golf courses and lakes closer to Hayden. All around the area there are Douglas fir and lodgepole pine, reaching towards the brilliant blue Idaho sky. It is a beautiful place. To get to Richard Butler's home, you must travel along a slight incline on a winding hundred-yard dirt path that branches off Rimrock Road. You cannot miss Butler's residence: a man carrying an AR-15 semi-automatic assault rifle stands guard at a fenced gate, just beside a hut that sports the sign "WHITES ONLY."

After arriving in the spring of 1973, Butler and his Identity followers built the chapel first. Then came the adjoining Aryan Hall. Next to be built was the office, which housed an elaborate printing press and storage space. Soon, there was a small school, and a few cabins for church members. (In June 1981, a bomb blast rocked Aryan Hall, causing what Butler said was $80,000 in damage. He blamed the militant Jewish Defence League for the bombing and immediately resolved to erect a 30-foot watchtower not far from Aryan Hall, where an armed Aryan would keep watch over Butler's flock.) Butler paid for all of the construction out of his own pocket, just as he had paid for the land.

In the first year at Hayden Lake, Butler and his followers often discussed political action. They wanted to find a secular way to advance the principles of the Identity creed. Butler's first political foray came in 1974: a brief flirtation with a local chapter of the Posse Comitatus, an ultra-secretive Identity organization. (Founded in 1969, Posse Comitatus takes its name from the Latin for power of the county.) Its members, found in rural areas in more than a dozen states, assert that there is no legitimate governmental authority above the level of the local sheriff. Butler's liaison with the Posse was unsuccessful, however, as was a brief linkage with the Louisiana-based National Emancipation of the White Seed. He continued his ministry in relative obscurity.

And then, in June 1978, Butler posted a sign at the entrance to his acreage. It read "ARYAN NATIONS." This, he decreed, was to be the political arm of the Church of Jesus Christ Christian.

In one of its earliest pamphlets, "Who What Why When Where Aryan Nations," the group described its raison d'être: "Aryan Nations is not a new right wing organization which has suddenly appeared on the scene. Aryan Nations is the on-going work of Jesus the Christ regathering His people, calling His people to a state for their nation to bring in His Kingdom! Hail His Victory! WE BELIEVE that the true, literal children of the Bible are the twelve tribes of Israel which are now scattered throughout the world and are now known as the Anglo-Saxon, Celtic, Scandinavian, Teutonic people of this earth. WE BELIEVE that there are literal children of Satan in the world today. These children are the descendants of Cain, who was a result of Eve's original sin, her physical seduction by Satan. WE BELIEVE there is a battle being fought this day between the children of darkness (today known as

Jews) and the children of light (God), the Aryan race, the true Israel of the Bible. WE BELIEVE in the preservation of our race individually and collectively as a people as demanded and directed by God. We believe a racial nation has a right and is under obligation to preserve itself and its members."

Two things distinguished the Church of Jesus Christ Christian Aryan Nations from the Posse Comitatus, the Ku Klux Klans and dozens of other far right organizations that had gone before it. First, it was both religious and secular in orientation at the same time; that is, unlike other rightist groups, it could comfortably accommodate those who entered the far right movement for either spiritual or earthly reasons. Butler was shrewd: his decade of experience in the white nationalist movement had taught him that Klansmen and neo-Nazis often spent more time battling each other than they did the real enemy. Butler's bright idea was to develop an organization sufficiently open to accommodate all points of view. So, if one embraced Identity, for example, one could join the Church of Jesus Christ Christian. If one did not, one could join the Aryan Nations alone. Or one could simply just hang out at Hayden Lake and join neither. The Church of Jesus Christ Christian Aryan Nations had become the first neo-Nazi umbrella group.

The second important distinction was that the Aryan Nations had rejected the century-old approach of, say, the Ku Klux Klan. No more would there be self-defeating and random acts of terror against blacks or Catholics or synagogues. Instead, the Aryan Nations had a broader and more apocalyptic vision. It favored the creation of what it called a whites-only "territorial imperative" in British Columbia, Alberta and the five most northwestern U.S. states. In this area, only white, able-bodied heterosexuals would be permitted to live. Once the territorial imperative was firmly established, Aryan Warriors would strike out and reclaim all of North America and, eventually, Europe. Non-whites would be deported to their places of origin, and Jews would be killed en masse.

Butler kept busy in the late 1970s, tending to his growing empire. Membership in the various Klan organizations was in decline, but interest in Identity and neo-Nazism was flourishing in the far right, which is just as susceptible to fads as mainstream society. As a result, Butler picked up many recruits during this period. He was becoming the spiritual leader to the entire North American far right movement.

Nazi-style uniforms were designed for the recently acquired male members of the church. A regular publication, *Calling Our Nation*, was sent out to members and subscribers. Memberships were sold for $15 to all those who were prepared to declare that they were "of the white Aryan race" and that they "further understood and agreed with the Aryan Nations' exclusion of Jews, Negroes, Mexicans, Orientals and Mongrels." Using his printing press, Butler also started to reproduce and sell books and leaflets written by Wesley Swift, Bertram Comparet and Adolf Hitler. Other items peddled included the infamous hoax pamphlet produced by the secret police of the Russian czar, "Protocols of the Learned Elders of Zion"; Aryan Nations belt buckles and coffee mugs; copies of *The International Jew*, the viciously anti-Semitic book written in 1920 by automobile pioneer Henry Ford; and, in 1978, a book called *The Turner Diaries*, which became an underground best seller.

The Turner Diaries was a novel about a far right revolution. Five years later, it would serve as the blueprint for the 18-month rampage of murders, bombings and robberies carried out by the clandestine Aryan Nations offshoot called the Silent Brotherhood, or, as it was sometimes known, the Order.

The unlikely author of *The Turner Diaries* was a bookish-looking scientist named William L. Pierce, founder and leader of the ultra-rightist National Alliance in West Virginia. A former university physics professor and American Nazi Party publicist, Pierce had written the 200-odd-page book (under the pseudonym Andrew Macdonald) partly to raise funds for the National Alliance and partly as a recruitment tool. On both counts, *The Turner Diaries* was wildly successful. In time, it would be sold at far right rallies, gun lobby meetings and through the mail by groups like the Aryan Nations. Although privately published,

THE RELIGION OF HATE 115

and impossible to find at mainstream bookstores, *The Turner Diaries* sold thousands upon thousands of copies. It is now in its fifth printing. For many young American and Canadian racists in the 1980s, it would serve as a powerful clarion call to battle—a call to begin the Aryan-led revolution Identity Christians believed was foretold in Scripture. The FBI called it "the Bible of the racist right." The National Alliance called it "a handbook for white victory"—and for some, it very nearly was.

The book is completely unlike any other literature ever seen in the racist right wing. Most of the pamphlets, booklets and texts produced by the white nationalist movement are monosyllabic drivel, rife with spelling errors, non sequiturs and historical revisionism. They profess to be factual; they are anything but. *The Turner Diaries*, on the other hand, is written with what can only be described as an uncharacteristic intelligence and style. Even though it is clearly a work of fiction, and even though it is regarded as such by all racists who thumb through it, *The Diaries* has dramatically transformed a whole generation of Klansmen and neo-Nazi activists, in both Canada and the United States. Some members of the Silent Brotherhood carried the book with them wherever they went.

The book tells the story, diary-style, of just over two years in the life of Earl Turner, a member of an underground racist terrorist group called the Organization. It begins in September 1991, when Turner and 2,000 like-minded men and women are fighting the Cohen Act, which has outlawed the private ownership of firearms. The government—or, as Turner calls it, the System—is employing gangs of blacks to confiscate weapons. But Turner and his cunning band of desperadoes are determined to overthrow the entire System at any cost. At the outset, Turner despairs of the huge task ahead: "Why didn't we rise up three years ago, when they started taking our guns away? Why didn't we rise up in righteous fury and drag these arrogant aliens into the streets and cut their throats then? Why didn't we roast them over bonfires at every street corner? Why didn't we make a final end to this obnoxious and eternally pushy clan, this pestilence from the sewers of the East, instead of meekly allowing ourselves to be disarmed?" If the Organization fails in its mission, Turner darkly muses, "there will be no white men to remember us . . . only a swarming horde of indifferent, mulatto zombies." Writes Turner: "It is a terrible, terrible task we have before us."

The Organization, which operates in a cell system, is made up of "units" whose five or six members are for the most part unknown to each other. Turner's particular expertise is the construction of home-made bombs; in his diary, he tells the reader, in great detail, how to find and assemble the materials needed for each, as well as how to properly store, handle and use firearms and explosives. With Turner's help, the Organization plots and carries out a bomb attack on the national headquarters of the FBI in Washington, D.C., killing 700 people. It bombs the offices of *The Washington Post*, because the press is a willing tool of the "political police," and kills one of the paper's Jewish editors at his home. It murders one of its own members, who refuses to murder a priest and a rabbi. It bombs television transmitters. It rains mortars on Congress during a presidential visit, killing hundreds more. It shoots a Tel Aviv-bound jetliner out of the sky with a bazooka. It bombs the city of Houston—"the Great Houston Bombings," Turner calls them—killing 4,000. It kills 300 at a cocktail party at the Israeli Embassy.

Midway through his blood-drenched white supremacist odyssey, Earl Turner learns of the existence of a small group of men who control the Organization, a group called the Order. Before being invited to join, Turner is injected with truth serum to determine if he is an informant. He is then obliged to read what is simply called "The Book," a 400-page Aryan magnum opus that details the past and future of the non-Jewish white race. Finally, in a secret ceremony replete with chanting, robes and sacred oaths, Turner is made a member of the Order. He is instructed to kill himself if he is ever captured by the enemy, and to never reveal its dark secrets.

In July 1993, the Order sends out terrorist units to simultaneously "hit targets all across the country, from Canada to Mexico and from coast to coast." The Aryan commandos direct their assaults against airports, highways, water and electrical utilities, telephone exchanges, gas storage depots and police stations. "The whole key to neutralizing the police—and to everything else, for that matter—was our work inside the military," Turner writes that month. "[Our] strategy hinged on our success in winning over a number of high-ranking military commanders." With substantial military help, the Organization deliberately provokes race riots and cuts off food supplies to all but the chosen few. Once it seizes control of a city, the Organization begins a program of shipping out non-whites. And then, on August 1, 1993, it makes its move.

"Today," Turner writes in the entry on that date, "has been the Day of the Rope—a grim and bloody day, but an unavoidable one. Tonight, for the first time in weeks, it is quiet and totally peaceful throughout all of Southern California. But the night is filled with silent horrors; from tens of thousands of lampposts, power poles and trees throughout this vast metropolitan area the grisly forms hang." The grisly forms are the corpses of people who have betrayed their race.

With military help, Turner and his Organization somehow secure a large number of abandoned nuclear warheads and missiles. Shortly thereafter, a group of Organization members conceal four 60-kiloton nuclear warheads in the Washington, D.C., area. Before they can be detonated, other Organization members kill more than 60,000 in Miami in an unprovoked nuclear attack, and an equivalent number in South Carolina. The "Revolutionary Command" issues a statement calling for the U.S. government to abandon its plans to respond to the threat posed by the Organization. There is a brief respite in the fighting. Then, a few days later, Baltimore is levelled by a nuclear attack, killing one million. "Two dozen" other such blasts destroy unnamed U.S. cities on the same day. Despite all the carnage, however, the System refuses to surrender. The Order learns of its plans to counter-strike. Writes Turner: "So we decided to preempt. We struck first, but not at the government's forces. We fired all of our missiles from Vandenberg (except for a half-dozen targeted on New York) at two targets: Israel and the Soviet

Union. . . . By hitting New York and Israel, we had completely knocked out two of world Jewry's principal nerve centers, and it should take them a while to establish a new chain of command and get their act together. . . . By provoking a Soviet counterattack, we did far more to disrupt the System in this country than we could have done by using our own weapons against domestic targets—and we still have most of our 60-kiloton warheads left!"

The entire planet slips into post-nuclear chaos, with Jewish pogroms being carried out on every continent. Writes Turner: "If the Organization survives this contest, no Jew will—anywhere. We'll go to the uttermost ends of the earth to hunt down the last of Satan's spawn." The book finally concludes with the November 9, 1993, entry, the day Turner leads a suicide mission against the Pentagon, flying a plane equipped with a nuclear warhead. The diary offers an Epilogue: "The only time, after November 9, 1993, the Organization was forced to detonate a nuclear weapon on the North American continent was a year later, in Toronto. Hundreds of thousands of Jews had fled the United States to that Canadian city during 1993 and 1994, making almost a second New York of it and using it as their command center for the war raging to the south. As far as both the Jews and the Organization were concerned, the U.S.–Canadian border had no real significance during the later stages of the Great Revolution, and by mid-1994 conditions were only slightly less chaotic north of the border than south of it."

And so the book ends—an astonishing paean to an orgy of violence, racism and anti-Semitism. Earl Turner "helped greatly to assure that his race would survive and prosper," the book's final sentence reads, "that the Organization would achieve its worldwide political and military goals, and that the Order would spread its wise and benevolent rule over the earth for all time to come."

Bob Mathews was 25 years old when *The Turner Diaries* first appeared in May 1978. He was also a member of the National Alliance, the organization run by the book's author, William Pierce.

The Diaries electrified him, and changed his life forever. By the spring of 1984, Mathews was, like Earl Turner, heading a secretive neo-Nazi terrorist group that called itself the Order. After recruits took a sacred oath in a barracks on his small farm in Metaline Falls, Washington, Mathews would hand each man a copy of *The Diaries*.

"Read it," he would tell them. "It's what we are all about."

Richard Butler learned his anti-Semitism and white supremacy at his father's knee, but where did Bob Mathews get his? It is difficult to provide any compelling answers about Mathews's brief life. Unlike many far right leaders, he studiously avoided the media. Like a flare in a dark night, he burned brightly with some odd, misplaced passion—and then, just as quickly, he was gone. On the outside, he was a fairly handsome, clean-cut man, the sort of fellow one would not look twice at on the street. But beating in his breast, Robert Jay Mathews nurtured a seething black hatred for Jews and non-whites and "the System." He would become, in just a few years, one of the most notorious anti-Semites and white supremacists North America has ever produced.

Where did his hate come from? According to those who knew him, it did not come from his parents. Robert Jay Mathews was born in January 1953 in Marfa, Texas, son to Johnny and Una who called him Robbie. While Johnny worked at a General Electric appliance store, Una would read to young Robbie and his two older brothers about different cultures. She wanted her three sons to be open-minded towards others. They were an ordinary American family with a slightly liberal bent. By all accounts, Robbie grew up in a supportive environment and he was well loved. He was certainly not abused, ignored or maltreated.

In 1964, the Mathews family was living in Phoenix, Arizona, where Robbie's father worked at a paper company. In October, *The Arizona Republic* carried a special advertising supplement produced by the John Birch Society. The far right group had been founded in 1958 in Massachusetts to "alert the nation" to the growing Communist menace. As Kevin Flynn and Gary Gerhardt recount in their authoritative biography of Mathews, *The Silent Brotherhood*, young Robbie was literally transfixed by the Birchers' 16-page tabloid insert. After a few minutes of study, he clipped a $5 bill to a coupon included in the tabloid, and sent it off to the John Birch Society for a membership. He was 11 years old.

His family was variously enraged or depressed by the youngest Mathews's fascination with the far right and guns and off-beat faiths. But despite their objections, he continued on his downward spiral, uncaring about or unaware of the consequences. In 1970, for example, as a junior in high school—and as one of the youngest members of the local John Birch Society chapter—he became a Mormon because he liked the haircuts and the conservative lifestyle and because he didn't like hippies. Some months afterwards, he was involved in a Mormon-led anti-tax movement, even though, at 16, he of course had not yet been asked to pay income taxes. And then, in 1972, young Robbie slipped entirely out of his parents' world and into another: he became involved with a paramilitary organization called the Sons of Liberty, which he had learned about through his tax-protest activities. The group, which was briefly investigated by both the Internal Revenue Service and the FBI, believed the IRS was doing the bidding of the Kremlin. It also believed that Jews had removed all of the gold reserves from Fort Knox, thereby rendering U.S. currency worthless, and the levy of taxes somehow unconstitutional. It is possible that Mathews may even have been the leader of the Sons of Liberty even though he was not yet in his twenties.

In 1973, at the age of 20, Mathews worked as a maintenance man at an Arizona mine. When he got home in the evenings, he would write letters to the IRS to inform them that income tax was illegal. The IRS, needless to say, disagreed; they filed Mathews's letters away for future reference. In that same year, Flynn and Gerhardt recount, Mathews filled out a federal income tax form and declared that he was supporting ten dependants. When the IRS saw that from a 20-year-old Phoenix resident recently graduated from high school, they pursued the matter. The U.S. Attorney's office filed a misdemeanor complaint against Mathews and secured a conviction. A judge issued a bench warrant for Mathews's arrest, and armed IRS agents went looking for him in July 1973. When the agents tracked him down at a 7-Eleven, Mathews tried to escape, rolling his pick-up truck in the process. He was caught, and thrown in jail for the weekend. In January 1974, on his twenty-first birthday, he was sentenced to six months' probation.

Mathews resolved to put Arizona behind him—and some mileage on his new pick-up. In the summer of 1974, he and a high-school chum decided to go on a road trip to the Pacific Northwest, to see if there were any mines looking for workers. After a few days of crawling along backroads in some of the most beautiful country Robbie Mathews had ever seen, they found Metaline Falls, Washington, a town of 400 or so a few miles south of the Canadian border—and a three-hour drive from Richard Butler's Church of Jesus Christ Christian Aryan Nations. Metaline Falls would become Mathews's new home.

There, Mathews worked in an area mine, Bunker Hill, and kept his distance from tax protestors and the like. He gave his family his word that his days of radical politics were over. His parents were deliriously happy about the change; his father sent him words of encouragement and some money to assist in the down payment on 60 acres of undeveloped land. But Mathews could not escape his past. In the spring of 1975, two Spokane FBI agents visited the mine to tell his employers about Mathews's tax-evading antics. The mine foreman did not care and soon forgot about the matter. Mathews, however, was livid. He sent a letter to the FBI's Seattle office in which he wrote: "Leave me alone, or I will respond in such a way that could be very painful to certain agents."

Poison-pen letters notwithstanding, Mathews seemed to keep his word to his parents. The next few years were spent clearing his land, taking bagpipe lessons across the border in nearby Nelson, British Columbia, and placing ads in the *Mother Earth News* for a "mature intelligent" woman to share his life. Through the ad, Mathews met a Wyoming National Park employee, Debbie McGarrity. A Kansas native, McGarrity was charmed by Mathews's boyish manner and his muscular physique. In February 1976, they were married. The Mathewses tried often, without success, to have a child, but Debbie could not carry one to term. It was a great disappointment, particularly for Bob, who seemed almost obsessed by the notion of fatherhood, which he often likened to "planting seed." So the couple placed their names with an adoption agency.

The Mathewses did not own a television so, in the long winter months, when he had more spare time, Bob Mathews read a lot of books. Many were unremarkable, but some were unusual, books like *Which Way Western Man*, a 1978 text about the decline of "white" civilization. It had been published by William Pierce's National Alliance. Within time, Mathews's old passion had consumed him once again. By 1980, he had read (and reread) *The Turner Diaries* and joined the organization led by the man who had written it.

But Mathews was frustrated: in the relative isolation of Metaline Falls, it was difficult to find other men of action who shared his views. So, in 1980, he drove down to Hayden Lake to learn more about the Christian Identity group based there, the one that had been receiving so much press attention for its First Annual Aryan Nations Congress. In one of his many trips to Idaho, Mathews met Daniel Bauer, a Hayden Lake man who was a member of the board at the Church of Jesus Christ Christian and editor of Richard Butler's *Calling Our Nation* publication. Bauer, then in his thirties, had been a member of a paramilitary outfit known as the Minutemen. During their heyday in the 1960s, the Minutemen were stridently anti-Communist, anti-immigrant and anti–gun control. Mathews was impressed with Bauer's far right credentials.

Bauer, who earned his living as a general contractor, was a friendly father of four who played armchair sociologist, chatting amiably about race and culture. He and Bob Mathews, then 27, were kindred spirits. Recalls Bauer: "Bob was a little younger than I, and he was a little less experienced in this regard: he worked and lived in a small community, very much like the small Canadian communities across the border.

These places are large enough to be established, but small enough where you don't really have a scope . . ." He laughs. "A scope of what's going on in the world, in the metropolitan areas. And when you travelled to larger communities, and you saw a picture that was a bit different than your own, and you saw things that disturbed you, you magnified them. You say to yourself that they don't have to be, or they shouldn't be. And it just seemed to me that Bob was pretty provincial in that regard. He didn't really have the big picture, or the whole picture."

In late 1981, as Bob Mathews was spending more and more time down at Hayden Lake, some good news came: he and Debbie were offered a son through the adoption agency. Elated, they named him Clint. In February 1982, Clint Mathews was baptized the offspring of an "Aryan Warrior" by Pastor Richard G. Butler in a ceremony at the Church of Jesus Christ Christian in Hayden Lake, Idaho.

The volley of .45-calibre bullets slammed into the torso and head of controversial radio talkshow host Alan Berg as he stepped out of his Volkswagen Beetle. It was 9:20 p.m. on June 18, 1984. The bullets ricocheted throughout Berg's body, shattering into lead fragments—severing his spinal column, ripping apart his heart and turning his brain into pulp. He fell onto the short concrete driveway at his Denver home without making a sound.

Bruce Carroll Pierce lowered the silenced MAC-10 machine gun and sprinted to the curb, where a yellow Volkswagen sedan awaited him. In the getaway car, behind the wheel, was David Lane. Also in the car were two other men: Richard Scutari and Robert Jay Mathews. Pierce jumped into the vehicle and Lane screeched away, towards Colorado Boulevard. Pierce, who had been introduced to Bob Mathews and the Silent Brotherhood by Dan Bauer, gave a broad smile. "Did you see that?" he said. "He didn't make a sound. He just went down like I pulled the rug out from under him." They all laughed.

The Silent Brotherhood had made its second successful assassination, and the four men were delighted. The crime of Alan Berg had been to criticize the far right on his radio program.

The first killing had taken place three weeks earlier, on May 26, 1984. The victim was Walter West, an Aryan Nations member. Because he liked to shoot off his mouth in bars, he was considered a security risk, and Mathews ordered his followers to kill him. The 42-year-old was lured to a remote wooded spot approximately two hours away from the Hayden Lake compound. As West stepped out of Richie Kemp's car, Kemp, then barely 21, smashed the back of his skull with a sledgehammer, twice. Incredibly, the blows did not kill West. So Randy Duey, one of West's closest friends and a Vietnam veteran, fired a shot from West's own Ruger Mini-14 into the man's forehead. The Silent Brotherhood members then buried West's body, which has never been found. A few weeks later, one of the men involved in the murder moved in with West's wife.

The Silent Brotherhood or, as it was sometimes also called, the Order, the White American Bastion, the Organization, the Company, or (Mathews's favorite) the Bruder Schweigen (the German for Silent Brotherhood) had come a long way in a short time.

Nine months earlier, in September 1983, a bizarre late-night ceremony was held. In the barn-like barracks Bauer had built at Bob Mathews's Metaline Falls home, the Silent Brotherhood was born. In its rituals, the group would bear more than a passing resemblance to Hitler's SS. Present for the swearing-in ceremony were Richie Kemp and Bill Soderquist, two men Mathews had met through the National Alliance, plus Aryan Nations members David Lane, Dan Bauer, Denver Parmenter, Randy Duey and Bruce Pierce. Ken Loff, Mathews's next-door neighbor and one of his closest friends, was also present. Most of the men were Identity Christians. Mathews explained to the eight—he called them kinsmen—that forming the group was step one. The next step would be to establish a list of common goals. The third step, he said, was to procure funds for the far right movement. The fourth step was recruitment of new members. The fifth step would be assassination of enemies of the white race. The final step was the creation of a guerrilla force to carry out acts of sabotage and terror in urban areas, just as Earl Turner had done.

Wordlessly, the group then assembled in a rough circle, standing around Loff's six-week-old daughter, Jamie Anne, who was placed in a blanket on the floor. The only light was provided by a few candles. In a scene reminiscent of *The Turner Diaries*, the men held hands and repeated the Brotherhood's oath, which Mathews had written for the occasion: "Let us go forth by ones and by twos, by scores and legions, and as true Aryan men with pure hearts and strong minds, face the enemies of our faith and our race with courage and determination. We hereby invoke the blood covenant and declare that we are in a full state of war and will not lay down our weapons until we have driven the enemy into the sea and reclaimed the land which was promised to our fathers of old, and through our blood and his will, becomes the land of our children to be."

The two murders Bob Mathews ordered in the spring and summer of 1984 were the culmination of a long string of crimes that started not long after that candle-lit night in Metaline Falls. On October 28, 1983, just as Earl Turner did in *The Turner Diaries*, Mathews, Duey, Pierce and Bauer robbed Spokane's World Wide Video, a store that sold pornographic publications and sex toys. They got away with $369. That was followed, in November, with the printing of bags and bags full of counterfeit money; this task was carried out by Bauer and a few others on Richard Butler's Aryan Nations presses at Hayden Lake. In the same month, Bauer produced a bomb the group hoped to used to blow up the Baron Elie de Rothschild during a Seattle speaking engagement; the assassination plans were abandoned, however, when Mathews concluded that killings would be premature. During this period, Mathews determined that the Silent Brotherhood's production of counterfeit currency, which was being overseen by Bauer, was too risky. (Pierce was arrested for distributing the cheap-looking currency but jumped bail in December 1983.) The bills were not perfect fakes by any means. Real currency would be needed to finance the Silent Brotherhood's campaign against the System. So, on December 18, 1983, on his own, Mathews robbed a City Bank branch in Seattle of $25,952.

The day before the robbery, Mathews, clearly worried about his chances of getting out of the bank alive, wrote a letter to the woman who had recently become his mistress, Aryan Nations adherent Zillah Craig. In it, he wrote: "[Tomorrow] will bring either victory or my death. Sometimes, in the dark hours of the night, I wish I was a normal man so I could enjoy life unhindered. But I know what future awaits our children unless I stand up like a man and fight. If enough of us stand up and fight then your two fine sons will have the future they deserve. They will be able to stand up and say: 'I am white, I am proud and I am free,' and no Jew or mudman will dare stand against them."

Mathews's Seattle robbery was a success, but the Aryan revolution prophesied in *The Turner Diaries* could hardly be achieved with a paltry $25,952. Mathews had big plans: more funds were needed to make them a reality. Silent Brotherhood member Thomas Allen Martinez, who helped to distribute the Brotherhood's counterfeit dollars in Philadelphia, says his former friend was fed up with waiting for the System to collapse. Like Earl Turner, he wanted action.

Martinez is a large, mustachioed former Pennsylvania Klansman who met Mathews at the September 1981 convention of the National Alliance in Arlington, Virginia. The pair became very close friends, and, two years later, Martinez was invited to become a member of the Silent Brotherhood. Shortly after that, he would become an informant for the FBI and a participant in the Witness Protection Program. Among neo-Nazis and white supremacists, he is not a popular man. One Aryan Nations member is serving time for plotting to assassinate Martinez; other far right activists have placed a bounty on his head, hoping to honor the Silent Brotherhood's oath and "separate" Martinez's head from his body. In a telephone interview from his home, somewhere in the United States, Martinez says: "I spent a lot of time with Bob Mathews. I was with him for three years in all, I guess. Few people really knew him well. . . . He was a real snake. He knew which buttons to push, you know? Sometimes you'll hear people say he was crazy, but he wasn't."

Martinez says that Mathews had a meticulous and detailed plan to destabilize the Zionist Occupation Government. The plan may well have succeeded, Martinez says, had the Silent Brotherhood leader not been surrounded by so many "nitwits." Martinez explains Mathews's objectives this way: "You could compare what Bob wanted to do to the Irish Republican Army. That's where he was headed. He wanted terrorism, and he wanted to fund the entire right wing."

The funding campaign began in earnest on January 30, 1984, when Bruce Pierce and another Silent Brotherhood member, Gary Yarbrough, robbed the Washington Mutual Savings Bank in Spokane of $3,600, a portion of which was dropped into the collection plate at Hayden Lake. On March 16, Pierce, Yarbrough, Mathews and Randy Duey held up a Continental Armored Transport truck in Seattle, getting away with $43,345. On April 23, the Silent Brotherhood ambushed another armored truck in a parking lot of a shopping mall in Seattle; they made off with $500,000 in cash and cheques. Portions of these monies were given to Silent Brotherhood members for what Mathews described as "salary." Portions were also sent off to Richard Butler and other far right leaders such as the National Alliance's William Pierce and Tom Metzger, leader of the White Aryan Resistance. But not all of the group's crimes during this period were directed at merely securing funds for far right organizations. For example, on April 29, Bruce Pierce bombed a synagogue in Boise, Idaho—just for kicks.

"I now despise what we tried to do," Martinez says ruefully.

Asked about the crimewave in which he, too, played a substantial role—and for which he served three years in a federal prison—Dan Bauer is evasive. With a few of his seven children playing in an adjoining room at his Hayden Lake home, he sounds penitent. "In retrospect, it was foolishness," he says. "It wasn't something that the man on the street supported—or ever would, actually. I can't help but think that we were out of step. Completely out of step. In a criminal sense we were out of step—that's obvious. But we were also out of step because we were attempting to counter the direction that society was going in. We weren't willing to accept the changes. I believe—and this is the bottom line—that it's pretty hard to stop society's clock. It's foolish to do that. And we were all part of the foolishness."

Following the murder of Alan Berg, "the foolishness," as Bauer put it, continued unabated. Mathews and the Silent Brotherhood were left feeling positively giddy after the talkshow host's killing. They immediately starting making plans for another armored car robbery. Relying upon information given to them by Charles E. Ostrout, a Brink's manager turned Silent Brotherhood member, Mathews planned to rob a Brink's truck outside the town of Ukiah, in northern California.

On July 19, 1984, while Aryan Nations members from all over Canada and the United States gathered up in Hayden Lake for the fifth annual World Congress, the Silent Brotherhood struck. Thirteen heavily armed members of the group stopped a Brink's truck on a steep incline just before noon; one of them stood in front of it, holding up a sign that read "GET OUT OR DIE." After Bruce Pierce—the only man not wearing a mask—fired a few shots through the truck's windows, the guards did as they were told. The trigger-happy Randy Duey also let loose with a few shots, narrowly missing one of the guards. The operation went as smooth as silk: some masked members calmly directed astonished drivers past the incredible scene, others monitored police and citizen's band transmissions, a few watched the guards, and the rest unloaded the bags of money, all $3.6 million of it. It was during this part of the robbery that Mathews made a fatal mistake: his 9-mm Smith and Wesson pistol slipped out of his belt and fell noiselessly to the floor of the Brink's truck. He would not notice its absence until much later, when it was already in the hands of the police. The gun, the FBI learned, was registered in Montana under the real name of one of the members of the Silent Brotherhood. Using that name, the FBI would ultimately track down every one of the group's members and send them to jail.

Every member, that is, except for Bob Mathews and the two Canadians who belonged to his Silent Brotherhood: Edgar Foth and Jim Mackey.

*

Edgar Foth drove his pick-up truck through the dusk, speeding out of U.S. Customs just across the border from Creston, B.C. Foth's friend, Jim Mackey, sprawled on the seat beside him, watching the scenery go by. It was the last week of September 1984, and some of the leaves had started to turn yellow and red. Foth and Mackey probably didn't speak much; Foth dislikes small talk. After a few years of inconsequential activity in the Canadian right wing, the pair had decided to abandon rhetoric and embrace action. They were heading down to Washington to meet up with their new friends in the Silent Brotherhood, at the Aryan Soldiers' Academy.

Foth had heard a few tantalizing stories about the group several weeks earlier, during the fifth annual World Congress at the Aryan Nations compound in Hayden Lake. Rumors about Bob Mathews's secretive paramilitary organization had been circulating in far right circles for much of the spring and summer of 1984. Foth, a large, beefy man who fancied guns, was tired of waiting for the Zionist Occupation Government to collapse on its own; like all of the men in the Silent Brotherhood, he wanted to accelerate the Day of Judgment. For most of the week-long congress in mid-July 1984, Foth played the role of guard. Walking the perimeter of Richard Butler's fenced property, he carried a semi-automatic assault rifle and scowled at reporters. "[Foth] is a nice guy," says Carl Franklin, the Aryan Nations chief of staff. "He's quiet and he's sober." In fact, Foth has volunteered for guard duty every time he has come down to Hayden Lake for a congress, Franklin says.

The 1984 Aryan Nations congress had attracted a substantial number of Canadians from British Columbia, Alberta, Saskatchewan, Manitoba and Ontario. Among these were future Canadian Aryan Nations leader Terry Long and Saskatchewan Aryan Nations boss Carney Milton Nerland. Another Canadian at the congress was Wagner Saende. At the time, Saende was between jobs. For seven years, he had been a teacher and vice-principal at Fleetwood-Bawden Elementary School, in Lethbridge, Alberta; later, he was vice-principal at Westminster Elementary

School in the same city. Midway through the congress, Foth and Saende attended a lecture by Jack Mohr, a retired U.S. Army colonel. Mohr was a former John Birch Society leader; on this day, he was speaking on behalf of the Christian Patriots Defense League, a group that advocated the establishment of armed bands of white Christian citizens.

Saende, interestingly, is now principal at the Elizabeth Settlement School, on a Métis reserve near Grand Centre, in northern Alberta. Saende says he travelled to Hayden Lake simply to hear Mohr, whom he calls "a super speaker." He claims that he does not remember Foth. Saende, who also says he does not have "much" sympathy for Nazism, has visited the Aryan Nations compound three times. "There are a lot of fine people down there," he says. "In 1984, I was mostly there to listen to Jack Mohr. I'm a fundamentalist, you know—the back-to-the-Bible sort of thing." Saende has been investigated by his employers at the Northland School Division, but they found no evidence that the mathematics teacher was preaching racism to his students—95 per cent of whom are Métis. Racism, said School Superintendent Colin Kelly, "is something we cannot tolerate from our employees. But in this case, we have had no indication of any wrongdoing on Mr. Saende's part."

At one point during Mohr's well-attended chat about urban terrorism, in which he gave his audience helpful pointers on how to derail trains and blow up roads, Saende asked for suggestions on how to steal blasting caps. Mohr, eyeing Saende's longish blond hair, mistook him for a woman. Saende and Foth laughed heartily. Later, when the conversation turned to Identity Christianity, Saende said the movement must deal harshly with priests and ministers who refuse to embrace the true faith. "We should tell them the truth," a Winnipeg newspaper later quoted Saende, "give them a week to repent, then execute them."

At the congress, Edgar Foth also renewed his acquaintance with Rev. Tom Erhart, a Calgary man who had been the second vice-president of Canada's Social Credit Party and was contemplating a run at the federal riding of Bow Valley. Like Foth, Erhart was a vociferous supporter of defrocked Eckville social studies teacher Jim Keegstra. Ed Foth and Erhart had both participated in pro-Keegstra demonstrations back home. "Ed's a big man [in the far right movement]," says Erhart. "A very big man." On the sunny July day they ran into each other, Foth, then not as well known in Canadian Nazi circles, showed Erhart and a few other Canadians a copy of a magazine that featured a photograph of him and two others waving placards on Keegstra's behalf.

When he was not on guard duty, Foth spent some time looking for a few publications he believed would be helpful to Keegstra's defence. Apart from "Did Six Million Really Die?" none of the books he wanted could be found at the Aryan Nations office. Foth was disappointed, but he had not travelled to Hayden Lake simply to pick up reading material.

The congress was scheduled to run from July 10 to 22. On the last day, after making contact with a few Aryan Nations adherents who gave him phone numbers belonging to members of the Silent Brotherhood, Foth donned a Klansman's robes and chatted with Erhart and another robed Klansman, Karl Leppert of Vancouver. The trio talked about Keegstra; they talked about how the Canadian media always did the bidding of the Jews. At the appointed hour, Foth and about 80 men and women were asked to form two long rows. When Michigan Klansman Robert E. Miles gave the signal, the two rows formed a circle around the 25-foot-high cross. The cross had been wrapped in gasoline-soaked burlap. Through an opening in the circle, and to the wail of bagpipes, 17 children stepped into the centre of the gathering of Klansmen and neo-Nazis. All but one of the children wore Klan robes. A few of the children, Foth knew, were Canadian.

"Hail victory!" Foth and the others screamed as Miles lit the cross with a torch. "Hail victory!"

Two months later, Edgar Foth and his friend Jim Mackey bumped over backroads in upstate Washington, approaching the outskirts of Bluecreek where Silent Brotherhood member Randy Duey—the one who had murdered Walter West in May 1984—had established a neo-Nazi training camp. At the camp, Duey produced pamphlets with such titles as "The Enemy's Organization," "The Purpose of the Aryan Soldiers' Academy" and "On Being Underground." The Aryan "academy" was being financed out of Duey's share of the Ukiah armored car robbery. Foth and Mackey were its first students.

As Foth and Mackey pulled up, Duey stepped out of his small trailer home to greet them. The Canadian recruits had arrived.

Edgar Foth was born in Edmonton in 1954. His parents, some say, were simple, quiet people who had come to Canada from war-ravaged Poland in the early 1950s. Along with Edgar, the Foths had three other children, two sons and a daughter. As a young boy, Edgar listened to his parents relate frightening tales about the treatment of refugees during World War Two. His parents, who spoke fluent German, made clear their sympathies were with the Third Reich and not Poland. "We also heard these stories from family members, and from friends of the family," says one of Foth's siblings, who did not wish to be identified. "Our parents were right in the middle of the war. They saw what was going on. They didn't agree with the history that was being told in Canada, but they were in a new country and they kept their mouths shut. But Ed really took these stories to heart."

According to friends, Foth has said that his father was a member of the Ku Klux Klan who stored his robes in a closet at home. William Foth is remembered as a stern, humorless man. "You never disagreed with him, or else," says another family member. "He was a difficult man to talk to." William Foth died of a heart attack in 1988.

The Foth children spent much of their childhood years in British Columbia, where their father worked as a laborer. After graduating from high school, Edgar took a job as a guard at the province's penitentiary in New Westminster. Foth, who had already displayed a keen interest in firearms and uniforms, loved the power that came with the job. But the money was not good enough. Farther east, in Alberta, the oil boom was on, and there was money to be made.

For much of the 1970s and early 1980s, Edgar Foth was what Albertans call a rig pig, that is, he earned his living working on oil rigs and petroleum-industry projects in the North. As a site supervisor for Esso Petroleum, he worked at the Norman Wells energy megaproject, seven hours north of Yellowknife by air. He and his brother Rob shared living quarters during this time. In 1978, at the age of 24, Foth had saved enough money to travel to Germany, to learn the truth about the war for himself. There, he stayed with relatives and spent time visiting museums. Lots of museums. He collected dozens of photographs of military helmets, uniforms and armaments. "It all started when he went on his little European vacation," recalls one family member. "He loves history, so he went to a lot of museums when he was over there. It was around that time that his opinion started to change."

Edgar's change worried his brother Rob, who remarked on it to other family members. In this period, Edgar Foth is believed to have made connections with the Western Guard, a Toronto-based neo-Nazi group. The Guard was formed in 1972 to lobby for a halt to all non-white immigration into Canada, the repatriation of non-whites and the enthusiastic promotion of Aryan culture.

Despite its name, the Western Guard never established a presence in Western Canada. When it drifted apart in the early 1980s, Edgar Foth was already looking for a new cause to believe in. He often tuned in to CJOY, an AM station based in Wetaskiwin, Alberta, a town just over 40 miles south of Edmonton. Every week, CJOY broadcast taped sermons by Phoenix preacher Sheldon Emry; about 30 other stations across Canada and the United States did the same. Before his death in June 1985, Emry was the leader of the Lord's Covenant Church, an Identity organization; he was also a close friend of Col. Jack Mohr. After receiving many complaints about the Emry programs, the Canadian Radio-Television and Telecommunications Commission (CRTC) ordered CJOY to stop broadcasting them. Foth was one of those who protested the CRTC action.

Foth is a large man, standing well over six feet. He is muscular and clean-cut, with wire-rim glasses, a mustache and thinning hair.

To many Canadian Aryan Nations supporters, he also looked a lot like an undercover police officer. "At first," one friend says, "some people thought he was a cop. They used to call him Ed the Fed. But not to his face." His crusade to have Pastor Emry's taped sermons returned to the air at CJOY convinced many Aryan Nations supporters that Foth was committed to the Identity cause.

In the summer of 1983, Foth met Gloria Mackey, recently divorced from an acquaintance of Foth's, Jim Mackey. Before and after their divorce, the Mackeys ran a business called Calmar Book and Video, located in a small town a short drive north of Calgary. "They were friends," says one woman who knew the couple. "They got along okay. He left her alone, and she left him alone, and that was that." In August 1983, Edgar Foth and Gloria Mackey discovered that they both had been invited to attend the same wedding in a nearby town. Foth offered Gloria a lift. It wasn't long before the two were romantically involved. In April 1984, Gloria got pregnant.

Foth kept his new girlfriend away from his friends in the far right. Whenever she expressed interest in learning about the Aryan Nations, he would tell her, "You don't want to get mixed up in it. And I don't want anything to happen to you." When alone with Gloria, friends say, Foth was a different man. "When they first got together," says one, "he was really nice to her. He was very gentle. He never drank. But he was a loner, always a loner. He never really trusted anybody—he was always looking over his shoulder. He was always expecting the worst. And he told her she was the only person he could ever trust."

During late 1983 and early 1984, Foth continued to work for Esso during the days, but his nights belonged to the Aryan Nations. For extended periods, Foth would simply disappear from sight. On some of these trips, strangely, he would take along his girlfriend's ex-husband. Asked why Foth would spend so much time with Jim Mackey, a friend recalls: "They got along fine. I don't know if they were best buddies or anything. But they got along. There were no fist fights, let's put it that way."

Following the July 1984 Aryan Nations congress, Foth converted to Richard Butler's Church of Jesus Christ Christian. Says one family member: "He started to get involved with the Aryan Nations, but [the Silent Brotherhood] was definitely a catapult for him. Some of those guys were Vietnam vets, like that Duey guy, and they wanted to fight what they thought was happening to their country. He was impressed by that."

At the Aryan Academy, Foth and Mackey spent more than a fortnight with Duey, discussing far right theory and engaging in some paramilitary training. Group members kept in touch with each other by telephone, using a complex code system devised by Bob Mathews; the Silent Brotherhood leader required them to contact the mobile "message centre" every day.

On October 19, shocking news swept through the Silent Brotherhood's membership: the previous day, Gary Yarbrough had been in a shoot-out with FBI agents at his Sandpoint, Idaho, home. Yarbrough had escaped, but the FBI had raided his house. There, the agents found a shrine to Adolf Hitler, blasting caps, dynamite, C4 plastic explosive, dozens of guns, coded documents about the Silent Brotherhood and, worst of all, the MAC-10 machine gun used to murder Alan Berg. Shaken, Mathews ordered all members of his organization to pull up stakes and meet in Spokane on the morning of October 20. The next day, a caravan of neo-Nazis headed up to Duey's camp in Bluecreek. That evening, a Sunday, Foth and Mackey joined 18 other members of the Silent Brotherhood in a huge mess tent on Duey's property.

The men listened approvingly as Yarbrough described his run-in with the forces of the Zionist Occupation Government. But the mood turned sombre when he told them that the gun used to kill "that Jew in Denver" was now in the hands of the FBI. Mathews tried to pep the men up, reminding them of the group's successes and telling them how to evade FBI surveillance teams. Transfixed, Foth and Mackey listened without saying a word. Mathews continued: "Kinsmen! We must strike back at ZOG for what it has done to our comrade Gary! True to our oath, we must repay the ZOG bastards for what they have done! We must march on Sandpoint and take back what the devils have confiscated! We must raid their offices if necessary to reclaim what is ours!"

Some of the members of the Silent Brotherhood were annoyed with their leader's outlandish rhetoric. The Canadians, they quietly noted, hadn't even formally joined the group yet. They could be informants. After some argument, Mathews reluctantly agreed that now was not the time to strike back at ZOG. Most of the men were ordered to remain at the Aryan Academy in Bluecreek; Mathews and Richard Scutari, meanwhile, left at midnight for a rendezvous with some Klansmen who wanted to join up.

Foth and Mackey remained at the camp with the others. There, Foth later recalled, the men went through tough training drills—camping in huge snowdrifts, eating foul-tasting army rations and improving their marksmanship in the sub-zero air. Many of the men grumbled about the spartan living conditions. A few left for nearby towns. For Foth and Mackey, the only bonus came when they were given their own Silent Brotherhood medallions. The medallions had been commissioned by Jean Craig, mother of Zillah Craig, Mathews's mistress and, as of that fall, the mother of his daughter, Emerant. The medallions were attached to a silver chain. On each was a battle axe below a scroll. Across the shield was engraved the words BRUDER SCHWEIGEN. The two were also given code names. Foth's was Norseman.

By the second week of November, Duey, Foth and Mackey had abandoned the Bluecreek camp and headed southwest to Oregon. After a meeting with Mathews at which they were instructed to find new safe houses for the group, Duey and his two Canadian recruits drove back north again, towards Seattle. The three men cruised along Interstate 5, past Seattle and Mount Vernon, Washington. They eventually found what they were looking for at Whidbey Island, in the Puget Sound. The island was about a one-hour drive from the Canadian border. With the help of an agent at Loganberry Hill Realty, Foth and Mackey picked a large chalet on Smugglers Cove Road. Using cash from the Ukiah robbery, the men rented that cottage and two others. The owner of Foth and Mackey's hideout was Larry F. Moore, an associate professor in the Faculty of Commerce and Business Administration at the University of British Columbia. In an interview, Moore says he instructed Loganberry Realty to deal directly with Foth and Mackey. Foth, says Moore, was "the fellow who rented the place, but I never did meet him. He claimed to be a writer with a back problem, recently divorced. He wanted a place to go and get peace and quiet, he said. He was the front man, of course, for the group that eventually came onto Whidbey Island. I was given a cash payment and a damage deposit."

Moore pauses, then laughs. "But the deposit didn't quite cover the damages done."

With very little prompting, the FBI agents and prosecuting attorneys who worked to bring about the demise of Bob Mathews's gang all agree: the Silent Brotherhood was the most effective domestic terrorist threat the United States had ever seen. But when those same individuals are questioned about the role two Canadian men played in the Silent Brotherhood, they become somewhat restrained. With the exception of Norm Stephenson.

In late 1983, Stephenson was an FBI agent based in Seattle. A colorful, plain-talking cop now retired in Arkansas, Stephenson used intuition to link members of the Silent Brotherhood to some of their armed robberies. And he was the agent who first learned about Bob Mathews's presence in Larry Moore's cottage. Asked about Edgar Foth and Jim Mackey, Norm Stephenson does not equivocate: "Yep. Those two guys were members of the Order. They weren't active in any of the robberies. They were members, however."

Stephenson says Foth and Mackey spent most of their time assisting Randy Duey at his Aryan Academy, producing pamphlets and practising their marksmanship. When their activities are compared to those of Mathews, Pierce and many of the others, Stephenson says it was "lightweight in nature," then adds: "But keep in mind that when Mathews and his crowd started out, they were law-abiding citizens.

There were only two of those guys out of that whole bunch, in fact, who had ever had any contact with law enforcement. Other than that, they were just Joe Blows off the street. But they had a real firm belief in what they were doing.

"The Canadians, Jim Mackey and Edgar Foth, were not in leadership roles at all. They were down there kind of hanging out."

Other FBI men are less precise, but they confirm the membership of Foth and Mackey in the Silent Brotherhood. Wayne Manis, a veteran Bureau member who was stationed near the Hayden Lake compound when Mathews was recruiting Aryan Nations members to join the Silent Brotherhood, says he cannot discuss Edgar Foth. "Edgar Foth was not charged in any of our indictments. Anybody who was not charged, I'm not permitted to discuss." Asked why Foth and Mackey were not charged, Manis says, "Primarily the problem with these unindicted individuals was direct evidence linking them to the criminal acts we were concerned with." He will say no more. Manis's boss, Alan Whitaker, the agent-in-charge at the Whidbey Island showdown, is even less forthcoming: "We were aware that Canadians were involved with the Silent Brotherhood. The investigation did not turn up any evidence that they had violated the laws of the United States."

One of the men who assisted in the prosecution of members of the Silent Brotherhood, Seattle attorney Peter Mueller, says "two Canadians"—he says their names were Jim and Edgar—were "brought to the group by Randy Duey." The man who led the prosecution team, Gene Wilson, now a U.S. magistrate judge in Seattle, will only say this about those two Canadians: "They joined, but they never got into any of the heavy stuff. Perhaps they got scared by what happened at Whidbey Island. In any event, there were a number of folks who started showing up and being attracted to this group in late 1984." He pauses. "It was the Canadians' good fortune, I suppose, that they split before things got very hot."

After the arrival of Foth, Mackey and Duey on Whidbey Island in mid-November 1984, things got very hot, indeed. On the evening of

November 23, Tom Martinez flew to Portland, Oregon, where he was met by Bob Mathews and Gary Yarbrough. Unbeknownst to Mathews and Yarbrough, however, Martinez had been a federal informant for about seven weeks and he was leading a heavily armed team of FBI agents straight to the leader of the Silent Brotherhood. Martinez agreed to lead the agents to Mathews only on the condition that his friend would not be hurt and that he not be arrested when Martinez was anywhere nearby. The FBI agreed.

Despite a massive FBI presence at the airport, Mathews gave the agents the slip. It was not the first time he had done so. The three men then rented rooms at Portland's Capri Motel. Martinez was given Number 14; Yarbrough and Mathews took Number 42. Later, while Mathews and Yarbrough slept, Martinez crept out to tell the FBI where the two men were staying. The next morning, Mathews stepped outside and spotted one of about 20 agents hiding in some bushes. He yelled, "Gary! Watch out!" and ran back into Room 42 as the FBI opened fire. From Room 14, Martinez watched helplessly, infuriated that the FBI had broken its promise to him.

After a few minutes of silence, Mathews charged out the door and bounded down to street level, bullets whizzing inches above his head. At the same moment, Yarbrough was attempting an ungraceful exit through the rear window. In his hands was a list of the Silent Brotherhood's members, along with their aliases and phone numbers. Waiting for him below was Libby Pierciey, a Philadelphia FBI agent who also happened to be Martinez's handler. Spotting her, Yarbrough yelled. "You fucking slut! You white whore, you fuck niggers. I'll remember your face, bitch. I'll remember you." A black agent stepped up, slapped handcuffs on Yarbrough and hustled him away.

In a letter received at the Aryan Nations compound in Hayden Lake on December 8, Mathews recalls what happened next: "The incompetence of these gun-toting bureaucrats never ceases to amaze me. Especially after their attempted murder and ambush of myself at a Portland hotel. First, let me say that the FBI was not there to arrest Gary but to ambush me. They didn't even know that Gary was in the room. The only reason they were able to find me was because a trusted friend in Room 14 was actually a traitor and an informant. The FBI has vast resources and the latest technology but the quality of their agents is going down hill with every new recruit. That's because most of the best white men in this country are starting to realize that, to be an FBI agent is to be nothing more than a mercenary for the ADL [Anti-Defamation League of the B'nai Brith] and Tel Aviv.

"When I stepped out of my motel room that morning, a gang of armed men came running at me. None of the men had uniforms on, and the only thing they said to me was 'Stop, you bastard.' At this, I yelled to Gary who was still inside and I leaped down the stairwell and took off running into the parking lot. A women [*sic*] agent shot at my back and the bullet missed and hit the motel manager. I rounded the corner of the motel and took off down the hill into a residential area. After running for two blocks I decided to quit being the hunted and become the hunter. I drew my gun and waited behind a concrete wall for the agents to draw near. When I aimed my gun at the head of the closest agent, I saw the handsome face of a young white man and lowered my aim to his knee and foot. Had I not done so, I could have killed both agents and still had left the use of my hand which is now mangled beyond repair and which I might very well lose altogether. That is the last time I will ever give quarter.

"As for the traitor in Room 14, we will eventually find him. If it takes ten years and we have to travel to the far ends of the Earth, we will find him. And, true to our oath, when we do find him, we will remove his head from his body.

"I have no regrets or apologies to make for Gary or myself. In fact, I am proud that we had the courage and the determination to stand up and fight for our race and our heritage at a time in our history when such a deed is called a crime and not an act of valor. . . .

"I am not going into hiding. Rather, I will press the FBI and let them know what it is like to become the hunted. Doing so, it is only logical to assume that my days on this planet are rapidly drawing to a close. Even so, I have no fear. For the reality of life is death, and the worst the enemy can do to me is shorten my tour of duty in this world. I will leave knowing that my family and friends love me and support me. I will leave knowing I have made the ultimate sacrifice to secure the future of my children.

"As always, for blood, soil, honor, for faith and for race. Robert Jay Mathews."

But Mathews did, in fact, go into hiding. Badly wounded by an FBI bullet that had struck him in his left hand, he quickly made his way to Brightwood, Oregon, where he hooked up with Richard Scutari and other members of his gang. Despite Scutari's protests, Mathews ordered the group to move to the safe houses on Whidbey Island. Scutari was opposed to the idea, because Whidbey Island lacked adequate escape routes. But Mathews was insistent. On the morning of Monday, November 26, Mathews, Scutari and a small group of Silent Brotherhood members travelled to the island. They arrived at the two-storey chalet just before noon; Edgar Foth and Jim Mackey stepped outside to help Mathews carry in his belongings. Later that same day, the two Canadians moved into another cottage.

Mathews spent the next two days writing letters to his family and friends. He had decided that his death was only a matter of days away; his fatalism made a few of his followers decidedly nervous. Some also noted that the FBI would not take long to find the hideout. On November 27, he wrote: "We declare ourselves to be in full and unrelenting state of war with those forces seeking and consciously promoting the destruction of our faith and our race." Mathews signed the declaration, as did Pierce, Duey, Scutari and nine others. (It is not known if Foth and Mackey signed, since most of the signatories used pseudonyms.) After the signing ceremony, the men surrounded Scutari's infant daughter, Danielle, and repeated the Silent Brotherhood's oath for the last time.

Two days later, Foth and Mackey visited Mathews at Larry Moore's cottage. They were leaving. Gloria Mackey, Foth's girlfriend, was eight months pregnant. "I don't want to leave her alone just before the baby comes," Foth said. "I want to head back, check up on her, then head back. But we want you to know that we will be back if you will wait for us." Foth and Mackey knew that if the Silent Brotherhood left the island, they would be impossible to track down again.

Mathews placed his good hand on Foth's shoulder. "Ed, go be with your woman. And I give you my word that I will be here until at least next weekend. I'll wait for you."

"We'll be back in less than a week, Bob," Foth said. The two Canadians said their goodbyes to the others, then they drove off.

By Monday, December 3, many of the Silent Brotherhood's members were also preparing to leave. Scutari pleaded with Mathews to abandon Whidbey Island. "I told Jim and Edgar I would wait here for them because the message centre is moving," Mathews replied. "If no one stays, we will lose contact with those two Canadian kinsmen who won't know how to contact us. I'll be all right." By Tuesday, only six members of the Silent Brotherhood remained.

Early on Friday, December 7, a day still known as Martyr's Day to thousands of neo-Nazis in Canada, the United States and Europe, Randy Duey picked up his phone. The line was dead. Hearing his name called on a bullhorn, Duey grabbed his Uzi machine gun and ran outside, then stopped dead in his tracks. "But you're all white men!" he said, then surrendered. A few minutes later, the Silent Brotherhood's counterfeiting team also surrendered.

Dozens upon dozens of heavily armed FBI agents and Special Weapons and Tactics, or SWAT officers surrounded Mathews's cottage. Mathews, however, would not budge. When telephone contact was established with him, the Silent Brotherhood leader gave his terms: "I want parts of eastern Washington, Idaho and Montana set aside as an Aryan homeland, where my kinsmen will be free to live as they choose." When the FBI refused Mathews's demand, he told them: "Do what you have to do."

The next day, Saturday, an eight-man SWAT team tried to capture Mathews. When the team stepped into the chalet, Mathews fired through the ceiling above them in a Z pattern; none, incredibly, were hit. The men beat a hasty retreat, and for a few hours the siege continued. Then, around dusk, the FBI command post ordered the SWAT team to lob three M-79 Starburst flares through a broken window. The idea, apparently, was to illuminate the house and drive Mathews outside. However, Mathews stubbornly stayed put, firing off rounds as the wooden chalet erupted in flame. Stores of ammunition started to explode. Within minutes, the flames had engulfed the entire structure, rising some 200 feet into the night sky. The shooting stopped.

The next day, after the ashes cooled, the remains of Robbie Mathews were found beside a bathtub. He had died for his race, his many followers would later write, just as Earl Turner had done. Burned into Mathews's chest was a gold medallion bearing the inscription "BRUDER SCHWEIGEN."

Edgar Foth sat in his trailer home in Calmar, Alberta. Gloria Mackey, who was about to give birth to their son on January 7, was happy Ed had returned home. As Gloria chatted with her mother, Foth flipped through the December 9, 1984, edition of *The Calgary Herald*. He found what he was looking for inside the first section. It was a six-paragraph story headlined: "House Burns after Battle With Fugitive."

"Shots were exchanged and a large fire broke out late Saturday at a house where a man believed to be a fugitive neo-Nazi had been under siege for two days by authorities, an FBI spokesman said," the story read. "The cause of the fire was not immediately known, nor was the fate of the house's occupant, said an FBI spokesman."

But Edgar Foth knew the fate of the leader of the Silent Brotherhood. He reread the news item a few times. Then he crossed into the bedroom and picked up the phone to dial a number in Caroline, Alberta. "Hello, Terry?" he said. "It's Ed. Listen, Terry, the paper says Bob Mathews is dead." He listened. "Yeah," he said. "Yeah."

"Listen, Terry, we've got a lot of work to do."

6

CANADA'S HIGH ARYAN WARRIOR PRIEST

About 90 miles northwest of Calgary, on a secluded acreage just out-side the town of Caroline, population 431, a bearded man sits at his kitchen table, drinking coffee. His mother washes dishes at the sink, while two of his three children race around his house, playing with a toy gun. There is nothing remarkable or unusual about the man's appearance. In his worn jeans and plaid shirt cut in the Western style, he looks like an average Alberta farmer. But he is not.

The bearded man is Evert (or, as he favors, Terry) Allan Long, High Aryan Warrior Priest of the Aryan Nations and a pastor in the Church of Jesus Christ Christian. And there is nothing average about Terry Long.

"As things get worse, as more and more racial dissension hap-pens, more whites will move into this area," he says, his voice even. "There will be race wars, and there will be revolution and anarchy. When that happens, we will have this area as a home from which we can branch out and force the repatriation of non-whites."

His words hang in the air like static. On the other side of the kitchen, his mother nods in mute agreement. But the Jews, Long is asked. What will happen to the Jews?

Terry Long shrugs and drinks some coffee with studied indifference. "Who knows. Scripture says they're going to be exterminated."

He makes eye contact for the first time. "The Jew is the ultimate in deception. They take the truth and turn it around to their advantage," he says, straight-faced. "The Jews are the ultimate abomination."

Terry Long, former Progressive Conservative member, former Social Credit supporter, former Western Canada Concept candidate, has found an ideological home. Terry Long has found the Aryan Nations.

Before he came along, the Aryan Nations in Canada was an organization of no consequence. Its handful of members took their cues from Aryan Nations bosses in the United States and did little on their own initiative. Until Terry Long. When he assumed the national leadership in 1986, the Canadian Aryan Nations was transformed into a national controversy—and has remained in the headlines, more or less continuously, ever since. Terry Long would prove himself to be one of the most capable leaders the Canadian racist right had ever seen.

He was, he admits, a conservative right from the very start. In the dusty countryside outside Red Deer, Alberta, where he was born in May 1946, young Terry Long earned extra money as a paper boy, delivering the Red Deer *Advocate* door-to-door. As he loped from one mailbox to the next, he would read the news stories coming out of Ottawa and Edmonton and he would shake his head in disgust. "I could never understand," he said years later, "why all the politicians were so liberal."

His father, Peter, was a truck driver, sawmill owner and farmer who always voted Conservative. His mother, Beatrice, was a Liberal. "I guess I'm an anomaly," Long says now, giving a rare laugh.

Long was raised in a family that was, according to all accounts, typical small-town Alberta. His father, while conservative, was hardly a racist; throughout the small central-Alberta community, Peter Long, a fourth-grade drop-out, was widely regarded as a man of honesty and integrity. In 1946, the year Terry was born, he purchased about ten acres of thickly forested land bordering the Clearwater River, a few miles west of Caroline. There, he built a modest panel-and-stucco wood-frame house in the woods, out of sight of the trucks speeding by on Highway 54. It was here that Terry and his older brother, David, born in 1938, spent their early years.

Just south of the house, in a clearing surrounded by wild roses and thick stands of pine, Peter set up a small sawmill operation. To make ends meet, he also bought a few head of cattle. In their shack on the banks of the Clearwater River, Peter and Beatrice Long prepared their two sons for the world with time-tested rural Alberta ideals: a dollop of independence, a distrust of government, and the Baptist faith. "They were quite sociable, hard-working folk," recalls Cliff Stalwick, pastor at the Church of the Living Faith in Caroline and an occasional minister to the Long family. "Peter was a big fella, very robust and an out-of-doors type. He had gone through a lot of tough times. To carve a living out of the woods, as he did, was very tough. They were never very well off people. It seemed to be a hand-to-mouth existence all the time for them, living in that old shack."

In 1953, when Terry Long was seven, his family moved south to Sacramento, where Peter had heard that life might not be as hard. There, Peter worked as a trucker and garage mechanic; his wife toiled at a supermarket check-out counter. Long would later recall that it was in Southern California that he felt the faint stirrings of what he now calls "racialist thinking." It was in Sacramento, at the tender age of eight or nine, that he says he first encountered members of the "colored races." Says Long: "I saw them for what they were. They were different."

By the mid-sixties, Terry Long had completed his high-school education in California as well as two years of college. He had revealed himself to be bright, with an aptitude for mathematics and electronics. In 1966, their enthusiasm for the United States diminished, Peter,

Beatrice and Terry Long returned to their tiny home outside Caroline. Marjorie McNeill, Beatrice's sister, says one of the reasons the family returned to Canada was that Peter, then in his late fifties, was nearing retirement and there was no Old Age Security plan in the States. (David Long remained in California, where he continues to live.)

Soon after the Longs' return, neighbors say, 20-year-old Terry was distinguishing himself as a hot-headed young man with an intolerant streak. His fuse was short, they say, and he often got in fights in bars. It fell to Peter Long to keep his son in line. Neighbors started to notice a growing tension between the two men. "Terry had that racist stuff in his thinking long before [joining the Aryan Nations]," says Stalwick. "But his father kept it at bay. After Peter died, though, Terry was free to do whatever he wanted."

In 1968, Terry travelled north to Edmonton to continue his post-secondary education. He enrolled at the University of Alberta and graduated with a bachelor's degree in science in 1972, with a specialization in electrical engineering. At U of A, he met his wife-to-be, Janice, who was then a pharmacy student. The two hit it off: like Terry, Janice was from a small central-Alberta town, Markerville. She didn't have a lot of fancy big-town ideas, and Terry liked that. On holiday weekends, when he was driving to Caroline to see his parents, Terry would give Janice a lift to her own family's home, just west of Caroline. The two married shortly after Terry graduated.

In 1973, the newlyweds purchased a farm just west of Bentley, Alberta. Bentley was a sunny little town with a population of a few hundred, located a few minutes' drive north of Red Deer. For the next few years, Terry and Janice Long mostly kept to themselves, tending their livestock, helping Peter Long with the family sawmill and voting Conservative. On occasion, Long would later say, he used his schooling to help design gas plants, sour gas plants and compressor stations for the petrochemical industry. In Bentley, the Longs started their family: a daughter, Sarah, came in the summer of 1974; then another girl, Rebecca, in 1978; and, to Terry's relief, a boy, Cody, in 1980. Although described as friendly by the few neighbors who remember him, Terry Long did not socialize much; instead, he says he devoted much of his spare time to an Edmonton-area Progressive Conservative Party association, where he was a director. Before long, he grew disenchanted with the Tories. "They had backroom guys making the decisions all the time," he says with disgust. "The PCs are based on the democracy principle. But democracy will never work."

On February 17, 1982, Long made up his mind to abandon the Conservatives. On that night, in a result that stunned the nation, Gordon Kesler was elected to the Alberta legislature in a by-election in the Olds-Didsbury riding. Kesler, who ran under the banner of Doug Christie's Western Canada Concept, was the first separatist ever to be elected west of the Ottawa River. The WCC was engaged in a struggle, Kesler later said, with unnamed forces "in control of vast numbers of megacorporations, banks, media and various union factions, as well as political movements." On a whim, Long attended Kesler's victory celebration, and was mightily impressed by the farmer's speech, in which Kesler proclaimed: "God is in this room. You can feel it."

In an interview many years later, Long recalled: "When Kesler said that, there were over a hundred people in the room, and about half a dozen TV cameras. And you could hear a pin drop. I knew that he was right. I felt humble. I started searching from then on."

Long's search led him, like Kesler, to Doug Christie's doorstep. Although Christie now insists that he did not recruit Long, it is clear that the right-wing Western Canada Concept was precisely the type of party the young man was looking for. He was persuaded to run for the WCC in the Lacombe riding in the 1982 provincial election.

Neighbors recall that, during the weeks leading up to the October 5 vote, Long was a surprisingly adept campaigner. His tongue planted firmly in cheek, neighbor and family friend Ray Paradis recalls, "Terry went to school a lot, you know. He knows a lot about politics and computers and things, but he never seemed to want to do a lot of work." As expected, the newly designated Progressive Conservative candidate, Ron Moore, easily outpolled the rest of the field, finishing with 5,141 votes. But Terry Long raised a few eyebrows in the Caroline area with his respectable second-place finish, capturing 1,340 votes. Long even beat New Democrat candidate Glen R. Nelson by more than 200 votes—a surprising result, given that the NDP has traditionally made up the Official Opposition in Alberta.

Although Terry Long lost the election, he gained a new circle of friends and acquaintances through his campaign for western separatism. These men would play significant roles in nudging Long towards the farthest extreme of the ideological spectrum, towards fascism and Nazism. Among them were three figures with connections to both the WCC and the Social Credit Party of Canada: one of Christie's clients, Eckville Mayor Jim Keegstra; Jim Green, regional director of the Socreds; and Rev. Tom Erhart, a Social Credit vice-president. Following his dismissal by the Lacombe County Board of Education in January 1983, Keegstra was elected second Alberta vice-president of the national Socreds, but within days, he was dismissed for his anti-Semitism by party national leader Martin Hattersley. Green and Erhart were also dismissed for endorsing Keegstra's views. (The three were later reinstated by the Alberta Social Credit Party, a move that led to Hattersley's own resignation and Terry Long's brief flirtation with the party.)

Green, like Long, lived in Bentley, which served as his retirement home at the time. Born in 1921, Green was a one-time member of the Royal Canadian Air Force and had worked as a merchant and a farmer to support his seven children. In Bentley, he employed Keegstra at his garage, where the defrocked teacher earned extra dollars working as a mechanic. When Long met him, Green had been a member of the Social Credit Party for some 20 years. In 1972, 1974, 1980 and 1984, Green had run for a seat in Parliament under the Socred banner. He lost each time. His 1984 campaign literature read: "Not only Canada, but this world, is going down the drain, unless it smartens up, returns to God, and obeys His commandments." Among other things, Green believed the Holocaust was a hoax.

The Reverend Tom Erhart was a shortish, balding man with a fringe of red curls and horn-rimmed glasses. He was a longtime Social

Credit supporter and another Holocaust denier. A resident of Calgary's posh Mount Royal district, Erhart also would have the distinction of being one of the first Canadians to attend one of the annual Aryan Nations world congresses, in July 1984. "I'm an Aryan," Erhart told a reporter for *The Winnipeg Sun* who attended the conference posing as a Nazi. "I'm not ashamed of it." Declining to discuss his enthusiasm for Aryan Nations doctrine, Erhart will say only that he is a minister of the Apostolic Church of the Pentecost, then adds that he is not preaching at the moment. His voice quavering, he says he is a fundamentalist Christian, but he does not accept many of the current fundamentalist points of view—particularly those concerning Jews. "Fundamentalists believe that the Jews of today are God's chosen people. People speak of them being indispensable. But the Jews of today, these are not the true Hebrew people. They have never had anything to do with Israel." He pauses. "And now they run the world."

Erhart says he was impressed with Terry Long from the very start. "He reminded me of a Clint Eastwood movie," he says, brightening. "He was the real rifleman, the real thing. He was hard and he was tough. He was true to his convictions."

With new friends like Keegstra, Green and Erhart—and with the convictions he formed as a youth in Sacramento taking on a larger significance in his life—Terry Long slipped further into the vortex of organized anti-Semitism and white supremacy. Throughout the spring and summer of 1983, his new friends lent him books and pamphlets that, for the most part, have been classified as hate literature by the Canadian government. While many of his neighbors busied themselves with planting crops or fishing for pickerel at nearby Gull Lake, Terry Long holed up in his room, thumbing through Arthur R. Butz's *Hoax of the Twentieth Century* or studying Ferar Fenton's 1902 revisionist bible, *The Books of the History of the House of Israel* ("This book foretells what is taking place right now and what is going to happen in the future," he says).

In the fall of 1983, the circle almost complete, Long abandoned his previous circumspection and went public in a blaze of racist and anti-Jewish frenzy. With the help of Jim Green and Tom Erhart, he formed the Christian Defence League, a group ostensibly created to raise money for Keegstra's looming court battle (and no relation to Reverend Swift's Christian Defense League in the States). Long was the first president of the league. In a news release issued on CDL letterhead, which curiously did not directly refer to Keegstra's approaching court case, Long wrote:

"The Christian Defence League of Canada is not an arm of the Canadian government and operates as a non-profit organization to give assistance to those whose civil rights have been violated by raw and excessive government abuse. The CDL of Canada was formed in September of 1983. The League was formed before any criminal charges were laid against anyone in this province for exercising 'freedom of speech,' and we have been successful in helping to meet the moral, financial and legal requirements which many more Canadians will probably require as we move closer to World Government."

Along with raising money for Keegstra, the CDL busied itself with activities that, it proudly admitted, were completely illegal. One such project, initiated by Long, involved smuggling copies of Butz's book across the border into Alberta. The copies of *Hoax* were purchased by Long and his CDL colleagues from the Institute for Historical Review, a California company that produced and marketed far right material. Long sported 50 of the books into Canada wrapped, he claimed, in copies of *Penthouse*. (When a bomb attack levelled the Institute for Historical Review's offices on July 4, 1984, Long devised a plan with Aryan Nations leader Richard Butler to transmit passages from the book through a computer network connected by long-distance telephone lines. The idea of using computer networks to transmit hate publications, which even Canada Customs officials grudgingly conceded was clever, was beyond the reach of the hate-promotion sections in the Criminal Code. Said Long: "The computer system is a beautiful solution, because if you have a modem and a printer, you can get all of this information in your own home. They can ban all the books they want. The more they seize this stuff, the better it is for us.

I'm not going to give in. If they think I'm going to go along with this horseshit, they're crazy.")

In the fall of 1983, some Canadian CDL supporters stumbled across the fact that another Christian Defense League had been in existence in Louisiana since 1977; others heard about an even older version, which had kicked around Southern California in the early 1960s. In its literature, they noted, the Louisiana CDL declared that its "ultimate aim must be to organize the White Christian majority, and to forge them into a force or movement that can sweep the anti-Christ from our churches and those that support the anti-Christ Jews from any political positions they may hold." Hearing that, some of Keegstra's supporters fretted about being seen as a branch of a too-radical U.S. organization.

The Canadian CDL members also had something else to worry about: during this same period, Terry Long was growing increasingly blunt, and his views increasingly extreme, surprising even the likes of veteran anti-Semites such as Keegstra, Green and Erhart. The league, Long told reporters at the time, was hoping to "provide vocal support for Christian individuals persecuted for revealing the conspiracy of Jew-Communists to form One World Government." One outspoken CDL activist, a 60-year-old former Medicine Hat mattress salesman named Frank Cottingham, was alarmed by that kind of talk. Cottingham said he was opposed to Long's "radicalism." Such radicalism, he said, unwittingly plays into the hands of the "agents of the conspiracy," whom he refused to name. Cottingham and others expressed concern that the league's president—and the apparent connection to the U.S. group, which some suspected had been Long's idea in the first place—could do more harm to Keegstra's defence than good; as a result, Long was asked to resign as president, to be replaced by Green. Green's treasurer role was then taken on by Keegstra and Cottingham.

Long will not discuss his apparent falling-out with Keegstra and Green. But he traces his conversion to the Aryan Nations Identity faith back to the summer and fall of that same year. "I got into this as a logical, thinking individual," he says, without the faintest hint of irony in his voice. "I looked at the evidence, then I turned to Scripture. This isn't pie-in-the-sky stuff. I didn't wave my arms and flutter up to heaven and praise the Lord. I arrived at a logical position based upon Scripture and the secular evidence. The two complement one another. The Identity perspective is the only scriptural interpretation that offers no contradictions. In the spring of '83, I was presented with it. And in the fall of '83, I confirmed my convictions at the conference."

"The conference," as he puts it, turned out to be a pivotal event in Long's life. It, along with the death of his father, would push Terry Long past the point of no return.

The humorous coincidence, apparently, was completely lost on the humorless men and women belonging to the Crown Commonwealth League of Rights. Their three-day meeting in Calgary ran from Saturday, October 29, to Monday, October 31, 1983—Halloween weekend. But there were to be no jokes about ghosts and goblins among this crowd.

Held in a hotel not far from Calgary's international airport, the conference attracted dozens of anti-Semites and white supremacists from all over western Canada and points beyond. For the most part, it took place behind closed doors. To the media, the event had all the hallmarks of a rinky-dink gathering of a few local wing-nuts, monarchists and survivalists. It was, however, anything but.

The league's Australian-born president, Eric Butler (no relation to Richard Girnt Butler), was appointed to fend off the queries of the few reporters in attendance. In a raucous press conference called for October 31, when most delegates had already left, Butler said the event "was basically just a family gathering." Among the subjects discussed by the family members, Butler admitted, was "the Zionist question." Said he: "The Jewish question is very important." And, in what Butler called "a very important statement of principles" released at the meeting's conclusion, the league intoned that "the future of Western Christian civilization" depended on, among other things, the destruction of the United Nations—and the mantle of leadership being assumed by "the people of Great Britain, Australia, New Zealand and the United States."

What Butler did not state at his press conference, and what most of the reporters covering it apparently did not know, was that the Crown Commonwealth League of Rights was Butler's co-ordinating body for a massive worldwide network of professional Holocaust deniers, racists and Hitler freaks. The CCLR, as it calls itself, is a decades-old umbrella group whose charter member organizations include the Canadian League of Rights, the British League of Rights, the Australian League of Rights and the New Zealand League of Rights. Its members like to think of their organization as a sort of conservative think-tank. Publicly, they disavow any connection to violent extremists such as those found in the Aryan Nations. But for many such extremists—Terry Long included—groups such as the League of Rights are a point of entry into the far right.

The CCLR's international affiliates include the neo-Nazi Liberty Lobby in the United States, South Korea's World Anti-Communist League and the pro-apartheid National Forum in South Africa. These groups are among the oldest and most powerful far right organizations in existence. And they had chosen a non-descript Calgary hotel in which to hold an "international conference."

To the fledgling neo-Nazi named Terry Long, the whole thing must have been somewhat akin to placing a banquet before a starving man. The place was buzzing with excitement. There was a lot of corridor talk about Zionist Occupation Government's latest outrage, Jimmy Keegstra's awful predicament, and an impressive little outfit grabbing headlines down in Idaho, the Aryan Nations. Long, who previously had been obliged to content himself with inconclusive discussions with small-town bigots and high-school drop-outs in the back of Jim Green's garage, was being given an opportunity to chat with the likes of Ivor Benson, a one-time adviser to the white supremacist government in Rhodesia and leader of South Africa's National Forum, and Ron Gostick, national director of the Ontario-based Canadian League of Rights, which the Canadian Jewish Congress has called "perhaps Canada's leading anti-Semitic organization." For a small-town Alberta boy with a racist bent, it was heady stuff. Terry Long was in Nazi heaven.

The highlight of the weekend came on Saturday night. The keynote speaker was billed as no less than "Brigadier General Gordon 'Jack' Mohr, National Defence Co-ordinator, Civilian Emergency Defence System."

Mohr was one of the most popular and able speakers on the U.S. far right circuit. Despite his claims to the contrary, the septuagenarian Mississippi resident was nothing more than a retired U.S. Army lieutenant-colonel, a member of the Christian Patriots Defense League and a former John Birch Society leader—and a man with a fondness for giving peculiar speeches about the need to create armed citizens' groups to "defend white Christian civilization." But Klansmen and neo-Nazis would travel great distances to hear Mohr, whom they apparently regarded as one or two steps removed from a deity. (Such was his celebrity, in fact, that when Denver radio talkshow host Alan Berg got into a heated argument with Mohr during a broadcast four months after the CCLR conference, an enraged Silent Brotherhood leader Bob Mathews reportedly made the decision to murder Berg.)

The title of Mohr's October 29 address was "The Brainwashing of Christendom." He began with a few folksy anecdotes about World War Two adversaries Erwin Rommel and George Patton, and then he warmed to his topic. "There has been very little moral, spiritual or physical progress made in the world, except under the guidance of the white race," Mohr told his audience, as Terry Long listened, enraptured. "So don't let anyone make you feel guilty because you are white. If this truth makes me a racist, so be it!"

Mohr went on to excoriate the Anti-Defamation League of the B'nai Brith ("An anti-Christ, anti-freedom organization!"), One World Government ("I understand that, in Canada, you have at least 108 parliamentarians for World Order in your government!") and international communism ("It was Jewish planned, financed and led—their leaders braggingly admit this!"). "In the States," said Mohr, "as it is in Canada, and I imagine in many of the other countries of Christendom, you can criticize most anyone, including the government, as long as you tell the truth. But this is not true when you deal with the Jewish question—even when your criticism is correct. When you have the courage to expose them, the roof of anti-Semitism falls on you.

"When will the free world wake up?" he asked his audience. "Will we take a stand when our ships of state founder on the internationalists' rocks? Will we wake up when Asiatic hordes goosestep down our city streets? Will we become alert to what is happening when they rape our wives and daughters and murder our sons? It will be too late then!"

The crowd gave Jack Mohr a standing ovation, and Terry Long gave him the highest praise of which he is capable. Says Long, misty-eyed, recalling that night: "Subsequent to the '82 election, I knew what was going on, but I wasn't totally fulfilled as to an alternative. I knew there was something else. And that night, Jack Mohr showed me the something else: Identity."

To Terry Long in the fall of 1983, his head swimming with questions about politics, race and religion, the pseudo-religion called Identity Christianity seemed to make a great deal of sense. Standing beside the sawmill where his father made a living for so many years, Long admits that Identity was not a mainstream choice. "As Christ said in Luke . . . I have, let's see." He pauses, scanning the woods, trying to remember the right words. "I have . . . let's see. 'Bring forth mine enemies and slay them before me.' So we're not your typical flutter-up-to-heaven Christians. We don't believe in rolling over and dying and turning the other cheek. We believe in fighting for our beliefs and our freedoms and our God."

Long was a man electrified by his new creed: the heavens had opened up, basking him in the glow of Identity truth. But back on Earth, where such things matter little, he was facing a uniquely secular dilemma: missed mortgage payments. The Longs were in deep financial trouble. "We were behind on one payment," Long says, his rage apparent. "We were making progress payments. But they shut us down. They didn't allow us time to catch up. That's the way they operate." Under foreclosure proceedings, Long's bank sued him for the approximately $40,000 outstanding under the terms of the mortgage. "We didn't fight it, so supposedly we owe them forty thousand," he says, refusing to name the lending institution. "We had tried to sell the place, and they refused three offers that would have reimbursed them totally for their mortgage. They refused all three."

To someone else, the foreclosure on Terry and Janice Long's property might have been yet another of the many such personal tragedies experienced by prairie farm families in the early 1980s, no more, no less. Or perhaps it might have been a direct consequence of Terry Long devoting too much time to the Western Canada Concept and the Christian Defence League and not enough time to his financial obligations. But to Terry Long, it was "straight politics"—Jewish politics. Says Long: "I have no doubt whatsoever. That's the way they operate. After I took my stand in support of Keegstra, we were more or less told to get out." The Long family had nowhere else to go, so Terry asked his father if he and Janice and the three children could move into the Caroline home. Peter said yes.

The winter of 1983–84 was a tense time in Peter Long's house, for a number of very good reasons. First, Terry's extremist views disturbed his father, say neighbors and family friends. Second, the house had not been built to accommodate seven people. Third, money was scarce. (One in-law pins much of the blame for this on Peter Long, whom she says had a lifelong love of attending auctions.)

While Peter Long was hardly a misty-eyed liberal, neither was he a crypto-Nazi. This set the stage for more than a few confrontations between father and son. Says Church of the Living Faith Pastor Cliff Stalwick: "I talked to one of their neighbors at the time, and he told me that Pete was not the radical. Terry, of course, had all of these ideas in his head against blacks and anyone who wasn't white, but

Pete wasn't that way. And none of us knew where Terry had gotten these awful ideas." Terry Long's aunt, Marjorie McNeill, agrees. She says that although Peter was occasionally "narrow-minded," he was no right-wing nutcase: "Pete did not have a lot of education. He was just a cowboy, really. But he never went as far as Terry."

Given time, some family friends say, Peter Long might have been successful in persuading his son to abandon the hateful religion he had embraced. But the elder Long did not get the chance. On April 9, 1984, a crisp spring morning, Peter and Terry Long were skidding logs. Peter was adjusting a guide blade when he stumbled and fell onto the head saw blade. Says Stalwick: "Somehow he lost his balance and fell. It cut him right down through the middle. It was terrible, just terrible."

It is said that Peter Long, age 74, died in his son's arms. Since that day, Terry Long has refused to discuss the incident with anyone, says Stalwick, who eulogized Peter Long at his funeral. Adds a Victoria lawyer who is a close friend: "Terry just won't talk about it. He just went into a shell afterwards." But neighbor Jim Martin later claimed that Long spoke to him about his father's death. "Terry told me his dad was still talking to him after he was cut in two. Something like that can't help but have an effect on a person."

Following his father's tragic death Terry Long, now navigating alone in some uncharted waters, started to devote his every waking moment to Christian Identity. Within time, his wife, his mother and even his children were spouting Identity theory to whoever would listen. In Caroline, few did.

The family's wholesale conversion to Identity was not without its burdens. In 1985, for example, Janice and Terry enrolled their two daughters, Sarah and Rebecca, in Cliff Stalwick's Living Faith Bible School in Caroline. One day, Stalwick recalls, Sarah showed up with a copy of Arthur Butz's *The Hoax of the Twentieth Century*. "She was showing the book to other students and talking to them about it, but we didn't know she was doing it," he says. "When we found out, we asked her to take the book home."

The next day, Terry Long barged into Stalwick's office, where the Pastor was meeting with a church elder. Long yelled a few earthy curses and lunged across the desk at Stalwick. "I saw it coming, so I was on my way in the opposite direction," Stalwick says now, laughing. "He hit me on the chest. It didn't hurt much." Stalwick and the church elder persuaded Long to calm down and agree to a meeting with the church leadership to arbitrate the dispute.

At the meeting, Stalwick and other church members explained that they did not want their school associated with books like Butz's. The Longs were not impressed. They announced that they planned to immediately withdraw Sarah and Rebecca from the school. "And we haven't seen them since," Stalwick says. (Long tells the story differently: he insists that Sarah was "kicked out of school" for taking the banned text to class. But other community members support Stalwick's version of events.)

At the time of Terry Long's conversion to Identity, the titular head of the Aryan Nations in Canada was alleged to be Lester Morris, a Bible-thumping shipping clerk living in Fort Langley, B.C. Long disputes Morris's claim to the leadership, saying that the B.C. man was merely a provincial Aryan officer. Whatever the case, it is clear that Morris was an ineffective leader. In the view of Aryan Nations founder Richard Butler, a better, more telegenic Aryan chief had to be found for Canada. Membership inquiries were growing there: a man with charisma and drive was needed to handle the burgeoning interest.

In mid-July 1984, three months after his father's death, Terry Long pulled into Hayden Lake, Idaho, for the fifth annual Aryan Nations World Congress. Also present were Tom Erhart; Wagner Saende; Klansman Karl Leppert of Vancouver; Carney Nerland; Jim Harding, an alleged founder of the Western Canada Concept from Alberta who asserted that blacks "come from another planet"; Lester Morris, who called Jim Keegstra "the most intellectual white man I ever talked with in Canada"; Alberta rightist Jim Mackey; and, last but certainly not least, Edgar Foth, who was, unbeknownst to many at the congress, a member of the Silent Brotherhood.

Along with the usual cross-lighting ceremony, there was a two-day guerrilla warfare course taught by Jack Mohr and Louis Beam. During his speeches, Beam would crack jokes about Alan Berg's death, which was then still unsolved. Said Beam during one speech: "Ask that Jew bastard in Denver. Only, you'll have to go to Hell to do it. Somebody reached out and touched him 14 times. Reach out and touch someone!"

At the congress, Butler and his lieutenants strutted about in their homemade polyester uniforms, glorying in the rapt attention of the huge media horde that had descended on Hayden Lake. The Canadian Aryan contingent particularly pleased them. Terry Long, Butler later remarked, had all the makings of an ideal Aryan Nations leader. "He has the ability to get across the point," said Butler. "He's very vocal in the intellectual way. He's articulate. I don't think we could find any-one better to articulate the cause of the white race." Privately, how-ever, Butler and a few other Aryan Nations leaders were worried. Conspicuously absent that weekend were a dozen or so men who tra-ditionally never missed the mid-July congresses—men rumored to be members of Bob Mathews's Silent Brotherhood group. As things turned out, Butler was right to be concerned. On July 19, during the five-day congress and hundreds of miles away in northern California, Mathews and a dozen other members of the Silent Brotherhood staged a daring broad-daylight armed robbery of a Brink's truck on a stretch of highway.

Long returned to Caroline flushed with victory and his glove com-partment bursting with illegal hate literature. Breathless with excite-ment, he spent the summer and fall reading about the Aryan Nations and searching for new members. One of those he signed up was Jim Martin, a 52-year-old former Eckville waiter who would later rent a shack on Long's property.

Martin shared Long's propensity for outlandish rhetoric. A dishev-elled-looking father of six, Martin said that he would "blow the brains out" of any non-white who attempted to court one of his daughters. Martin, who had been separated from his wife for some time, insisted that he was a captain with the Canadian armed forces in

Korea and that he personally killed 150 Communists. When tracked down at his tiny log cabin, he told one Calgary reporter: "A lot of our members are actually crack shots. I would defy 20 Mounties to try and find one of them in the bush. They can go out there and survive just as easy as they can in downtown Rocky Mountain House."

Whether Terry Long had been successful in attracting many more bona fide members than his immediate family and Jim Martin was an open question. Richard Butler, however, was impressed; he decided to make Terry Alberta leader of the Aryan Nations. On November 14, 1984, he dictated a letter to his secretary, Janet Hounsell, which read:

> Greetings Aryan Warrior Priest!
> It is with great joy we receive you into the ranks as an officer leader in the army of the King of kings.
> Each who takes His yoke upon him must do so with the full knowledge that our honour is measure [sic] by our loyalty and fidelity to His infinite purpose.
> Our highest duty is to serve for the life of our people.
> May the blessing of Yahweh be ever with you.
> Hail His Victory!"

Attached to the letter was what Butler called a Leadership Certificate for Church of Jesus Christ Christian Aryan Nations. When he received Butler's letter and certificate, Terry Long was thrilled. On Aryan Nations letterhead, he immediately typed up a crude-looking press release. After briefly highlighting his involvement with the Christian Defence League and the Western Canada Concept, he introduced the Canadian media to the Church of Jesus Christ Christian:

> Aryan Nations is an Identity Christian movement which believes that northern European peoples comprised of Anglo-Saxon, Celtic, Germanic, Basque, Nordic, Slavic and Lombard peoples are the lost tribes of Israel having migrated to their present locations following the two great dispersions

of biblical Israel in 720 and 585 B.C. Adequate documentation is available to prove that Communism is Jewish in origin and is presently controlled by the Jewish elite. Since
Jew-Communists in their own publications advocate the
take-over and annihilation of Western Christian civilization
through the extermination of the white race, Aryan Nations
in accordance with God's seventh commandment advocates
and works for the racial purity of true Israel.

The release was sent to newspaper and magazine offices across
Alberta. Terry Long then waited for prospective members to ring his
phone off the wall. And he waited. And he waited. And, apart from a
brief item titled "The Right to Hate" in the January 7, 1985, edition
of the magazine *Alberta Report*, no media organization took notice
of Terry Long's new job. But the Ku Klux Klan did.

On November 13, Long met in Calgary with self-anointed Alberta
Klan leader Teàrlach Dunsford Mac a'Phearsoin. Mac a'Phearsoin was
the owner of the copyright on the various Klan symbols; he offered to
sell Long the rights to the emblems for $6,000. The next week, Mac
a'Phearsoin confirmed his offer to Long in a registered letter as well as
a telex. On November 26, the Alberta Aryan Nations leader wrote to
Mac a'Phearsoin to politely refuse the Klansman's overture. The Aryan
Nations had entered "the fifth era," Long told Mac a'Phearsoin, meaning it had largely abandoned all propagandistic recruitment ventures
and was now directing its energies at developing a small, cell-based
organization as secretive as it was terroristic. "The organization. . . con-
sequently has become much more serious and action oriented than at
any time in the past," Long wrote. "Such status in my opinion leads
one to preclude the option of going public. The organization is no
longer simply fraternal. It must, given the present critical status of our
people, of necessity be elitist, militant and private."

Mac a'Phearsoin, for his part, does not deny that he attempted to sell
the Klan symbols to Long. But, ever the philanthropist, he claims that
he tried to persuade Long to pursue "legitimate things, constructive

things, things that didn't require opposing anyone or exterminating Jews or any of these things." In a 1986 interview, Mac a'Phearsoin sniffed with distaste at Long's written response. "Of course, his answer was he rejected that. In effect, what he said was that the movement has to be violent."

By the summer of 1985, things were also going poorly for the Aryan Nations organization. The annual congress was cancelled after the indictments against members of Bob Mathews's Silent Brotherhood. Up north, Alberta's own High Aryan Warrior Priest was experiencing an equally difficult time. Bills were not being paid. No more than about 20 local men had joined the Aryan Nations. And neighbors who had once been friendly were starting to resent Long's odd little religion. (He did not help his cause when he declared in the *Alberta Report* "Right to Hate" story that Caroline was "the red-neck capital of Alberta.") Matters came to a head on August 12, when Long's fondness for both free speech and ale got him into a fight in a Caroline bar. The Aryan Nations leader was given a good going-over in the resulting rumble, and "severely injured," one of his friends said. Bruised and fed up, he complained to the RCMP and stopped talking to the media. For almost a full year, Terry Long disappeared from public view. He was seldom seen in Caroline, although Janice continued to work part-time in an area pharmacy.

And then, in late June 1986, as Long was making preparations to attend the July 11 to 13 Aryan Nations World Congress in Hayden Lake with his family, he received a phone call. A reporter from *The Calgary Herald* wanted to meet Long to learn how the Aryan Nations in Canada was handling the bad publicity that had resulted from the Silent Brotherhood prosecutions in Seattle. Still chafing from the previous summer's embarrassment, Long at first rebuffed the reporter. But after a few more phone calls, Long reluctantly agreed to meet. "You can come up after we get back from the congress in Hayden Lake," Long said. He would be there for ten days.

The *Herald* reporter, with a photographer in tow, appeared at the Caroline acreage in late July. Long was in an expansive, cheery mood: he had just been designated Canadian leader of the Aryan

Nations, Church of Jesus Christ Christian, at the group's sixth World Congress in Idaho. The congress had been called to discuss the establishment of a whites-only "territorial imperative" in Alberta, British Columbia and five northwest American states. Escorting his guests around his property while wearing a "WHITE PRIDE" trucker's cap, Long said that "just short of" 500 men, women and children had participated in the event. (More reliable estimates place the attendance at 150.) Also attending the congress was 73-year-old John Ross Taylor, the Aryan Nations' "ambassador" to Canada. "He's a friend of mine," said Long. "It's his intention to move out here. In his words, Toronto is dead. There is no hope for Toronto or Ontario. The colored immigration has taken over in the east."

The *Herald* reporter was surprised by Terry Long. When he relaxed, the lanky, bearded farmer spoke with confidence and ease; his manner was almost engaging. He was decidedly not a run-of-the-mill Hitlerite crackpot. Said Long: "The mood at the congress was one of defiance and victory. The congress was a victory for us, what with all the intimidation that has been going on. The federals have taken out the C.S.A. [Covenant, the Sword and the Arm of the Lord]; they've taken out the Posse Comitatus; they've taken out the Order. The number one organization they have wanted to take out was the Aryan Nations, because the Aryan Nations was in the leadership position for the right wing. By the success at the congress, by the attendance there, we've shown that we won. The battle may be won, but the war is still going on."

Long said the Hayden Lake compound was swarming with reporters and police and what he called "undercover FBI Jew agents." Despite that, the weekend proceeded as planned. On Saturday, July 12, there was a cross-lighting—"You notice I said cross-lighting," Long stressed, "not cross-burning"—in which his three children participated, in pint-sized Klan robes. The children were led in an oath to their "race" by Robert Miles, the Midwest organizer for the Aryan Nations. (Traditionally, the cross-lighting ceremony is used to initiate members into the Ku Klux Klan. Standing before the blazing cross in the klavern, or meeting place, the prospective Klansmen would take the oaths of obedience, secrecy, fidelity and "klannishness." The burning-cross ritual has been appropriated by neo-Nazi groups like the Aryan Nations simply because it is such a big hit with the far right crowd.)

At the July 12 cross-burning, Long, decked out in a three-piece pale blue suit, was asked to step into the Inner Circle, which was made up of seven hooded men. As one of the so-called Officers of the Night, Long's responsibility, among other things, was to indoctrinate children into the Aryan way. "The Officers of the Night accept responsibility for the youngsters, and accept responsibility for passing on information to the youngsters," he said. The reporter noted that Long's son, Cody, was no more than six years old. Was the frightening ritual the best place for such a young child? Long shrugged. "Children initially react to it with trepidation and anxiety. But within a short period of time, they accept it as being the truth. They accept it like the rest of us, as a breath of fresh air." He pauses. "Especially my daughters, who have seen how hypocritical the establishment and their phony apostate ministers can be. They have readily accepted the Aryan Nations."

For the *Herald* reporter, Long's approach to fatherhood was stomach-churning, but it was hardly front-page news. He sensed there was something Long was not saying. Given the Aryan leader's enthusiasm for the Hayden Lake compound, was it possible that he was planning a similar venture in Caroline? As Long strolled around his acreage, chatting with his two guests, the reporter played a hunch. "This area looks like it would be ideal for a training camp, like Pastor Butler has in Idaho." Long slowed a bit and gave a thin smile. "Sure it is," he said. There was a long pause. "It could develop into something like that."

The *Herald* reporter and photographer quickly exchanged glances. A few minutes later, after listening to Long pronounce on Identity and the coming racial holy war, the reporter tried again: "Mr. Long, are you thinking of building your own training camp here?" Long stopped and surveyed the trees.

Finally: "We're . . . getting it together," he said, sounding reluctant. "We've already started working on the structure." Long escorted his guests to a clearing, just south of his house, obscured by stands of pine. It was surrounded by barbed wire. The Aryan leader pointed out an area precisely 32 feet by 16 feet that had been set aside in the centre of the clearing for a bunkhouse and, beside it, a parking lot for visitors. The Caroline acreage is a better area than Hayden Lake, Long said. "It's more isolated, it's less populated. We're in closer proximity to the mountains. We've even got river frontage," he said, pointing east to the Clearwater. "It's totally wooded, right from the mouth to the source."

The training camp—and the bunkhouse to accommodate what Long referred to as 20 Canadian "Aryan warriors"—had been planned for two months. Long had cleared space for the bunkhouse and cut some of the necessary lumber with the help of two local men, Will and Ray Paradis. The Paradis brothers' father, Bill Sr., was a member of the Aryan Nations. "The objective," said Long, leaning on the saw that had claimed his father's life two years before, "is to be identical to the Hayden Lake compound. This site would be a focal point for the church itself. There has to be a focal point for people to congregate and develop their motivation. We've had people who have come here and stayed in the house. Now they will have a place to stay on their own. It's better. They can stay as long as they want.

"Most people," he continued, "would come here to be with other whites."

But would the training camp ever be completed, Long was asked. Was he really serious? Said Long: "I'm not going to speculate what's going to happen. We're going to go one step at a time. I mean, the Jew patrol authorities may throw me in jail in three months, right?"

The *Herald* pursued the story. Neighbors confirmed Long's plans; many said the Aryan leader had been periodically boarding swarthy-looking visitors with out-of-province licence plates. Other inquiries were made, with the RCMP and Caroline residents. There was little doubt: Long was, in fact, planning to establish an Aryan warrior training camp. The Calgary *Herald* put the story on the front page of its August 5, 1986, edition. That report—plus two more front-page stories in the next two days—threw Terry Long into the centre of a national controversy.

The "Jew patrol authorities"—the Royal Canadian Mounted Police—did not, as things turned out, throw the Canadian Aryan Nations leader in jail. But in the succeeding days, he may have wished they had. Dozens of reporters descended on his property to interview him. More than 100 very critical letters were written about Long to the *Herald*. A coalition of church and anti-discrimination organizations formed to thwart the Aryan leader's plans. The Alberta Legislature unanimously passed a motion condemning Long. On the other side of the country, the leader of the Jewish Defence League, Meir Halevi, darkly warned Long to abandon his camp, or else. A huge anti-racism rally was held in the town of Sundre, not far from Caroline; almost the entire population turned out. And, to top it all off, the province's attorney-general, Jim Horsman, even threatened to "crack down" on Long. He told reporters: "It is not permissible in Canada to set up private armies . . . anybody that advocates violence in our society should be brought to task."

At first, Terry Long said he welcomed all the attention. Standing at the gate to his property, by the "NO TRESPASSING" sign, he cheerfully gave scores of interviews about his hopes for the training camp. But one week after the *Herald* broke the story, Long was getting annoyed. Prank callers were telephoning at all hours. Neighbors were upset, particularly about their community being depicted by the news media as another Eckville, and were talking about an informal boycott of Long's sawmill business. And the RCMP were starting to pay unannounced visits. The media attention and the RCMP surveillance, said Long, "are definitely deterring people from learning about us. I think that is what they are trying to do. It's pure blatant intimidation." The culprit, not surprisingly, was the same group that had foreclosed on his Bentley farm—"the most powerful group in the world: international communism and international finance capitalism. They're two heads of the same snake."

"It's a pain in the neck," Long said of the most powerful group in the world. "I can't get anything done around here."

At the end of September 1986, after almost two months of unabated Aryan mania in the local, regional and national media, the Jewish Defence League made good on its threat. On a beautiful Indian summer afternoon, with no clouds in the sky and the Innisfail RCMP far down the road, Long was visited by Canadian Jewish Defence League leader Meir Halevi and U.S. league leader Irv Rubin. The confrontation was hardly spontaneous; Long and Halevi had been sniping at each other in the Alberta media for days. At the appointed hour, from behind his fence, Long was passing out Aryan Nations pamphlets to the two dozen reporters and photographers present. As if on cue, a car screeched up carrying Halevi, Rubin and Edmonton JDL supporter David Strauss. Without delay, Halevi and Rubin jumped out and set about taunting Long, daring him to step onto Highway 54. Looking somewhat uncomfortable, Long refused, saying "that would be inflaming the situation."

Along the perimeter of Long's fence, five or six unidentified men stood holding rifles, watching Halevi pray while Rubin ridiculed Long. "This is a fine specimen of Aryan manhood," Rubin said. "They look like something you'd drag out of a gutter." At Long's side, Aryan Nations member Bill Paradis, Sr., swayed back and forth, clutching a battered old rifle. Paradis pointed the rifle in the direction of Halevi and a cluster of reporters. A Calgary *Herald* reporter told Paradis he did not believe it was loaded. Without saying a word, Paradis pulled back the rifle's bolt and displayed a shell in its chamber. He then pushed the barrel into the reporter's chest for a few moments, grinning.

Long pointed at Rubin. "This guy is a well-known JDL terrorist," he said. "I think he ought to be taken out and hung for treason, and so should 90 per cent of all Jews."

"Your mentality killed 6 million of my people," Rubin spat back. "It's a good thing you're behind a fence, like an animal."

Long said "17 million more" Jews would be exterminated in the future, adding: "I'm not advocating it. God is."

After a few minutes of this sort of thing, Long turned his attention to Halevi. The two exchanged a few unpleasantries while the cameras rolled.

"Show us how you goose-step," Halevi said, while Long leaned on a fencepost.

"I don't goose-step," said Long. "I'm not German, I'm Irish. Also I'm an Aryan and proud of it. I'm certainly not a kike."

At that moment, Halevi lunged across the fence, and narrowly missed slamming his fist into Long's face. Long jumped back, his hands shaking; Paradis lifted his rifle to firing position and shouted, "Hey! Don't push the fence down!" Long, looking jarred, said, "Leave the fence alone." Cameras clicked and television people jockeyed for better position. Across the road, a carload of Innisfail RCMP officers watched, motionless.

As perhaps its participants had anticipated, the Aryan Nations/Jewish Defence League encounter made all of the national television broadcasts. Terry Long, meanwhile, filed another complaint with the RCMP, this time demanding that Meir Halevi be charged with assault. The RCMP declined.

Try as he might, Terry Long could not match the headline-grabbing Aryan summer of 1986. The years 1987, 1988 and 1989 were comparatively quiet ones for Canada's own High Aryan Warrior Priest.

But he had a few ideas, just the same. Mimicking his Toronto Aryan pal John Ross Taylor, who had been broadcasting racist and anti-Semitic messages through a Western Guard phone number since 1977, Long advertised his own hate line in the Red Deer *Advocate*. The plan, which was hatched at a meeting of Canadian Aryan Nations members at Long's property in December 1986, was a cheap and effective way to spread the Aryan gospel. For the cost of the classified ad and the $41 he paid Alberta Government Telephones every month, Long could recruit members and get his message out. The ad ran from February to May 1987 in the Classified section of the *Advocate*. "Church of Jesus Christ Christian-Aryan Nations recorded messages: 343-0216."

The first message, which featured the voice of Red Deer Aryan Nations member Randy Johnston, described Canada's immigration policy as "national suicide." If the policy is not changed, Johnston squeaked, Canada's "once-proud Anglo-Saxon heritage will be washed away by a flood of instant Canadians." A couple of weeks later, Long and Johnston elected to try their hands at some clumsy satire: "Welcome to the hate-infested Church of Jesus Christ Christian Aryan Nations. We have given up fighting for white rights because our bleeding heart politicians have refused to allow whites to show their racial pride. From now on we are forced to promote hatred against Caucasians." Canada's anti-hate laws, Johnston declared, would result in no less than "the genetic extermination of [the white man's] holy seed."

In the next few months, Long and Johnston took aim at Tamils, Sikhs, Vietnamese and, of course, Jews. Judaism, callers were informed, was "anti-Christian, satanic and synonymous with international communism." Other messages trumpeted the unique achievements of Jim Keegstra, New Brunswick anti-Semitic writer Malcolm Ross and Austrian chancellor Kurt Waldheim; some depicted immigrants as "pre-human" who should be sent "back where they came from." The messages were dutifully changed every Sunday. Callers were encouraged to write to Long's post office box in Caroline, where they could purchase books that "explained another side of history."

Johnston later told a Canadian Human Rights Commission official that he did not write any of the messages. In fact, he said, the offending scripts were penned by Long. The messages averaged 30 seconds in length. They were picked up by Johnston every Sunday at the Aryan leader's Caroline acreage. Long, who had mentioned to Johnston that he "liked his broadcast voice," maintained near-total editorial control over content. Johnston informed the Human Rights Commission employee that he sometimes "refused" to read some messages, but admitted that no changes were made without Long's approval.

In the fall of 1987, with the provincial government of Don Getty displaying remarkable disinterest in Terry Long and his band of hatemongers, Alberta officials at B'nai Brith Canada moved against the hate line. First, the B'nai Brith asked Alberta Government Telephones to pull the plug on the Aryan Nations message, but the provincially owned utility refused. Next, the B'nai Brith asked the Red Deer *Advocate* to stop printing Long's classified ad. It, too, refused. The Alberta Human Rights Commission also concluded that it could do nothing about the hate line, because telephones are a federally regulated responsibility. In January 1988, an exasperated Deborah Glaser, regional director of the B'nai Brith's Alberta and Saskatchewan branch—along with her predecessor, David Goldberg, and three other Albertans, one of whom, Robert Nealy, was black—made a formal complaint to the Canadian Human Rights Commission. Some 12 weeks later, the commission agreed to hear the complainants—in October 1988. (Commissioner Max Yalden said the delay was chiefly due to the *Advocate*'s refusal to release the billing address of the Aryan Nations. The CHRC eventually obtained the address through a search warrant issued against the *Advocate*. The commissioner, apparently, was unaware that Long's mailing address was mentioned in every single taped message.)

After reading about the B'nai Brith's complaint in the *Advocate*, Terry Long again showed that, for some Aryan Warriors, discretion is the better part of valor. He conferred with Johnston, and the two quietly switched off the Aryan Nations line in February 1988. Still, the federal Human Rights Commission proceeded with its investigation into the complaints. In October, in an Edmonton courtroom, the three-member commission, led by former University of Calgary Law School dean John McLaren, met to listen to a sampling of Long and Johnston's messages. Long and Johnston did not appear, nor did they send lawyers to represent them. The commission was a "kangaroo court," Long snarled at one reporter. Months afterwards, in July 1989, the commission released its decision on the case. It ruled that Long's messages were discriminatory and likely to cause hatred, and ordered Long and Johnston to cease and desist. The order was filed with the Federal Court, ensuring that Long could be cited for contempt if he ignored the ruling.

But Terry Long, if nothing else, was inventive. He would find a new way to stamp his hateful creed on the public consciousness. And, in early 1989, an opportunity presented itself on his doorstep in Caroline: a tattooed, 250-pound opportunity that passed bad cheques.

The 23-year-old Texas native named Howard Pursley was one tough-looking customer, covered as he was with scars and tattoos. One arm featured tattoos of a skull-and-crossbones and the word "MERC"—as in "mercenary"—while the other bore a Viking above the caption "ARYAN WARRIOR." Facing jail time for writing ten rubber cheques in and around Dallas, Pursley consulted with his fellow Identity Christians at the Church of Jesus Christ Christian in Hayden Lake. They advised him to high-tail it up to Terry Long's spread, which Pursley promptly did, slipping across the border into Alberta in January 1989.

In Alberta, Pursley occupied himself working, without a visa, at a moving company. He spent much of his spare time at Terry Long's acreage, where the two men would drink beer and use Menachem Begin posters for target practice. In February, Immigration officials learned of Pursley's presence in Canada. Worrying about both his size and his propensity for violence—Pursley has a long criminal record in the United States—Immigration officials brought along an armed Mountie to help them arrest the American at the motel where he was living. But Pursley surrendered without incident.

Once in captivity, and at Terry Long's urging, Pursley threw an unexpected curve at the Department of Immigration: he claimed he was a refugee, fleeing persecution in the United States for his religious beliefs. The culprit, he alleged, was the FBI, which Pursley said was oppressing Richard Butler's flock. Pursley had been a member of the church since 1986. If nothing else, the refugee claim was inventive. Only once before had an American citizen applied for refugee status in Canada. Long posted a $1,000 bail bond, and Pursley was released from the Calgary Remand Centre until his case could be heard, on February 14.

On that day, Pursley's first action was to request that only reporters from *The Calgary Herald* and CBC Television be permitted to observe the proceedings. The hearing was adjourned to February 23 because Pursley, while evidently having spent some considerable time thinking about media coverage of his story, had spent no time at all on finding and retaining a lawyer. At the February 23 hearing, a two-man immigration board quickly determined that there was no credible basis for Pursley's claim of FBI persecution. He was ordered deported on April 8. An attempt at an appeal, filed three days after the hearing, was unsuccessful. So the reluctant 23-year-old Aryan Nations adherent was shipped back to the United States. (Pursley reattempted entry on April 22, but the Calgary-bound Greyhound bus he was riding was stopped by the RCMP at Milk River, Alberta, just past the border. Pursley was once again deported back to the United States. In July 1989, a Texas judge sentenced him to 18 months in prison for passing the bad cheques.)

It was around this time—the summer of 1989—that some lawmakers and anti-racism activists reluctantly started to admit that they had been wrong: Terry Long was not going to go away. When *The Calgary Herald* published its extensive profile of Long in August 1986, some members of the Alberta Jewish community were harshly critical of the newspaper. Terry Long is an aberration, they said; without the glare of publicity, he and his rag-tag group of Nazis will wither and die. Stop writing about them. *Alberta Report* called the *Herald*'s coverage "The Aryan Conquest of the Media." Even the magazine *Saturday Night* got into the act in 1987, calling the *Herald*'s stories about the Aryan Nations a lot of "tall tales."

As things turned out, the nay-sayers were emphatically wrong on two counts: one, the media coverage had not helped Terry Long, and two, Terry Long was a stubborn man with no intention of folding his tent. On the positive side of the ledger, it can be noted that the flurry of media scrutiny derailed Long's plans for the Aryan Warrior training camp, perhaps indefinitely; moreover, the resulting community-led backlash drove him onto welfare for many months. But one unfortunate fact could not be escaped: despite the many setbacks he and his group experienced, Terry Long refused to give up. Through his efforts, the Aryan Nations Canadian membership grew to almost 200 men and women, mainly in the three westernmost provinces. It also grew to be what was one of the largest and most extreme neo-Nazi groups in Canada. Long had become an unqualified hero to skinhead and other Nazi organizations from British Columbia to the Atlantic provinces. And, among American racists and anti-Semites, he was regarded with considerably more respect than the man who had "ordained" him in 1984, Aryan Nations founder Richard Butler. Long had achieved the status—and, in some instances, exceeded the status—of the likes of Jim Keegstra, Ernst Zundel and Malcolm Ross.

But he was an angry man, with a need to prove himself worthy of the title High Aryan Warrior Priest. His chosen vehicle was a man named Keith Rutherford.

On April 14, 1990, with about five minutes to go until midnight—and five minutes to go until his sixtieth birthday—Keith Rutherford sat on the couch in his television room on Bonneville Court in Sherwood Park, Alberta, watching a hockey game. The playoff match between the Edmonton Oilers and the Los Angeles Kings was into its second overtime period. Rutherford's wife, Lois, had gone to bed. But like most residents of Edmonton and its environs, Rutherford had elected to watch the game until its bitter end. He sat in his undershirt, smoking a cigarette.

The doorbell rang. Keith and Lois Rutherford were not in the habit of receiving guests late at night, but Rutherford was not concerned. Sherwood Park was a peaceful, law-abiding Edmonton bedroom community. Besides, two weeks earlier, at about 3:00 a.m., an inebriated man had ambled down the quiet cul-de-sac where the Rutherfords had lived since 1963. The drunk had knocked on their door to ask for some directions. So, as he walked up a short flight of stairs to the main floor, Keith Rutherford assumed the unexpected guest was another wayward drunk.

He opened the door. Standing on the first step was a young man with a shaved head. Through the screen door, Rutherford could see that the young man—who looked to be barely out of his teens—was wearing a black T-shirt with something written on it, a pair of shiny military-style boots with red laces and a navy blue nylon bomber jacket with what appeared to be an eagle holding a swastika. Although he did not know it, Keith Rutherford was making his first face-to-face encounter with a neo-Nazi skinhead. The name of this skinhead was Daniel Joshua Sims.

Frowning, Rutherford opened the door.

"Are you Mr. Rutherford?" Sims asked.

"Yes," Rutherford said.

"Are you the Mr. Rutherford who worked for Moscow Radio?"

Rutherford squinted at the dark figure. "No, son," he said. "I never worked for Moscow Radio."

"Well," Sims said, undeterred, "were you ever involved with a story about a man in Winnipeg who ended up hanging himself?"

"Well, kind of," Rutherford said, remembering. "I never worked for Moscow Radio, son, but I was involved in a story a little bit like that in Winnipeg. But why do you ask? Who are you?"

"That man was my grandfather," Sims said. "And you shouldn't have done that."

"Son, you can think what you like, but I think we did the right thing," Rutherford said, suddenly feeling uneasy. He edged back towards the door.

"You shouldn't have done that," Sims repeated. A moment passed when neither man said a word, and then Sims lunged forward, kicking at Rutherford. One of his boots struck a shin and Rutherford stumbled down the front steps. Rutherford bent forward, trying to protect himself from Sims, who was now trying to kick the older man in the genitals. Rutherford called out to his wife: "Lois! Get the police!" As he reached ground level, Rutherford saw movement in the periphery of his vision. Standing to his left, in a shadowy corner at the front of Rutherford's home, was another large skinhead, Mark Allan Swanson. Swanson seemed to be holding something in his hands.

And then, there was pain. Swanson smashed Rutherford in the face with a large wooden club he had brought along for precisely that purpose. The blow landed on his good eye, the right one. Recalls Rutherford: "The pain was excruciating. There was unbelievable pain, and then nothing. It was just like squeezing a grape; it burst inside. That's what happened to my eyeball. It shattered my retina."

Keith Rutherford had been blinded in his right eye, for good. He lurched towards a stand of pine trees, holding his face, blood spurting out between his fingers. He gasped for breath. "They've got my eye, Lois! Call the ambulance!" Lois Rutherford was already on the phone in the kitchen, speaking to a 911 operator.

Silent, Sims and Swanson watched Rutherford for a second or two, and then they turned and jogged away. Two other skinheads who had been observing the assault from behind a truck parked in Rutherford's driveway, Wayne Granfield and Paul Planiden, also started running down Bonneville Court. The group raced towards Granfield's big four-door 1974 Meteor, parked around the corner. As their boots echoed on the asphalt, one of them yelled: "Up with white power!" The group jumped into the car, where two more skinheads, Trinity Larocque and Scott Fuhr, were waiting. "What happened?" Larocque asked. Fuhr squealed away from the curb and started driving west, towards Edmonton.

Sims was, in Swanson's words, "really happy." He said, "I kicked him so hard, I snapped his neck, the old bastard." He laughed.

Swanson seemed less buoyant. He sat quiet for a moment, until one of the skinheads asked him what had transpired. "Dan and the old guy were arguing, and it was getting pretty bad," Swanson said. "So I hit him."

"We did our part for the cause," Sims said, with finality. When a police officer later asked Scott Fuhr what Dan Sims had meant by this remark, Fuhr replied that "the cause" that had motivated Sims and Swanson to blind Keith Rutherford was "the preservation of white culture."

There was silence. The car sped westward, along the Sherwood Park Freeway. Fuhr stopped at a red light, and another car pulled up alongside. The driver of the other car looked over and saw six grim-looking skinheads. One of them appeared to have a swastika tattooed onto his forehead.

At about 1:30, while Rutherford was being examined by a team of doctors at the University of Alberta Hospital, the carload of skin-heads pulled up outside their rented home at the corner of 89th Street and 114th Avenue. Inside the house, there were lots of National Socialist posters, dozens of pro-Nazi tracts scattered on broken-down couches and an old rifle hidden upstairs. Sims and his friends called this place the Skin Bin. It was the Edmonton headquarters of ultra-violent pro-Nazi group called the Final Solution Skinheads. The group said hello to Daryl Rivest, an enormous skinhead who had drunk himself into a stupor during the hockey game and passed out on the floor. "They were all jumping up and down and yelling and screaming," Rivest would later recall. "They were in a great mood." The skinheads tossed back a few beers and some Irish whiskey while they reviewed the night's events. All of them were in fine spirits, but Sims, in particular, was clearly delighted. "We finally did something right," he said. "We finally got someone who deserved it."

Sims remarked that he would now have something to brag about at the Adolf Hitler birthday party—the 101st—that was taking place in a few days' time in Idaho. The skinhead was "totally hyped up" after the attack on Rutherford, Rivest recalled. "He enjoyed it." Wayne Granfield told the police that "we were all in, like, a giddy mood."

Sims, all of the skinheads admitted, had been talking about Keith Rutherford for weeks. Sims had heard the man's name at Terry Long's place. Long, in turn, had been given Rutherford's name by someone at the Aryan Nations armed compound in Hayden Lake, Idaho. Long maintained a list of "enemies" on a computer at his home in Caroline, Alberta. The list contained the names of dozens of Canadians, among them Alberta Human Rights Commission chair-man Fil Fraser, Jewish Defence League leader Meir Halevi and Keith Rutherford. "Dan was really happy about [the attack on Rutherford]," Swanson told police five days after the assault. "He really wants to get ahead in the Aryan Nations. I heard Dan on the phone to Terry Long about it. He was telling him what happened."

In a September 1991 court hearing, former Final Solution member Brett Hayes would testify under oath that a group of Edmonton skins visited Long's isolated acreage in March 1990, a month before the assault on Rutherford. In attendance were Sims, Hayes, Trinity Larocque and a member of the Canadian Armed Forces, Matt McKay. Recalled Hayes: "[Terry Long] was just explaining about this person that murdered this Nazi, and that we should find this problem and get rid of it. Terry Long was saying to us . . . that this is the lowest form of crime that somebody could do to a white supremacist, and he wasn't very happy about it. He said: 'That Rutherford,' that is all he said. He didn't say first name or anything like that. He just said 'Rutherford,' [and] you know, I just got the idea, the hint, that something is going down. Something was going to come down."

Dan Sims, at least, understood Terry Long's cryptic musings. And he knew precisely what was going down. At 19 years of age, Daniel Joshua Sims was a committed neo-Nazi. A slight figure who did not do well in fights, Sims more than compensated for his awkwardness with an unswerving devotion to the cause. The previous year, in fact, he had been placed on the Aryan Nations payroll. To clear up any uncertainty, he even had a swastika tattooed onto his forehead. Along with being an Identity Christian, Sims was also a member of the Church of Jesus Christ Christian Aryan Nations; the Alberta Independent Knights of the Ku Klux Klan; the National Socialist Action Party; the Brotherhood of Racial Purity; White Aryan Resistance; Viking Youth; SS Action Group; the Aryan Resistance Movement; and, of course, the Final Solution Skinheads. He was also an honorary member of Britain's National Front and the Scottish Storm Trooper Skins. For the privilege of belonging to so many hate groups, Sims paid upwards of $800 a year in dues.

In February 1990, a few weeks before Sims assaulted Rutherford, an *Edmonton Sun* reporter tracked him down in front of the Eaton Centre. There, Sims was handing out copies of "The Thunderbolt," a hate sheet published by the National States Rights Party, in Marietta, Georgia. As his friends Michelle Evers and André Lemieux looked on, Sims told the reporter that pro-Nazi skinheads were misunderstood. "We're not violence-prone," said Sims, apparently with a straight face. "We just don't go around beating up people unless we're provoked."

What, then, provoked Dan Sims to attack Keith Rutherford? What provoked the Aryan Nations to place Rutherford's name on its "enemies" list? At 4:00 a.m. on April 14, as he sat at his kitchen table with his wife Lois, Keith Rutherford, bone-tired but unable to sleep, tried to answer that one question. What had provoked two strangers to attack him on his own doorstep? That the young men were pro-Nazi skinheads, Rutherford now had little doubt: the swastika patches on Sims's jacket and the "Up with white power!" cry were fairly compelling pieces of evidence. But why? What had he done to them?

Keith Rutherford had a good idea what had brought the skinheads to his door in the middle of the night. Thirty years before, he had been a popular young disc jockey at Winnipeg radio station CKY. At just 30 years of age, Rutherford, CKY's late-night man, had already been working in the radio business for more than a decade. He started out in Medicine Hat, when he was 19. From there, he criss-crossed the prairies, working at stations in North Battleford, Calgary, Brandon, Yorkton and then, finally, CKY. With 50,000 watts of power, it was one of the best-known radio stations in the west; on a good night, one could hear it as far away as Alberta. After many expressions of interest, CKY hired Rutherford to be "The Voice in the Night," host of a dusk-to-dawn show that featured dedications, requests and some news.

One Saturday night in late August 1960, the chief engineer phoned Rutherford with some very hot news, indeed. While fiddling with a short-wave radio at home, the engineer said, he had picked up a segment of "Moscow Radio," a regular English-language program broadcast by the Soviet government. The program, the engineer told Rutherford, dealt with Nazi war criminals living in Canada. And it had identified a man living in the Winnipeg suburb of St. James as a Nazi war criminal.

Rutherford searched through the Winnipeg phone book and found the man's name: Alexander Laak. "It's a hell of a story," Rutherford told the engineer. "But we have to get the tape." Using directory assistance, Rutherford had reached Moscow Radio within a few hours. After discussing the matter with an English-speaking man at Moscow Radio, Rutherford was told he would be sent the tape containing information about Alexander Laak. Within a week, as promised, the tape arrived in the mail. Rutherford promptly handed the tape over to his bosses at CKY. After that, he recalls, "I was completely out of the story. I had nothing more to do with it."

CKY checked the story. Estonian by birth, Laak was the owner of a brick-laying business he ran out of his St. James home. He had immigrated to Canada in 1948; he lived with his wife, Daisy, and his two sons. In September 1942, CKY concluded, Obersturmführer Alexander Laak had, in fact, overseen the mass murder of 3,000 German and Czech Jews at a railway station near the Jagala death camp. Later reports linked Laak to the murders of some 300,000 Jews and gypsies at Jagala. On September 3, CKY broadcast its story about Laak, which the Estonian man denied. Then, on September 6, Laak's wife found him hanging in the garage of their home. Recalls Rutherford: "There was an investigation of his death and the police ruled it was suicide, and I believe it was. That was the end of it, I thought."

Rutherford was wrong. Six months later, an unidentified RCMP officer called the disc jockey at his home in St. Boniface. The Mounties wanted to know why Rutherford had contacted Moscow Radio to request the tape. "I kind of chuckled and said: 'Because I wanted them, why else would I phone?' That didn't please the RCMP guy too much." With McCarthyite determination, the RCMP officer proceeded to question Rutherford about his involvement in the youth wing of the Cooperative Commonwealth Federation (CCF), about his mother's association with the turn-of-the-century Winnipeg labor movement, and whether the brother of one of his teachers in Saskatoon

Kelly Lyle (*left*), leader of the ultra-violent Final Solution skinheads, is considered one of the most dangerous members of the skinhead movement in Canada.

Manitoba Klan leader Bill Harcus (*top left*) and former Aryan Nations enforcer Brett Hayes (*bottom left*) with other skinheads in Winnipeg, 1989. Harcus is now in hiding. Hayes leads the Calgary chapter of Skinheads Against Racial Prejudice (SHARP).

This poster was circulated by Mission, B.C.'s Aryan Resistance Movement.

(Larry MacDougal)

(Larry MacDougal)

Canadian Jewish Defence League leader Meir Halevi takes a swing at Aryan Nations leader Terry Long at Long's Caroline, Alberta, property in September 1986. Silent Brotherhood member Edgar Foth stands between them in the background, holding a camera.

Terry Long in his favorite trucker's cap, Caroline, Alberta, July 1986.

Saskatchewan Aryan Nations Leader Carney Milton Nerland (*above*) confronts Auschwitz survivor Sigmund Sobolewski at the September 1990 Aryan Fest in Provost, Alberta. Kelly Lyle stands between the two men, and is seen wearing sunglasses.

(*left*) Canadian Silent Brotherhood member, Edgar Foth, strikes a pose. Foth was one of two Canadian members of this Aryan Nations terrorist offshoot.

(Scot Magnish/Courtesy *The Ottawa Sun*)

Canadian Church of the Creator leader George Burdi on the night of May 29, 1993, when a neo-Nazi riot took place on Parliament Hill. Burdi is one of the most able far right leaders to appear in the last decade.

Heritage Front leader Wolfgang Droege, one of the most persistent and vocal members of the far right, has been a successful recruiter of young people.

(Dave Chan)

A few of the youthful faces belonging to Donald Andrews's Nationalist Party of Canada in 1989. Some of these young people will go on to play leadership roles in the growing hate movement.

A pro-Nazi publication from the Ottawa chapter of the Aryan Resistance Movement in 1989.

CANADA AWAKE! No. 2

White Pride

CANADA

AWAKE

THE KNIGHTS OF THE KU KLUX KLAN Confederate Hammer Skins

RACIAL NEWS and *VIEWS*

(Scot Magnish/Courtesy *The Ottawa Sun*)

A young skinhead sporting a swastika armband poses with an unidentified child in August 1992 at La Plaine, Quebec.

(Jeff Speed)

(*above*) Aryan Nations supporter and
Canadian Armed Forces member
Matt McKay on duty in Belet Huen,
Somalia, 1993.

Matt McKay wearing a Hitler T-shirt and
giving a Nazi salute in his Winnipeg barracks. Behind him is a swastika banner
he was permitted to display.

(CP)

had been a conscientious objector during World War Two. After jousting with the Mountie for a few more minutes, a bemused Rutherford hung up. It would be his last contact with the Alexander Laak story for 25 years.

On an evening in May 1985, Lois and Keith Rutherford sat in the living room of their tidy home on Bonneville Court, watching the news. Some months before, in February, the federal government had established a Commission of Inquiry on War Criminals. Headed by Quebec Superior Court judge Jules Deschênes, the commission had been set up to determine whether Joseph Mengele and other Nazi war criminals had attempted to enter Canada after the war. On this particular night, Keith Rutherford recalled, an RCMP official was telling a CBC interviewer that the Mounties had "no knowledge" of any Nazi war criminals living in Canada. Upon hearing this, Rutherford went through the proverbial roof. "Well, that's a bloody lie," he told his wife. "How can they say they didn't know about it when they questioned me about one of these people in 1961? The story was common knowledge in Winnipeg. They can't have it both ways. They either knew about it or they didn't."

Displaying the same sort of resolve that had prompted him to seek out Moscow Radio during the height of the cold war, Rutherford phoned the city desk at *The Edmonton Journal*. He related his story to an editor, who assigned a reporter to visit him. On May 9, 1985, the story ran with the headline "War Crime Tales Confirm Man's Suspicions Since '50s." In it, Rutherford was quoted as saying: "The RCMP said there was absolutely no truth to [the Alexander Laak story]. They said it was something cooked up by the Russians. But three days after we played the tape on the air, the man went into his garage and hanged himself. Why would a man living in Canada hang himself if he was innocent?" Rutherford said he planned to hand the Moscow Radio tape over to the Deschênes Commission.

The story produced little reaction in Edmonton. But 90 miles south, in a house on the edge of Red Deer city limits, it caused a minor sensation. In May 1985, a former Eckville, Alberta, teacher named Jim

Keegstra happened to be in the middle of being prosecuted on the charge that he had willfully promoted hatred against Jews in his classroom. Keegstra's lawyer, Doug Christie, spotted the *Journal* story and was moved to write to the newspaper's editor. "Mr. Rutherford seemed delighted that, three days after the tape was played on the air, the man went into his garage and hanged himself," Christie wrote in the letter published on May 16. "When the Soviet propaganda tentacles can reach around the world and be believed, where is there safety for freedom-loving people? Today the Deschênes Commission is giving a platform for Soviet propaganda. . . . If it is [our] intention to use the state to spread terror via KGB evidence, why don't we just adopt the KGB as our security force? On the other hand, looking at Canada today, maybe we already have."

Rutherford does not know who, ultimately, made the decision to seek retribution for Alexander Laak's death. But Rutherford believes the two items published in *The Edmonton Journal* left a very unfavorable impression with the Aryan Nations. He says: "I am either on file somewhere, or somebody kept those clippings. But they obviously were the reasons for my attack. [Dan Sims] isn't Laak's grandson. Somebody sent him. Somebody told him about me." Rutherford, Sims's friends say, is right. After Aryan Nations leaders Terry Long and Edgar Foth spoke to the Final Solution gang about Rutherford in early 1990, Daryl Rivest interpreted the discussions to mean "go and bash his head in."

It was 4:15 a.m. Still euphoric over the courageous way he and a friend had beaten and kicked a 60-year-old man in the dark, Dan Sims decided to have some more fun. He dialled Rutherford's number as half a dozen skinheads looked on. Unbeknownst to Sims, however, the Sherwood Park RCMP detachment was already monitoring Rutherford's phone line. The RCMP reasoned correctly that the attackers would phone to find out their victim's condition.

Disguising his voice with what he hoped was a British accent, Sims told Rutherford that his name was Paul and that he had done "a lot for the cause." Rutherford asked what cause. Sims replied that he had worked with National Socialist groups in Scotland, Wales and England. "How do you stand?" Sims asked. "Everyone knows where I stand," Rutherford said, and then his wife hung up.

A few minutes later, there was another call. This time, Sims abandoned the fake British accent. Identifying himself as one of the men who had "visited" Rutherford at midnight, Sims said: "We'll be there again to get you, you fucking kike." He hung up.

Then, a third call. "It's your move, motherfucker!" Sims bellowed. "We'll be back, you fucking kike."

Then, at about 5:30, Sims called again. Claiming to be Alexander Laak's grandson, Sims repeatedly called Rutherford "a fucking kike." At this point, her patience at an end, Lois Rutherford grabbed the phone to tell Dan Sims to leave her husband alone. "I'm not interested in talking to you," Sims sneered. "Put Keith back on."

"I won't do that," Lois Rutherford said. "Are you aware that these calls are being traced, and that the RCMP are listening to you?" At that, Sims quickly hung up.

But RCMP officers had already traced the calls to a run-down section of downtown Edmonton, where they knew a notorious group of neo-Nazi skinheads lived in a rented house. The skinheads, they also knew, had lengthy criminal records. Armed with that information—and with a call from the man who had seen the six skinheads speeding along the Sherwood Park Freeway a few hours before—the Mounties questioned everyone who lived in the Skin Bin. On April 18, Swanson was arrested. And, after eluding capture for more than a week, thanks largely to the assistance of Edgar Foth, Dan Sims was arrested on April 22 in downtown Edmonton. At the time, he was wearing a curly wig, a baseball cap and a T-shirt that read: "Join the army, travel to exotic distant lands, meet exciting and unusual people, then kill them."

On June 14, Sims and Swanson appeared in Sherwood Park Provincial Court to plead guilty to assault and aggravated assault, respectively. Edgar Foth and Terry Long were on hand to offer friendly waves and moral support. Keith Rutherford, who had been under police protection but had not been consulted by the Crown Attorney's Office, was furious to learn that a plea bargain had been struck. Sims was being offered 60 days; Swanson, meanwhile, was to get eight months. Says Rutherford: "[An RCMP] constable was trying to convince me that they wouldn't get anything more than that anyway. But I wouldn't hear of it. And they said: 'Well, you have nothing to say about it.' The case was blown in two minutes." Sims and Swanson pleaded guilty. Swanson was promptly whisked off to the Grand Cache Correctional Centre. Sims would be released in just a few days, having already spent about six weeks at Edmonton's Remand Centre.

Following a huge media outcry in which anti-racism groups and Jewish community leaders rallied to Rutherford's side, the Crown Attorney's Office came to realize that it had made a grave mistake. It appealed the sentences, and was successful in obtaining longer jail terms. But by then, Sims was long gone. He now lives in the United States, recruiting for the Aryan Nations.

Keith Rutherford, meanwhile, continues to live in his tidy home on Bonneville Court in Sherwood Park. In September 1990, he launched a $2.5-million lawsuit against Terry Long, Edgar Foth, Dan Sims, Mark Swanson and all of the others who participated in the attack that left him blind in one eye. Rutherford has learned a lot about the Aryan Nations plot against him but he also knows that it is unlikely he will ever see a penny. Still, he perseveres, speaking out against racism at community hall meetings, giving interviews, seeking intervenor status in human rights hearings that concern organized hate groups.

"My life will never be the same," he says now, in his deep broadcaster's voice. "The Keith Rutherford who went to the door that night was different than the Keith Rutherford who came back in. Inside of a minute and a half, my life was changed forever."

He pauses to light a cigarette. "If you are without prejudice, you are a pretty fortunate person, a pretty unique person. Before all of this happened, I had some hang-ups, too. I had some petty prejudices, like everybody does," he says, then stops. "But now I have been on the other side. Now I have been on the receiving end of unbridled, unreasoning, illogical hatred. And if you're not on the receiving end of hate, it's hard to understand.

"These young men did not know me. They didn't have their facts straight. They didn't know anything about me. And yet they were willing to go out and maim me because they thought it was necessary to further their cause. Unless you're on the receiving end of that hate and that violence—the violence that results from hate—you can't fully understand. Now, I understand."

There was little doubt that Terry Long had come a long way since his days as a Western Canada Concept candidate and a Christian Defence League founder. He was more radical, more media-savvy and, as a consequence of the Rutherford incident, much more feared than he had ever been. Said Richard Butler: "Terry Long has everything it takes to lead people, to motivate them, to teach them. The man is committed to an ideal, and that ideal is the preservation of his people." When all the praise and accolades are mentioned to him, Terry Long shrugs. "It's a job that has to be done, and I said I'd do it." But what would he "do" next?

In early 1990, around the time of the assault on Keith Rutherford, Terry Long renewed his acquaintance with Carney Milton Nerland, a Prince Albert, Saskatchewan National Socialist. The two men had met at the July 1984 Aryan World Congress at Hayden Lake, where Nerland, then a squat, moon-faced teenager with a dream to own a gun shop, informed Long that he was a Nazi as well as a member of the KKK. Over the years, the pair had kept in touch over the telephone. In September 1989, some time following Nerland's own conversion to Christian Identity, Long appointed him the Saskatchewan leader of the Church of Jesus Christ Christian Aryan Nations. In the coming months, the two men busied themselves with beefing up the Canadian Aryan Nations' membership lists. The task was not as difficult as it had been during the lean years of 1984 and 1985; skinheads with Nazi leanings were signing up in droves. "In the past year," Long said in a summer 1989 interview, "we've obtained members from all across Canada from the skinhead movement. We're very impressed with them. This thing has progressed from just a handful to tens of thousands in just the past two years. It's totally spontaneous, and the Jews can't stop it, and that's what really bugs them."

A few months after the Rutherford attack, the two men set to work on an event designed to bring together the new skinhead members and some of the older western Canadian racists. This event, as things turned out, would also bring to an apparent end Terry Long's very public tenure as Canadian leader of the Church of Jesus Christ Christian Aryan Nations. It would be the event that would shatter the Canadian Aryan Nations organization, split up Long's family and drive Terry Long into hiding, with the RCMP hot in pursuit.

In the summer of 1990, Terry Long and Carney Nerland decided to hold a two-day Aryan Fest in Provost, Alberta.

7

PROVOST, AND TWO MEN WHO WERE THERE

Provost, Alberta, is a quiet, out-of-the-way little place. During the week, people who live there farm the dusty land or work for oil companies. On weekends, the men fish for trout and perch at Gooseberry Lake down south or Dillberry Lake up north. It is, by all accounts, an unremarkable central-Alberta town of about 2,000 people, six restaurants, three banks, three motels, two car dealerships, one hotel and a big outdoor swimming pool. Provost—which is not pronounced the French way, locals say, but with the *st* pronounced—is about 20 minutes' drive east of the Saskatchewan border.

On most Wednesdays and Saturdays, residents of Provost can be seen loading their garbage into the back of their pick-ups, then driving four miles west on Highway 13, in the direction of the local PetroCanada station. They get to the sanitary landfill along a gravel secondary road.

On the Saturday in question—September 8, 1990—a damp red ribbon is fluttering from the PetroCanada sign. Near the entrance to the landfill, a few more red ribbons can be seen.

Some locals gaze at the ribbons and mutter to themselves; others curse. On any other day, the red ribbons would be forgotten as quickly as they are spotted. But not today. On this day, the Provost residents know, the ribbons have been left to help members of the Ku Klux Klan, the Aryan Nations and the Final Solution Skinheads find their way to the property of Ray and Janet Bradley. An Identity Christian and a member of the Aryan Nations, Bradley is the leader of a previously unheard-of group called the Brotherhood of Regular People, or the Brotherhood of Racial Purity, or just BHORP for short.

Curious—in some cases disbelieving—a few people drive one mile north to Bradley's property. Long before they arrive, they can see that all of the rumors and whispers are true.

Raymond Maxwell Bradley bought his property in Provost in April 1986. Most of the time, he used the acreage as a base of operations for his business, Bradley's Porta-Weld Limited. He kept to himself. Viewing his domain from the road that runs alongside it, one sees a tidy one-storey home with white panelling and black shutters, just behind a stand of trees. A few cars and trucks are parked near the house, their licence plates splattered with judicious amounts of mud. Just north of the house is a large two-vehicle garage. Tacked to the side of the garage, above a Laidlaw waste container and a metal tool shed, there is a six-foot by three-foot Nazi Battle Flag, on loan from the Saskatchewan leader of the Aryan Nations. Spotlights will be trained on the flag when dusk falls. Off in Bradley's field, a 30-foot-tall metal cross has been erected; it has been welded together by Bradley and his two sons, Wade and Ray, Jr., and Bradley had used a crane to lift it in place. The cross has been wrapped in burlap sacks and soaked with 100 gallons of diesel fuel to ensure that it burns for a long time.

Down the driveway, at the road, a large white sign has been fastened to the gate. On one side of the sign, in foot-high black letters, someone has used a stencil set to spray-paint a few words: "KKK WHITE POWER! 1990." On the right side of the sign, they have stencilled "BHORP WELCOME'S [*sic*] ARYAN-NATIONS."

Leaning over the top of the sign—which will, by the time the weekend is over, become perhaps the most-photographed piece of plywood in the history of Alberta—there are Terry Long, leader of the Aryan Nations in Canada; Kelly Scott Lyle, founder of Calgary's Final Solution Skinheads; and Carney Milton Nerland, the Saskatchewan leader of the Church of Jesus Christ Christian Aryan Nations. At this moment, Nerland is wearing black sunglasses, a brown shirt, a tie and a swastika armband. The Prince Albert gun dealer calls it his Schutzstaffel uniform. His belly hangs over an Aryan Nations buckle purchased in Hayden Lake. He is cradling a Winchester pistol-handled pump-action 12-gauge "Police Defender" shotgun, which happens to be loaded. On his belt he carries an SS ceremonial dagger. His chubby little face twisted into a sneer, Nerland stands at the end of the gate, bellowing at Sigmund Sherwood Sobolewski, a Holocaust survivor who is carrying a sign that reads "RACIAL HATRED LEADS TO AUSCHWITZ." For his one-man protest at the neo-Nazi rally, Sobolewski, a Roman Catholic, has donned a replica of the uniform worn by prisoners at the Auschwitz concentration camp. Standing a dozen feet away, Sobolewski challenges Nerland to remove his sunglasses.

"Come and take them off, you fucking war hero," Nerland says, as his friends at the gate laugh. "You survived Auschwitz, you'll survive me."

Nerland hands his shotgun and a bayonet to a masked skinhead. "Come here and take my fucking glasses off, you fucking war hero, you piece of shit," he says to Sobolewski, as Kelly Lyle laughs.

"You're one of the ones they didn't work to death, you parasite," Nerland says, a fleck of spit at the corner of his mouth. "You fucking weren't able to work in the camps good enough to feed the Nazi war machine. What the fuck are you doing over here, you piece of shit? You lying son of a bitch. You tell everyone they got what, 20 million people at Auschwitz? Why don't you tell me they made fucking soap out of your auntie and fucking luggage out of your uncle. They made luggage out of him. I've got it in the fucking trunk of my car. I've got luggage made from your fucking uncle."

  The assembled neo-Nazis erupt in peals of laughter; Sobolewski and a few other protestors, meanwhile, stand mute for a few moments, catching their breath, overwhelmed by Nerland's spew of hatred and abuse. Shaking their heads, the locals climb back into their pick-ups and pull away. Overhead, the sky is flat and grey as metal.

  Welcome to Alberta Aryan Fest 1990.

Provost, of course, was not the first such gathering of its type. The first known meeting of organized white supremacists took place more than a century earlier, in April 1867, in Nashville, Tennessee. The infamous 1867 rally brought together hundreds of members of the embryonic Ku Klux Klan to discuss responses to the U.S. government's Reconstruction policy, a policy that saw, among other things, the abolition of the Confederate state governments and the registration of black voters. From all over Tennessee, Alabama, Georgia and Mississippi, alarmed Klansmen travelled to Nashville to rally against Congress and the Union. In Nashville, the Klansmen paraded about in their robes, waved guns, burned crosses, drank a lot of whiskey, and listened to speeches by their new Imperial Wizard, Confederate cavalry general Nathan Bedford Forrest.

  In the intervening hundred-odd years, white supremacist and anti-Semitic rallies have not changed much. Whenever there is a gathering of far-rightists in Canada or the United States—usually in rural areas, in the spring or summer—there is a lot of dressing up in Klan robes or homemade Nazi uniforms. If local law permits, there is the burning of a cross or two. There is plenty of drinking, and not a little flaunting of knives, clubs and guns. And, finally, there are numerous animated speeches about the threats posed by race-mixing, liberalism and the international Jewish conspiracy.

  The purpose of the rallies is three-fold. First, they serve as great boosters of morale, reassuring lonely Klansmen and neo-Nazis that, despite all appearances to the contrary, they are not alone, that there are many others like them. Second, the rallies in some ways are not unlike meetings of Rotarians or Legionnaires or other such groups:

they give the far right an opportunity to raise funds, discuss the issues that concern them and, significantly, recruit members. Finally, the rallies help the personalities who make up the racist right to achieve one of the most important objectives of all: they help to scare people, particularly non-white and Jewish people.

Since the late 1980s, summertime neo-Nazi and white supremacist rallies have become a virtual commonplace in rural Canada. In their wake, they have left behind tiny communities convulsed with fear, loathing and self-doubt. Minden, Ontario, in July 1989, hosted by former Canadian Nazi Party leader John Beattie; Metcalfe, Ontario, in July 1990, hosted by former Canadian Knights of the Ku Klux Klan adviser Ian Verner Macdonald; Provost, Alberta, in September 1990, hosted by Terry Long's Aryan Nations and Ray Bradley's BHORP; La Plaine, Quebec, in August 1992, hosted by the Montreal chapter of the Invisible Empire of the Knights of the Ku Klux Klan; an August 1993 Heritage Front rally in Montreal that drew more than 200 neo-Nazi skinheads. Few of these places are remembered for what they were previously known for—say, good fishing, or farming, or nice campgrounds. Instead, in Canadian far right circles, these well-attended rallies have become popular enough that Nazis and Klansmen need only mention that they spent a few days at Metcalfe, say, or Provost, and their rightist colleagues will know precisely what they are talking about. In many cases, the men, women and children who attend the rallies travel hundreds of miles to be with their so-called kinsmen; at the July 1990 Metcalfe rally, for example, skinheads, Nazis, Klansmen and others came from as far away as Alberta. A few even risked crossing the border and drove up from various northeastern states.

The Provost Aryan Fest was not particularly well attended, nor did Adolf Hitler appear to anyone in a vision. But Provost was significant because of the troubles it caused Terry Long and his Canadian Church of Jesus Christ Christian Aryan Nations—and because of the precedent-setting human rights hearing that it gave rise to. It was also significant because it brought together, for perhaps the first time, all of the prairie provinces' neo-Nazi luminaries. The event began inauspiciously enough on August 17, 1990, when Terry Long sat down at his manual typewriter at his kitchen table and tapped out the following letter on Aryan Nations letterhead:

> Comrade:
> You and your White friends are invited to the first annual Alberta Aryan Fest to be held 8 Sept., 1990, 4 miles west of Provost, Alberta, at the acreage of AN Leader Ray Bradley. Festivities will begin at 1:00 p.m. on Saturday and will include speeches, taped music and fellowship followed by a steak supper and cross lighting. Festivities will end at 1:00 p.m. the following Sunday. Bring a tent or R.V. and a sleeping bag as well as $10 for the cost of the meal. All Klansmen bring your uniforms. HAIL VICTORY!!!
> Terry Long.

Long added a handwritten postscript: "P.S. Please confirm your attendance and do not talk to the media."

On the other side of the page, Long sketched out a small map of the various routes to Bradley's property, indicating where the red ribbons would be. He then drove into Caroline to photocopy 40 invitations. He mailed off 30 or so to various Aryan Nations members and supporters: Kelly Scott Lyle and Debbie Macy of the Final Solution Skinheads; Aryan supporters Tom Erhart and Ryder (Rob) Robinson; Aryan Nations hotline enthusiast Randy Johnston; and, of course, Saskatchewan Aryan Nations leader Carney Milton Nerland. A few invitations were kept by Long to be handed out personally. These went to Edgar Foth and various skinheads. Long would later say he "bypassed the mail [to] save money." (Strangely, one invitation made its way to Calgary's Harvey Kane, executive director of the Jewish Defence League of Canada—although Long vigorously denies that he or any of his supporters sent it.)

Long recalls that his first contact with Ray Bradley came in the summer of 1989, when the Provost welder sent him a letter expressing an interest in the Aryan Nations. In his letter, Bradley said he wanted to purchase some Aryan Nations patches as well as some Identity literature. For the next few months, the two men communicated through the mail or by telephone. Says Long: "Mr. Bradley was developing his knowledge with regard to the conspiracy, the Jewish conspiracy, and with regard to Identity. . . . The purpose of those communications was for the purpose of conveying knowledge and just general fellowship."

In September 1989, Long and his wife, Janice, drove to Saskatoon for meetings with Carney Nerland. After Long designated Nerland his official Saskatchewan leader in a small ceremony, the Longs headed west, to Ray Bradley's acreage in Provost. It was their first face-to-face meeting. Long told Bradley that the isolated property would be ideal for a meeting of Aryan Nations members. In the months that followed, Long, Bradley and Nerland discussed the idea of an Aryan Nations rally often, growing increasingly excited about the controversy it would cause.

The controversy was not long in coming. On the morning of Tuesday, September 4, Long was working in the basement of his home in Caroline, while Janice was upstairs, listening to Ron Collister's morning show on Edmonton radio station CJCA. Collister started to read Long's Aryan Fest invitation on the air; Janice rushed to the top of the stairs to call her husband. The two listened as Collister read the entire letter. The next day, Long was called by *Edmonton Journal* reporter Rick McConnell about the Aryan Fest. Long refused to comment. Undaunted, McConnell raised the issue with Alberta Solicitor-General Dick Fowler, who told a scrum of reporters at the provincial legislature that he could not stop the event. "They're crazy, all of them, the Aryan Nations. Crazier than hell," Fowler said. "[But] they have that right . . . and I will defend that right for them. That doesn't make them any less crazy."

Following Collister's broadcast, word of the impending Aryan Fest spread through Provost in a matter of hours. Sgt. Peter Zacour, a spokesman for the Provost RCMP detachment, did not appear pained by the news. "If there are criminal matters that transpire, we'll take the appropriate action. Otherwise, we'll stay out of it," he told McConnell. A few town residents also dismissed the Aryan Nations plans as a meaningless publicity stunt. But many others were worried. One of the largest expressions of concern came on the morning of Friday, September 7, at Provost Public School, when more than a hundred students dressed in black to protest the Aryan Fest. The demonstration involved students in Grades 7 to 9, and had been the idea of a few young men in Grade 9.

At 9:00 a.m. on September 7, school principal Wally Herle read a message over the school's intercom system: "As you know, an assembly is being held near Provost this weekend. This news item has gathered a great deal of attention—in Provost, Alberta, and beyond. You can show your opposition to it, as many of you are doing here today. You can speak your feelings on it. You are free to do this. It is a freedom of citizens of Provost, Alberta, and Canada. As many of you know, racism is not sanctioned within society. It does not reflect the values which we endorse in this country and this school. Our entire educational system is geared towards tolerance, multiculturalism, rights of minorities and non-racist practices. . . . I am sure many of you have questions in your minds—'what if' this, 'what if' that, what's going to happen after this? I, too, have many questions in my mind, and not many answers. It is unfortunate for Provost, for its residents, that this is occurring. You may wish to discuss this further with your families. I support what you students are doing here today."

That night, as Provost grew dark, unfamiliar trucks and cars slipped through town, heading west towards Ray Bradley's acreage.

Saturday dawned to a downpour. At about 9:00, a van driven by Sigmund Sobolewski stopped near the PetroCanada station on Highway 13. (The owners of the PetroCan station had hired extra security in case there was trouble during the weekend.) Sobolewski, born in 1927, was a resident of Fort Assiniboine, Alberta, where he owned a hotel. He had been the eighty-eighth prisoner to enter Auschwitz. His father, he says, was a member of the Polish intelligentsia; in 1940, when the elder Sobolewski was very ill, the Gestapo came to take him away. When they saw that his father was near death, they took 17-year-old Sigmund instead. Sobolewski was imprisoned for four years at the notorious death camp; he says he was not treated as harshly as his fellow Jewish prisoners, thousands of whom he watched die with his own eyes.

For his planned protest at Ray Bradley's acreage, Sobolewski had donned a replica of the uniform worn by prisoners at Auschwitz. In the spring of 1985, he had worn the same uniform while passing out anti-Nazi leaflets outside the Red Deer courthouse, where Jim Keegstra had been prosecuted for willfully promoting hatred against Jews. In the van with him were David Strauss, an Edmonton man who was an occasional member of Meir Halevi's Toronto-based Jewish Defence League, and Harvey Kane, executive director of the Jewish Defence League of Canada, a group unrelated to Halevi's organization. Kane, a retired Canadian veteran, had formed his own branch of the JDL in Calgary in 1986 in response to Terry Long's announced plans to establish an Aryan Warrior training camp in Caroline. Gruff, affable and plain-spoken, Kane was the unofficial leader of the delegation to Provost.

The van pulled over near the gas station. The three men peered through the windows into the rainy morning, trying to spot the red ribbons that marked the road to Ray Bradley's place. After a few wrong turns, Sobolewski found the service road. Recalls Kane: "We drove down the road to Bradley's place, but there was nobody around. They were all in the garage, holding their meeting. Nobody was outside." The trio decided to head back to Highway 13 to begin their protest.

They stood in the rain—it was "pouring cats and dogs," says Kane—for about half an hour, carrying signs Kane had prepared. A few pick-ups drove past and honked their horns. At about 10:00, *The Calgary Herald* reporter Sheldon Alberts drove up, accompanied by *Herald* photographer Mike Sturk. The group chatted for a few minutes, then headed out to Bradley's acreage. When they arrived, the area once again appeared to be deserted. Kane's group concluded it would be a good time to inform the RCMP that the Jewish Defence League was in Provost to protest the Aryan Fest. When they arrived at the RCMP detachment's headquarters, no officer was present, and the door was locked. Says Kane: "So we went back. By that time, a few people had started showing up—mainly locals. We parked the van and walked over to the gateway with our signs. And that is when the skinheads started coming out of the garage and towards the barrier. And they had guns."

Kane, Sobolewski and Strauss—who by now was wearing a ski mask to hide his identity—walked up and down the roadway with their signs while the skinheads shouted taunts at them. The *Herald*'s Alberts and Sturk were there, as were television crews from Alberta CBC and CTV affiliates. Like Strauss, most of the skins were wearing masks or bandanas over their faces. The young neo-Nazis, it rapidly became obvious, were highly agitated by Sobolewski's Auschwitz uniform. Most angry was Kelly Scott Lyle, leader of the ultra-violent Final Solution Skinheads. Lyle—who has been convicted of aggravated assault and for desecrating Calgary's House of Israel synagogue—was wearing sunglasses and a Brownshirt uniform, complete with an authentic Nazi armband.

"Why don't you go play victim somewhere else," Lyle shouted at Sobolewski. "We all know you're full of shit."

"You're full of shit yourself," Harvey Kane told Lyle.

"You're all Zionist conspirators," Lyle said, walking away from the gate, as a Randy Travis song blasted through a loudspeaker system. Ray Bradley had rented the system for the Aryan Fest; later, Randy Travis would be replaced by taped speeches of Aryan Nations founder Richard Butler, as well as James Wickstrom, a Pennsylvania Identity preacher who, for a time, led the Posse Comitatus.

After a while, it started to rain again. Some of the protestors retreated to their vehicles, but Harvey Kane and Sigmund Sobolewski stood their ground. As the rain grew heavier, a 1971 black Lada sedan was spotted barrelling down the road, heading directly towards Kane and Sobolewski. The two men jumped out of the way. As the gate was being pulled back, Kane spotted Carney Nerland in the driver's seat. In the back seat was a gangly young man in a Nazi uniform, Gary Voycey, a former Armed Forces reservist from Saskatoon. (Voycey was an Aryan Nations spokesman for the Saskatoon area who posessed an ability to "raise quite a stink," Terry Long wrote in a letter to Harcus's former partner, Dennis Godin.) And in the passenger's seat was none other than Bill Harcus, the Manitoba leader of the Knights of the Ku Klux Klan. Harcus, a resident of Winnipeg, was an Identity Christian and a follower of Terry Long, whom he idolized. As the Lada sped through the gate, splashing mud over the assembled journalists and protestors, Harcus yelled: "White power!"

Recalls Kane: "When Nerland saw Sobolewski in his Auschwitz uniform, he went completely berserk. He was screaming and yelling obscenities and insults, and things got pretty heavy. We see-sawed back and forth, and then Sobolewski got into the interior of the farm. You could see that [the Nazis] were ready to take some action, so I went onto the farm property and got him the hell out of there. The last thing we wanted was to be responsible for causing injuries to bystanders and other people."

At this point—just before noon, Kane recalls—things cooled down. Kane retreated to Sobolewski's van to make a few notes. Although no more than about 30 or 40 white supremacists and neo-Nazis were present at the Aryan Fest, it was clear to Kane that all of the far right's prairie leadership had gathered for the event: Terry Long, Edgar Foth and Tom Erhart from Alberta; Carney Nerland from Saskatchewan; and Bill Harcus from Manitoba. It was unprecedented for so many neo-Nazi leaders to be present in one place. But the RCMP were nowhere to be seen, despite their earlier promises of "appropriate action." Says Kane bitterly: "The RCMP were a joke. I later told [an RCMP commanding officer] in Red Deer that Harcus had been there, for example, and they pretended that they had never heard of him."

After adjourning to a Provost motel for lunch, Kane, Sobolewski and Strauss returned to the Aryan Fest with Brad Clark, a freelance reporter then representing *Alberta Report* magazine. Clark, a Briton with a master's degree in journalism from the University of Wales, was hoping to take a few photographs of the Aryan Fest. Kane walked over to the gate to chat with Kelly Lyle and a few other skinheads. "If you guys want to invite us to your barbecue, we wouldn't mind sitting down and breaking bread with you," Kane told Lyle, "as long as we're not going to be the main course." In spite of himself, Lyle laughed at Kane's bravado. Clark, meanwhile, stood a few feet away and pulled out a meter to check lighting conditions. As he did so, one of the masked skins yelled, "Hey! No pictures! No pictures!" Within seconds, five armed skinheads had jumped from behind the barrier and surrounded Clark. One grabbed the reporter's camera away; Kelly Lyle pumped a shotgun and pointed it at him.

"My first reaction was to go and grab the camera, too," Kane says. "The next thing I know, I'm wrestling with four or five skinheads for possession of Clark's camera. One of them said they were going to confiscate the camera and smash it. So I told them to take out the film instead." Seconds later and from somewhere behind him on the road, Kane heard Clark yell. The skinheads had taken the writer's tape recorder and were refusing to give it back.

Across Bradley's lawn, Terry Long was walking towards the sound of the disturbance. He had his "WHITE PRIDE" trucker's cap perched on his head and a bemused expression on his face. Kane called to him. The JDL leader told Long what had transpired, calling it "robbery at gunpoint on the Queen's highway." Long mumbled a few words to his followers and walked away. Kane again demanded Clark's belongings, but the skinheads stood at the gate, laughing, refusing to turn over the tape recorder. With no other option, Kane, Clark, Strauss and Sobolewski left to file a complaint with the RCMP. As Clark climbed into his car, one of the skinheads said to him: "We'll see you again, on deadlier terms."

When the RCMP duty officer finally returned to his office—90 minutes after the arrival of Clark, Kane and the others—the four men filled out complaint forms. But the Mounties never laid charges in the incident, and nor, apparently, did they investigate it.

Meanwhile, assaults on journalists and protestors continued throughout the day. One female reporter was sexually assaulted by a masked skinhead who leaned through a car window and mauled her breast. Nerland and Lyle repeatedly pointed loaded weapons at reporters and protestors. At one point, in an exchange that would take on far greater significance, Nerland held up his 12-gauge shotgun and stated: "This is Native birth control." Later, Nerland aimed the shotgun at Kane's stomach and said: "A 12-gauge cuts a person right in half, it's just great for preventing further Jewish births. It's a way to customize the womb."

Kane was shoved and spat at by Final Solution skinhead Brett Hayes, Bill Harcus's former roommate and one of Terry Long's "enforcers." Kelly Lyle pushed Calgary television reporter Rick Boguski off the driveway. Protestors were repeatedly shoved and threatened by armed skinheads; in some cases, they were photographed by the skins, and their licence plate numbers were recorded. Later that night, gunshots could be heard from the field behind Bradley's house.

Finally a massive Final Solution skinhead named Michael Joseph Bertling swaggered onto the roadway and straight towards a cameraman for CFCN. Bertling, from Edmonton, stood well over six feet and wore a shiny black nylon bomber jacket with "CANADIAN SKINHEADS" stitched on the back. He was known as Joey to his Aryan comrades.

"You want me to shove that camera up your ass?" he said to the cameraman. Bertling knocked the camera, pushing its operator backwards. He then shoved another cameraman, grabbing the camera's lens and hurling him towards a truck. Rick Boguski tried to intervene, saying: "We are not looking for trouble here." Bertling whirled on Boguski, snarling: "Then what the fuck did you come here for, then? You want trouble here?" A half dozen times, Bertling lunged at the cameramen, saying: "I'll shove those fucking cameras up your ass" and "Fucking take those cameras and go home." Boguski again tried to calm Bertling, saying: "If there's nothing to shoot here, then we're gone." Bertling paused and leered menacingly at Boguski. "Oh, there's lots of things to shoot around here. You're damn straight. Things like you."

For reasons known only to itself, the RCMP declined to lay charges in any of these cases, most of which are well documented in news photographs and videotape—notwithstanding the fact that the Criminal Code has one or two things to say about provocative display of loaded weapons, pointing of loaded weapons at human beings, discharge of weapons outside firing ranges, theft, assault, sexual assault and the uttering of death threats, and notwithstanding the fact that there was no shortage of formal complaints.

Shortly past 9:00 p.m. on that Saturday, more than 20 people had started moving through the fields towards the metal cross planted in the soil north of Bradley's house. A few of the Aryan Fest crowd, such as Carney Nerland and Bill Harcus, wore white Klansmen's robes; others sported Nazi uniforms. Edgar Foth could be clearly seen in the black-and-red robe normally worn by a Klan wizard, or regional Ku Klux Klan leader. His face was not masked. At about 9:20, Foth yelled, "Come on, boys! Get in the circle!" Foth lit his torch, then stepped forward to set fire to the diesel-soaked burlap. It burst into flame. Other torch-bearers lit their own torches on the cross, then stepped back to form a haphazard circle. The group made Nazi salutes and bellowed "White power!" a few times. Foth yelled "Sieg!"—to which his fellow Aryans responded "Heil!" This was repeated five times. Foth called out "Forward march," and the group started to circle the cross.

They halted. "What do we want?" Foth yelled. "White power!" the group screamed. "When do we want it?" he yelled. "Now!" they replied. After a few more lusty "White power!" and "Sieg Heil" choruses, the group assembled on one side of the burning cross and joined Foth in screaming "Death to the Jew!" four times. They then broke into applause.

While the cross burned on, the group moved back to Ray Bradley's garage to drink more beer. Some of the skinheads shot off a few rounds into the sky—and, apparently, in the direction of *Herald* photographer Mike Sturk, who was then standing on the roadway at the point closest to the burning cross. At the gate, Gary Voycey fondled a shotgun and smoked a cigarette. As reporters clustered around him, he shrugged and squinted into the bright klieg lights. He talked about how *Mein Kampf* had inspired him; he talked about his gun.

"We're nothing but a bunch of guys getting together and having a good time," he said, and shrugged again. "That's all."

Poorly attended as it was by the "bunch of guys," the Provost Aryan Fest was a dramatic event in Alberta's 115-year history. Never before had organized white supremacy manifested itself so visibly. Never before had the trappings of neo-Nazism been so openly flaunted in a province that prided itself on tolerance and multi-culturalism.

On the front page of the Sunday, September 9, *Herald*, Mike Sturk's photograph of the cross was prominently featured with the headline "Cross Blazes in Shame." The anonymous headline writer's choice of words were not inappropriate. All over Alberta, citizens reacted with anger and revulsion when they read how armed and masked pro-Nazi goons were permitted to charge onto public roadways to threaten, abuse and assault protestors as well as members of the media. That they did so with impunity merely magnified the rage of Albertans. Within a matter of days, Letters-to-the-Editor columns and phone-in shows were flooded with expressions of shock and disbelief. On September 13, the Alberta Human Rights Commission issued a resolution that condemned, "in the strongest possible terms, the existence and activities of the Aryan Nations and the doctrine of aggressive racism it promotes." The same week, Calgary Liberal MLA Sheldon Chumir, a noted civil libertarian, blasted the RCMP for their "totally inadequate presence" at the Aryan Fest. (In a bizarre twist of logic, Alberta Solicitor-General Dick Fowler blamed the media for the criminal acts that took place at the Aryan Fest, stating that some of the incidents "could have been avoided if the press hadn't been there.")

In virtually all of the news stories and photographs that recorded the event, one figure appeared again and again: the chubby man who wore a Nazi armband and repeatedly pointed a shotgun at protestors and reporters. The man who had told Sigmund Sobolewski: "We're making a gas chamber here today—and if you stay around long enough . . . we'll put you in it." The man who used the alias Kurt Meyer—taken from a long-dead German war criminal—but was most widely known as Carney Nerland.

Until the Aryan Fest, Nerland was a virtual unknown. After it, he was transformed overnight into a one-man Nazi media personality. Thereafter, every time the Provost rally was written about—and it was written about often in 1990 and the next two years—Carney Nerland was seen front and centre, goose-stepping about in his home-made Schutzstaffel uniform, spitting hate and venom. Media, police and not a few neo-Nazi types wanted to learn more about him.

Carney Milton Nerland was born on September 30, 1965, in North Battleford, Saskatchewan, and spent the first eight years of his childhood in Rouleau, a small town southwest of Regina, about a half-hour's drive off of the Trans-Canada Highway. His father, Bob, was a large man with large appetites; he was known to pilot motorcycles around town wearing a genuine German World War Two helmet. His mother, Vera, was a quieter sort, but a devout Jehovah's Witness. Nerland had one older brother, a quiet boy named Alfen, and an outspoken sister, Hayley.

In 1973, when young Milt—he now prefers Carney—was eight years old, Big Bob moved the family to Prince Albert. Compared to Rouleau, Prince Albert (pop. 35,000) seemed a veritable metropolis to Carney Nerland. With the exception of a few months spent in the southern United States in the mid-1980s, he would remain in Prince Albert for close to two decades. Nerland attended Prince Albert Central Institute and, later, Carlton Senior High but he eventually dropped out of Carlton. "In high school, Carney was always going to the library and looking up as much as he could about Germany and Hitler and the Second World War," recalls one woman who attended school with him. "Carney was really different, even back then. Always different."

Schoolmates and neighbors note that the Nerland family's home life was far from routine. Though they lived in the middle-class Crescent Heights district in Prince Albert, they were considered oddballs in the Saskatchewan town, where everyone knew everyone else. Says one neighbor: "Those kids grew up in a very strange family. None of us kids were allowed to hang around with them. When we saw them coming, we were told to cross to the other side of the street."

In 1984, when he was 19 years old, Nerland, like many other latter-day white supremacist leaders, was smitten by the writings of David Ernest Duke. Nerland was drawn to the Knights of the Ku Klux Klan, the Louisiana group that Duke had incorporated and established in 1975. (Duke left the KKK in 1980 to found the National Association for the Advancement of White People, turning over the leadership of the Knights to Don Black. Despite Duke's decision to abandon the Klan, the group continued to use his earlier writings as recruitment tools.)

In July 1984, Nerland made his way to Hayden Lake for the fifth annual Aryan Nations World Congress. There he met the Canadians who would make up his social circle for the next few years: Terry Long; B.C. Aryan Nations leader Lester Morris; Edgar Foth; and a dozen or so other Aryans, among them Tom Erhart. At the congress, Nerland had fun attending lectures about urban terrorism. At one point, he had his picture taken: the photo shows him in jacket and tie, grinning, standing behind Pastor Butler's pulpit, the stained-glass rendering of the Aryan Nations logo glowing above his head. Significantly, it was at the congress that Nerland also met Karl Hand, Jr., leader of the National Socialist Liberation Front (NSLF).

The NSLF was, in the view of the Anti-Defamation League of the B'nai Brith, "the most violent of the Nazi splinter groups" then in existence. It was founded in California in 1969 by an American Nazi Party lieutenant. For the 1970s, the front carried out diverse acts of terror against its enemies—among them the February 1975 bombing of the California offices of the Socialist Workers Party, a Trotskyite group. In 1981, Hand, who had previously served time in prison in

New Jersey for shooting into the home of a black family, and was also the former national organizer of Duke's Knights of the Ku Klux Klan, took control of the National Socialist Liberation Front. He moved the NSLF to Metairie, Louisiana, and declared it "a revolutionary movement that has repudiated mass tactics and has instead embraced armed struggle and political terrorism." He became the NSLF's "commanding officer."

In the early 1980s, Hand set up a group he called Street Action, whose approach and clothing aped that of Hitler's Brownshirts. In the fall of 1984, following the Aryan Nations congress, Nerland flew to Metairie at Hand's request. Nerland would soon become what he called a "serving captain" in Street Action. He received weapons training and says he participated in violent encounters with members of the U.S. Jewish Defense League; he reportedly also passed out recruiting materials at regional fairs and contributed to the NSLF's official organ, the *National Socialist Observer*.

In the United States, Nerland networked with a variety of American neo-Nazi groups and gun dealers. Among the ultra-rightists were Donald V. Clerkin's Euro-American Alliance; William Pierce's National Alliance; and the New Hampshire branch of the Nazi Party. In his travels as Karl Hand's captain, Nerland also met with the owners of dozens of army surplus stores. He would inquire about the availability of hand grenades and the far right's firearm of choice, the Ruger .223-calibre Mini-14. Mysteriously, during this same period, Nerland also made trips to Chile, ostensibly to purchase antiques and antique coins. Some Prince Albert residents speculate that he travelled to South America to meet with former German Nazi officers known to be in hiding in remote parts of the continent. During one trip to Chile, he met his future wife, Jackie; the two were married there in 1987.

After one extended visit to the NSLF's Louisiana headquarters in late 1985, Nerland flew from New Orleans, connected with a Continental Airlines flight in Houston and landed at Calgary's international airport on November 6. There, a suspicious Canada Customs officer instructed him to report to Christopher Sowden, an Immigration official.

Nerland presented Sowden with a Louisiana driver's licence as well as a U.S. Social Security card bearing the name Kurt Meyer. Unbeknownst to Sowden—as it would be to all but a few war buffs—Kurt Meyer was an interesting choice for a pseudonym. The real Meyer had been a young divisional commander of the Twelfth SS Panzer Hitlerjugend. At his command, 18 Canadian prisoners of war were shot to death near Caen, France, in June 1944. After his capture, Meyer was convicted of war crimes and ordered executed by a firing squad; the sentence was later commuted to life imprisonment. He was released in 1954.

"What is your purpose in coming to Canada?" Sowden asked Nerland.

Nerland shrugged. "I'm going to be visiting some friends in Edmonton and the Red Deer area."

When Sowden pressed Nerland for more detail, he was evasive. He told Sowden he might visit Regina, Vancouver, Victoria or Nanaimo instead. He started to pull business cards from his briefcase.

Sowden asked Nerland his occupation. Nerland replied that he was working part-time as a baker, and then he seemed to change his mind, stating that he was working at a flea market in Louisiana "seasonally and part-time." He also told Sowden he had been born in New Jersey. Sowden examined "Meyer's" airline ticket; it was a one-year open return and it cost approximately $500. Asked how much money he planned to spend in Canada, Nerland said, "About $500." Sowden asked Nerland how much he earned in his job. Said Nerland: "Last year I made about $3,000."

One-third of his yearly wage on an ill-planned trip to Canada? Sowden knew that Nerland was either lying or very stupid. He started peppering Nerland with further questions. At one point, Nerland bragged that he "normally" carried a Walther P .38-calibre handgun in his belt. "But I was told that I should leave it in the U.S., because that isn't legal in Canada. So I left it in Louisiana."

The conversation continued. Sowden asked Nerland to empty his briefcase. With reluctance, "Meyer" did so. In the briefcase was a wide variety of material, including: cassette tapes with such titles as "Interrogation Techniques" and "Adolf Hitler on Victory," and others in German; a dozen or so photographs of Nerland and other Street Action members in Nazi uniforms, holding automatic weapons (in one of the photos, Nerland could be seen smashing the head of a mannequin with a rifle butt); dozens of business cards for arms dealers; Aryan Nations belt buckles; badges representing various white supremacist groups; and a ceremonial dagger. (How Nerland was permitted to carry a dagger onto an airplane in both New Orleans and Houston has never been explained.)

Examining a Nazi Party membership card made out in Kurt Meyer's name, Sowden asked Nerland if he was a member of the Aryan Nations. "No," Nerland said, quickly. "I'm a member of a historical re-enactment society. That's what these pictures are all about."

"But why do some of the photos show you engaged in combat training, Mr. Meyer?"

Nerland said nothing. Sowden took a few more notes, but he had already made up his mind. "Kurt Meyer" was inadmissible under the Immigration Act; Sowden ordered him photographed and detained. The next morning, he was put on a Continental Airlines flight back to Houston.

The unsuccessful trip to Calgary was to be one of Carney Nerland's last missions as a captain in Karl Hand's Street Action. In December 1986, Hand was convicted of attempted murder and sentenced to 15 years' imprisonment. He now passes his days behind bars at Louisiana State Prison, hailed as a "prisoner of war" by U.S. neo-Nazi groups. Despite the efforts of his wife, Mary Sue, Hand's National Socialist Liberation Front fell apart soon after his trial.

In time, a leaderless Carney Nerland made his way back to Prince Albert with his Chilean-born wife. Jackie gave birth to a daughter, Stephanie, in 1989. But the Nerlands' marriage was not to be a happy union. In a sworn statement given to Prince Albert police in February 1991, a friend of Jackie Nerland stated: "Once . . . Carney had pulled a big gun on her and told her he would use it on her if she didn't smarten up. . . . She said to me he would kill her if she left him or tried to leave. Jackie has also told me when she gets back to Chile she is not returning to Canada because she feared for her life." This woman reported seeing many bruises on Jackie Nerland's arms and back and added that the white supremacist's wife was forbidden to leave the couple's apartment on Nineteenth Street West: "If she were to leave, she would get a slap or a kick." On one occasion in the spring of 1990, the woman told police, she spotted Nerland violently pulling his wife out of their car—a battered black 1971 Lada—and down a hill to their apartment. Asked about the incident later, Jackie told the woman that her husband had given her a "licking" because dinner had been late.

Another Prince Albert woman, Fay Harrison, told police she too had seen multiple bruises on Jackie Nerland's body. The two met in 1990, when Harrison gave English-language lessons to the Chilean. Said Harrison: "Jackie Nerland seemed frightened of her husband. . . . [Her] stated intention was to go to Chile and stay there as long as she could."

Confronted by Prince Albert police with the sworn affidavits, Nerland denied abusing his wife. Jackie not surprisingly also rejected the wife-beating charges. In sworn statements, the two described their relationship as "close and loving." Said Jackie: "It is not true that I am fearful for my life. . . . I deny the allegations [that] my husband Carney Milton Nerland has hit me, causing bruises. It is not true my husband ever threatened me with a gun. We have had no special problems in our relationship and there have been no problems involving alcohol, drugs, violence or anything else."

Violence, however, was indisputably part of Nerland's life. By 1985, Prince Albert police were quietly observing his comings and goings, puzzling over his connection to an ultra-violent Louisiana neo-Nazi group. By 1990, they were actively investigating Nerland and two Calgary men for the production and distribution of viciously anti-Semitic and anti-Native hate propaganda. (At the time, Nerland was making ends meet by selling vacuum cleaners door-to-door in Regina.) And then, inexplicably, they gave him a licence to sell guns.

In early 1990, Nerland and a Saskatchewan businessman, Darwin Alvin Bear, opened Northern Pawn and Gun Shop at 167 River Street West in Prince Albert. Nerland would run the gun side of the enterprise; Bear would handle the pawn shop. Bear, however, did not spend much time at Northern Pawn and Gun, so Nerland pretty much had complete control of the place. Eventually, the gun shop would serve as a meeting place for neo-Nazis, white supremacists and gun nuts from all over the prairie provinces. Here and there, Nerland tacked up Nazi flags and photographs of Adolf Hitler; he also played videotapes of Hitler speeches. He did a brisk business trading in Nazi memorabilia, buying and selling from Calgary's Bill Treleaven and other merchants of militaria across the prairies.

In retrospect, Carney Nerland's life was a seeming maze of contradictions: for example, his Chilean wife was no Aryan; his business partner was a status Indian from the Montreal Lake Reserve; and his landlord, Arnold Katz, was a Jew. Before he got into trouble with the law, Nerland would insist that he did not hate any particular racial or ethnic group. Like many neo-Nazi leaders, he would claim that he did not hate anyone; rather, he loved his own race. Arnold Katz, for one, says that he never felt that Carney Nerland hated him.

Katz occupied a fur and scrap-metal trading post next door to Northern Gun and Pawn. It was called Katz Brothers Furs. Katz, who is a jovial man in his seventies, says Carney Nerland was always "a very nice fellow" in his presence. "He was a smart fellow," he says. "But if I had known what kind of fellow he really was, I wouldn't have rented the place to him. No way." On the one occasion he spotted pro-Nazi material in Nerland's shop, Katz asked why it was there. Nerland told him it was only for history buffs. For the most part, Katz says, he was more curious about why police cruisers were always parked outside the Northern Pawn and Gun Shop, which was open for about nine months. When asked about the police, Nerland would only say: "They're here to do business. They're buying guns from me." But why were the police buying guns from a man they were investigating for hate promotion? Why did they give a licence to purchase restricted weapons to a man they knew had been a member of the most violent neo-Nazi group in the United States?

On the afternoon of Monday, January 28, 1991, the mysterious relationship between Carney Nerland and the police grew more inexplicable. In a shack on the Whitefish Reserve, northeast of Prince Albert, a Cree trapper named Leo LaChance gathered together five sad-looking squirrel pelts and one weasel pelt he had snared a few days before in his Big River trap lines. LaChance wrote a note to his brother, David, that read: "Gone to P.A. Back Wednesday." He tugged the frayed curtains across his windows and turned off the lights. He was a poor man; apart from the house itself, all that the trapper owned was a bed, a table and a chair. LaChance stepped outside, pausing to fasten the door with a piece of string so that his German shepherd, Sport, would not get out. LaChance was wearing a long winter coat, but no gloves or mittens. Squinting against the cold, he reached into his pocket, where he found 30 cents in change.

Moving towards the highway, Leo LaChance knew that it was time to do some trading at Katz Brothers Furs.

About 12 hours later, Nerland sat before Prince Albert Police sergeant Peter Mesluk in the Criminal Investigations Division interview room. Mesluk told Nerland that he had the right to obtain and instruct counsel without delay; he told him about his rights under the Charter. Nerland leaned forward. "I want to co-operate with you guys. I won't give you any problems. I want to talk."

Mesluk reached for a notepad with "PRINCE ALBERT POLICE WARNED STATEMENT" inscribed at the top. "What do you have to say, Carney?" he asked.

"Well, basically, nothing happened," Nerland said. "There's really nothing to say."

Mesluk told Nerland that police officers were preparing to search Northern Pawn and Gun Shop and that Darwin Bear had already given them permission to do so. Nerland stirred. "Well, you know, I think I can help you guys," he said, then paused for a long time. "Um, what would happen if this was just an accident? What would happen to the guy who was involved? What would this guy be charged with, if the gun, uh, had gone off accidentally?"

There was a bit of murmuring, and one of the detectives present, Sgt. Gerry Novotny, handed Nerland a copy of the Criminal Code, opened to the section on firearms. Silent, Nerland flipped through the Code while Mesluk, Novotny and Cpl. Bruce Parker watched him. He looked up at Mesluk. "How much time would someone get for accidentally shooting off a gun?" he asked.

Mesluk shrugged. "Everything depends on the circumstances, Carney. We have to know what went on before we can say it is going to be this charge or it's going to be that charge."

Nerland nodded. "All right," he said. "I'll give you a statement. You can start writing." For the next 31 minutes, Nerland told his story, pausing only to drink coffee or answer a clarifying question from Mesluk.

"I am part-owner of Northern Pawn and Gun with Darwin Bear. On January 28, 1991, I opened the store by 11:00 a.m. Darwin came by the store today at around 4:00 p.m. and he stayed more or less till around 5:00 p.m. I continued on business until around 6:00 p.m. when it started to gear down to close-up. I was a little bit late because I was cleaning up and doing paper work. I was putting stuff away and a couple of gentlemen came in. They were both males and white, I would say they were in their late twenties. I really didn't feel awfully comfortable with them there. There was two of them. I was hoping they would get the hint to leave, and [so] I continued working. What I mean is, I'm putting guns away in my safe, in a gun locker, I'm taking guns off the display board and I'm putting them in the safe. I've got my back to these guys and I'm hoping they leave. All the while they were touching things and handling weapons. The one wearing the dark coat picked up . . . well, I couldn't see what he had picked up as my back was turned, as I was putting things away.

"It was at this time I heard a shot go off. I didn't hear any screams or glass break. I turned around and this guy had a dumb look on his face and he passes the gun, an M-56 [7.62-mm semi-automatic rifle], to me and smiles at his friend. I took the gun, removed the magazine, placed the gun in the gun closet and I put the clip on the counter. I would think the casing is on the ground somewhere. This gun is actually a folding-stock rifle and shoots a 7.62-mm shell, a pistol shell. At this point, I'm traumatized. I didn't know what to do. There are two of them and one of me, and like I said, there were no other persons in the store. Just me and these two guys. I don't recall an Indian being in the store after 6:00 p.m. The only other person that came in was a fellow that wanted to borrow the phone. He wondered if there was a phone he could use and he stated something to the effect that someone had fallen on the ice.

"I wanted to get out of this situation. I just told him no. Well, I just shook my head no. He left, then they guy looked at me and said: 'Keep your fucking mouth shut.' This was the guy that had shot the gun, [the one] wearing the dark jacket. The two guys shuffled off and I quickly finished my business, set my alarm and closed. I just wanted to get out of there."

Without comment, Mesluk scribbled on the pad for a few more seconds. He looked up at Nerland. "What more can you tell us about these two guys?" he asked.

"One guy had a red jacket, mid-length past his waist," Nerland said. "Average-length hair, under 200 pounds. The guy with the darker jacket . . . [it was] mid-length. Under 200 pounds. Brown hair, shorter hair cut."

"These two guys were unknown to you, right?" Mesluk asked.

"Yes," Nerland said.

"Where do you keep the ammunition?"

"I keep it either on the counter or in the case," Nerland replied.

"What about this particular 7.62-mm ammo?" Mesluk asked.

"I must have ten boxes of it," Nerland said. "And in close proximity, I have spare magazines. And they . . . I believe one of them was loaded. It wouldn't have had more than one shell in it. This is what I think might have happened. It's the only explanation I can think of. The guy saw a clip and put it in. Like I said, these guys were picking things up as I was trying to put them away."

While he gave his statement, Nerland appeared confident to the three police officers. He did not stumble or contradict himself as he related his account of the evening's events; nor did he say anything that seemed to be dramatically at odds with the facts as the officers then knew them. But the fact is that virtually every word that slipped from Carney Nerland's lips in the CID interview room was a bald-faced lie. Nerland lied about his relationship with the two men who were in Northern Pawn and Gun that night. He lied about the presence of Natives in his store that night. He lied about the number of shots that were fired. And, most significantly, he lied about who fired them.

Within a week, Prince Albert police, the Saskatchewan Crown Attorney's Office, Provincial Court Judge T.W. Ferris and even the accused gun shop owner would agree that Carney Milton Nerland had lied about his role in the death of Leo LaChance on that bitterly cold night in January 1991.

Court records show that at about 5:15 p.m., as Whitefish Band Chief John Keenatch's Chevrolet Cavalier approached the John Diefenbaker Bridge in Prince Albert, Leo LaChance said: "Drop me off here. I have to go."

Keenatch pulled to the side of the road. Silent, he and his daughter Patsy waited as LaChance got out; the Cree trapper appeared unsteady, and there seemed to be a faint odor of Lysol on his breath. They watched him as he wobbled through the snow towards River Street. Keenatch had picked up LaChance at the side of Highway 55, near Debden, about an hour before. As they drove east, through Canwood, Shellbrook and Holbein and on into Prince Albert, LaChance had said nothing. Keenatch watched the retreating figure for a few more moments, and then he drove on into Prince Albert.

When LaChance arrived at Katz Brothers Furs about 15 minutes later, the front door was locked. Arnold Katz, who had known

LaChance for years, recalls that he had quickly closed up shop only a few minutes before the trapper's arrival. (Asked what he thought of LaChance, Katz says: "He was an Indian. I get lots of Indians in here.") No one will ever know, of course, what went through Leo LaChance's mind at the moment he found Arnold Katz's window darkened and his shop's door locked, or what persuaded him to step into the place next door. With the temperature hovering at about 21 below zero Celsius, perhaps he merely wanted to warm up for a minute. Perhaps he thought he could pawn his pelts.

Wordlessly, LaChance opened the shop door and stepped inside. Watching him were three men: Carney Nerland, standing behind the counter; Russ Joseph Yungwrith, a prison guard who had attended Carlton Senior High with Nerland; and Gar Wallace Brownbridge, also a Corrections Canada employee. Two days before, Brownbridge had spoken to Nerland about his desire to purchase a pistol; he and Yungwrith were there that night to discuss when the shipment of pistols would be arriving, and what it would cost to pick up a leather holster for the pistol Brownbridge had in mind. The three men were chatting about the Persian Gulf War—and, apparently, drinking rum and Cokes—when Leo LaChance appeared.

After a protracted silence, LaChance turned to Brownbridge. "I want to sell a .303," he said.

"You want to sell a .303?" Brownbridge asked.

"I want to sell a .303," LaChance repeated.

"How much do you want for it?" Brownbridge asked, but LaChance did not answer. Brownbridge asked LaChance what he wanted.

"Ten bucks," LaChance said.

"If you sell a .303, make sure you have the magazine," Brownbridge said.

At that moment, an explosion was heard. LaChance, Brownbridge and Yungwrith jumped and turned towards Nerland. He was holding a Soviet-made Tokarev T-56 semi-automatic rifle, its smoking muzzle pointed towards the floor. Seconds ticked by. While the three men watched him, Nerland, his face expressionless, fired another shot into the floor of Northern Pawn and Gun. The smell of cordite filled the air.

Without saying another word, Leo LaChance started towards the door of the shop, his facial expression one of "disgust," Brownbridge would later recall. LaChance, he said, opened the door and waved his arm dismissively in Nerland's direction, then stepped out into the night. Says Brownbridge: "The door closed and immediately I heard another gun shot. I then turned to Milton and saw him holding the gun [at] chest level, pointed towards the Coke machine, which is next to the door. . . . Milton said something like: 'I didn't have three rounds,' or 'I didn't know it was loaded,' something to that effect."

Brownbridge was immediately concerned, but not about Leo LaChance. "You better not have shot my car!" he said, then walked to the door and peered through the window. He could see nothing wrong with his car; he returned to the counter, where he told Nerland it was "stupid" to fire a gun indoors.

Crown Attorney John Field would later tell a Saskatchewan Court of Queen's Bench judge that police and the prosecution "came to the belief that this was a non-intentional killing." This conclusion greatly bewilders many people, years afterwards. Even Nerland's longtime friend Russ Yungwrith told police: "In my head, I was hoping he had not been hit, but because of the close proximity of the times, places and circumstances, I felt in my heart that the fellow was hit." Yungwrith, of course, was right; one does not need to be a ballistics expert to know what the reasonable consequences of Nerland's actions were. (Minutes after he fired the third bullet, in fact, Nerland told Yungwrith and Brownbridge, "If I shot that guy, my business is fucked. I'm fucked.") Leo LaChance had been shot by Carney Nerland but, inexplicably, Prince Albert Police and the Saskatchewan Crown attorney came to the conclusion that Nerland, who knew more than a little about firearms, did not "intend" to shoot him.

The third bullet smashed through Leo LaChance's left arm, then entered the left side of his chest, where it perforated his diaphragm, spleen, splenic artery, pancreas, gallbladder, liver and right abdominal wall. Its deadly flight complete, the bullet came to rest in the external muscles of LaChance's right chest wall. Holding his sides, bleeding internally and in massive shock, LaChance stumbled about 30 feet east of Nerland's shop, where police believe he retrieved his little bag of pelts. Somehow, he stumbled for another 70 feet or so along River Street West. He then fell violently to the snow-covered sidewalk in front of Hewitt's, another pawn shop.

Kim Koroll, a technician with the Prince Albert engineering department, was driving along River Street when he saw Leo LaChance go down. Koroll pulled over and saw immediately that the man was bleeding profusely. Koroll ran to Northern Pawn and Gun, where Yungwrith and Brownbridge were helping Nerland close up. He told Nerland, who was still behind the counter, that a man had fallen on River Street and needed an ambulance. He asked to use the phone. Nerland refused. After finding no telephone at a nearby A&W restaurant, Koroll eventually located a pay phone and dialled 911. An ambulance arrived at 6.42 p.m., almost half an hour after Leo LaChance was shot by Carney Nerland. By that point, it was too late. Seven hours later, the Cree trapper died on an operating table at Royal University Hospital in Saskatoon.

In the next few days, many curious events took place. At about the time LaChance was being rushed to Saskatoon for medical care he could not obtain in Prince Albert, Gar Brownbridge was at Russ Yungwrith's home, where the two Corrections Canada employees happily played some Nintendo games. But at the same hour, Carney Milton Nerland was driving around town in a dark green Dodge sedan with a big bear of a man named Roy McKnight. McKnight had been in Northern Pawn and Gun an hour or so before Leo LaChance was shot. Following their cruise through the snow-covered streets of Prince Albert—they discussed only the Persian Gulf War, McKnight says—Carney Nerland went to Prince Albert police headquarters to give his false statement.

A few hours after his interview with the police, at about 4:00 a.m., Nerland tried to remove a locked file of what he called "customers' names" from Northern Pawn and Gun, but police officers guarding the shop refused to let him do so. Two days later, however, Roy McKnight popped in to Northern Pawn and Gun, said hello to the police officer standing guard there, picked up the files of "customers' names" and walked out. No one tried to stop him. The files, which sources say contain the names and addresses of Aryan Nations and Ku Klux Klan members from across Canada, were never seen again.

In the months following the shooting, Native groups speculated that Carney Nerland was able to secure a light sentence because he had been a police informant.

On the morning after the shooting, Russ Yungwrith was listening to Prince Albert radio station CJNN, getting his children ready for school, when he heard a story about a Native man who had been shot the night before on River Street West. Panicked, he immediately contacted Gar Brownbridge, and the two men decided to consult a lawyer. At about the same time Yungwrith and Brownbridge were getting some legal advice—1:30 p.m.—Nerland phoned Prince Albert police to tell them that his father was in town. Sounding very polite, Nerland asked for permission to travel to "Big Bob's" home near Veteran, Alberta, to look at a van he was interested in purchasing. Police gave him permission to do so. About an hour later, while Nerland was en route to Veteran, Brownbridge and Yungwrith related their own accounts of the events the night before. At this point, Prince Albert police officers started to realize that they may have been mistaken to let Nerland leave Saskatchewan. Six hours later, this was confirmed when police in Regina and Prince Albert received two anonymous CrimeStoppers tips to the effect that Nerland planned to travel to Alberta and then slip out of Canada.

The next day, RCMP officers arrested Nerland at his father's home, which is a short distance southwest of Ray Bradley's place in Provost. When he was arrested, the Mounties found 20 crisp new $100 bills in his wallet.

On Thursday, April 11, 1991, Carney Nerland pleaded guilty to the charge of manslaughter in the death of Leo LaChance. As a consequence, there would be no witnesses called and no exploration of the strange circumstances surrounding the case—just a joint submission from the Crown and Nerland's Legal Aid lawyer. Asked by Court of Queen's Bench Justice W.F. Gerein whether he had anything to say before the passing of sentence, Nerland said: "I do regret the tragic loss of life. It was my own irresponsibility and dangerous use of a firearm and I accept my responsibility."

The next day, Gerein gave his decision, noting, "I have come to the conclusion that what happened on the date in question had nothing to do with the beliefs which you possess as a result of being a member of a white supremacist organization."

It is interesting to note that, in the course of giving his decision, Gerein talked for a few moments about a statement Nerland had made on February 5, 1991, to Prince Albert Cpl. Howard Darbyshire, on the way back to the local remand centre from his bail hearing. The statement was later read into the court record by Crown Attorney John Field. After hearing it, Gerein told Nerland: "I cannot be certain that the remark truly represented your feelings. In any event, even if it did, it would not necessarily follow that those feelings or attitudes were operative at the time of the offence."

And this is the statement that Nerland made to Darbyshire: "If I am convicted of killing that Indian, they should give me a medal, and you should pin it on me." Later, it was learned that Nerland had also told Darbyshire: "I'm not eating any gook food made by a Chinaman. I'd starve first."

Justice Gerein gave Nerland a sentence of four years' imprisonment. Like Teàrlach Dunsford Mac a'Phearsoin before him, Carney Milton Nerland had narrowly escaped the punishment some say he richly deserved.

In late November 1993, a three-member board of inquiry issued a report stating, among other things, that shortcomings in the Prince Albert police investigation had been "unfortunate and serious" and criticized prosecutors for "so quickly embracing the . . . accidental shooting theory."

The inquiry, which had been appointed by the Saskatchewan government, investigated the LaChance shooting for more than a year. The inquiry's 75-page report pulls no punches. "[Prince Albert police] did not recognize when they should have that racism may have been the motivating factor for the actions of Nerland. Not only should this have been recognized, but it should have been followed by further investigation of Nerland's association with and activities as a member of the Church of Jesus Christ Christian Aryan Nations," the report reads. "We also believe prosecutors erred in concluding that Nerland's white supremacist views had nothing to do with the shooting. They apparently did not recognize the connection between the shooting and Nerland's racial beliefs."

In a decision that stunned many, Carney Milton Nerland was released from jail on December 15, 1993, into the RCMP witness protection program. Nerland was placed under RCMP protection following his release from the Stony Mountain Penitentiary. Said Alphonse Bird, Chief of the Prince Albert Grand Council: "Aboriginal peoples, minorities, Jews—they're all victims in this case, and they're not being protected. It's the perpetrator who's being protected now."

At about the time that the door on Carney Nerland's cell at Stony Mountain Penitentiary was slamming shut on him, bringing to a halt, however briefly, any meaningful discussion about the unanswered questions in his case, the Provost Aryan Fest was coming back to haunt Terry Long and Ray Bradley. On December 18, 1990, slightly more than a month before Leo LaChance's murder, Jewish Defence League of Canada executive director Harvey Kane consulted a Calgary lawyer, Hal Joffe, and swore a complaint with the Alberta Human Rights Commission. In the complaint, made under the anti-discrimination provisions of Alberta's Individual Rights Protection Act, Kane stated:

> On September 8, 1990, I was personally at Provost, Alberta, and in particular at a farm near Provost, Alberta. I

saw Terry Long on the property along with a number of other men. I saw a swastika flag displayed in full view on the barn and I saw a sign that said 'KKK White Power.' Although I did not physically see the cross burning on September 8, 1990, I did see video footage on a CFCN-TV television broadcast on September 9, 1990, which showed the cross burning. . . . I believe that the Provost meeting and the activities referred to above were organized, sponsored, encouraged and performed in whole or part by members of the Church of Jesus Christ Christian Aryan Nations, including Terry Long. I believe that the above display took place on land owned and/or occupied by Ray Bradley, and with his knowledge and consent. I allege that, in displaying or causing to be displayed before the public and assembled media such representations as a burning cross, swastika flag, and KKK White Power the Respondents did violate Section 2 of the Individual Rights Protection Act.

Kane's complaint was followed by six others, all identically worded. Among those who filed complaints were retired Edmonton broadcaster Keith Rutherford, who had been partially blinded by neo-Nazi skinheads in an April 1990 attack; Joffe, the lawyer who advised Kane, and the former leader of a Calgary-based anti-discrimination group; and Jack Downey, a Canadian veteran who had briefly staged a one-man protest at the Provost rally. Elaine McCoy, the Alberta cabinet minister responsible for the province's Human Rights Commission, told the media she was "very proud of the Albertans who came forward and registered the complaints."

In mid-January, the commission's manager of field services wrote letters, sent by double-registered mail, to Terry Long, Ray Bradley and the church to which they belonged. In the letters, she told the two Aryan Nations adherents about the complaints against them. She also requested "early meetings . . . [to] facilitate a timely conclusion of the investigation and/or resolution of the dispute."

Long and Bradley were not impressed by the Alberta Human Rights Commission, or by anything it had to say. In his response on Aryan Nations letterhead, sent the same day he received notice of the complaints, Long made an argument that he would make repeatedly in the months ahead. "The meeting to which the complaints refer was held on private property and all signs and symbols relative to that meeting were also on private property. Neither the press nor the media were notified of the meeting by us and indeed were not welcome, so if some of your complainants were appalled by that media coverage, I suggest that you people harass the media rather than us."

Ray Bradley's reply, received at the Edmonton offices of the commission a few days later, was hand written by his wife, Janet. It repeated most of the points raised in Long's letter, but added that the complaints were "ludicrous" and that those who had shown up at the rally uninvited were "clowns." Said Bradley: "The complaints are nothing more than mental terrorism to keep like-minded people from gathering and worshipping in the religion of their choice. Please excuse my ignorance if by chance a law was passed in our multicultural society prohibiting Aryans the right of free assembly and the right to practice their religious beliefs. . . . This letter will end all communications on my part in regard to this matter."

Bradley was not kidding. In Alberta, he was not heard from again. In November 1991, Bradley and his wife packed up their belongings and moved to Castlegar, a town in central British Columbia near the Washington border. There they purchased a plot of land in the Kootenay District, where Ray Bradley now runs a welding business.

But for Terry Long, it was not the end of the matter. Far from it. Just as his Saskatchewan lieutenant, Carney Nerland, had met defeat at the hands of the legal system in Prince Albert, so too would Long in Edmonton. After considering the matter for more than three months and after concluding that Long and Bradley were not about to apologize or make reparations to Harvey Kane, Hal Joffe or the other complainants, the Alberta Human Rights Commission decided to act. On May 2, Labour Minister Elaine McCoy agreed to establish a three-member panel to look into the Provost rally; on the same day, commission chairman Fil Fraser called the Provost event "repugnant." A few weeks later, the panel's members were named by McCoy: Tim Christian, the dean of the Faculty of Law at the University of Alberta; Calgary lawyer Cheryl Daniel; and Dr. Knut Vik, an Edmonton doctor.

In early July, the three members of the panel huddled in Edmonton to authorize the placement of newspaper advertisements about the case and to discuss where the hearings should take place. Concerned about the Aryan Nations' propensity for violence, a room on the third floor of Edmonton's law courts was eventually selected because the building offered the best security and facilities. Finally, the inquiry set a date for all parties to meet face-to-face and deal with preliminary matters: Wednesday, July 24, 1991.

On the appointed day, Terry Long and Ray Bradley did not show up. But many others did. Among them was Rosemary Walker, the mother of Daniel Sims, the neo-Nazi skinhead who assisted in the assault on Keith Rutherford. Also present at the first hearing were lawyers representing the Canadian Jewish Congress and the Canadian Association of Journalists (CAJ). The CAJ was seeking intervenor status to protest the treatment of journalists assigned to cover the Provost rally. After listening to arguments about what should be done in Long and Bradley's absence, inquiry chairman Tim Christian ruled that it would be improper to continue and ordered that further attempts be made to encourage the two men to attend. Although the Human Rights Commission may have had trouble locating Long, the media did not. Those who telephoned him at his home in Caroline located Canada's Aryan Nations leader within a matter of minutes. Asked if he planned to attend the next hearing, Long told one reporter: "I'd be happy to attend and testify if for no other reason than that the government doesn't expect me to." Long added that he would be surrounded by skinhead bodyguards when he showed up.

Later that same week, Long drove to Red Deer to apply for Legal Aid so that he could be represented by a lawyer during the inquiry. In his one-page application, he described himself as a "self-employed sawmill operator." He wrote that he and his wife were on social assistance, which provided them with $1,175 a month; with all other income sources included, Long informed a Legal Aid officer that his family made "approximately" $14,500 a year. He listed his van and a Canadian Imperial Bank of Commerce joint account as assets, giving him a worldly wealth of $1,800.

A few days later, Long's application was refused in writing by a Legal Aid Society of Alberta manager who noted that the Edmonton Regional Legal Aid Committee had "resolved to deny coverage. In their opinion, the consequences of the hearing do not warrant the appointment of counsel." Long later said he was told that, because he could not be imprisoned under the provincial human rights legislation, it was not necessary to provide funds for his defence. Long appealed the society's decision, but this too was unsuccessful. Many Alberta lawyers, among them the head of the inquiry, Tim Christian, expressed surprise at this decision.

At 9:30 on the morning of August 12, the hearing reconvened in Edmonton. The atmosphere was electric. As promised, Long was there, sporting a powder-blue polyester leisure suit with an Aryan Nations patch stitched onto one shoulder. As he strode into the courthouse carrying a briefcase full of hate propaganda and legal papers, Long was surrounded by a group of skinhead followers. At breaks in the proceedings, these skinheads obligingly gave Nazi salutes to photographers gathered outside the court building. One of the skinheads was Joey Bertling, the Final Solution Skins member who had threatened television cameramen at the Provost rally. Also assisting Long were Aryan Nations members Foth and Rob Robinson, who were seen throughout the day, and the days that followed, conferring with the Aryan Nations leader and ferrying papers around the courtroom. After preliminaries, murmurs could be heard when Long stood to introduce his "counsel" to the board of inquiry: none other than John Ross Taylor, former leader of Toronto's Western Guard and the Aryan Nations' "ambassador" to Canada.

Taylor's job was to question Long when he chose to take the stand to introduce evidence. As a lawyer, he left much to be desired. Often, he could be seen wavering at the respondents' table, his lined face pinched in a frown as dozens of his arguments were ruled inadmissible by the inquiry's chairman. For example, late in the proceeding, Taylor failed in an attempt to introduce a U.S. military report, telling the inquiry: "I'm not a lawyer, although my father was, and I don't know just how to, maybe, put this into the proper legal setting, but this is a vital piece of information to anybody who isn't on what we call the Communist side."

Significantly, Ray Bradley did not attend any of the hearings, and the Board of Inquiry decided to waste no further time in trying to locate him. Strategically, Bradley's absence was helpful to Long; it allowed him to claim, without contradiction, that the Aryan Fest had been organized by Bradley alone.

The courtroom, filled as it was with three dozen neo-Nazis, a handful of anti-racist punk rockers and a battery of news reporters and photographers, took on a decidedly bizarre ambience. Matters that should have occupied a few minutes took hours. Many of the skinheads tried to engage Christian and his fellow panellists in staring contests. And legal arguments were complicated by the presence of a large number of lawyers, representing the CAJ, the Jewish Congress, the Legal Education Action Fund, the University of Calgary Group for Research and Education on Human Rights and, later, the Canadian Congress of Black Women.

At first, Long appeared somewhat ill at ease at the hearing, his voice faltering, his tone ranging from aggressive to acquiescent. But in the next few days he grew more confident. While he was clearly no master of courtroom procedures, Long demonstrated a surprising degree of competence during the hearing, on occasion even catching experienced lawyers in errors of fact or law. He had visibly aged since the summer of 1984, when he had embraced Identity: his hair was peppered with more grey, and it was thinner; his face was lined and drawn.

In one of its first orders of business, the panel listened as Long recounted Legal Aid's refusal to indemnify him. With his family on welfare, Long told the hearing, he and his wife were obliged to sleep in their van so that they could attend the hearing. He could not afford to drive the 150 miles between Caroline and Edmonton every day, he said. "I'm indigent," he told the hearing. "The personal expense for me to take part is prohibitive. I'm talking about having enough money to pay for the gas." What Long called "social ostracism" had resulted in his inability to get a job anywhere. He requested that the hearings be moved to Red Deer or that he be provided with money to cover his expenses.

The panel opted for the latter and resolved that it was appropriate to give Long funding to pay for his expenses. He would be provided with daily witness fees of $10, plus accommodation costs and mileage. Long thought this was only fair, telling reporters at a break, "I'm the only one in that stinkin' hearing who's not getting his expenses paid." Not surprisingly, JDL leader Harvey Kane disagreed, asking, "Why should I pay my own executioner with my own tax dollars?"

By letter, Long informed the inquiry's counsel, Calgary lawyer Neil Wittman, that he wanted to subpoena Labour Minister Elaine McCoy, Human Rights Commission chairman Fil Fraser, Edmonton *Journal* staff writers Rick McConnell and Sherri Aikenhead, and Carney Milton Nerland. He would later request the presence of Louis Beam, Jr. After discussing the demand with his colleagues, Christian ruled that all but McCoy should appear to answer Long's questions and added Provost *News* editor Richard Holmes as well as *The Calgary Herald* reporter Sheldon Alberts to the list (Beam never appeared). Arguing that McConnell and Aikenhead did not have first-hand information about the Provost rally, *The Edmonton Journal* attempted, unsuccessfully, to overturn the ruling in Alberta's Court of Queen's Bench. In the end, Long never called Aikenhead or Fraser.

The preliminary matters disposed of, the historic inquiry into the Provost Aryan Fest got down to business. First to testify were various Alberta Human Rights Commission officials, who detailed the complaints, the background and the procedures that the commission had followed as they dealt with Long and Bradley. Then, on August 26, Terry Long himself took the stand for the first time. Under questioning by Taylor, Long wasted little time in getting to his main argument—namely, that the rally was private, and, as such, the offending symbols had not been displayed publicly: "At no time did I or anyone else associated with the Church of Jesus Christ Christian Aryan Nations deliberately contact the press with regard to this meeting. I don't know where they got the information with regard to our meeting, but at no time did we directly contact the press. In fact, I stressed to the press that it was a private meeting by invitation only."

Long hoped to persuade the Board of Inquiry that it had no jurisdiction to proceed any further. When invited by inquiry member Cheryl Daniel to give evidence as to why, Long said: "Those signs were placed on the gate by Mr. Bradley and his organization, Brotherhood of Regular People. They were not placed by Aryan Nations. . . . As I pointed out in my first letter to the commission in response to their charges, the signs were used for religious . . . as religious symbols, and to show pride in our own racial and cultural heritage. [They] were in no way intended to reflect discrimination on any other racial or religious group. That's it."

Like much of what Long and Taylor argued during the hearing, the jurisdiction objection was unsuccessful. In its 13-page written decision dealing with Long's motion, the board certainly implied that the May 2 press release—a release that had so infuriated Long—signalled the beginning of the inquiry and was issued too soon. But it did not accept Long's argument, for example, that this hasty move was evidence of the commission having reached a decision before all the evidence was in.

After hearing from Alberts, Holmes and a couple of the protestors about what they saw on that rainy September weekend at Ray Bradley's acreage, the inquiry listened to the testimony of all of the complainants. Some had not been present at the Aryan Fest, so they testified that what they had seen on the television news or read in Alberta's newspapers had caused them great distress. There were no surprises, although Harvey Kane provided one of the hearing's snappiest quotes while being cross-examined by Terry Long. "What about people that believe the Earth is flat, should they be prosecuted?" Long asked Kane. Without blinking, Kane shot back: "They're harmless, you're not."

Not long after the Board of Inquiry's hearings were under way, it became clear to most participants that Long and his fellow travellers would not hesitate, when it suited them, to bend the truth. In fact, the inquiry later dismissed many statements made by Long and others as unreliable. Social Credit candidate Tom Erhart, for example, was called by Long to testify about what took place at the Provost Aryan Fest. But Erhart was so evasive, and so forgetful about important details, he quickly became a figure of ridicule.

After two weeks or so of this type of thing, the inquiry had degenerated into equal parts vaudeville camp and Beckett play. Little new ground was being broken: the complainants, with few exceptions, had the same story to tell. After the initial shock wore off, the hearing grew increasingly and surprisingly dull.

The monotony of hate changed, however, on August 29, when the man everyone had been waiting for—Long's star witness, Carney Milton Nerland—came to town.

Security, which had been tight throughout the hearing, was increased dramatically for Nerland's appearance. Every spectator was scanned by metal detectors, and briefcases and purses were all thoroughly searched before anyone could enter the courtroom. At 9:30 a.m., as the standing-room-only crowd waited, chatting quietly, a side door abruptly opened and out stepped Carney Nerland and two nervous-looking police officers. Nerland had changed since the Provost Aryan Fest, videotapes of which had been played often during the inquiry. His hair had grown to collar length, and his mustache had given way to a full beard. He seemed to have lost a little weight during his time in Stony Mountain Pen. A few moments passed; not a sound could be heard. Then, grinning, Nerland gave the rigid-armed Nazi salute. A half-dozen skinheads leapt to their feet to return the gesture, as some spectators recoiled in astonishment and horror. Terry Long merely smiled.

After being sworn in, Long started to question Nerland. The two men appeared to have prepared well for Nerland's appearance. Nerland seemed to be providing rehearsed answers calculated to support Long's case. For example, Nerland repeated Long's claim that the Aryan Fest had been the brainchild of Ray Bradley and that Long had played no supervisory role. As they reviewed videotapes of the rally, Long asked Nerland if he was "proud" of the swastika armband he wore during the event.

"Definitely," Nerland said.

"What significance does it have for you?"

"Personally, it symbolizes not only the proud tradition of the Aryan peoples that stood against world Zionism and Judaism, but it also symbolizes our religious and racial heritage as well," Nerland testified.

Calling himself "security supervisor," Nerland admitted that he had provided most of the weapons brandished at Provost. He had carried them to Bradley's acreage in the trunk of his black Lada. With a straight face, he denied that he, or anyone else, pointed weapons at protestors or members of the media, adding that protestors crossed onto Bradley's property "on a number of occasions." He shrugged off the sexual assault of a female reporter, claiming the assailant had been a member of BHORP who was drunk. Asked by Long if Sigmund Sobolewski or Harvey Kane had been invited to the Aryan Fest, Nerland shook his head vigorously. "From all my experience in the years I've been a National Socialist, we usually never invite Jews or Holocaust war-hero survivors to any of our gatherings."

"You mentioned the Holocaust," Long said. "How do you feel about the Holocaust?"

"I personally feel that it is the biggest misshapen, misrepresented, sickish joke of the twentieth century," Nerland said, shifting his ample frame.

"So do you believe—"

Nerland interrupted. "An absolute offence against the intelligence," he said.

"Do you believe the Holocaust actually happened?" Long asked.

"I don't believe it occurred in any shape, way or form as they presented it."

After a lengthy exchange concerning Identity dogma, Long turned his attention to the symbols that had been displayed on Bradley's property. What Nerland had to say was the very centre of Long's argument: that the Provost Aryan Fest had been a private, by-invitation-only event. As a result, no symbols had been displayed to the public—and, even if they had been, the symbols were religious in their origin.

"The name Adolf Hitler," Long said. "Does that have any religious significance to you?"

"To me, personally, it does," Nerland said. "Adolf Hitler, as far as I'm concerned from my research and what I've read in the Bible . . . I would consider Adolf Hitler to be Elijah the Prophet, the Prophet sent forth by God in the last days."

There was silence. A few spectators could be seen shaking their heads in disbelief. One man held his face in his hands; he appeared to be weeping. After a lengthy silence, broken only by the sound of lawyers flipping pages, Long asked: "During previous testimony, the words 'White Pride' were denigrated by one of our Jewish witnesses. Would you tell us what the words 'White Pride' mean to you, in terms of your religion?"

Nerland drew himself up in his seat. "White pride, in my estimation, is something that would be the opposite of being ashamed or having disdain for your race." He paused. He seemed deep in thought. Perhaps he was thinking about his wife, Jackie, who was a non-white—and who had petitioned for a divorce from her husband of five years. "I'm not at all ashamed of my racial background. I believe that the white Aryan peoples of Western Europe are the most gifted people on Earth, that they have enlightened the world in their culture and their technological advances. And I feel no shame just saying that I'm proud to be white, and I make no apologies whatsoever."

Nerland took a breath. "I don't think we have to be ashamed of what the Jews say we did to them 50 or 60 years ago. Or what the

Natives say we did to them via the Hudson's Bay Company, or what certain slave dealers, many of whom were of Jewish persuasion, did to the American negroes in the South."

Long started to wind up. Next was the question many had been waiting for. "Do you hate Native people, Mr. Nerland?"

Nerland shook his head. "No, I don't hate them," he said. "I hate many of the things they do. I hate . . . I hate the way that they feel that they should be better treated than average Canadians. I do not believe they want equality. They want to be treated better than everyone else."

In one final memorable exchange with R.S. Abells, counsel for the Canadian Jewish Congress, Nerland expanded on Article 8 of the Aryan National State Platform, which had been published in an edition of Richard Butler's *Calling Our Nation* and entered as an exhibit. The provision called for "a ruthless war" to be waged against non-Aryans. Said Abells: "Presumably, sir, in order to wage a ruthless war, the church is going to require more than the 30 or 40 people who attended in Provost, is that correct?"

"Well," Nerland shot back, "there's a lot more than 30 or 40 people that attended that particular function in Provost. In fact, if you were to bring us all up on these bogus charges in front of a commission like this, I don't think you'd have enough jails or policemen to incarcerate us all."

Abells pressed on. "In the killing of Mr. LaChance," he said, "were you engaged in the ruthless war that's advocated in the Aryan National State Platform?"

Nerland exploded, his face red, his fists clenched. "I personally object to that question on the grounds that I was tried in front of a Queen's Bench Court judge, okay? And it was totally clear to anyone that was involved in that incident that it had nothing whatsoever to do with that platform! It's erroneous on your part to even ask that question!"

Abells walked back to his seat. "Mr. Chairman, at present, these are all the questions I have of this witness." After a brief discussion about security matters, Nerland was permitted to leave, and he gave one last Nazi salute to his followers on his way out.

The next day, Carney Milton Nerland was returned to his cell at Stony Mountain.

Friday, September 13, 1991, was an unlucky day for Canadian Aryan Nations leader Terry Long.

From his perspective, it started well enough. During the course of a lengthy examination-in-chief by his counsel, John Ross Taylor, Long was able to relate to a captive audience, in minute detail, why Adolf Hitler was Elijah the Prophet; why the Nazi salute "indicates openness, friendship and no secretiveness whatsoever"; why the burning of crosses signifies "the victory of our people over the children of darkness"; and why his country had become what he called "the Soviet Peoples' Republic of Canada."

There were a few tricky moments, however, such as when he was asked to explain why some of his followers had chanted "Death to the Jew" on Ray Bradley's acreage. Looking distinctly uncomfortable, Long denied he had participated in the chant, then added: "Yahweh is stating in [the King James Version of the Bible] that . . . the children of Satan will be exterminated. I'm not saying it, the church is not saying it, the church does not teach it. The Holy Bible says it. And anybody can read it in the Holy Bible."

"Is that related to the cry we have just heard or the shout we just mentioned?" Taylor asked.

"I can't speak for everybody there," Long replied, "but that's what I get out of it. And again, I didn't say it."

Long also took pains to distance himself from the behavior of those assigned to provide security at the Provost rally. "Many of those who attended that meeting have had death threats and have had aggressive moves, aggressive actions directed towards them," he said. "So there was a definite need of security. What I was in disagreement with was the use of weapons at the meeting . . . and I pointed out before that I wasn't in charge of the meeting. I didn't host it. I disagreed with the use of weapons, however. But I couldn't do anything about it because it wasn't my meeting."

At the lunch break, while Long waited outside the courthouse with a few supporters, a man stepped up to him. "Mr. Long?" the man asked. "Yes," Long said. The man handed him a document and walked away. Long opened it and read the cover page. It was a notice of claim, issued a few days earlier in Alberta's Court of Queen's Bench. Keith Rutherford, the Edmonton broadcaster who was blinded in one eye by two of Long's followers, was suing him—for general, punitive and special damages totalling $2.5 million. Also named in the suit were Mark Allan Swanson, the skinhead who had swung the club that struck Rutherford; Daniel Joshua Sims, who also participated in the attack; Edgar Foth; Rob Robinson; Long's wife, Janice; Aryan Nations founder Richard Butler; Final Solution Skinheads leader Kelly Lyle; four other neo-Nazi skinheads; and the Church of Jesus Christ Christian Aryan Nations. Long, Foth and a group of skinheads studied the document in amazement.

After the hearing reconvened, and after Terry Long and his followers had recovered from the shock of Rutherford's statement of claim, the Canadian Aryan Nations leader was seething with anger. On the witness stand, Long could not resist mentioning Rutherford, who was sitting in the spectators' area. Taylor asked him about the legal document. "That's a notice of civil action against myself and the church by Keith Rutherford," Long said, contemptuous. "I received it today just before this current session opened. And as far as I'm concerned, it's another form of harassment towards our church. It's religious persecution."

For Long, the day went from bad to worse. After a few hours of blistering cross-examination by a number of lawyers, inquiry chairman Tim Christian decided to adjourn. Before doing so, he asked counsel present for further submissions.

"There is one matter, sir," said the commission's senior counsel. "I would ask that the board make a direction to this witness that by Monday morning, the opening of the hearing, he produce all of the documents and records that relate to this matter—including membership lists."

Christian nodded. "That order will go. Mr. Long, do you understand the order?"

"Which documents in particular?" Long asked.

"Well," Christian said, "you better bring the box of documents
you have that might relate to this matter."

"Okay," Long said, looking confused. He added that he would
"make inquiries" about documents he did not possess.

The hearing adjourned and the spectators started to file out,
unaware that they were laying eyes on Terry Allan Long for the last
time. He was about to disappear.

On Friday afternoon, a sombre Terry and Janice Long drove back to
Caroline, where they were soon joined by John Ross Taylor, Edgar
Foth and a few others. After discussing the matter at length, Long
made up his mind: he would not provide the Board of Inquiry with his
membership lists, even if it meant being found in contempt. On
Sunday morning, a Canadian Press reporter telephoned Caroline and
reached Long at home, where, unbeknownst to the reporter, he was
packing his bags. "This is nothing more than an inquisition to divulge
information that should be private," Long told the reporter. "Not only
is my religion being raked over the coals but now they have instructed
me that my membership list is being subpoenaed. They want it there
Monday morning."

What did he plan to do, Long was asked. "If they want to put me in
jail for defending my religion and the supporters of my church, then
that's up to them. They're going to have to send the KGB out here to
get me."

Even if they had wanted to catch him, "the KGB," as Long called
the RCMP, would have been too late. By the time the Provost inquiry
resumed on Monday morning, Terry Long, as one Alberta newspaper
headline put it, was "long gone." On September 16, a defaulting witness warrant was issued by Tim Christian requiring "all peace officers
in Alberta [to] arrest and bring the witness, Terry Long, before the
Board of Inquiry to give evidence in this proceeding." That evening, a

group of RCMP officers searched Long's property, but no one was home. The next day, at about 9:00 a.m., two plainclothes Mounties and a group of uniformed officers were greeted at Long's property by John Ross Taylor. Taylor told the RCMP officers that if Christian lifted the arrest warrant, "I will be in a position to get things on the road again."

"But," Taylor added, hastily, "that is only if Mr. Long makes contact with us, which is something I can in no way guarantee."

The RCMP would return to Long's property many times in the weeks and months that followed, but to no avail. The trail had gone cold. Janice Long and her three children remained in the house. Terry Long, however, was gone.

For a time, sources say, Long lived under an assumed name with his brother, David, in California. Wisely, he kept away from the Aryan Nations compound at Hayden Lake, knowing that the FBI would probably be looking for him there. During his absence, Janice became an Aryan leader in her own right, sending letters to publications of the Church of Jesus Christ Christian, and taping hate line messages for the Manitoba KKK.

In March 1992, almost as an afterthought, the Board of Inquiry released its 112-page report, ordering Terry Long and Ray Bradley to "refrain in the future" from displaying swastikas, "white power" signs, burning crosses and "signs or symbols indicating an affiliation with the Ku Klux Klan." The Board of Inquiry then abandoned its six-month-old arrest warrant against Long. Said commission chairman Fil Fraser, "We're not in the pound of flesh business."

To Terry Long, it seems, that did not seem to matter. He kept away from Alberta in general and from Caroline in particular. He kept in touch with his family by phone. By late 1992, however, there were multiple sightings of the Canadian Aryan Nations leader in south-central British Columbia, between Castlegar and Salmon Arm—two towns where militant Identity Christian groups were known to be active. In December 1992, Long's wife and two youngest children, Rebecca and Cody, moved to British Columbia to be with the fugitive leader (Long's wife left him in 1993). The eldest daughter, Sarah, remained in Alberta to pursue her university studies, while Long's mother, Beatrice, continued to live in her trailer home on the family's acreage. Edgar Foth, meanwhile, moved into the Longs' home, where he gave Calgary and Edmonton skinheads arms training.

And just down the road, on Highway 54, two brothers mused about their famous neighbors. One of them, Will Paradis, Jr., says this of Janice and Terry Long: "As far as I know, they were really good people. Everyday people, you know?"

Nodding, Paradis's brother, Ray, agrees. "But the family is all gone now. And I don't think you're going to see Terry around here again for a while."

He was wrong.

There are many anti-Semitic and white supremacist organizations in western Canada. But it would be unfair to conclude, as many central Canadian observers have done, that the west maintains a monopoly over organized hate. The evidence shows that this is emphatically not the case. Every region of Canada has recently experienced a growth in hate activity.

In the west, hate groups subscribe to divergent creeds and philosophies. Some, like the Church of Jesus Christ Christian Aryan Nations, find solace in so-called scripture. Others reject religious dogma and pursue a secular agenda. All of these groups, however, endorse one position above all: violence. Western hate groups have distinguished themselves for their willingness to commit acts of violence. Only the ferocity of the skinheads found in the province of Quebec comes close.

The western hate groups also distinguish themselves in another way: they are not primarily home grown. White supremacists and anti-Semites found in the west have numerous links to like-minded individuals and groups in the United States. Some, like the Aryan Nations and the Ku Klux Klan, are simply branch plant operations that have their origin in American states. As such, they often lack sufficient autonomy to do what they believe needs to be done.

That said, western hate groups are sophisticated in their use of technology, in their recruitment efforts and in their organization. Terry Long's Aryan Nations, for example, has pioneered the use of computer technology to ship banned texts back and forth across the Canada–U.S. border. All of the established western hate groups have successfully tapped in to the growing neo-Nazi skinhead "market." And, with few exceptions, the groups coexist more or less peacefully. More than once, in fact, organizations that compete for the same membership base have assisted each other. Alberta Aryan Nations leaders, for example, have gone out of their way to provide rhetorical support to the Manitoba Knights of the Ku Klux Klan and British Columbia's Canadian Liberty Net. (Some cross-Canada co-operation has also taken place: in January 1991, for example, Heritage Front security chief Grant Bristow travelled west to solicit Terry Long's help in unifying the country's white supremacist movement. When they met, Long spoke to Bristow of his hopes to set up a Canadian Aryan Computer Network. A later meeting involving Long, Bristow and Wolfgang Droege in May 1991 saw further discussion of such a network, which Long hoped would include a "hit list." Ernst Zundel contributed names to be added to the list — one of which was Jewish Defence League leader Meir Halevi. The hit list eventually contained 22 names, many of them Jewish. As late as February 1992, names were still being placed on the list. At Janice Long's insistence, for example, Keith Rutherford's name was placed on it at this time.)

Are the western hate groups growing stronger? Yes. Are they growing more violent? Yes. Has the law been effective in controlling them? Probably not. As the prosecutions of Carney Milton Nerland, Bill Harcus and Teàrlach Mac a'Phearsoin show, police agencies and Crown attorneys in the west often lack the means or the insight to fight the growing tide of racism. And, as the Alberta inquiry into the Provost Aryan Fest demonstrates, human rights commissions have also been somewhat less than effective.

As hate groups in western Canada and elsewhere become more organized, Canadians should become aware that their violence only too easily can infect mainstream society.

8

THE WOLFIE AND GEORGE SHOW

One quiet Thursday evening in early March 1981, in the kitchen of an untidy house at 1439 Dundas Street in Riverdale, in Toronto's east end, a group of about 20 men and women stood about drinking beer and chatting. The group crowded into the smallish kitchen, filling every square inch of space.

At the appointed hour, a handsome young man stepped forward and gave the signal. Conversation stopped. A scratchy cassette tape could be heard, and then a distinctive Louisiana twang filled the room.

"The plain truth is, our race is losing," declared the voice on the tape. "We're losing our schools to black savagery, losing our hard-earned pay to black welfare, losing our lives to no-win red treason and black crime, losing our culture to Jewish and black degeneracy, and we are losing our most precious possession, our white racial heritage, to race-mixing."

The taped speech by David Duke, founder and leader of the Knights of the Ku Klux Klan, went on to describe how all major governmental institutions in the United States were controlled by a Jewish-Communist conspiracy. It described how African-Americans—Duke usually called them "niggers"—were being used as pawns by Jews in the campaign against the white majority. Hearing these things, the men and women of the Canadian Knights of the Ku Klux Klan nodded enthusiastically; some clapped their hands, others gave fascist salutes. "Right on!" one man said. "Right on!"

After the taped speech had concluded, a diminutive, stocky man pushed to the front of the kitchen, near the sink. Surveying the room, scratching at his goatee, the little man smiled and raised his hand. "Okay, okay," Wolfgang Droege said, in his distinctive German accent. "Okay, thank you very much for coming to the regular Thursday-night meeting of the Canadian Knights of the Ku Klux Klan." For the next few minutes, as his audience listened in respectful silence, Droege attempted to give the taped David Duke speech a Canadian spin. He explained that, just like in the United States, the Canadian government was a willing puppet of an international conspiracy of Jews. He described how Canadian immigration laws were being used to attack the white race. He told how the Holocaust was a massive hoax, designed to make white men feel guilty and to give Canadian Jews more power. Everyone applauded.

The men and women of the Canadian Ku Klux Klan took to some socializing. After a few minutes, Wolfgang Droege made his way across the kitchen to the latest recruit, a lean young man with a talent for writing. Alexander McQuirter, the youthful Grand Wizard of the Canadian Klan—and Droege's boss—had told his German-born lieutenant to get to know the writer. McQuirter, who slept easy with the knowledge that he knew most everything, did not know that the writer he had taken into his organization was Neil Louttit, a reporter with *The Toronto Star*. Louttit was working undercover, hoping to expose the inner workings of the largest and most-powerful Ku Klux Klan to appear in Canada since Saskatchewan in the 1920s and 1930s. Louttit figured that people wanted to learn more about the telegenic Alexander McQuirter and his sidekick, Wolfgang Droege. So, in early

1981, with some reluctance, the *Star* decided to send Louttit in to find the real story of the Canadian Knights of the Ku Klux Klan.

Droege and Louttit chatted for a little while, and then Droege handed the writer a thin booklet. Its title was "Did Six Million Really Die? The Truth at Last." Louttit flipped through it. The 30-page document, which called the Nazi-led mass-murder of 6 million Jews a hoax, was written in 1974 by a leader of Britain's neo-Nazi National Front. In the intervening seven years, "Did Six Million Really Die?" had been reprinted in several languages and distributed throughout Europe, North America and the Middle East. It is easily one of the most comprehensive postwar attempts to attack the reality of the Holocaust, an event neo-Nazis correctly regard as a major impediment to the rehabilitation of the reputations of Adolf Hitler and his Third Reich. The copy Droege gave to Louttit had been printed by another German-born man, Toronto publisher Ernst Zundel.

"If you want to really be a Klansman," Droege told Louttit, "you should read this. It will give you the historical facts."

Louttit nodded, murmuring that he was indeed interested in learning the facts. But one "fact" unknown to both Neil Louttit and Wolfgang Droege that night was that Droege was only a few days away from being arrested by a posse of FBI agents just outside New Orleans, Louisiana. On April 27, 1981, Droege and Canadian Klansman Larry Jacklin—as well as eight other U.S. white supremacists, were taken into custody in the woods near New Orleans. In their rented boat was a huge cache of weapons and other material: 33 guns and rifles, 20 sticks of dynamite, 30 blasting caps, 5,000 rounds of ammunition, battle fatigues, rubber rafts, a few large-calibre machine guns and a number of Confederate and Nazi flags. The plan, apparently, had been to travel some 2,000 miles to the small Caribbean island of Dominica, slip ashore at the capital of Roseau, lay waste the island's police station and dispose of Prime Minister Mary Eugenia Charles. Thereafter, Droege and his friends would restore to power the country's right-wing premier, Patrick John, and establish a neo-Nazi haven within the Western Hemisphere. Droege, for his part, hoped to establish a cocaine-processing plant on the island to finance white supremacist groups.

Their tongues planted firmly in cheek, the FBI called their undercover investigation "The Bayou of Pigs." It was a complete success. In May, a U.S. federal grand jury indicted Droege and his friends for violating various weapons laws as well as the U.S. Neutrality Act. In court, federal prosecutors and the FBI established that Droege et al. had conspired to overthrow a friendly government and, if necessary, kill any person who got in their way.

Shortly before he was arrested in Louisiana—and around the time he met *Star* reporter Louttit—Droege told a Toronto radio reporter why he was participating in the plot to overthrow Dominica's government. (The reporter, strangely enough, did not file his story until after the coup attempt.) Said Droege: "I consider myself a little bit of a rebel in society. And, like, I'm not content to have a nine-to-five job. I want to live a real life. You know, I want excitement and adventure in my life."

It is not known if the aborted coup resulted in any excitement or adventure for Wolfgang Droege. It did, however, result in three years behind bars in a U.S. prison.

Notions such as equality and multiculturalism never had much currency with Wolfgang Droege. From virtually the moment of his birth in 1949 in Forchheim, Bavaria, young Wolfgang seemed destined to achieve some sort of distinction as a committed neo-Nazi, a devoted disciple of Adolf Hitler and an observer of the twin ideologies of white supremacy and anti-Semitism. "I've had these same views since my early childhood," he says matter-of-factly. As a boy, Wolfie—as he came to be known to his Canadian friends—listened to his father, Walter, as he described his wartime efforts in the Luftwaffe on behalf of the Third Reich. Wolfie loved hearing these stories, and Walter loved telling them. Even more entertaining were the tales spun by his grandfather Werner. Werner Droege was a successful man who owned two hotels—Hotel Frankenhouf, in Forchheim, and Café Blattnersberg, near Nuremberg—and who happened to have been a friend of one

Julius Streicher. Before he was hanged for various war crimes in 1946 at Nuremberg, Streicher achieved distinction as a hardcore pornographer and leading Nazi—and as a patron of the elder Droege's Café Blattnersberg. Strolling through the Bavarian woods with his grandfather, with whom he lived from 1957 to 1963, Wolfie was entranced by the exploits of Hitler and Streicher. At the age of eight, he resolved that he, too—like his father and like his grandfather—would grow to be a Nazi. In time, he would get his wish, and become perhaps the most powerful neo-Nazi leader Canada has known in the postwar years.

By 1961, Wolfie's mother, Margot, had relocated to Canada and remarried another German to start a new life, bringing with her the Droeges' youngest son, Werner. Wolfie continues the story in his thick German accent: "I came to Canada when I was about 13 years old, in 1963. After living here for about four years, I went back to Germany. I thought I could maybe make a go of it there. I got a trade, working in a hotel, but I had a difficult time adjusting. I had become used to the Canadian way of life and Canadian values. In Germany, you know, there is much more discipline. Much more is expected of you. As a result I was kind of rebellious. Because of my rebellious attitude, I refused to cower before the people who were supposed to be my bosses. I had a difficult time."

During his stay in Germany, Wolfie's budding neo-Nazism had become a good deal more obvious. With the encouragement of his father and his grandfather, the teenager's views on Jews and non-whites had grown more extreme. More than once, in fact, he had attended meetings of Adolf van Thadden's pro-Nazi National Party. In 1967, he assisted van Thadden's group—which Droege says was "very nationalist, but not extreme"—in pre-election preparations. When he returned to Canada, Droege says, his mother and his stepfather implored him to be less outspoken. Spouting anti-Semitic or anti-black epithets will not endear him to prospective employers, they told him. But he was not interested in such faint-hearted advice. Wolfgang Droege was not one for compromises or half measures. Droege's Nazi fervor grew markedly one evening, when he caught an episode of the acclaimed CBC television program "This Hour Has Seven Days." The program featured an interview with George Lincoln Rockwell, the leader of the American Nazi Party. Droege was entranced by Rockwell and his unflinching pro-Nazi sentiment. He says, "My lightning bolt on the road to Damascus? I would say it came when I saw Rockwell. He was amazing."

Droege's mother was not happy about her son's growing attachment to extremism and extremists. Her son, conversely, was growing even more rebellious. "So within a few weeks of my return, I decided to take off and go up to Sudbury," recalls Droege. "I found a job there working for the International Nickel Company. It was a place to work, and get away."

In Sudbury, Droege joined the steelworkers' union and worked as a smelterer at one of the world's largest producers of nickel, copper and other precious metals. He was 18. Job conditions at INCO, he claims, were less than ideal. With a group other workers, most of them young like him, Droege decided to organize a wildcat strike. "We just walked out, a section of us, and we went over to the union office and said we're on strike. INCO is a huge operation, and when one department walks out, everything comes to a virtual standstill. It was a one-day thing," he says, chuckling at the memory of how Wolfgang Droege— one of the most conservative people ever to set foot on Canadian soil—had been a radical trade unionist, if only for a short while.

Droege remained in Sudbury for slightly less than two years. Then, during a six-month work stoppage in 1969, he decided to move on. "I didn't see much point in sticking around, so I came back to Toronto. Of course, by that time, my family was pressuring me, telling me I had to get a trade. They told me I had to do something with my life. So, as a result, I got involved with the printing trade." Droege found work as an offset press apprentice at Ready-Set Business Forms in Don Mills. At the time, he lived at home with his mother, brother, stepfather and three stepsiblings. As in Sudbury, he became involved with a union, this time the Graphic Artists International. "I had about three years of experience, but I was not a journeyman printer yet. But the union asked me to become the shop steward and negotiator." He adds that, once again, he led his fellow workers in a brief strike action. He laughs again, finding all of this union militancy hugely amusing. "It's funny," he says, "because I would consider myself probably to be a conservative, although I never voted along party lines. I voted for the candidates. Sometime I actually voted NDP!" More laughter.

Then, Wolfgang Droege's life changed forever. In the fall of 1974, while having a few beers at a bar called Maloney's in downtown Toronto, Droege met a man he had heard a lot about: Donald Clarke Andrews.

Born with the name Vilim Zlomislic in 1942 in the Serbian region of what was then Yugoslavia, Andrews came to Canada at the age of ten. As a youth, he was an excellent student who liked to read. He attended Ryerson Polytechnical Institute under a scholarship and, in his spare time, volunteered with various social democrat groups. Then, in the mid-1960s, alarmed by Soviet expansionism, Andrews became a dedicated anti-Communist. In February 1967, he and two other men, school teacher Paul Fromm and University of Toronto student Leigh Smith, formed the Edmund Burke Society. The group was named after an arch-conservative British parliamentarian; in time, it grew to include about 1,000 members, almost all from the Toronto region. Along with communism, which it loathed with a vengeance, the Edmund Burke Society opposed immigration, sex education, welfare, homosexuality, abortion, big government and Pierre Trudeau.

The Burkers infiltrated left-wing groups and they organized dozens of counter-demonstrations whenever leftists were gathering to protest something. Often, brawls ensued, such as one bloody encounter between the Edmund Burke Society and Viet Cong supporters in April 1968, and another with anti-war protestors in May 1970. Andrews, who delighted in such conflicts, called the violence "militant conservative activism." Some members of the group were convicted of bomb threats, break-ins, thefts, arson, vandalism and countless assaults. At the start, the Burkers were singularly devoted to the anti-Communist cause. By 1968 or so, however, the group's official organ, *Straight Talk*, was describing the African people as "completely primitive" and describing the Holocaust as an "allegation."

The stage was set, at this point, for the conversion of Donald Andrews's Edmund Burke Society to Donald Andrews's Western Guard. At a council meeting in February 1972, the Burkers agreed to the name change. They concluded that it was necessary for two reasons. First, too many Canadians were confusing them with the U.S.-based John Birch Society. Second, and perhaps most significant, the organization had expanded its list of enemies to include Jews and non-whites. Shortly thereafter, both Paul Fromm and Leigh Smith resigned, expressing concerns about nascent pro-Nazi musings among the Western Guard membership. Smith, who moved to Ottawa and much later became involved with Preston Manning's Reform Party, recalls why he abandoned the Andrews group: "It's been a painful thing in my life. I should be proud of what I did, but I have a hard time feeling good about it. . . . I was and am a conservative and a right-winger. But I wasn't a racist."

As Smith and Fromm left, other men who were racists—men who had been associated with John Beattie's Canadian Nazi Party, like John Ross Taylor, Jacob Prins and Martin Weiche—joined up. The bulk of the Western Guard's membership was male and based in and around Toronto, although British Columbia and Alberta contributed a few recruits. (Edgar Foth, the future Canadian member of the Silent Brotherhood, was one of these "write-in members," sources say.)

By August 1972, the Western Guard was using *Straight Talk* to editorialize in support of what it called "a white Canada." From that point onwards, and with moderates like Leigh Smith long gone, the group was overtly racist. Evidence of this is easy to locate in the pages of *Straight Talk*, which featured articles with titles such as "Race is the Real Issue," "White Power," "Mongrelization of Toronto," "Negroes Massacre Whites," "Race Pollution," and "Canada—A White Man's Country." Simultaneously, the group grew more anti-Semitic, as well: references to "the jewdicial system" started to appear in *Straight Talk*,

244 WEB OF HATE

kosher food laws were attacked and Jews were referred to as the instigators of international communism.

In 1973, the group established a telephone hate line, the first of its
kind in Canada. Some of the messages were sufficiently racist to
result in a 1979 Canadian Human Rights Commission hearing, which
found that they were discriminatory enough to merit shutting down
the hate line.

If that was not enough, Western Guard members started to deco-
rate construction-site hoardings with a variety of similarly unpleasant messages, among them "RACISM IS NOT EVIL," "MORE NIGGERS,
MORE CRIME—KILL RACE MIXERS," "HAPPY BIRTHDAY ADOLF HITLER,"
and the old stand-by, "WHITE POWER." The group's extremism was
not confined to rhetoric; in its actions, too, the Western Guard was
much more violent than the Edmund Burke Society had ever been.
At one memorable April 1974 event, members attacked a group of
black students at the University of Toronto. In the ensuing clash, a
number of black Canadians were assaulted and more than a few
were sprayed in their faces with harmful chemicals.

It was at this time that Wolfgang Droege, encouraged by what he
had heard about the Western Guard, decided to learn more about
these rebellious Canadian racists. Droege recalls his 1974 meeting
with Andrews at Maloney's Bar: "I came up to him and said: 'Are
you Don Andrews?' And basically we engaged in a conversation.
And then we became friends. We talked a lot about politics, but we
became more social friends. Shortly thereafter, he was trying to get
me involved in the Western Guard, which I did. I was an activist,
and I was promoting the cause. My whole life, from that point on,
was devoted to promoting the cause. I was always racially conscious, but I just hadn't made any contacts. But that night I contacted someone who I realized was very conscious racially and that
was Andrews."

Andrews laughs at the memory. "He probably heard me pontifi-
cating at the bar. His views were similar to mine. He seemed like an
intelligent, middle-class guy. He went on to be an integral part of our

operation. He did have the intellect, plus the bully factor—he was one of our strong-arm guys at the time."

In May 1975, less than a year after joining the Western Guard, Wolfgang Droege had his first run-in with the law. He painted racist slogans along the route of an African Liberation Day march in downtown Toronto. The slogan read "WHITE POWER—690-7777." The phone number belonged to the Western Guard's hate line. Recalls Droege, with obvious pride: "I ended up getting 14 days in jail, and basically I was the first person ever to be convicted here in Toronto for racialist activity. The sentence was fairly stiff considering what I had done. I got 14 days in jail, I got two years' probation, I got a two-year curfew where I could not be out of my residence between 12 and six in the morning." He pauses and adds with a laugh: "And I broke that every single night."

Then, a few weeks later, another run-in with the law: as he walked to court to answer charges of mischief and damage to private property arising out of the African Liberation Day incident, Droege spotted a photographer from *The Toronto Sun* tabloid. The photographer, ironically enough, was David Somerville, later the leader of the conservative lobby group called the National Citizens' Coalition. Says Droege: "I was walking along, on the way to court at City Hall, and Somerville snapped our picture. So what happened was I went up and knocked him to the ground . . . In those days, I was a lot wilder. I didn't mind getting into it, to scrap." Droege is not exaggerating: after Somerville ran off, the Western Guard "activist" jumped on a streetcar and headed over to *The Toronto Sun*'s offices on Front Street. He bolted past security guards and into the *Sun*'s newsroom. Recalls Droege, with a smile: "I threatened some of them right there. To get me out of there, one of the editors asked me to meet with him in a boardroom. Nobody really wanted to get into a fight with me, and I was intimidating some people. So they got me into a boardroom and sat down to discuss my grievance, and the next thing I know, the cops arrive." For that, Droege was found guilty of assault and fined $100.

All of his efforts on behalf of the white race were getting Wolfgang Droege attention, but not the sort of attention he wanted. RCMP officers started to pop by Droege's employer, Ready-Set Business Forms. "That put a lot of pressure on me, of course," says Droege ruefully. "I was really having problems at the time."

So was Droege's leader, Don Andrews. By 1975, the Western Guard leader had been charged on four occasions for offences ranging from assault to issuing death threats. But each time, he was acquitted. Then, in mid-1976, Andrews and another Western Guard member, David (Tarzan) Zarytshansky, dreamt up a plot to launch a terrorist bomb attack on the Israeli soccer team during an exhibition match at Varsity Stadium.

"After he was arrested and got his [18-month] sentence," Droege says of Andrews, "he was not allowed to be involved in the Western Guard any more. So he was gone for two years."

Droege did not sit on his hands while Andrews was behind bars. In 1975, he had met a young Western Guard member named James Alexander McQuirter. At the time, McQuirter was only 16. Born in North York, Ontario, in May 1958, he came from a middle-class family and was the eldest of five children. At about the age of 14, while enrolled at York Mills Collegiate, he started to read so-called racialist literature. Soon, he was attempting to convert his peers at school to racism; his parents, meanwhile, forbade him to discuss racial issues at home. Recalls Droege: "McQuirter was a very smart fellow. He was young, articulate and intelligent. Very capable, with a lot of ideas. We met, and we started to form a close friendship. We had the same feelings about Andrews. We felt he was trying to play this role of dictator and that he was not interested in working for our race or the advancement of our race. He just wanted a group so he could be the boss of it. He just wanted to be a mafia don."

Andrews, not surprisingly, rejects this criticism: "A lot of Germans have an attitude problem when it comes to the right wing. They want to be in charge of everything—and, if they were, they would just go and lose it a third time." He pauses. "He got to be buddies with

McQuirter, who wanted to do all sorts of wild things. Wolf assisted him in that."

In the mid-1970s, the Ku Klux Klan maintained a small and fairly ineffective presence in Ontario. Two of Droege's friends were members of different Klans. Jacob Prins was the self-proclaimed Grand Dragon of the Invisible Empire Knights of the Ku Klux Klan, which was headquartered in Ohio; another Western Guard member, Armand Siksna, who was born in Latvia in 1944, moved to Canada in 1957 and called himself "a true Nazi," had written to the Knights of the Ku Klux Klan in Louisiana to obtain permission to start up a klavern in Toronto. Siksna received the go-ahead from the man who single-handedly built the modern KKK in the United States, David Duke.

David Duke was a shrewd manipulator of the media. Born in Tulsa, Oklahoma, in 1951, Duke had been a member of the Ku Klux Klan since his adolescence. Clean-cut, polite and dressed in a suit and tie, the Grand Dragon of the newly-founded Knights of the Ku Klux Klan travelled to various American states to raise the profile of his "non-violent" Klan. In television appearances, he was articulate and effective; he abandoned the crass name-calling favored by more-traditional Klan leaders and said he frowned on lynchings and cross-burnings. The media, in turn, gave Duke legitimacy by inviting him to debate the likes of Rev. Jesse Jackson and helped his cause by constantly remarking on, among other things, how "normal" he was. In very little time, a "new age" Klan was born, one that was outwardly, at least, soft and fuzzy and friendly, and one that attracted membership inquiries from all over the United States and even parts of Canada. Some of these early members would go on to lead violent neo-Nazi and white supremacist groups of their own.

Duke was always interested in developing klaverns in Canada, but he was unsure how to go about doing it. In March 1971, he travelled to Toronto to meet with a few local racists; a requested meeting with provincial Attorney-General Roy McMurtry was rebuffed. In February 1972, a few Western Guard members, among them Don Andrews,

Jacob Prins and John Ross Taylor, attended a Duke rally in suburban Detroit. Still, the new Klan did not seem to catch on in Canada; there was a need, first, for a Duke-style leader with Canadian citizenship, a Canadian male who was media-savvy, good looking and smart.

Enter James Alexander McQuirter. In September 1976, Wolfgang Droege, John Ross Taylor and McQuirter attended Duke's International Patriotic Congress of neo-Nazi and white supremacist groups in New Orleans. McQuirter and Taylor travelled together in Taylor's car while Droege travelled by himself. During his journey south, Droege met with a number of prominent American far right leaders. Among these were Jesse Benjamin Stoner, chairman of the National States Rights Party, and the cofounder of this anti-Semitic organization, Edward R. Fields. In their organ, *The Thunderbolt*, Stoner and Fields were not ambiguous about their anti-Semitism: "What is required?" one July 1972 issue asked. "Every Jew who holds a position of power or authority must be removed from that position. If this does not work, then we must establish the Final Solution!!"

At the New Orleans hotel where the Knights of the Ku Klux Klan event was taking place, Droege met David Duke in an elevator. The two hit it off immediately. Recalls Droege: "From that point on, we were close friends. I was highly impressed with Duke." They have remained friends ever since and Duke contributes a regular column to *Up Front*, the Heritage Front's official newsmagazine.

In one speech he gave to the 600 white supremacists in attendance, Duke said: "The white people have to unite if we are to save ourselves! There is no other organization! There is no other hope. . . . We want a constitutional amendment against niggers. . . . The American people are searching, are reaching out, for a movement to carry forth their ideals, their values, the dreams they have in their hearts! And the Ku Klux Klan is their movement!" After the speech, there was a cross-burning outside New Orleans, where Duke led his troops in chants of "White Power."

The congress—which Droege now describes in reverent tones, as if he had witnessed a miracle of some sort—had a profound effect on both him and Alexander McQuirter. Recalls Droege: "At that point, I joined. I told Duke I would be his man in Canada. McQuirter took a little longer, but eventually he joined too. And so we decided if Duke needed any help, we would promote the organization here in Canada. We felt Duke was the most capable individual to lead our fight." Duke, in turn, provided McQuirter and Droege with the names and addresses of a few dozen Canadians who had contacted him to seek information about the Knights of the Ku Klux Klan.

Rejuvenated, Droege and McQuirter returned to Canada. During the days, McQuirter busied himself with the Canadian militia, while Droege continued his work as a printer; in evenings and on weekends, however, the pair organized on behalf of David Duke. They contacted the men and women on Duke's lists, and held small, secretive meetings at homes around Toronto. In April 1977, the Canadian Knights of the Ku Klux Klan secured some media coverage when Droege persuaded Duke, who was then visiting a group of Klansmen in Buffalo, New York, to tour through Toronto. As expected, the resulting news coverage attracted more recruits.

In January 1978, a teacher at Cardinal Newman Roman Catholic High School, in Toronto's suburbs, invited the Klan to speak to his American Civil War class. Recalls Droege: "At that point, we had done a little bit of literature distribution, we had set up a post office box, we had done a few things that had gotten attention behind the scenes. But when we were invited to go to the Catholic high school, it attracted a lot of attention. When we got there, of course, the invitation had been cancelled on us. So we held a demonstration." Among those who participated in the demonstration was former Western Guard and Edmund Burke Society member Paul Hartmann. (Hartmann, a former Western Guard member, died in June 1986 under mysterious circumstances in his Toronto home from a shotgun blast to the throat. His wife, Rita Anne Kelly—after recuperating, as she put it, "from the vicious murder of her husband"—would go on to dabble in far right causes, leading the Ottawa-based Northern Foundation and acting as a director of REAL Women of Canada.)

Two months later, in March 1978, McQuirter and Siksna were charged with conspiracy to distribute hate literature. When Siksna's College Street apartment was raided by Metro Toronto police, officers found swastika flags, boxes of KKK propaganda and several copies of *Mein Kampf*. Says Droege: "After that, things kind of subsided for a while. We decided it would be a good time to go out west. McQuirter's father was in the car business, you see, and he was going to give us dealer's licences to sell cars. So we went out to Vancouver and got into the car business." The two Klansmen rented an apartment in North Vancouver and started to visit some of the men and women named on David Duke's Canadian mailing list. Whereas the used car trade did not appeal to Droege and McQuirter, white supremacist agitation clearly did. "We were selling cars here and there, but we didn't really do too well at it," says Droege. "So McQuirter and myself started visiting some of these people. That's how we got started. We eventually had meetings. For the first time ever in the post–World War Two era, there was a racialist organization in western Canada. We did much better out there [than in Toronto]. Here in Toronto is the toughest recruiting ground there is in Canada."

Back in Toronto, Don Andrews had served his jail time and was devoting himself to yet another white supremacist group, the Nationalist Party of Canada. For much of 1978, Droege and McQuirter put their plans to build a Canadian Knights of the Ku Klux Klan on the back burner. McQuirter returned to Toronto to serve on the Nationalist Party's executive council, and Droege remained in British Columbia to organize on Andrews's behalf. He worked in Victoria at a printing plant called Capital Business Forms.

As had happened in 1976, McQuirter and Droege grew weary of Andrews's megalomania. In 1979, they let their memberships in the Nationalist Party lapse, and returned their attention to the KKK. Years later, Western Guard founder Donald Andrews remains sceptical about McQuirter and Droege's Ku Klux Klan. He says, "I didn't believe any of it. I thought it was just a lot of publicity-grabbing."

In April 1979, Droege organized a publicity-grabbing B.C. tour by David Duke, during which he conducted more than 30 newspaper, television and radio interviews. "[The tour] was quite successful. We got massive publicity," Droege recalls now. "A Conservative member of Parliament told Duke I should be his advance man, his promoter." Interest in the B.C. branch of the Klan boomed as a result, Droege says. Then, in September, Droege flew to Louisiana to attend a Knights of the Ku Klux Klan leadership conference. He remained in Louisiana for two weeks to assist Duke in one of his state senatorial election campaigns, in which the Klan leader captured more than 30 per cent of the popular vote, finishing second in a three-man race.

By October 1980, Droege says he had been forced out of his printing job. "The provincial government was putting pressure on the owner, and he was getting problems getting government work due to my organizing on behalf of the Klan." Droege left the firm and, like McQuirter, devoted himself to working full time on Ku Klux Klan recruitment.

Tension notwithstanding, the Canadian Knights of the Ku Klux Klan continued to grow at a rapid rate. The pair were greatly assisted in this by the Toronto news media, which produced an avalanche of stories in June 1980 when the Klan's phone number was found listed in the Metro Toronto phone book. The phone line was installed at McQuirter's east end rowhouse. McQuirter later told Julian Sher, author of *White Hoods*, a look at Canada's KKK: "It was nothing planned, really. We had the phone installed so we could print up some literature. The news media really blew it up and did all our work for us."

In one fawning profile in *The Ottawa Citizen* in July 1980, a staff reporter, evidently expecting the Klan leader to burn a cross or shoot a non-white in her presence, describes McQuirter as "shy" and "better suited to a milk commercial." The *Citizen* writer declares, "Alexander McQuirter doesn't look like a racist." A December 1980 Canadian Press story that ran in a number of newspapers across the country struck a similarly artless tone, describing McQuirter as the "youthful, unlikely-looking leader of the Canadian Knights of the Ku Klux Klan," a leader who "speaks with the lofty ideals of a boy scout counsellor." With this sort of uncritical media coverage, it is no surprise, perhaps, that McQuirter and Droege were attracting hundreds of inquiries from potential members. Stanley Barrett, in his seminal work on the Canadian far right, *Is God a Racist?*, estimates that there were approximately 2,500 committed Klan members and activists at this time.

Many of these new members were, by Ku Klux Klan standards, very young. Droege oversaw a massive recruitment campaign in urban B.C. schools. A number of Vancouver high schools as well as the University of British Columbia and the B.C. Institute of Technology were targeted. Those who responded received information packages mailed from Louisiana and application forms for the Klan Youth Corps. In Ontario, meanwhile, McQuirter was leading an effort to distribute Klan propaganda in Durham-area high schools.

In time, Droege and McQuirter built up a membership base in every Canadian province. Though members of white supremacist organizations tend to be marginal individuals who achieve little, if anything, in some cities, the Klan's supporters were hardly stereotypical. According to McQuirter, the Knights of the Ku Klux Klan attracted members of the news media, Armed Forces and various police agencies. In Vancouver, for example, a bright young UBC student, Ann Farmer, became the Klan's provincial spokesperson and, later, Droege's live-in girlfriend. Back east, in Ottawa, McQuirter secured the assistance of Ian Verner Macdonald, a man who had been a senior member of the Canadian diplomatic corps and who was friendly with the likes of Senator Eugene Forsey and Progressive Conservative Party leader Robert Stanfield. Macdonald, a wealthy land-owner in Ottawa with a penchant for writing letters to the editor, admits he acted as an "adviser" to McQuirter.

Says Macdonald: "When Alex would visit Ottawa, generally if I had a spare room, I would let him use it. We would talk about social problems and develop ploys to publicize his point of view. We weren't plotting any revolutions or insurrections. . . . In some ways, some of the Klan's comments ring very true. Any sensible Canadian who has the interests of the country at heart would want the borders controlled, for example. The potential for the white population to be completely overwhelmed is too real and too great to be ignored." Although Macdonald denies he was a member of the Canadian Knights of the Ku Klux Klan, McQuirter told *The Ottawa Citizen* that his followers in the national capital raised a great deal of money, and wrote many letters to the editor, on behalf of the group. The Ottawa klavern was filled with "intellectuals" in sensitive government jobs, McQuirter told the paper.

In the Canadian Knights of the Ku Klux Klan's handbook, in the chapter titled "Primary Objective," the Klansmen note: "We are not playing a game with only a few trinkets at stake. We are locked in a life and death struggle for the survival of the white race. The objective of the Klan is to form not only an effective white racialist political movement, but to grasp power." But to grasp power, McQuirter and Droege knew, the Ku Klux Klan would be little help. Its name conjured up unhelpful images of lynchings and cross-burnings. Realizing this, David Duke had left the Knights of the Ku Klux Klan earlier in 1980 to form the National Association for the Advancement of White People. Impressed, Droege and McQuirter talked about forming a similar organization in Canada, but they could not agree on a name.

Out of convenience more than anything else, they discussed merging with Don Andrews's Nationalist Party of Canada. In September 1980, a 13-point formal merger of the Klan and the Nationalist Party was signed "to promote co-operation in the white nationalist ranks." But the agreement did not last long. In a few weeks' time, it was abandoned by both sides. Recalls Andrews: "It fell apart. They weren't really interested in merging. It was more a case of a complete takeover."

As Droege and McQuirter continued to cast about for some way to energize the Canadian Knights of the Ku Klux Klan, an American man contacted Don Andrews with a bright idea. Michael Perdue claimed to be a mercenary with a long involvement in various U.S. Klan cells. In the fall of 1979, he travelled to Canada to discuss with Andrews the prospect of overthrowing Maurice Bishop's Marxist government on the Caribbean island of Grenada, which had previously deposed Sir Eric Gairy. Andrews, who had long advocated the idea of a white supremacist haven and sanctuary off the coast of North America, loved Perdue's idea. He introduced Perdue to Wolfgang Droege. Recalls Andrews: "My idea was to launch an invasion of Grenada, like Ronald Reagan finally did a few years ago, and to use Dominica as a launching pad. So I sent Wolfgang down there to talk to some mercenaries I knew, but he wasn't all that serious about following instructions. He formed his own plan, which was the Dominica [coup] thing."

Asked about this, Droege sounds annoyed. "I guess he didn't like the idea of him being cut out of the action. Andrews is one of those people who will never really do anything himself. He'll do a lot of talking, but he will never do anything. He's an instigator but not a doer."

Unlike Andrews, Perdue supported Droege's change of plan. Perdue met with former Dominican prime minister Patrick John and concluded an agreement that would see John returned to power. In exchange, Perdue and his friends would control the Dominican army and exploit the island's resources with John's blessing. Droege was sent to Dominica in December 1979 to tidy up loose ends with John. Later, he and Perdue travelled to Las Vegas and other U.S. cities to locate investors for the scheme. Some $75,000 was raised. Perdue's ten-man force included Droege, Ontario Klansman Larry Jacklin, future Knights of the Ku Klux Klan leader Don Black and seven other "mercenaries" with links to U.S.-based neo-Nazi and white supremacist groups. McQuirter assisted in planning the coup and was given the code name Red Dog Three. His job was to travel to Dominica and bring a number of vehicles to a spot near the capital's beach for use by the mercenaries.

When Dominica's government learned of a planned coup d'état, Patrick John was imprisoned. But Michael Perdue and company decided to go ahead with their plan. Says Droege: "I talked to some

FBI agents later, after it was all over, and they told me they thought it was hare-brained at first. But they said they later realized it could have been feasible. It was easy."

Easy or not, before they even left the United States, Droege and the others were arrested by FBI agents at a marina outside New Orleans. He pleaded guilty to a charge of violating the U.S. Neutrality Act and was given a three-year sentence. He was sent to a medium-security correctional facility in Sandstone, Minnesota. Says Droege: "Considering prisons, it wasn't so bad. It was 30 to 35 per cent non-white, but I didn't have any real problems."

With his second-in-command behind bars, the Grand Wizard of the Canadian Knights of the Ku Klux Klan was lost. In the summer of 1982, Alex McQuirter suddenly quit the organization he had helped to create. A better, more-moderate vehicle was needed if a white nationalist state was ever to be realized in Canada, he declared. Droege's former girlfriend, Ann Farmer, took over as Grand Wizard. Farmer, who had previously been the secretary-general with the B.C. branch of the Klan, had been brought up in South Africa with a lasting appreciation of apartheid. She was an ineffective leader, however, and lacked the ability to communicate with what Droege calls "blue collar" Klansmen. With Droege and McQuirter gone, the Canadian Knights of the Ku Klux Klan was effectively dead. In August 1982, McQuirter and Armand Siksna were charged with conspiracy to murder another Klansman. Later that year, after being found guilty on the conspiracy charge, McQuirter pleaded guilty to conspiring to commit a crime outside Canada's boundaries. For that, he received two years. Along with the murder conspiracy charge and a counterfeiting charge, McQuirter would not see the light of day until 1989, when he was released to the care of a halfway house in the Toronto area.

Droege, meanwhile, remained in prison in the United States. Upon his release in May 1983, he immediately travelled to Vancouver to pick up where he left off with Ann Farmer. By August, he had replaced Farmer as leader of the Ku Klux Klan. "I became leader, and initially a number of people expressed interest in getting things going again," Droege says. "But after the experience I had had . . . in prison, I had time to reflect quite a bit and I had matured. I knew that the Klan was not the way to go." Droege puttered around Vancouver for a few months. Then, in early 1984, he returned to the United States.

For a neo-Nazi, 1984 was an exciting year. The Aryan Nations offshoot, the Silent Brotherhood, or the Order, was looking for capable men to carry out Bob Mathews's racial holy war against the Zionist Occupation Government in the United States. During that year, Droege lived in St. Paul, Minnesota; Birmingham, Alabama; New Orleans, Louisiana; and Los Angeles. When asked how he kept himself busy, he is deliberately vague. "I spent time with people who were really political," he says. One of these people was Bill Riccio, an organizer with the KKK. Riccio had done time for a weapons offence in 1979 and had been one of Wolfgang Droege's fellow mercenaries in the ill-fated Dominica coup. He, like his friend Droege, had received a three-year sentence. As a consequence of all of this jail time, Riccio was well regarded within the movement—and, most importantly, by Bob Mathews, who met him shortly after his release at the 1983 Aryan congress at Hayden Lake.

Riccio was one of the best orators in the radical right. He lived in the small town of Centrepoint, outside Birmingham. Droege spent many weeks there, discussing the Silent Brotherhood's plans for a violent neo-Nazi revolution. Through Riccio, Droege was introduced to Mathews and one of his lieutenants, Richard Scutari. Mathews was familiar with Droege's far right credentials, and the two men got along well. Sources confirm that Mathews asked Droege to act as a recruiter for the Silent Brotherhood. Droege, however, was nervous. He told Riccio he opposed Mathews's plan to "skin alive" Morris Dees, leader of the anti-racist Southern Poverty Law Center, and bowed out. "I don't want to go back to jail," he told Riccio.

But whether he liked it or not, jail was where Wolfgang Droege was headed, and for a very long time. In November 1985, as he disembarked from a flight in Huntsville, Alabama, he was stopped and searched by federal agents. Found in his possession was a Teflon dagger, which was invisible to most airport security scanners. Also in possession was four ounces of cocaine. Asked why a man who preaches against violence and drug use was in possession of such things, Droege sounds uncomfortable. "The Teflon knife was given to me as a present by a movement leader from North Carolina. He just gave it to me. I didn't even want it," he explains. "The cocaine . . . Well, it was like the Dominica case. I was looking to finance the movement. I'm not a user or anything. Our means are limited, you know, and I was looking for other means to finance us."

At his trial in Birmingham, Droege was found guilty of trafficking and a weapons offence. He was sentenced to 13 years in prison. "The sentence was politically inspired," Droege says. "The National Security Agency tried to pressure me into co-operating with them. They wanted me to give them profiles [of neo-Nazi leaders]. They offered me a job and U.S. citizenship if I helped them, and they said I would never have to testify. I told them I couldn't do it. There was just no way. But that meant they were going to stick it to me."

Droege was transferred to a maximum security prison in Lompoc, California. Once there, he made contact with the members of the Aryan Brotherhood, a neo-Nazi group that recruits in federal prisons across the United States and maintains links to the Aryan Nations and other far right organizations. Droege was given his own cell and did not experience any significant problems. He killed time playing cards, watching television and, when the prison mailroom workers were being less than diligent, reading racist propaganda. Often, he received letters from David Duke, Aryan Nations "prison ambassador" Robert Miles and White Aryan Resistance leader Tom Metzger. In April 1989, having served one-third of his sentence without incident, Droege was released. He was deported to Canada and told never to return to the United States.

In Toronto, the racist right treated Wolfgang Droege like a war hero. He was invited to welcome-home parties, and feted around town. Nationalist Party leader Don Andrews, in particular, was delighted to see his old friend back in Canada. "When I came back, we resumed our friendship," says Droege. But the two men did not remain friends for long. In September 1989, at Andrews's suggestion, Droege travelled to Libya with a group of 17 Nationalist Party members. Andrews remained in Toronto. The Libyan government of Mu'ammar Qadhafi had been funding Andrews's group since at least April 1987, when a number of his members travelled to Tripoli for a "peace conference" to commemorate a U.S. bombing raid. Qadhafi liked the white supremacists because, like him, they believed in separate racial states and they despised Jews.

As they strolled through the ruins outside Tripoli, Droege, Grant Bristow and other disgruntled Toronto racists had many discussions about setting up a militant white supremacist group and about Don Andrews's domineering ways. Droege and a few of the others decided to form a new and better Canadian white supremacist organization. In attendance with Droege in Libya were Grant Bristow, recently recruited as a CSIS informant; Nicola Andrews, then wife of the Nationalist Party leader; and Max French, who would achieve fame in September 1994 when—as a candidate in the Scarborough mayoralty race—he was expelled from the Reform Party. (Eventually Andrews's Nationalist Party would be completely dominated by Droege's new hate group. Andrews would remain virtually invisible until August 1994, when the Nationalist Party scored a publicity coup. Andrews duped city leaders in Halifax and Victoria to proclaim "European Heritage Week" in October 1994. Andrews's "European Heritage Week" poster, which featured a photo of Hitler, even drew a positive response from Buckingham Palace.) On their way back to Canada, the rightists passed through O'Hare International Airport in Chicago at about 2:00 p.m. on September 4, to transfer planes. When Droege realized he would be obliged to deal with U.S. Customs—after being told by Alitalia that he would not be required to do so—he refused to get off the plane. Airline personnel had to escort him off. Customs immediately detained him on the grounds that he had violated the conditions of his early release from prison. Droege was taken by U.S. Immigration and Naturalization Service officers to a federal correctional centre in downtown Chicago, where he remained for two days. After again promising not to return to the United States, he was driven to the border crossing at Niagara Falls.

Back home, Droege held low-key meetings with his new group in his apartment. They discussed their plans for their new group, and they discussed a name: the Heritage Front. On September 25, 1989, the group was formed at a meeting attended by Gerry Lincoln, Grant Bristow and James Dawson. Droege and Bristow were originally expected to work "behind the scenes as 'silent' executives," Bristow later told CSIS — but that is not how things worked out. Dawson registered the Heritage Front on October 2. The group would have four levels: at the top, the Brethren — Droege, Bristow and Lincoln. The second level, the Executive Council, included the Brethren, Dawson and various "rising stars." The third level was made up of card-carrying members. And the fourth level would be comprised of supporters and subscribers to the Heritage Front newsletter.

In the early days, Droege had a variety of wild-eyed plans. One scheme envisioned Front members buying up property in the Peterborough area, controlling the town council and legislating whites-only bylaws. Another plan, modelled on the exploits of the Silent Brotherhood, would see Heritage Front members robbing armored cars and black drug dealers for funds; selective violence would also be used against so-called "race traitors." (Droege also hoped to emulate Don Andrews and obtain monies from the Libyan government of Mu'ammar Qadhafi, and asked Grant Bristow to assist him in this task.)

In November 1989, the Heritage Front went public. Droege, Lincoln and a few others travelled to Ottawa to attend a conference of the Northern Foundation, a rightist group founded in 1987 by Ottawa resident Gareth Llewellyn. Droege had chosen a good place for his coming-out party. As CSIS later noted, the Northern Foundation conference was "beneficial in allowing the Service to monitor Droege's launching of the Heritage Front."

The Northern Foundation's vice-president was Rita Anne Hartmann, widow of former Western Guard activist Paul Hartmann. Hartmann had moved to Ottawa in 1989 with her six children, two of whom were skinheads who would go on to recruit on behalf of the Heritage Front in the national capital. The Hartmann family lived in a huge home at 25 Delaware Avenue, in the well-to-do Golden Triangle neighborhood. (She later changed the number to 27 to avoid police detection.) From there, as the Northern Foundation's vice-president, Hartmann maintained connections with neo-Nazi groups across North America. In 1989, she gave a 1,000-name list of groups to a shocked National Foundation member to add to the Foundation's mailing list; half the names belonged to organizations such as the Aryan Nations and the Knights of the Klu Klux Klan. In early 1990, she maintained Nationalist Party of Canada membership forms in the Northern Foundation's computer system. In March 1990, she wrote to the ultra-violent Confederate Hammerskins of Tulsa, Oklahoma, using an alias she favors, Eleanor Cameron. Out of the same address, Ann Hartmann busied herself with REAL Women of Canada. Hartmann, who has a law degree from the University of Toronto, provides legal advice to REAL Women. In April 1989, for example, she gave an anti-feminist speech to a Realwomen conference at the Radisson Hotel in Ottawa.

Not all of the Northern Foundation's members were neo-Nazis. (In fact, Hartmann insists that she is not, pointing to a letter she once wrote praising conservative David Frum, who happens to be Jewish.) Along with the Heritage Front, the group's inaugural conference was attended by a well-known Conservative MP; a founder of *Alberta Report* magazine; a senior representative of the Alliance for the Preservation of English in Canada; and a columnist for *The Toronto Sun*. Yet many of those associated with the Northern Foundation would go on to play key roles in the Heritage Front, among them Steve Dumas, the foundation's research officer, who would write a regular column in the Front's *Up Front* publication under the pseudonym Steve Baker; Geoff Lupton, who had made an unsuccessful attempt in 1989 to establish a Nationalist Party club at Carleton University and who used the pseudonym Geoff Edwards when working on behalf of the

Heritage Front; and Eric (Stilts) Hartmann, son of Paul and Anne, who was moved to pen an anti-abortion editorial for Droege.

"The Northern Foundation conference was the start of it all for the Heritage Front," recalls Droege. "From that point on, things really took off." So, in September 1991 at Toronto's Latvian Hall, after some two years of behind-the-scenes organizing and discreet recruitment, the Heritage Front held its first public meeting. After a few good-natured remarks by Droege, a young man was called to the stage. He stood behind the podium, complete with the distinctive "HF" logo. He looked awkward in an ill-fitting jacket.

"My name is George," the young man said. "I'm a member of the Heritage Front and I've decided to remain silent no longer."

On the last day of June 1993, George Burdi eases himself into a chair at the Ottawa Courthouse, where he has just made his first appearance on a charge of assault causing bodily harm. A few minutes earlier, wearing a shiny double-breasted suit and a bored expression, Burdi, the leader of the Canadian branch of the virulently racist Church of the Creator and Wolfgang Droege's second-in-command, listened as a justice of the peace told him to return for another hearing in late July. Burdi nodded and ambled out of the crowded courtroom. The assault charge related to an alleged attack on a young woman in downtown Ottawa on May 29, the night Burdi and his band Rahowa were in town to play a few numbers for the Aryan faithful. After conferring with his lawyer, Robert Selkirk—and after chatting with longtime Ottawa anti-Semite Phillip Belgrave, who has popped by to offer moral support—Burdi sits on a chair in the courthouse cafeteria. He sips his coffee, awaiting a writer's questions, which he will handle with the aplomb of a veteran politician.

He is a large man, standing about six feet and weighing in at about 200 pounds. His dark hair is cropped close to his head. Even when he wears a suit, it is clear that he is a very muscular fellow who regularly works out. Burdi's face, which is still young, is littered with dozens of eruptions of acne, all ostensibly caused by the ingestion of a variety of steroids. Burdi and his Church of the Creator (COTC) followers take steroids, police say, and they work out regularly and avoid unhealthy foods. They want to be strong and fit on the day that the racial holy war begins. Police officers in Toronto and Ottawa, who take Burdi and his colleagues very seriously, say that the muscle-bound boys of the COTC are among the biggest and fiercest trouble-makers they have seen in a long time.

Around the world, in Sweden, South Africa, the United States and 31 other countries, COTC members—they call themselves Creators— have been convicted in dozens of murders and vicious assaults. In one such incident in Neptune Beach, Florida, in 1991, a Church of the Creator "reverend" calmly shot and killed a black Gulf War veteran who had merely suggested that he stop handing out racist literature in a supermarket parking lot; a COTC leader, who had been court-martialled out of the Green Berets after raping and murdering a Vietnamese girl in 1966, was later charged with being an accessory after the fact. Overseas, in the same year, two Creators were killed in a shoot-out with South African police, after they used automatic weapons and grenades to murder an officer who had been probing their links to an arms-smuggling network.

George Burdi is an articulate and intelligent man, and he is clearly in love with himself. As he sits in the courthouse cafeteria, expounding on the byzantine theories that form the basis of his pseudo-religion, he states with a straight face that he was born "with some kind of destiny" and that virtually no one "can beat me in a debate." Burdi does not seem to mind that his loud voice is attracting attention. In fact, he seems to be counting on it.

"This society is ripe for a change," Burdi says. "White people are very discouraged in Canadian society. They're very disillusioned with mainstream politics. They're looking for answers following the race riots in Toronto and what happened last summer in Los Angeles. Things like that are only necessary illustrations of what we've been trying to say all along. There is an unprecedented wave of violence against whites by non-whites. Non-whites are more prone to violence, they bring drugs wherever they go. When you talk about modern-day problems, when you talk about the drug problem, when you talk about the rise in crime, when you talk about problems in the economy, so much of that is connected to the tremendous percentage of non-whites."

All of this is undoubtedly racist, but it lacks the verbal directness of, say, Aryan Nations leader Terry Long or some of the leaders of groups such as the Aryan Resistance Movement or the Final Solution Skinheads. When he is in Canada, Burdi's public pronouncements are often like this. They are tempered with oblique references to statistics and poetic flourishes—and never any unpleasant phrasings, like "kike," or "nigger" or so on. In interviews, Burdi often appears to be striving to achieve a reasonable middle ground with his listener, his deep voice full of courtly inflection, his eyes wet with sincerity.

But when he is with his pals, when there are no pesky newspaper reporters within earshot and he is safely ensconced within the bosom of the COTC's headquarters in the United States where the First Amendment permits him a greater degree of candor, Burdi is a good deal less ambiguous about such matters. In the January 1992 edition of *Racial Loyalty*, the official organ of the Church of the Creator, he wrote an interesting essay titled "Enter the Racial Holy War," using his pseudonym, Rev. Eric Hawthorne. He says he picked the name Hawthorne because it sounded like "a leader, an idea-maker." In his now-infamous essay, Burdi quotes Friedrich Nietzsche, whom he adores, and he passes on a few memorable lines worth quoting. "It was white men of courage, white men of strength, white men of fury and blazing anger that conquered the world, and it is exactly the same type of WHITE MEN that will win it back. As Adolf Hitler said, terror can only be broken by terror."

When questioned about the marked difference between what he says when he in the States and what he says when in his home town of Toronto, Burdi shrugs, as if the answer is obvious. "The main reason is that we are a U.S.-based group and therefore the U.S. constitution protects us and lets us say what we want," he says, perhaps

WEB OF HATE

unwittingly demonstrating why Canada's hate laws are a good idea. "We can write our version of the truth in the United States. This has enabled racial ideologies in the States to be a lot more radical than they are in Canada. You would see a lot more radical ideologies coming out of Canada if it weren't for the hate laws that prevent it."

As he discusses the coming racial holy war in a way that permits no doubt, no equivocation, George Burdi remains a mystery. How did this young man, the son of a well-to-do Toronto family of Armenian descent, the product of private boys' schools, come to embrace what is generally regarded as one of the most extreme of the right-wing extremist groups? How did a boy whose best friend was a Filipino, and who was popular enough to be elected vice-president of his high school's student council, find it in himself to write: "White man! You have cowered and trembled at the feet of primates, pygmies and rats for long enough! NOW RISE! RISE AND LET THEM FEEL THE WEIGHT OF YOUR BOOT ON THEIR NECKS, LET THEM COWER BEFORE YOU!" How did George Burdi become the Rev. Eric Hawthorne?

George Burdi was born in June 1970. His father, who asked that he not be named, is a self-employed businessman operating a firm out of the family home in Woodbridge, Ontario, a community north-west of Toronto. With his broad face and his piercing eyes, George is said to be the spitting image of his father. He was an altar boy, and he read the Bible while still in his early adolescence. "He is a bright kid," the elder Burdi says of his son, and he is correct. As a boy, Burdi was encouraged by his parents, particularly by his mother, to read as many books as possible. During one two-week family vacation in California in 1982, Burdi recalls reading close to 20 books. "My mother would never consider money spent on books to be poorly spent," he says. "I used to thrive in book stores. I had a thirst to learn." He wrote lots of poetry, he earned straight As and he excelled at sports; many of his teachers seemed to adore him. His Grade 5 teacher at St. Gerard's School in Mississauga, for example, told his mother that young George "was going to be someone very important in the future."

In the summer of 1985, Burdi enrolled at De La Salle College School in Toronto, a Catholic boys' school whose pupils were required to wear uniforms and who typically were the children of the suburban upper-crust. In 1986, in Grade 10, Burdi met Lee Hardy, a history teacher at De La Salle who would have a tremendous influence on his thinking. Hardy, who now teaches at a school in Vancouver, says his favored approach in the classroom is to encourage his students to speak their mind as often as possible and to be unafraid to challenge conventional wisdom.

George Burdi, Hardy says, never hesitated to speak his mind. While this was generally positive, Hardy recalls, "I remember a few times I got upset with him because he wouldn't see any other point of view." At this point, Hardy says, Burdi was not openly racist; in fact, Hardy recalls that Burdi's closest friend was a bright Filipino youth. There was one incident, however, that foretold a change. On certain "special" days, De La Salle College's administrators permitted the students to wear something other than their school uniforms. On one occasion, Burdi and another student, Joseph, wore Nazi-style uniforms. "For Joseph, this was a way of attracting attention," Hardy recalls. "But for George, it was no joke. Any type of philosophy that tied in to the Nazis, George was always front and centre."

In Grade 11, Burdi was taught by a teacher whom he describes as "very cynical about society, but very well read." This man, Burdi claims, told his students that if they wanted to obtain a genuine education, they should drop out of school and read 100 books. On a list the teacher gave to his students, were 100 of the best books ever written. With this list in hand, Burdi started to devour Shakespeare, Plato, Shaw, Doestoevsky, Schopenhauer and, significantly, Friedrich Nietzsche. For 16-year-old George Burdi, reading the German philosopher on his own, without any knowledgeable adult to give some context to what was printed on the pages, Nietzsche's musings about the "instinctive aversion to Jews . . . these impudent people," their "vulgar souls" and the "affirmative Aryan religion" were electrifying. Recalls Burdi: "Nietzsche had a dramatic, powerful effect on my thinking. I remember sitting up to five, six in the morning, watching the sun come up and reading Nietzsche and all about the Superman and the will to power." He pauses. "Every living thing seeks to dominate; that is the nature of all higher life. That was what Nietzsche wrote, and it had a very profound effect on me. It made me view things from the perspective that strength was not something that could be evil. I learned to think beyond good and evil. Strength and power and the great historical figures who had lived before were to be respected for their strength and power. And whether there had been brutality or love used in the creation of their power base, it was all admirable. I started to learn about people like Alexander the Great, which led to Napoleon, which led to Adolf Hitler."

Which led to Ernst Zundel. In 1986, the year he was staying up late to read Nietzsche, Burdi started to date a girl from a nearby all-female Catholic school. This girl, whom Burdi will not name, knew many of the people who made up Toronto's neo-Nazi scene, people like Western Guard activist John Ross Taylor and Citizens for Foreign Aid Reform leader Paul Fromm, ex of the Edmund Burke Society. With Nietzsche's observations about Aryanism and the Superman fresh in his mind, Burdi was eager to meet as many National Socialists as possible. "She introduced me to Ernst Zundel," he recalls. "I started to work with Zundel, and I started to learn about Holocaust revisionism. I worked on his computer a lot. I typed his newsletters, and I went to his house as often as I could."

At Zundel's fortified, cramped home on Carlton Street in downtown Toronto, Burdi met many of the men who had led the forces of anti-Semitism and white supremacy in Ontario for decades. On one occasion, Burdi was even given an opportunity to meet David Irving, the British author who claims that Hitler was unaware of the Holocaust and who disputes the existence of gas chambers at Nazi concentration camps. When he was given an audience with Zundel himself, Burdi would ask the German-born publisher questions about race, Jews and the Holocaust. "Whatever his shortcomings may be," Burdi says of Zundel, "I knew him to be a very intelligent man. He expressed himself very eloquently. The time I spent with him I would ask questions and just listen. And soon, the only way I understood National Socialism was as a creative, positive force and ideology."

Burdi was placed in Lee Hardy's history class in his third year at De La Salle College. Right away, Hardy noticed there had been a physical change. In Grade 10, Burdi had been "physically small," Hardy says; by Grade 12, he had become muscular and bulky. After class, Burdi would discuss weightlifting with Hardy, who also coached the college's football team (Burdi played for the team for a season). With weightlifting magazines tucked under his arm, Burdi would insist that he was not taking "roids," as he called them. But Hardy was not so sure—nor was Burdi's younger brother, Andrew, who was also enrolled at De La Salle College. "George is weird," Andrew Burdi told Hardy. "He's gone off the deep end, and he's heavily into this weightlifting stuff."

There was a change in attitude, as well. Burdi had become cocky and belligerent, Hardy recalls. On one occasion, while a student teacher was leading the history class, Hardy sat at the back of the room to observe the discussion. The topic was Hitler and Nazism. When Burdi was given an opportunity to speak, he stood and stated that the Holocaust was grossly exaggerated. (A few weeks later, to perhaps emphasize the point, he brought in a copy of "Did Six Million Really Die?" for his classmates to read.) "The Holocaust is not reported on accurately," Burdi said. "Besides, I think it was a good policy. The Jews are a bunch of crybabies." Burdi went on in a similar vein for the next ten minutes, even quoting David Irving once or twice, until Hardy felt obliged to intervene.

"Excuse me, George," the teacher said. He pointed out that the extermination of 6 million Jews was a fact so notorious, so well established, that to question the Holocaust was to engage in bad research, or worse. He pointed out that, along with the Jews, hundreds of thousands of non-Jews—gypsies, German dissidents and resistance fighters—were exterminated by Hitler's forces. Burdi was unmoved, however. "That's insignificant," he said.

"At that point," Hardy recalls, "I got very upset. I made it very clear to him that he had taken things out of context, and I pointed out how he had taken things out of context. But I must say, he was doing an excellent job of manipulating many of the students in the class. A couple of them were even agreeing with him. So I said: 'George, you can sit down now.' That got him mad. He was red in the face."

After the class had been dismissed, Hardy spoke privately with Burdi. "I believe in revisionist history," Burdi told his teacher. "The things I said have been proven scientifically."

"George," Hardy said, exasperated. "Where are you getting this stuff?"

"I have friends," Burdi said, his eyes scanning the floor.

Some of those friends, police say, were members of the ultra-racist Church of the Creator and soon-to-be members of the embryonic Heritage Front. In 1989, after graduating from De La Salle College, Burdi enrolled in political science classes at the University of Guelph. There, he was drawn ever deeper into the racist right. He attended lectures only infrequently; most of the time, he hung out in university bars and coffee houses. In that same year, a friend lent him a copy of the Church of the Creator's *Racial Loyalty*. It was his first encounter with the COTC. The publication, Burdi recalls, "actually scared me, it was so radical. It just turned me off, it was just psycho." He laughs. "But then, as time went on, and when I was still at the University of Guelph, these ideas that I had read didn't leave me. They had sort of planted a seed of doubt and a lot of ideas in my mind, and I wanted to find out more about them. I wrote a letter to them right away and I sent away for *The White Man's Bible*."

This "bible" was written in 1981 by the Church of the Creator's founder and self-described Pontifex Maximus, Ben Klassen. Klassen was born in a Dutch-Mennonite community in the Rudnerweide in the Southern Ukraine; his family emigrated to Chihuahua, Mexico, in 1924, when Ben was 14. Eighteen months later, they moved to the wheat fields of Saskatchewan, where some of Klassen's relatives had taken up residence a year before, and Klassen grew up on a farm. At

19, he became a schoolteacher, but after teaching for two years, he went on to acquire degrees in science and electrical engineering. In 1945, he moved to California and became a U.S. citizen in 1948. For most of his life, he sold real estate, and became fairly wealthy as a result. In 1958, he settled in Florida and, eight years later, he was elected to the lower house of the Florida State Legislature on a platform that was anti-busing and anti-government. Then, recalls Klassen, "I became extremely concerned about the racial turmoil developing in America and the rapid mongrelization of our formerly white America."

For a time, Klassen ran a bookstore called American Opinion, out of which John Birch Society propaganda was distributed. Later, he had a falling-out with the Birchers, whom he believed were not radical enough. The society was "a smokescreen for the Jews," Klassen declared. In 1973, he founded the Church of the Creator, in Lighthouse Point, Florida. In that same year, he wrote and published his first book, the 512-page anti-Semitic magnum opus titled *Nature's Eternal Religion*. In it, Klassen outlined the COTC's credo: "We completely reject the Judeo-democratic-Marxist views of today and supplant them with new and basic values, of which race is the foundation. . . . We mean to cleanse our own territories of all the Jews, niggers and mud races, and send them back to their original habitat." To Klassen, Christianity was "a suicidal religion"; his was called "Creativity." (Unlike Identity, Creativity rejects any and all notions of a Christian deity; COTC publications often ridicule Identity, in fact.) Klassen occupied himself with building a neo-Nazi organization that was rigorously militant and devotedly violent.

In 1981—a year before he moved his "church" to a one-acre lot in Otto, North Carolina—Klassen wrote and published another book, *The White Man's Bible*. Possessing this 452-page tome, which Klassen described as "a powerful religious creed and program for the survival, expansion and advancement of the white race," is illegal in Canada. Scanning its pages, one can see why. It is one of the most anti-Semitic and racist books ever to be produced in North America in this century. In it, Klassen calls upon his fellow Christ-hating

"Creators" to build "sound minds in sound bodies in a sound society." Writes Klassen: "Working towards the niggerization of America is the Jewish race. Pushing, clawing, propagandizing with a fury unparalleled in history, the Jews are working towards their ultimate historic goal—total enslavement of all races of the world—and every Jew a king." Christians, meanwhile, "worry about spooks in the sky instead of struggling for their own survival and advancement." The anti-Christian sentiments expressed in *The White Man's Bible* are—even for the racist right—controversial.

But to George Burdi, who had been moving away from the strict Roman Catholicism of his youth for some time, the rantings of the founder of the Church of the Creator were inspirational. After reading over *Nature's Eternal Religion* and *The White Man's Bible*, Burdi telephoned the COTC's headquarters in Otto to speak with Ben Klassen. Klassen was impressed by this articulate young Canadian, and in January 1990, he agreed to pay for the cost of Burdi's travel to and from North Carolina. Burdi recalls: "I went by myself on the bus. I got a view of the armpit of America, on that bus. It was disgusting."

Burdi says the site of the Church of the Creator compound in the Blue Ridge Mountains—or, as they are known, the Smoky Mountains, due to the prevalence of fog in the mornings—was a beautiful place. "It was the most peaceful, tranquil time of my life. The outside world disappeared. It was a mental and emotional cleansing period. I focussed only on what I was doing down there.

"I spent many hours with Klassen, listening to him. It was a great learning experience."

Back at the University of Guelph, George Burdi was supposed to be learning things of a more conventional nature, but the Church of the Creator had transformed the first-year political science student. He was radicalized.

After completing one year of studies at university, Burdi dropped out. The Paul Fromm incident—and the vicious anti-Semitism and white supremacy of *Racial Loyalty*—had changed him, perhaps for good. Racism consumed him; soon, all of his waking hours were devoted to the cause. Burdi returned to Toronto and started hanging out with neo-Nazi skinheads downtown. Says Lee Hardy: "Our students reported bumping into him downtown every once in a while. He was making himself quite visible with the skinheads. They saw him getting into fights with people."

The change worried Burdi's parents as well. "His mother and father are quite soft-spoken people," says a person who knows the family well but did not wish to be identified. "And they just couldn't understand what had happened to him." In 1990, there were many fights in the Burdi household, as the family struggled to understand what had happened to their eldest son. The Burdis were not racist, and they could not comprehend the sea change in him. Asked about this period, George Burdi is contemptuous and cruel. "My parents, my family weren't thinkers. I don't take resistance of that sort seriously. Someone who is a television junkie, what type of ideas do they have that are original? I've never heard an intelligent, truly objective statement from any one of my family members." His father, meanwhile, valiantly continues to defend his son, notwithstanding the harshness of his remarks. In the only interview he has granted to date, the elder Burdi says: "George has his thoughts about certain things that are going on in Canada. But the translation [in the media] has been a little different than what the real truth is. As far as I am concerned, Canada is the way it is. Canada is a melting pot and it can't be changed."

He pauses, then adds: "George is a little more boisterous and opinionated than most people in Canada. He spoke up, and as a result, he got himself into a spot of trouble that he could not get himself out of easily."

George Burdi, however, was not interested in what his father had to say. He moved out of the family home, and into a series of flophouses he shared with other racists, some of them members of the Heritage Front, some of them soon-to-be members of the Church of the Creator. In the fall of 1990, he and three other COTC members formed a racist band called Rahowa (short for Racial Holy War). They started to practise. Given the experience a decade earlier of British pro-Nazi skinhead band Skrewdriver, Burdi reasoned that a rock band could reach a more-youthful audience with the racist message—and, he hoped, attract a few new members. He was right.

On Saturday, December 8, 1990, the band played at a racist get-together in Toronto, which happened to be the first-ever Heritage Front public rally. The top-secret meeting was called to mark Martyr's Day, the sixth anniversary of the death of Bob Mathews, leader of the Silent Brotherhood. (The rally became public in April 1991 when the Canadian Jewish Congress made public a videotape of the rally.) In attendance at the Martyr's Day event was Paul Fromm, who stood beside a Nazi flag and stated: "We're all on the same side. We know who we are, but we must also know who the enemy is. We're up against an enemy, as I see it, the equivalent of an army of occupation . . . and the only way we are going to regain our country is through unity, unity, unity." Speeches were given by members of the Women's Aryan Union and a small neo-Nazi skinhead group known as Canadian Alliance.

Then, at evening's end, Rahowa played a few numbers for about 20 minutes. One song featured Burdi yelling "Nigger! Nigger! Nigger!" while the crowd responded with chants of "Out! Out! Out!" In a letter sent to *Racial Loyalty* by Heritage Front cofounder Gerry Lincoln, the event was described in this way: "Rounding out the evening's activities, the COTC music band Rahowa performed an inspiring set of their own compositions, that appealed to even seniors in the audience, like the Canadian activist John Ross Taylor." On New Year's Eve, Rahowa played again, this time in Montreal. Approximately 200 skinheads attended the performance, Burdi says, adding that 20 copies of *The White Man's Bible* were sold.

In December 1991, the group recorded a four-song demo tape—"White Revolution," "Triumph of the Will," "Race Riot," and "Victory Day." It concluded with a spoken-word message, "Call to Creators," penned by Burdi. Later, 100 copies were made and sold at Rahowa concerts. In early 1992, COTC concluded a recording deal with Rebelles Europeans, a white supremacist record label, but no tapes were ever released. In the spring of 1993, Burdi's group was signed by Resistance Records, a Detroit-based label. Burdi says he acts as an "agent" for the company, which was formed with $50,000 in seed money offered by U.S. racist organizations. Eight other racist bands have been signed to the label, with names like Nordic Thunder, Aggravated Assault, Aryan and the Voice.

By 1991, the Rahowa concerts—and Burdi's dexterity with the media—were paying off for both the COTC and the Heritage Front. Droege and Burdi's efforts were attracting international attention: in March 1991, for example, Droege travelled to Munich with Grant Bristow to attend a pro-Nazi conference that had been sponsored by Ernst Zundel. There were cells of COTC members in Whitby, Scarborough and Burdi's home town of Woodbridge. The increasing influence of the Canadian branch of the COTC is seen in the pages of *Racial Loyalty*, which is produced in North Carolina. In the May 1991 issue, a Toronto man calling himself the "Reverend Norman Saxon" describes how Burdi gave him a copy of *The White Man's Bible* to read: "Before I finished this monumental work of yours, I had ceased to be a Christian and was on my way to becoming a member and a reverend of the one and only true white racial religion—Creativity. RAHOWA!" In the same issue, Burdi sends a "report from Canada." In it, he describes the New Year's Eve performance by Rahowa—and the Heritage Front Martyr's Day rally. He then writes: "Let's face it, people. Although many organizations expose part of the problem, Creativity provides us with the Final Solution, the total creed and the program to reach the stars with. It is truly our only hope. . . . Creativity recognizes the separation of Church and State concept as Jew-spawned poison. Religion is nothing more than the organized declaration of the highest values of a people. How could any government act independently of the value system of its people without being guilty of treason?" In the August 1991 issue, Toronto's Carl Alexander announces the establishment of the COTC's post office box in Woodbridge.

Around Toronto, COTC posters started to appear. One featured a sketch of a COTC warrior hoisting the group's flag. The poster read:

"Don't get mad—GET EVEN. ENOUGH IS ENOUGH. Learn the TRUTH, write now! CREATIVITY—THE WINNING FORMULA—DEFEND THE WHITE RACE . . . FOR A WHITER, BRIGHTER WORLD, JOIN THE CHURCH OF THE CREATOR."

It is perhaps ironic that, for much of 1991 and 1992, Burdi had no official status to represent himself as a Church of the Creator "leader." Although he clearly had Klassen's ear (he travelled to COTC compounds in Wisconsin and North Carolina for special guerrilla training about a dozen times during this period, federal agencies say), and although he was frequently profiled by the media (in 1992, Burdi was interviewed in disguise on an episode of "Geraldo" and was featured in a "Now It Can Be Told" segment), he had yet to be designated the COTC's Canadian leader. "Reporters kept asking me my title, whether I was leader, who was the leader in Canada and on and on," recalls Burdi. "Finally I just let them say that I was the Canadian leader." But it was not until September 1992, Burdi notes, that he was elevated to the COTC's Leadership Council.

In the fall of 1991, Burdi's new friend, Wolfgang Droege, was particularly busy. The Heritage Front hate line was established. Members infiltrated the Beaches-Woodbine Reform Party constituency association. There was the first public Heritage Front meeting to which the media had been invited. And, in the same period, U.S. Aryan Nations lieutenant Sean Maguire and Grant Bristow were arrested by a police SWAT team in the latter's car—the trunk of which contained a shotgun and a semi-automatic rifle. (Maguire was later deported, and Bristow was released because he carried the necessary firearms permits.)

It was around this time—in the fall of 1991 in particular—that members of Toronto's incestuous racist right community started to observe a curious development. George Burdi, Canadian leader of the Church of the Creator, had become best of friends with Wolfgang Droege, leader of the Heritage Front. Although Burdi was approximately half Droege's age, and although the two led organizations with starkly different approaches—the COTC was openly hostile towards other racist groups, particularly Christian ones, while the Heritage Front operated as an umbrella for a large number of neo-

Nazis and white supremacists with all manner of philosophies—they forged a strong alliance that persists to this day.

The Nationalist Party's Don Andrews, who is held in contempt by Burdi and Droege, observed the pair from afar. He says the relationship between the two men reminds him of the one that existed between McQuirter and Droege in the early 1980s. "It's interesting," says Andrews. "Burdi needs some seasoning, but I think he will be a good leader one day. He reminds me of myself when I was younger, actually."

Another observer, Bernie Farber, the Canadian Jewish Congress's expert on hate groups, agrees that Burdi and Droege have become virtually inseparable since late 1991. He says with a laugh, "They have become the Wolfie and George show."

Wolfgang Droege and George Burdi jointly oversee a growing racist empire. Its methods of recruitment, fund-raising and media manipulation are as organized and as professional as any one of the better-known non-governmental agencies that advance the cause of auto workers, drug companies or baby seals. Recalling the triumphs of the Canadian Knights of the Ku Klux Klan, police sources say Droege has again placed himself firmly in control of the Heritage Front/Church of the Creator organizational efforts, while Burdi has used his nimble tongue—and the novelty of his racist rock band—to attract media attention à la Alex McQuirter. (COTC's so-called Security Legions have played an additional role, acting as muscle at Heritage Front rallies and serving as Droege's bodyguards.) From the fall of 1990 until the summer of 1993, when a series of arrests shook the Heritage Front and Church of the Creator to their very foundations, Droege and Burdi were Canada's best-known and most-powerful racist leaders. During this period, no one—not the Aryan Nations' Terry Long, not Bill Harcus of the Manitoba Knights of the Ku Klux Klan, not Tony McAleer of Canadian Liberty Net, not any of Quebec's disputatious Klan groups—came even remotely close.

Droege and Burdi achieved this distinction through good old-fashioned Aryan hard work—and a few attention-grabbing gambits.

One of the most effective vehicles has been the Front's slick official magazine, *Up Front*. A survey of the publication's various articles provides a good chronological summary of the activities of the group and, to a lesser extent, the Church of the Creator. *Up Front* is important because it is the primary way the Heritage Front reaches the majority of its members and supporters—some 2,000 in all, across Canada. Only the Heritage Front's hate line comes close as a propaganda tool.

The first issue of *Up Front* was published in December 1991. Under a jazzy red-and-blue logo, it sported a large photograph of David Duke beside the legend: "RIGHT DOESN'T WIN EVERY BATTLE BUT RIGHT ALWAYS TRIUMPHS IN THE END." The magazine was edited by Heritage Front cofounder Gerry Lincoln, who penned an editorial designed to create the impression that the group—and its publication—would avoid the crass name-calling so popular with white supremacist groups of the past. Wrote Lincoln: "As individuals, and as a movement, we need to strive for a certain level of maturity which is decidedly lacking in many instances. We must learn that we are only as effective as the message that we convey and the image that we create in the minds of the general public. . . . Yelling 'Nigger!' will get you absolutely nowhere. People will not respect an ill-disciplined person, no matter how lofty his motivation." In time, however, this genteel attitude would give way to a coarser tone.

Elsewhere in the same issue there was an unsigned article about Duke. The article quoted Droege as saying that the Knights of the Ku Klux Klan founder was "the most dynamic white racialist leader in America!" There were columns by Carleton University student Steve Dumas and another called "Turner's Diary," a less-than-subtle reference to the ultra-violent novel that inspired the Silent Brotherhood. On one page, there was even an approving quotation from Mu'ammar Qadhafi's *Green Book*.

The second issue, published in January 1992, contained a letter by—and photograph of—David Lane, the Silent Brotherhood member who was given 40 years' imprisonment for his role in Bob Mathews's far right conspiracy and, later, 150 years for his assisting in the murder of

Alan Berg. Wrote the Heritage Front in response to Lane's letter: "Mr. Lane is an inspiration to patriots everywhere." There was also an article coauthored by Elisse Deschner, a giggly 18-year-old Romanian immigrant whose real name is Elisse Hategan; Hategan would achieve distinction in July 1993 by being only the fourth person in Ontario's history to be charged with willfully promoting hatred (Donald Andrews, of course, was one of the first). In late 1993, Hategan would turn police informant against the Front, linking its members to the fire-bombing of an anti-racist activist's Kitchener home, numerous beatings, and even the "breaking into" of telephone answering machines. After testifying against Wolfgang Droege, the charges of promoting hatred were withdrawn in June 1994. A full page was given over to Richie Kemp, the Silent Brotherhood member who in 1985 received a 60-year sentence for racketeering, conspiracy and armored car robbery.

It was while the third issue of *Up Front* was being readied for publication that Wolfgang Droege encountered his first difficulties as head of the Heritage Front. In February, he received a double-registered letter from the Canadian Human Rights Commission stating that the commission had received a complaint from the Native Canadian Centre regarding the Heritage Front's hate line. (The centre had previously made a complaint about the hate line to a municipal committee on race relations.) The commission's director requested Droege to prepare a defence to the allegations. The Heritage Front worked itself into a paroxysm of rage and indignation. Among other things, it circulated leaflets calling on its members to write letters of protest to the commission. Then, in the March 1992 issue of *Up Front*, Droege stated that the telephone messages, recorded by chain-smoking Heritage Front member Gary Schipper on a regular basis, some months after it was established in the fall of 1991, in the bathroom of his east end home, were aimed at "liberal types" and not Natives.

The hate line, which had been operating for several months, featured messages that were, notwithstanding Droege's claims, textbook examples of white supremacist dogma. It was to be stopped by court actions—and inactivity—seven times over the next three years. In

June, the commission ruled that there was merit to the Native Centre's complaint and decided to hold an inquiry into the matter in October 1992. In its June 9 message, Schipper—a confirmed welfare cheat—ridiculed the author of the complaint, anti-racism co-ordinator Rodney Bobiwash. Bobiwash, said Schipper, "is demeaning to his own proud people . . . this maniac is attacking this pro-white hot line . . . this tragic and macabre imposter, complete hogwash Bobbi, if the Heritage Hot Line is unplugged, then so is free speech for white Canada. We will fight back with equal force and conviction against this quasi-judicial farce, we will march on the Human Rights Commission again and again!" In a message recorded the same week, Schipper calls Bobiwash a "coward," "dishonorable," a "professional victim" and "a cigar-store idiot." Another message stated: "Anyone can get scalped, so get ready!"

Apart from the phone line controversy—which would continue in hearings for many months to come and would see the Heritage Front refusing to obey an injunction to shut down the messages—the third issue of *Up Front* was notable for an anti-abortion column by Eric (Stilts) Hartmann, the son of Northern Foundation leader Anne Hartmann. In it, Hartmann, who would go on to provide the voice for Ottawa's own Heritage Front hate line in 1993—a line it shared with the leader of the Ottawa branch of the neo-Nazi National Alliance, Les Griswold—declared that whites are "at war" against abortionists. The article was significant because it directly linked Hartmann's Northern Foundation to the Heritage Front for the first time since the November 1989 founding convention of the foundation in Ottawa. The fourth issue featured quotations from Ernst Zundel and *Stop Apologizing*, the massive white supremacist book penned by Jud Cyllorn, the former aide to Bill Vander Zalm.

The fifth issue of *Up Front*, published in June 1992, featured a cover story on the Toronto race riots, which came on the heels of the acquittal of Los Angeles police officers charged with beating black motorist Rodney King, and provided ample evidence of Droege's and Burdi's increasing militancy. In his editorial, Gerry Lincoln blamed the riots on "insane immigration policies, out-of-control welfare spending and affirmative action programs."

Tucked inside that issue of *Up Front*, significantly, was an appeal for funds by the editor, Gerry Lincoln. In the undated letter, Lincoln noted that the Canadian Human Rights Commission ordered the Front to stop "communicating . . . by telephonic means, messages that are likely to expose persons to hatred or contempt by reason of the fact that those persons are identifiable on the basis of race, national or ethnic origin." In his appeal, Lincoln wrote: "Fighting these charges promises to be a long and expensive process. . . . So we are asking you to please contribute whatever you can to this very important fight in the envelope provided." The legal battle was having consequences.

The cover of the sixth edition of *Up Front* carried a large photograph of White Aryan Resistance (WAR) leader Tom Metzger, who, along with his son John, was illegally smuggled into Canada by armed Heritage Front members. In a five-page article by Gerry Lincoln, complete with photographs of both Metzgers, the Heritage Front described its efforts to run the two neo-Nazis across the border on the evening of June 26, 1992. The group entered Canada at a Fort Erie border crossing; the Metzgers told border guards they were entering Canada to shop. The following evening, the two men addressed a Heritage Front rally at the Latvian Hall on College Street, witnessed by close to 200 cheering neo-Nazis from all over Ontario and New England. The *Up Front* account of the event quoted Metzger as saying WAR was "very upset with the way they have been treating free speech for Aryans in Canada." Metzger heaped praise on Ernst Zundel and Droege, and urged the assembled rightists to make better use of computer and fax technology to disseminate racist propaganda. Metzger was followed by Burdi, who thanked the Metzgers by reading from "In Flanders Fields."

After the rally, the Metzgers climbed into Droege's car. The trio was heading to a party north of Toronto when an RCMP tactical squad stopped their vehicle and arrested the Metzgers. They were held on an Immigration Department warrant alleging that there were

280 WEB OF HATE

grounds to suspect they had entered Canada illegally to commit an indictable offence, namely violating the country's hate laws. The police investigation was led by federal Immigration officials and involved the RCMP, Metro Toronto police, the Ontario Provincial Police and the FBI, as well as police in Los Angeles and San Diego. After the Metzgers' arrest, the Heritage Front mounted a "vigil" at the Don Jail. Following a deportation hearing, they were deported back to the United States on the evening of Thursday, July 2.

The deportation enraged Tom Metzger. On one of July's White Aryan Resistance telephone hate messages, he took aim at Canada: "One of this month's specials is the seditionist, revolutionary and downright nasty Canadian speech that Tom Metzger gave sponsored by the Canadian Heritage Front in Toronto. Yes! The speech that, uh, that branded Tom and John Metzger a national security threat by the Canadian iron heel in Ottawa. A speech that got high-ranking Canadian politicians out of bed in the middle of the night." In the weeks that followed, WAR organized what it called "Operation Canada"—a series of boycotts against Canadian-owned businesses operating in the United States.

Along with an anti-Semitic column by former Texas KKK Grand Dragon Louis Beam, Jr., the August 1992 issue carried a lengthy account of Wolfgang Droege's involvement with the Reform Party. In late February 1991, a reporter exposed in the *Sun* the fact that Droege and four other Heritage Front activists maintained memberships in Toronto-area Reform Party riding associations. Immediately thereafter, Reform leader Preston Manning ordered the group expelled. (The following year, Manning also expelled Northern Foundation president Anne Hartmann for her racist views.) Two of the racists had been appointed to the executive of the party's Beaches-Woodbine riding association; one of these, Alan Overfield, had acted as security at various Heritage Front rallies and—as police learned in November 1992 when they raided his home—maintained a huge stockpile of weapons. Included in the weapons cache were bazooka-style anti-tank rocket launchers, machine guns, assault riles, semi-automatic handguns, bayonets, ammunition and even a few hand grenades. Overfield had enlisted the assistance of Droege, Peter Mitrevski, Grant Bristow and other Front members to provide security at a number of Reform Party rallies in the Toronto area starting in May 1991. "Preston Manning has given us some hope," Droege later told *The Toronto Star*. Also involved in the Beaches-Woodbine riding association were Heritage Front members James Dawson and Nicola Polinuk, Don Andrews's estranged wife.

The expulsions enraged the Heritage Front, which saw the Reform Party's policies as very similar to, if not indistinguishable from, its own. How could a party that went on the record opposing immigration policies that "radically alter" Canada's ethnic make-up turn around and shun a group like the Heritage Front, Droege asked, when the Heritage Front supports the very same approach? Privately, spokesmen for B'nai Brith and the Canadian Jewish Congress admitted that Droege had a good point. In a lengthy article about the Reform Party controversy, *Up Front* stated that Manning and his followers were a pro-white organization that lacked the courage of its convictions: "The Heritage Front threatened the cosy power position of the establishment which Preston Manning and his sycophants now enjoy." The article featured a cartoon of a smiling Droege beating Preston Manning in a boxing ring.

Ironically, the cartoon was not far from the reality. In its December 1994 report into the Grant Bristow controversy, the Security Intelligence Review Committee concluded that Droege secretly wished to discredit the Reform Party. His rationale was simple. "As far as Droege was concerned," SIRC wrote, "the Reform Party was threatening the momentum of the white supremacist movement . . . Droege held a view common to those in the extreme right that the same situation occurred in the United Kingdom when the Conservative Party undermined [the British neo-Nazis'] momentum. Droege wanted to prevent the same situation from happening in Canada." Other white supremacists and neo-Nazis who were aware of Droege's plan, and evidently supported it, included Gerry Lincoln, James Dawson, Ernst Zundel, Peter Mitrevski, Terry Long and Bristow.

Wrote SIRC: "Preston Manning was seen by the white supremacists as an agent of the Zionist Occupation Government, and appeaser of the masses like Margaret Thatcher."

Following the swearing in of the new Parliament, some Reform MPs seemed intent on demonstrating that they *were* a "threat" to Droege's consituency: one, Werner Schmidt, quoted Hitler approvingly in a householder; another blamed Jamaicans for the (fictional) increased crime rate; a third, Herb Grubel, likened Natives to "spoiled children"; and in October 1994, Myron Thompson told an approving Reform convention that he "hated" homosexuality.

The October 1992 issue of *Up Front* highlighted another event that revitalized Ontario's neo-Nazi movement and was a boon to the Heritage Front and the Church of the Creator: the September decision of the Supreme Court of Canada to declare the law under which Ernst Zundel had been charged to be unconstitutional. In its judgment, the court's majority likened what Zundel did—denying the Holocaust and vilifying Jews and non-whites—to an environmental activist mistakenly stating that "the rainforest of British Columbia is being destroyed." The high court's majority, perhaps unaware that there is an appreciable difference between a bona fide mistaken statement about trees and the repeated endorsement of genocide, sent the Heritage Front into an orgy of self-congratulation. Following the judgment, police and social activists noted that *Up Front* became more extreme in its slander of Jews and non-whites. In its cover story on the case featuring a photo of a smiling Zundel beside the banner headline "E.Z. DOES IT!" Gerry Lincoln penned a three-page article about the case, which he called a "landmark decision" that "put to an end [a] nine-year nightmare of terror."

The December 1992 issue carried a cover story on British Holocaust denier David Irving, who entered Canada illegally in October 1992 for a three-week cross-Canada tour. Irving's lawyer, Doug Christie, tried unsuccessfully to prevent him from being deported on the evening of Friday, November 13, 1992. In *Up Front*, the Heritage Front encouraged its readers to contribute to Irving's defence fund, which was being run out of an Adelaide Street post office box.

The cover of the next issue, published in January 1993, lampooned a book about the links between neo-Nazis and foreign governments, *Unholy Alliances*. The lengthy article, by Ottawa white supremacist Steve Dumas, discussed what he asserted was "hatred for the white race." In an interview, the 27-year-old Dumas—a Quebecer with a close relationship to Northern Foundation leader Anne Hartmann, and who, along with Northern Foundation member Geoffrey Wasteneys, was a prodigious writer of "pro-white" letters to the editor—says he contacted the Heritage Front in the fall of 1991 to volunteer his services as a writer: "The Jews have a country of their own—is there anything wrong with that? No, there's not. We want our own country."

On the morning of January 25, 1993, the day that the Canadian Human Rights Commission opened its inquiry into the Heritage Front's hate line, an anti-racism rally was scheduled at Queen's Park. But the rally quickly degenerated into a full-blown riot as members of the far left Anti-Racist Action (ARA) group battled with police. (The ARA is a collection of Trotskyites, Marxists and other left-wingers who insist that force should be used to deal with fascist groups.) The police had been attempting, with not much success, to keep the protestors away from Wolfgang Droege, George Burdi and about 30 Heritage Front members who were heading to the commission hearing. Droege was to be represented at the inquiry by Ken Ernst, a 22-year-old university chemistry student.

Two people were arrested at the demonstration, and the bloody clash was front-page news across the country. As a consequence, it was a tremendous success for the Heritage Front. By casting themselves in the unlikely roles of victims, Droege's group succeeded—against all odds—in making both the police and the anti-racist protestors look bad. The hotline, meanwhile, continued to operate.

The March 1993 issue of *Up Front* carried a detailed report about the January 25 riot. In it, the Heritage Front acknowledged the public relations value that came with the event: "Our hotline was literally ringing off the hook for the next two weeks, with calls of support from all over Canada and border communities in the United States." The same issue contained a column by Dennis Mahon, a White Aryan Resistance activist and Church of the Creator "white beret" who had previously spoken at a February 1992 Heritage Front rally in Toronto before being deported. Mahon attempted to enter Canada again in late January 1993. But before he could meet with Droege, the Oklahoma-based racist leader was arrested at Pearson International Airport and later deported.

The May 1993 issue of *Up Front* contained photographs of Burdi at the April 17, 1993, performance of Rahowa at a Toronto warehouse. The event was filmed by MTV for a special segment on racist rock bands. At one point, a bare-chested Burdi—in a take-off on the old Nancy Sinatra hit "These Boots Are Made for Walking"—bellows: "One of these days these boots are going to stomp all over Jews!" (The next day, Droege, Burdi, Zundel, Jacob Prins and former Canadian National Socialist Party leader Martin Weiche gathered with more than a hundred Heritage Front and Church of the Creator members to celebrate Hitler's birthday at the Latvian Hall.) The May issue featured no fewer than four photographs of Burdi giving speeches or singing, all signifying the growing role of the COTC leader in the Heritage Front.

Later in April, Burdi and Droege travelled to Ottawa to announce the establishment of a Heritage Front chapter for the National Capital Region. Two of its identified spokespersons would be Nicole Poirier, a former federal public servant, and high-school student Len Langill, who would show up in a photograph in the August 9, 1993, issue of *Time* magazine, no less, at a neo-Nazi rally in Pennsylvania.

Droege and Burdi were pleased with themselves. Encouraged by their Ottawa media coup, the pair decided to organize a Rahowa concert in the nation's capital in late May. Nicole Poirier was instructed to contact the Ottawa-Carleton Boys and Girls Club. The club is located in a residential area just west of downtown. Poirier, who was noted for an intense hatred of blacks, called on May 8. She told the Boys and Girls Club that she wanted to rent its Nepean Street hall for a private dance; she did not mention that she planned to fill the hall with dozens of pro-Nazi skinheads. From its Toronto base, the Front then told the press that a Rahowa concert would take place in Ottawa on Saturday, May 29. It would not, however, say where the concert would be taking place.

On the afternoon of the appointed date, Burdi and his band showed up at the Boys and Girls Club and started to unload their equipment off the back of a battered pick-up truck. At this point, the RCMP, the Canadian Security Intelligence Service and the hate crimes unit of the Ottawa police force all knew, with reasonable certainty, where the white supremacists would be gathering. Because the event was not strictly illegal, the police did not interfere. They did, however, stake out the old brick building that served as the Centretown headquarters of the Boys and Girls Club.

At about 7:00 p.m., five blocks southeast, 500 protestors gathered at Minto Park to protest the Heritage Front rally. In attendance were SHARP skins (Skinheads Against Racial Prejudice), Trotskyites and the federal New Democrat candidate in the riding. Throughout the day, members of the International Socialists and the Ottawa District Labour Council had been cruising city streets, looking for large concentrations of skinheads, police or both. At about 7:30, the anti-racist activists concluded that something was about to take place in the three-block-wide area between Lebreton Flats and Nepean Street.

By 8:00 p.m., Droege, Burdi and approximately 60 skinheads were safely tucked inside the hall at the Boys and Girls Club, ready to go. The Church of the Creator's black-shirted "Security Legion" had set up guard posts around the building. Meanwhile, a club employee who watched the skinheads arrive en masse—and feared for his safety—locked himself in a second-floor office and started phoning the club's director of programs, Tim Simboli. By that time, the anti-racist demonstrators had made their way across downtown to the intersection of Bay and Percy streets, just behind the main entrance to the Boys and Girls Club. The protestors carried banners with slogans such as "RACISM IS THE REFUGE OF THE WEAK AND THE AFRAID" and "SAVE OUR LAND! SMASH THE KLAN!" Many chanted: "Hey, hey! Ho, ho! The Heritage Front's got to go!"

Two police cruisers were parked end-to-end across Percy Street to keep the protestors away from the Boys and Girls Club. The dozen police officers present—among them two members of the force's bicycle patrol—fanned out along the front of the building, canisters of pepper spray at the ready. One officer stood at the front door with an enormous German shepherd. The crowd by now had grown to well over 600 people. Some of the protestors hurled curses at the police, demanding that they be allowed to confront the members of the Heritage Front and Church of the Creator. The police, somewhat understandably, did not think this was a very good idea. Suddenly, at 8:25, the crowd surged forward, overwhelming the police. The protestors moved to within 40 feet of the front door and the tension was palpable.

Inside, Burdi's band had taken to the stage. They started to hammer away at their instruments, the sound throbbing through the thick brick walls. The skinheads chugged beer and made fascist salutes. Rahowa ripped through their repertoire.

Outside, meanwhile, eggs started to rain down on the police; a few of the protestors threw rocks, breaking windows above the entrance. Things were getting decidedly out of control. Alicia Reckzin, a tiny mother of two who had been one of the founders of the Ottawa chapter of Anti-Racist Action, spotted Ottawa Heritage Front member Len Langill through club's glass doors. "Come on, I'll take you now, you fuckers," screamed Reckzin, who had previously called for a non-violent demonstration. Her boyfriend, Ottawa SHARP skin Liam McCarthy, joined in, yelling: "Come on! I'll fucking kill you! Real skinheads aren't racists!"

By 8:45, along with more rocks and eggs, fist-sized cherry bomb firecrackers were being thrown at the feet of police. The resulting explosions sounded like gunshots. The cherry bombs, one officer grimly noted, were powerful enough to blow off the fingers of anyone who strayed too close. A few protestors also threw bottles and pushed against the officers who were attempting to maintain a semblance of order.

Some of the anti-racist protestors had now accomplished what, under any other circumstances, should have been impossible: they were making the Heritage Front's members look good. The Trotskyites, SHARP skins and Anti-Racist Action members were itching for a fight; if the Heritage Front did not appear, the police would do. As if to drive home the point, they chanted: "Cops and Klan go hand in hand!"

At 9:00 p.m., after a discussion with the Boys and Girls Club's program director, Tim Simboli, police moved inside to tell Droege and Burdi that their party was over.

At 9:15, when it had become clear that a full-scale riot was imminent, 15 uniformed members of the Ottawa Police Department's riot squad appeared from the east. They marched, single file, to the front of the building, batons drawn. The squad was greeted with a chorus of boos and a new barrage of eggs, but the police officers were unmoved. Their presence had the desired effect. Within ten minutes, the International Socialists had called it a night, and the rest of the crowd started to thin out. At 9:55, even the club-wielding members of Anti-Racist Action seemed prepared to move on. One of the ARA's Toronto leaders grabbed a megaphone and told her followers that "we shut down their fucking rally." The rally, of course, was anything but shut down. But to the ARA, this was a moot point.

"Nazis off the street—that's what we want!" the woman said. "Unfortunately, we do not have the forces to accomplish this right now! Therefore, we should leave in an orderly fashion and not hand a victory over to the cops and the fascists!"

The ARA protestors dispersed, some heading west, towards Bronson Avenue, others heading east, towards Bank Street. At 10:35 p.m., on cue, the riot squad stomped to the Percy Street entrance to the Boys and Girls Club and formed a human wall. Simultaneously, the 60-odd neo-Nazi skinheads poured out of the building, bellowing "White power!" at the few remaining protestors. The Heritage Front and Church of the Creator members scrambled down Percy Street, a small group of reporters and photographers in hot pursuit. A few blocks south, on Cooper Street, the skinheads spotted a group of about 50 anti-racist protestors who had been tailing them from Bronson Avenue, to the west.

Scot Magnish, a reporter from *The Ottawa Sun*, was jogging down Cooper Street when the two sides converged. "The ARA decided to cut them off at the pass," Magnish recalls. "They came in at Cooper Street and, as they did this, the Nazis, the Heritage Front supporters, were coming the other way. The two sides see each other, and this roar goes up, and they start charging each other. Beer bottles start flying. Some of the Heritage Front guys had baseball bats and boards. As they reached each other, the ARA guys realized they were outnumbered and started screaming: 'We're outnumbered! We're outnumbered!' They turn around and start running the other way. And this hail of beer bottles comes down all over the place."

Cooper Street residents could be seen peeking through the blinds of their living-room windows, watching the neo-Nazi skinheads swagger towards Bank Street. Some of the skinheads were urinating on lawns; others were bellowing racist slogans at police. Cooper Street resident Arthur Wilczynfki, an assistant to Shirley Maheu, then the Liberal Party's human rights critic, stepped out of his front door to see what was happening. "I'm not going to put up with this crap on my street," Wilczynfki said.

At Bank Street, the neo-Nazis—led by Droege and Burdi—turned and headed north, towards Parliament Hill. As cars sped by, the Heritage Front and COTC members made fascist salutes and yelled "White power!" at those who lingered long enough to stare.

Ottawa Front member Nicole Poirier whirled on the reporters who were following. "Are you guys on the wrong side of the tracks or what?" she shrieked, her eyes wild with some kind of private madness. "I'm getting fucked by black people, eh? Yeah, you fucking gay people, fuck off!"

At the corner of Cooper and Bank streets, the neo-Nazis paused while a few of their members urinated on an automated teller machine. Arthur Wilczynfki approached one of the skinheads who was wearing a bandana across his face. "You are a goddamn coward, with your mask and your bullying," Wilczynfki said, looking utterly fearless. "Why don't you get the hell out of our city?" Appearing startled, the skinhead, who stood a full head taller than Wilczynfki, backed away. Across the street, another young man yelled: "You're all filled with hatred!"

Unperturbed, the skinheads moved on, Wolfgang Droege leading at the front, George Burdi giving impromptu interviews at the rear. Asked where the ad hoc neo-Nazi parade was headed, Burdi laughed. "Beats me," he said.

A few minutes later, Droege's destination became obvious: Parliament Hill. As the group marched across Wellington Street, one of the skinheads stopped beside a car waiting at a stoplight. The driver was a black man. Leaning against the car, the masked skinhead pointed, and said "You're next." When the traffic light turned green, the black man sped away, his tires squealing. The skinheads laughed.

At about 11:30 p.m., after giving speeches on the Hill, Droege led his troops along the north side of Wellington Street. The anti-racists, meanwhile, kept to the south side, maintaining a respectful distance. Curses were traded back and forth. About eight police cruisers shadowed the two groups; some officers warned passers-by, especially non-whites, to move away as quickly as possible.

The skinheads gathered by the front doors of the Château Laurier hotel, as guests scrambled away. Across the street, near the war memorial, the anti-racists chanted more slogans. A few threw rocks across the street.

Then, at precisely 11:40 p.m., an animal roar filled the air and the skinheads charged towards their detractors, dodging through traffic. "Holy shit!" one police officer yelled. For the next half hour, anarchy reigned along Elgin Street; in places, blood covered the sidewalks. In a matter of seconds, groups of white supremacist skinheads had descended on the slower-moving leftists. Some used their feet and fists; some used small billy clubs they had hidden in the folds of their bomber jackets. As tourists and partygoers looked on in horror, the neo-Nazis savagely beat and kicked whoever got in their way.

One young boy, perhaps no more than 14 or 15, was standing near the ticket office at the National Arts Centre when a group of skinheads approached him. After shoving him, one of the skinheads, a dark-haired Front member who had led the parade down Bank Street with Droege, kicked the boy in the face. He fell to the ground, bleeding from his mouth and nose. Within 30 seconds, police appeared out of nowhere. In a blur of movement, they tackled and handcuffed the Front member and then they threw him into the back of a paddy wagon. A few minutes later, one skinhead approached Alicia Reckzin of Anti-Racist Action, gave a fascist salute, then assaulted her, breaking her nose. Throughout the downtown core, at least five other assaults took place. In one case, Heritage Front members dragged a homeless man by his hair down Slater Street, then kicked him unconscious.

At about midnight, Wolfgang Droege, looking very pleased with himself, led the Heritage Front and COTC members westward.

Their work done, Droege's troops were heading back to their cars, which had been parked on side streets near the Boys and Girls Club. On the way, Droege paused to speak with two reporters. He was smiling.

"I saw people lying in the street, but I don't know what happened to them," Droege said. "The thing is, we never picked up a rock first. They started throwing rocks at us. We said we weren't going to take the first step. We said to the police, let us go out the front door, we'll take care of the problem ourselves. We've got 60 or 70 people inside, just about all of them strapping young guys. But the police insisted."

As George Burdi looked on, Droege said, "We certainly didn't want it to come to this. But they were asking for it."

George Burdi slapped Droege on the back. The two men turned and walked off into the night.

Less than a month later, Burdi was charged with assaulting Reckzin, causing bodily harm. Within days, racists across the United States started up a legal defence fund for him; the fund was organized by COTC members in Los Angeles, FBI sources say. Others charged with assault were Dan Roussell and Geoffrey Sandes, both Ottawa residents. Sandes was imprisoned for three months, placed on three years' probation, and prohibited from associating with racist groups. Roussell received 45 days and three years' probation.

Not even two weeks after the Ottawa riot, the Heritage Front and the Church of the Creator suffered a greater blow. On June 9, the security chief of the Church of the Creator, former Canadian Airborne Regiment member Eric Fischer, was charged with kidnapping, forcible confinement and assault. Along with his brother Carl (Elkar), Fischer was Burdi's right-hand man; CSIS was aware that Fischer had been recruiting within the Canadian military as early as September 1992. Police said a disillusioned member of the Heritage Front had been kidnapped by three men and was taken on a terrifying three-hour van ride around Toronto in which he was tortured for information about missing membership lists. The men allegedly threatened to kill the victim by injecting window-cleaning fluid into his veins. Later, the bleeding and bruised 22-year-old—now under police protection—was dropped off at a hospital. A few hours later, heavily armed members of the Metro Toronto police force's Emergency Task Force surrounded a bungalow on Maxome Avenue, in North York. The house was home to six Church of the Creator members, among them George Burdi. When police stormed into the house to arrest the COTC trio, they found a 12-gauge shotgun, a .45-calibre semi-automatic and a .22-calibre pistol.

A few days later, more trouble. In Toronto's east end, on the evening of June 11, more than 200 anti-racist protestors descended on the run-down rented Bertmount Avenue home of Gary Schipper, voice of the Heritage Front hate line. The group, mostly made up of members of Anti-Racist Action, pelted the house with rocks and eggs and even threw a child's tricycle through a picture window. A few hours later, Droege met with members of his group who were eager to retaliate. About 40 members headed down to Sneaky Dee's, a bar at College and Bathurst streets, known as a haunt for Anti-Racist Action members. Seeing the hulking skinheads pour in, many patrons of the bar scrambled out the door. After about 20 minutes, many of the skins started to leave. One, known only as Adrian, left the bar alone and encountered a group of ARA activists on the north side of College Street.

Droege and two of his veteran members, Chris Newhook and Peter Mitrevski, were patrolling the area in his small car, looking for skinheads who might be in trouble. They spotted Adrian being beaten and pulled up. In the resulting melee, one ARA member was struck in the face with a beer bottle. Another was struck in the face with a flash-light, breaking his jaw in three places. Newhook started swinging a bat at some of the ARA members, who themselves were swinging bicycle chains.

Newhook was later charged and, in August, found guilty of posses-sion of a dangerous weapon—a baseball bat covered with Nordic runes and SS lightning-bolt insignia. He was sentenced to a year in prison. Droege was charged with possession of a dangerous weapon and assault causing bodily harm and ordered free on $15,000 bail only on the condition that he did not associate with Heritage Front mem-bers. Mitrevski was also charged with assault and freed on a $10,000 bail bond.

The twelfth issue of *Up Front*, published in August 1993, dis-cussed, in bloody detail, the May 29 riot in Ottawa. In it, the Heritage Front bragged about the assault on Alicia Reckzin. The anonymous author wrote that Reckzin "was promptly treated to an instant nose job" by "a couple of our men."

With Droege likely to get jail time if convicted for the assault and the Human Rights Commission contempt citation, with Burdi facing an assault charge and a charge of causing a disturbance following a street fight in Ottawa with a group of Iranians, and with senior mem-bers contemplating the very real prospect of a long prison term, the Wolfie and George show may be in its final act. Droege is now con-fined to his Scarborough apartment, unable to associate with the group he helped to create and unable to talk about it to the media. Burdi, meanwhile, has moved back into his parents' home, where he has sworn to sharply reduce his white supremacist activism.

One federal Immigration official who masterminded the deporta-tions of White Aryan Resistance activist Dennis Mahon, as well as David Irving and John and Tom Metzger, puts it this way: "Things were going very nicely for these people for a long time. But then, in the space of about three weeks, all of their senior members and leaders all got charged. It is now reality-check time for these guys. We know from internal sources that they are in a state of total disarray. For them, this is serious stuff."

In August 1994, the cover of one of those "internal sources" nestled within the bosom of the Heritage Front was dramatically blown: Grant Bristow, the Front's security chief, was revealed to be a paid informant of the Canadian Security Intelligence Service (CSIS).

Coming in a traditionally slow-news month, the Bristow allegation—which was neither confirmed nor denied by CSIS, as is its custom—caused a media sensation: it sent the spy agency into damage-control-mode for weeks; it gave rise to suggestions that Bristow (and, by extension, CSIS) had "spied" on the Reform Party, the CBC and various Canadian Jewish leaders; and it dashed any neo-Nazi hopes that Wolfgang Droege and George Burdi would be able to revitalize the remnants of the Heritage Front and the Church of the Creator.

Because neither CSIS nor Grant Bristow were talking to any reporters—Bristow and his wife Kim abruptly abandoned their Mississauga home shortly before the story broke—no one could know, for sure, whether any of the allegations were true. But that did not stop media outlets from turning the Bristow/CSIS story into headline news in the summer of '94.

What little is known about Grant Bristow is intriguing. Along with Droege, he was a co-founder of the Heritage Front and an outstanding security chief. And, by making use of cunning and an impressive array of high-tech espionage gadgets, Bristow successfully kept police agencies distant from the Heritage Front's leadership until the summer of 1993.

Following his April 1989 release from a U.S. prison, Wolfgang Droege returned to Canada, where he renewed his acquaintance with a number of members of Donald Andrews's Nationalist Party of Canada. In late April, Bristow was invited to Andrews's mansion to meet Droege. At the meeting, Droege—who had returned to Canada with little more than the clothes on his back—was offered accommodation, food and shelter. Shortly thereafter, Droege went to work as part-time bailiff for one of Bristow's contacts, Nationalist Party member and gun afficionado Alan Overfield. Bristow and Droege became friends. By July 1989, Bristow had told his CSIS handlers that Droege—who was looking for a more radical white supremacist vehicle than Andrews's Nationalist Party—was musing about forming something called the "Society for the Preservation of the White Race." By August, the favored name had changed to the "White Heritage Front." The "white" designation was later dropped.

Droege liked Bristow. Bristow—who described himself as a "security investigator"—stood well over six feet, sported a moustache, and kept his hair in a neat, military-style cut. He was a reformed alcoholic. When pressed about his origins, Bristow would say that he was an only child, born in Montreal in February 1958, and that his parents were dead. None of this was true: in fact, he was born in Winnipeg, he had at least one brother, and his parents, who were very much alive, had separated during his youth.

Those who knew Bristow recall that he seemed to be paranoid, and almost obsessed with security matters. He surfaced in the Toronto area in the mid-1980s, taking security jobs where he could. In 1989, the year he and Droege met, Bristow was working in the loss prevention department at a security and brokerage firm called Kuehne and Nagel. It was at Kuehne and Nagel he would meet his future wife, Kim Vilon, a secretary. It was also while he was working at Kuehne and Nagel that he would carry on most of his white supremacist activities, only to be dismissed in 1993 when his superiors learned about his position in the Heritage Front. In August 1989, Droege asked Bristow—along with Gerry Lincoln—to join the Front's powerful "inner clique," the Brethren. Bristow agreed.

Those who know Bristow also recall something else: he did not hesitate to profess to despise Jews, non-whites and race-mixers. In fact, he was an outspoken bigot, loudly proclaiming his hatred of all but the likes of Ernst Zundel. He was just what Droege was looking for.

The two men cemented their relationship in August and September

1989, during the all-expenses-paid trip to Libya to celebrate the twentieth anniversary of the revolution that brought Mu'ammar Qadhafi to power. Also in attendance were Andrews's wife, Nicola, and their three-month-old son; future Heritage Front lieutenant Peter Mitrevski; June and Max French; Wayne Elliot; James Dawson; Anne Ladas; in all, seventeen members—ten men, seven women—who were members of the Nationalist Party of Canada.

The white supremacists flew from Toronto to Rome, then from Rome to Malta. There they were loaded onto a converted prison ship and kept in what one member called "a dungeon," separate from left-wingers also heading to Tripoli. Once in Libya, the group stayed at Camp Qadhafi, a tent village a few miles outside the Libyan capital. Bristow spent much of his time shadowing Droege, even taking a few tourist-style photos of the former Klan leader browsing in Tripoli's *souk* market.

Shortly after their arrival, the Canadian neo-Nazis were told by their Libyan hosts they would soon be required to wear Qadhafi-style green uniforms and march in a parade in a nearby stadium. Although Anne Ladas and Max French were eager to comply with the Libyan directive, Droege adamantly refused, apparently regarding the Libyans' demand as offensive. His stance "stimulated a groundswell of support" for his leadership, Bristow would later inform CSIS. Droege's contempt for the gun-toting Libyans greatly impressed many of the white supremacists, and marked the beginning of the end for Don Andrews and his Nationalist Party of Canada.

When returning to Canada on September 4, Droege sat beside Bristow. When Droege noted that Andrews had booked the group to return through Chicago, he was livid. As a condition of his early release from Lompoc Prison in California, Droege had agreed not to return to the United States.

"What are we going to do, Wolf?" Bristow asked him.

"Probably get arrested," Droege replied.

Droege was correct. Once their country of origin became known—it is illegal under U.S. law to visit Libya—all of the Nationalist Party delegation were arrested by officers of the U.S. Immigration and Naturalization Service. In custody, they were strip-searched and had their body cavities probed for contraband; the videotapes they had shot in Tripoli were confiscated by the FBI. The entire group was interrogated over a period of several hours. Later, all of them—except Droege—were allowed through passport control.

Using $1,000 that had been given to the Nationalist Party by Mu'ammar Qadhafi's government, Bristow retained a lawyer for Droege, then returned to Canada. Two days later, Droege himself was permitted to return to Canada through a border crossing at Niagara Falls. Back home in Toronto, Droege conferred with Bristow. "Tensions were high in the Nationalist Party of Canada after the trip to Libya, particularly among those who had gone there," Bristow told CSIS. "People were generally tired and fed up."

By late 1989, Bristow could be seen busying himself as the security chief of the newly-formed Heritage Front. CSIS had formally targetted the extreme right in 1990 as a counter-terrorism measure. Concerned about what a CSIS document declared was "a noticeable shift" towards violence among white supremacists and neo-Nazis, CSIS needed a reliable source who would provide them with intelligence about their "leaders' capabilities in gaining support for their extremist political doctrine in 1990 and beyond. Financing, offshore direction and support, as well as the connections to other groups, will be included as objectives of our investigation." But who could be recruited to take on such a daunting mission?

Grant Bristow had been known to CSIS as early as March 1986, when he passed along some information about the activities of a few Toronto-based consular officers from an unidentified "foreign country." Two of the consulate's officers were later deported.

In February 1987, CSIS's Toronto office asked Bristow to develop a relationship with members of the city's burgeoning far right. By November 1988, around the time that CSIS was getting very "worried about growing [neo-Nazi] recruitment activities," it was noted that Bristow had acquired a number of contracts in white supremacist circles. Bristow, who CSIS regarded as "an outgoing, gregarious individual who was easy to get along with," was asked to take on the far right file full-time.

As the Front's security chief, Bristow was good at his job. Among his specialties were harassment campaigns—for example, breaking into the voice mailboxes and answering machines to steal names and phone numbers of the Heritage Front's adversaries. Often, he travelled abroad to attend neo-Nazi rallies, such as the Aryan Nations' annual World Congress. At these events, he would promote the profile of the Heritage Front, and exchange information with neo-Nazi and white supremacist leaders.

When the Bristow-as-spy story was made public in August 1994, an avalanche of media allegations soon followed. Among them: that Bristow spied for CSIS on postal workers in Toronto in 1989 (in fact, he was merely retained by Kuehne and Nagel to retrieve lost packages); that he spied for CSIS on the Reform Party at rallies in 1991 and 1992 (in fact, Bristow had been asked by Alan Overfield to act as security at a few party events in the Toronto area); and, finally, that he spied for CSIS on CBC researcher Howard Goldenthal in the spring of 1993 (in fact, CSIS had obtained details about Droege's conversation with Goldenthal concerning racists in the Airborne Regiment through non-"human sources"—probably telephone wiretaps).

Only one case of "spying" was verifiable—and it had nothing to do with CSIS. In May 1993, while researching *Web of Hate*, this writer was told that Bristow, using one of his aliases, "Trevor Graham," was posing as a researcher for the book, and attempting to gain access to Canadian Jewish Congress files concerning the neo-Nazi movement. I had previously been given access to those same files.

After consulting with police in Ottawa, who told me that the impersonation attempt would assist Metro Toronto police in bringing Bristow to justice, I called a detective associated with that city's anti-hate unit. Initially, the officer was excited about the prospect of charging Bristow. The detective explained that Bristow had led a "charmed life," always seeming to escape the law—even in 1992, when restricted weapons were found in the trunk of a car transporting Bristow and an American Aryan Nations leader. He said he would get back to me.

The officer didn't. Many days later, when I tracked *him* down, the officer sounded nervous. Despite his earlier enthusiasm, the detective said no action would be taken against Bristow. He thanked me for my concern and hung up.

"Did they decide against charging Bristow because they didn't think the evidence was good enough?" one Canadian Jewish Congress official later asked. "Or was it because he really was a CSIS spy, and they wanted to protect him? I don't think we will ever know."

*

In December 1994, many of the questions surrounding the Bristow case were answered in an exhaustive report by the Security Intelligence Review Committee (SIRC), the government-appointed CSIS watchdog. Unlike many other such reports, which are typically cluttered with bureaucratese and obfuscation, the SIRC report—which ran to more than 300 pages—was unusually frank and clear. It began with a quotation from C. S. Lewis: "Dream furniture is the only kind on which you never stub your toes or bang your knee." This set the theme for the report itself, which found that while Grant Bristow may have occasionally strayed too close to breaking the law, the work undertaken by Bristow and his CSIS handlers in 1989 "deserved praise."

Wrote SIRC: "We are satisfied that both [Bristow] and his handlers in this 'affair' discharged their duties in a competent and reasonable manner. Both men, throughout this period, believed that they were doing valuable work helping to protect Canadian society from a cancer growing within. They deserve our thanks."

In preparing its report, SIRC interviewed or contacted 121 people, many of them more than once. It pored through a mountain of documents, including "every CSIS file, every internal memo, all reports, threat assessments, reports to the Minister, reports to police forces and other government agencies, and all other documents having anything whatsoever to do with the 'Heritage Front Affair.'"

Making use of names, dates, places and facts—all elements that had been largely absent from the early reporting on the Bristow/CSIS connection—the report dispassionately blew to bits innumerable media claims alleging Bristow spied on the CBC, postal workers and the Reform Party of Canada, among other things. Of the CBC allegation, first printed by *The Toronto Star*, SIRC's members were blunt: "CSIS did not spy on the CBC, its journalists or any other employees." Of the postal workers' allegation: "We have conducted detailed reviews of all CSIS activities and all of its targets for ten years. We were aware, therefore, that the CBC's story that CSIS was spying on, or had spied on, the postal workers was not true . . . we have seen no evidence whatsoever that CSIS investigated the Canadian Union of Postal Workers." (To its credit, CBC later retracted the story.)

The Reform Party allegation—namely, that Bristow had spied on Preston Manning's movement at the behest of the then-Conservative government of Brian Mulroney—carried a certain amount of political difficulty with it. If even only partially true, it was an explosive story—a massive political scandal. SIRC's members were therefore aware that anything less than a thorough airing of the facts would be dismissed by Manning as a whitewash (ironically enough, on the day of the report's release, Manning did precisely that). As such, SIRC devoted much more time to verifying this allegation. In its report, the committee painstakingly reviewed every piece of innuendo and gossip relating to Bristow and the Reformers. It found that, after learning of Droege's secret plan to discredit Preston Manning, CSIS had ordered Bristow to observe four rules. First, he was told he was not to join the Reform Party. Secondly, CSIS was concerned about any unpleasantries the Front had planned. If any such events were about to take place, Bristow was instructed to inform his handlers immediately. Thirdly, he was only to collect information on what the Heritage Front was doing *to* the Reform Party, and nothing about what the Reform Party *itself* was doing. And, finally, he was explicitly forbidden from reporting on the Reform Party itself.

SIRC found that Bristow observed these rules to the letter. While

SIRC was somewhat critical of CSIS for taking "too long" to instruct Bristow to keep his distance from the Reformers, it also dismissed media claims that Bristow spied on the party. Wrote SIRC: "Our review of the documentation at CSIS and our interviews of employees have established beyond a reasonable doubt that [Bristow] did not report on any Reform Party activities. There was absolutely no credible evidence that CSIS was acting on the basis of political direction when [Bristow] reported on the activities of the Overfield security group."

Finally, after interviewing this writer about Grant Bristow's "Trevor Graham" ruse, SIRC spoke to Bristow, who was—and remains—in hiding. The Review Committee's members found that Bristow *had* represented himself to at least one Toronto Jewish group—the Jewish Student Network—using the false name. Wolfgang Droege told SIRC, under oath, that Bristow "felt it was important for us to find out as to what information [the Jewish Student Network] possessed. So he was going to try to infiltrate them or at least try to gather information from them."

Bristow denied this, telling SIRC that the Heritage Front leader had been the one who had suggested investigating the Jewish Student Network. After making a few half-hearted attempts to acquire some membership data—using this writer's name—Bristow told his CSIS handler about the incident, and moved on. SIRC did not comment on the matter positively or negatively.

9

SKINHEADS

With their close-cropped hair, their skin-tight Levi's, their clip-on braces, their Ben Sherman shirts and their sartorial trademark—eight-eyelet Air Wear Doc Marten boots, in black, brown or cherry and shined to a mirror finish—the skinheads have always inspired fear. Fear, after all, was the skinheads' *raison d'être*. As University of London professor Dick Hebdige notes in Nick Knight's photographic retrospective, *Skinhead*, the skins were "designed to make anyone who has even the smallest stake in the present scheme of things cross over to the other side of the street."

Later, of course, the skinheads would become known for other things, among them a penchant for neo-Nazism and white supremacy. But in the beginning, on the cluttered, noisy streets of southeast London in 1966, skinheads were about a look, and not much else. And the look—what Hebdige calls "aggressively proletarian, puritanical and chauvinist" in his own ground-breaking book, *Subculture: The Meaning of Style*—was indeed fearsome. As one British writer put it in the early days: "The sight of cropped heads and the sound of

heavy boots entering the midnight bar or dance hall is cause for sink-
ing feelings in the pit of the stomach." For many British in the late
1960s—and for many more in the present—these scarred, tattooed
and hard-living young men were the very personification of Fear.

It was not always so. The skinheads' sociological antecedents were
the Teddy Boys, a distinctive youth subculture that swept Britain in
the early 1950s. The Teds were young men drawn exclusively from
the British working class who escaped the monotony of schooling or
dead-end unskilled labor jobs with a style of dress that was as inspired
as it was iconoclastic. The Teddy Boys favored long Edwardian coats,
tight trousers, suede shoes, bootlace ties and greased-back hair, in the
style of Elvis Presley and Gene Vincent. To the likes of Presley and
Vincent they were devoted, cramming into sweaty dance halls to
swing to Presley's "Heartbreak Hotel" or Vincent's "Be-Bop-A-Lula."

The Teddy Boys, however, were not just about dancing, or dressing
up like dandies. The Teds were energetically, and unapologetically,
racist, beating up non-white immigrants whenever and wherever possible. In particular, they terrorized Britain's West Indian community,
ostensibly because they feared the loss of jobs—jobs that, on most
other occasions, they professed to loathe. The Teds figured prominently, Hebdige notes, in Britain's 1958 race riots. But that was to be
their last hurrah.

In the 1960s, the Teddy Boys were overtaken by a new subculture,
the Mods. These young men and women made up a somewhat more
exclusive underground movement that favored snappy Italian suits,
oversized army parkas and neat haircuts. During the day, the Mods busied themselves with mind-numbing clerical jobs and the like. But at
quitting time—and especially whenever a long weekend rolled
around—the Mods hopped onto their elaborately decorated Vespa or
Lambretta scooters and slid into a nether world of boutiques, cellar
clubs and record shops. For fun, they were not above the odd beach
resort riot. But unlike the Teddy Boys, whom they despised, the Mods
were proudly anti-racist. They were, in fact, great admirers of blacks.
They snatched up soul records imported from the United States—gems

like James Brown's "Papa's Got a Brand New Bag"—and they whipped themselves across the dance floors with amphetamine-enhanced abandon. Writes Hebdige: "[To the Mods] work was insignificant, irrelevant; vanity and arrogance were permissible, even desirable qualities, and a more furtive and ambiguous sense of masculinity could be seen to operate. . . . It was the Black Man who made all of this possible: by a kind of sorcery, a sleight of hand, through 'soul,' he had stepped outside the white man's comprehension."

Like all good things, the Mods could not, and did not, last. By 1966, they had split into two distinct groups. One was more self-consciously trendy, with a fondness for art school and the Carnaby Street scene. The other group, called the Gang Mods—or, most often, the Hard Mods—favored a tougher look and a tougher lifestyle. The Hard Mods, writes Nick Knight, "needed clothes that would not get torn in a fight, which would stay pressed and neat, and which would identify them in a crowd. Donkey jackets, army greens, tough working jeans, industrial boots and braces fitted this need."

By 1972, the skinheads could be seen everywhere on the streets of London. This time, they would remain. Their uniform, too, would remain unchanged: tight, rolled-up jeans; suspenders; the trademark haircut; and, of course, Doc Marten boots. Docs, as they are known, were developed by a German podiatrist named Klaus Martens who wanted a sturdy and comfortable shoe for people who were on their feet all day. For decades, Doc Martens were tremendously popular in Britain, worn by policemen and housewives alike. They were first spotted on North American sidewalks in 1974, when Canadian shoe designer John Fluevog imported a few pairs for sale at his Vancouver store. It was these distinctive boots, above all else, that skinheads cherished. Sometimes they would kill for them. In the 1980s, special significance was also attached to the laces used by racist Doc Martens' enthusiasts. Red laces on Doc Martens meant the wearer was a neo-Nazi. White laces meant that he or she was a white supremacist. Yellow laces, reportedly, came to mean the owner had killed a police officer.

304 WEB OF HATE

Interestingly, a growing number of young women came to be associated with the skinhead movement at this time. Along with the Doc Martens and heavy eye-liner, these women were distinguished by their distinctive hairstyles: shaved on top, à la skinhead, but with a fringe framing the face. The fringe was often bleached blond, for that Aryan poster girl look. On a good day, a skingirl's hairdo bears a striking resemblance to a Lhasa apso.

The skins, like the Teddy Boys before them, were self-consciously proletarian, violent and racist. By the summer of 1972—and as if in confirmation of the end of their uneasy alliance with the Rude Boys (West Indian Youths)—the skinheads were leading unprovoked attacks on second-generation blacks in Liverpool and elsewhere. Like the Teds, this new generation of skinheads professed to be pro-British; they sported Union Jack tattoos; and, with greater and greater frequency, they terrorized non-white immigrants, whom they saw as a threat to their economic security. It was inevitable that the skinheads would start to attract the attention of recruiters from the pro-Nazi British Movement and the National Front. Using dollops of anti-immigrant, anti-Communist, anti-Semitic and anti-IRA sentiment, the British Movement and National Front lured more than a few skinheads into their ranks.

Four years later, in the summer of 1976, the skinheads—racist and non-racist—were experiencing a dramatic renaissance thanks to the burgeoning punk rock movement. The skins, however, were a full-fledged youth subculture of their own. Although they would occasionally socialize with the punks, who favored spiked hair, Mohawk cuts and a characteristic brand of political nihilism, they also patronized their own musical heroes. Groups in the skinhead musical pantheon included Madness and bands on the Two-Tone record label. Madness played many of the old ska numbers first made famous by Prince Buster and others; the group's motto was "Fuck art—let's dance!" It was, however, strongly anti-fascist.

Another tremendously popular band with the skinhead crowd in the late 1970s was Sham 69. Led by the charismatic singer Jimmy Pursey, Sham 69 was no ska or bluebeat revival group. As with the early Clash and Sex Pistols recordings that inspired it, Sham 69 offered its fans—called the Sham Army—gloriously raw punk-style anthems. "Skinheads are back!" Pursey would declare at various Sham 69 gigs, until that cry started to attract skinhead British Movement and National Front members. Following a disastrous concert at the London School of Economics that was disrupted by neo-Nazis, Pursey and Sham 69 abandoned the skins, just as Madness had done. For a time, a few other British bands boasted skinhead followings. Some, like Bad Manners, favored the ska sound, which featured choppy, echo-laden guitars; many others, such as Cockney Rejects and Angelic Upstarts, were second-generation punk rockers. But all condemned the growing fascist inclinations of their skinhead followers.

This left the skinheads searching for a new set of musical heroes. In time, the skinhead "market" seized on a gritty new musical phenomenon, called Oi, which was an old Cockney greeting. The Oi trend, which was championed by *Sounds* magazine and almost no one else, was raw, fast and basically tuneless. Despite that, Oi bands drew huge skin followings. Not all were racist; some, like Cocksparrer and Oi Polloi, were in fact proudly anti-Nazi. However, the most popular, and most racist, of the Oi bands was Skrewdriver. Led by Ian Stuart Donaldson, a burly National Front organizer, Skrewdriver churned out noisy pub-style chants with lyrics like the ones found in "When the Boat Comes In":

> Put up a fence,
> Close down the borders,
> They don't fit in,
> In our new order.

In another Skrewdriver hit, the subtly titled "Nigger Nigger," Stuart, as he is known, bellows:

> Nigger, nigger, get on that boat
> Nigger, nigger, row!

> Nigger, nigger, get out of here
> Nigger, nigger, go go go!

With the neo-Nazi skinhead set, Skrewdriver's most popular song was "White Power":

> I stand and watch my country
> Going down the drain
> We are all at fault now,
> We are all to blame.
> We're letting them take over,
> We just let them come,
> Once we had an Empire,
> Now we've got a slum.

Along with the records, Skrewdriver's White Noise organization sold tapes, videos, badges and T-shirts. Out of these sales, the National Front realized a substantial income. Within time, other skinhead bands started to make their way into small recording studios to memorialize other Skrewdriver-style gems. Some of the better-known British skinhead bands included Brutal Attack, Skullhead, Prime Suspects, Sudden Impact, and British Standard. Eventually, the Oi phenomenon made the jump across the English Channel to Europe. There, skinhead bands popped up in Sweden (Ultimathule), France (Brutal Combat) and Germany (Bohse Onkelz).

The transition from ska-loving Hard Mods to violently racist skinheads was complete. For a decade, British Movement and National Front organizers had dedicated themselves to skinhead recruitment. Their efforts paid off. By 1980, the British skinhead movement was almost entirely fascist; a decade later, the same could be said of the North American skins. While it remains true that not all skins are fascists—the Skinheads Against Racial Prejudice (SHARP) are a notable exception—it is also true that the vast majority have had some degree of involvement in racist activity.

Most observers of the skinhead phenomenon assert that the racist skinhead movement did not spread to North American shores until about 1984, when the Chicago-Area Skinheads (CASH)—or, as they were known then, Romantic Violence—rented a post office box and started marketing pro-Nazi propaganda and T-shirts. But the fact is that isolated groups of neo-Nazi skinheads were active in major Canadian and American cities as early as 1980. In the spring of 1980, for example, the vibrant Calgary punk rock scene was shattered by the increasing visibility of violent pro-Nazi skinheads at privately organized concerts. In Ottawa and Toronto in the same year, Rock Against Racism concerts were organized by local punkers and left-ists to voice concern about, in part, the growing pro-Nazi element in the Canadian alternative music scene.

By the mid-1980s, Canadian racist leaders, whose temples had been growing decidedly grey under their pointed white hoods, were recruit-ing skinhead members on a wide scale. The hate movement leaders regarded the skinheads as ideal recruits because they were everything those same leaders were not: they were young, they were numerous and they were more than willing to do battle with the enemy. Conversely, the skinheads were attracted to the Canadian hate move-ment because it provided them with those things they desired the most: a sense of identity, a common set of goals and a legitimization of their bigotry. As the British Movement and the National Front had recog-nized a decade earlier, it was a match made in racist heaven. Overnight, the influx of skinheads revitalized a Canadian hate movement that had been experiencing little or no growth.

Racist leaders in Canada and the United States do not often agree on much. They are a fractious, catty group who frequently spend as much time criticizing each other as they do Jews or non-whites. But on one point, there is unanimous agreement: for them, the skinhead movement was a godsend.

Richard Butler, of the Church of Jesus Christ Christian Aryan Nations, calls the skinhead/hate movement union "inevitable" and "Divine will." "It's happening not only in Canada and the United States, it's happening in Belgium and Holland and France and Norway and Sweden and Australia and New Zealand and South Africa. It's happening wherever white men are. All of a sudden the white race is beginning to awaken. After World War Two, you in Canada were forced to let in anything that walked and give them welfare. [Non-whites] are raping the citizens of Canada, raping the citizens of the United States. They are trampling across your borders to destroy your culture and everything else. I think the young people are now starting to awaken to that fact."

Carl Franklin, Butler's likely successor and the Aryan Nations' lacklustre chief of staff, says skinheads "are the best recruits you can get." He says the Aryan Nations has sponsored many Youth Fests at its Hayden Lake headquarters. One such event in April 1991 attracted 20 Canadian skinheads, he says, adding: "They are very receptive to our message. A lot of them aren't getting answers from their teachers or ministers or parents. The young are the quickest to learn, and they are the future of the racist right. In my opinion, we have one of the best generations of white youth in history, right now. They are primed to take their homelands back. I don't think anything will stop them."

White Aryan Resistance leader Tom Metzger, whose Fallbrook, California, hate group has built up a formidable network of neo-Nazi skins across the United States, agrees. But he is openly critical of hate movement leaders who, he says somewhat disingenuously, "manipulate" the skinheads. "I just don't want to see the old right wing—that has been a failure for 50 years—take a whole new breed of young people down the same path they've been on," says Metzger with a straight face. "Many of these people in the right wing use the skinheads. Once they saw that the skinheads were around, they said, 'Yep, we'll pick these guys up and use them for bodyguards and so on and so forth, and if anything goes wrong, we'll say it's their fault.' Which has happened on several occasions. That to me is disgusting. A lot of these older guys wouldn't sit down in their own houses with the skinheads, but they'll use them just to get their muscle."

Terry Long, whose Canadian Aryan Nations' branch in Alberta has acquired more skinhead support in western Canada than any other hate

group in that region, says skinheads "are very much the new generation." And he insists that he, for one, has invited many skinheads to
his home, where they have bunked down when on the run from the
law. Says Long: "The skinheads are rejecting everything that their
fathers and their grandfathers have taught them in the last 50 years—
all of the lies that they've been taught. They realize the hypocrisy of
our current system, and they're reacting by accepting everything previous generations have rejected—in particular Adolf Hitler and
National Socialism. They figure that if their fathers didn't like Adolf
Hitler, then Adolf Hitler must be good, and they're absolutely right."

Long likens the sharp growth in neo-Nazi skinheads—the B'nai
Brith's League for Human Rights estimates there are now more than
1,000 in Canada—to the intifada uprising in Palestine. "The skinheads are a spontaneous uproar, a rejection of everything that our
present so-called democratic system stands for, which is only democratic for Jews, queers and niggers. We've now got a number of
skinhead members. Since 1987, we've obtained members from all
across Canada from the skinhead movement, and we're very
impressed. This thing has progressed from just a handful to thousands in just the past two years. It's totally spontaneous, and the
Jews can't stop it, and that's what is driving them crazy." He pauses.
"They are the new order."

Back east, the refrain is much the same. Don Andrews of the
Nationalist Party of Canada met with dozens of skinhead recruits once
a week in a Metro Toronto doughnut shop from 1987 to 1990. Pressed
about these recruitment drives, Andrews says: "Okay, we've been
meeting in various doughnut shops and Druxy's and McDonald's and
what have you. We had over 75 skinheads in one McDonald's a few
Saturdays ago. We just come in and have a coffee with the skinheads,
and they are all over the place and they are very mannerly. They are
learning to be the new princes and princesses of the future." He laughs.

Another central Canadian right-wing leader is Paul Fromm. A
Toronto public school teacher for two decades, Fromm cofounded the
Edmund Burke Society with Andrews in 1967 and the Western Guard in

1972. He currently leads two far right groups, the Canadian Association for Free Expression and Citizens for Foreign Aid Reform, and recently was disciplined by his school board employers for speaking at a December 1990 Heritage Front rally commemorating the death of Silent Brotherhood leader Bob Mathews. Fromm, who held a "Dominion Day celebration" with Toronto skinheads in 1989, says: "There's no doubt about it, a lot of young people are getting involved, and a lot of them are skinheads. When I first got involved in the right wing, it used to be something of a joke that, if you were under the age of 40, they'd appoint you the head of the youth wing. Certainly some groups on the right had trouble attracting young people. I would say that, since 1986 or so, is not really the case any longer."

Canadian skinhead Peter Mitrevski offers the last word on the subject. Mitrevski, born in 1967, is already a veteran in Canadian racist circles, having served on the Nationalist Party's Advisory Council as well as the Heritage Front's organizing staff. Asked why he became a racist skinhead, Mitrevski reflects for a moment, then says: "You look around today, and the white faces are disappearing. Every other race has a homeland. Why shouldn't we?"

Asked what he knows about the good old days in Britain, when skinheads/Hard Mods weren't racist at all and everyone got along, Mitrevski laughs. "I've always liked the music, so I shaved my head in 1987," he says. "But times have changed.

"If there is anything to be done, the skinheads will always be there. Nobody else is going to help the white race. We have to make the move ourselves. And we skinheads are making our move right fucking now."

One muggy evening in July 1989, Mark Bauer and his three skinhead buddies sprawled on a few chairs at the back of the General's Pump, a British-style pub on Sussex Drive in downtown Ottawa. Waiting for their guest—a writer—to set up his tape recorder, they order a few pints of Toby and Carlsberg and crack unfunny jokes about the police and the justice system.

"I don't believe we are committing any crime," says Bauer, who is the leader of the Ottawa chapter of the Aryan Resistance Movement (ARM). "I believe we are trying to establish a belief in white pride— not white supremacy or bigotry. We are true racists, not bigots."

Bauer's three chums, who refuse to identify themselves, giggle about their leader's coy references to crime and criminals. Bauer and his friends apparently believe that the writer does not understand the significance of unflattering references to particular judges. But in this, as in other things, they are incorrect.

One month before, Bauer—along with his friends Brian McQuaid, 19, of Southgate Road in Ottawa, and a 16-year-old young offender who cannot be named under federal law—were in court to face a charge of criminal negligence causing bodily harm. In September 1987, the three crammed into the cab of a pick-up truck and cruised the back- roads of Manotick, a small community south of Ottawa. At Cars Bridge, near Bond's Marina, they fired off seven .22-calibre bullets at a boat docked below in the Rideau River. They caused $1,000 damage.

Later, as they neared Manotick Station Road, the three young men pulled out the .22 and opened the truck window again.

Bauer or one of his friends pointed the gun at the home of Jaajpe Ladan, one of Manotick's few non-white immigrants, and fired. At that moment, Ladan was sitting in her living room, watching televi- sion. She was struck in the face by a bullet. Hearing the living-room picture window break, Bauer and his pals roared off into the night, laughing. Incredibly, Ladan would recover from her injuries.

Seven months later, the crime was still unsolved. But in May 1988, the Crimestoppers program broadcast a small segment about the attack on local television stations. A few days later, an anony- mous caller telephoned the Ontario Provincial Police to name Bauer and his friends as the gunmen. After their arrest by the OPP, the skinhead trio pleaded guilty in Provincial Court.

In the hearing, there was no discussion of the significance of three neo-Nazi skinheads shooting a non-white woman in the face. Nor was there any discussion of the fact that the three accused maintained links to ultra-violent far right organizations, and whether that fact was perhaps an aggravating factor that the presiding judge should consider.

Instead, James Harbic, lawyer for the young offender, in effect told the court that his client was just as much a victim as Jaajpe Ladan. "Up until he was sixteen, or sixteen-and-a-half, [the young offender] always appeared to be a well-rounded adolescent," Harbic told the court. "However, he then fell in with an unfortunate peer group."

Calling gun-toting neo-Nazi skinheads "an unfortunate peer group" is, some might argue, a bit of an understatement. But, as defence counsel, Harbic was simply doing his job—and doing it well. Jaajpe Ladan got a bullet in the face; while Mark Bauer and his friends got a judicial slap on the wrist. The three were handed two-year suspended sentences and ordered to keep away from each other.

A few weeks later, sitting in a dark corner at the General's Pump, Bauer and his buddies toss back a few more beers. Bauer, who was born in October 1967, is a confident and articulate young skinhead. He sports close-cropped dark hair and no visible tattoos. A product of public schools in Nepean, a small community next to Ottawa, Bauer became active in white supremacist circles in 1986, when he was 19. "Back in '86, Mark was getting pretty powerful with local skinheads," says Liam McCarthy, who founded the Ottawa branch of Skinheads Against Racial Prejudice when he was 16. "By 1987, he was starting to get people off drugs and shit. He was pretty dedicated." Another anti-racist skinhead, Scott Bristow, recalls that Bauer's neo-Nazi skinheads numbered about ten or twelve in 1986. All of them, except Bauer, lived in a rented property they called the Warehouse, on York Street in downtown Ottawa. "They all hung out around the Byward Market back then," recalls Bristow. "They were just skinheads back then. There was no Ku Klux Klan or Heritage Front or anything like that. It was all based on the British skinhead movement. It wasn't a North American Nazi skin thing at all."

From the start, Bristow and McCarthy agree, Mark Bauer distinguished himself as a natural leader. He counselled his peers who were experiencing trouble at home or at school; he loaned them money when they needed it; and, most of all, he lectured them about the perils of drug abuse. Says Bauer of drugs: "We don't want any of that kind of lifestyle. A lot of skinheads are just punk rockers with shaved heads and boots, and they walk around saying they are skinheads. We are the skinheads. We are the real skinheads. We are working-class, white, racially conscious youth. That is a skinhead: white working-class youth. Anybody who is proud of his race and culture and heritage is just going to fuck up his life by doing drugs."

They seem impressed with themselves, these young skinheads. In just a few months, they have come far.

The Ottawa branch of the Aryan Resistance Movement—a loose grouping of neo-Nazi skinheads with its base in Mission, B.C.—went "public" in March 1989, when "moderate fascist" David Irving came to town. One bitterly cold night, Irving was taken to the Château Laurier Hotel by two prominent local anti-Semites, Ian Verner Macdonald and Ingrid Beisner. Macdonald, a former Canadian trade diplomat, was also a policy adviser to the Grand Wizard of the Canadian Knights of the Ku Klux Klan; Beisner is a Kemptville, Ontario, housewife who raises funds for Toronto neo-Nazi Ernst Zundel and prints up copies of "Did Six Million Really Die?" on a photocopier in her basement.

Irving's speech in a gilt drawing room drew more than 300 Holocaust deniers and anti-Semites. Irving described himself to them as a "hardcore disbeliever" in the gas chambers used to exterminate Jews at Auschwitz. His audience applauded wildly at every anti-Semitic remark he made, and they snapped up autographed copies of his books. At the back of the room, keeping a watchful eye over the proceedings, were Mark Bauer and a half-dozen broad-shouldered members of his chapter of the Aryan Resistance Movement.

At the end of the evening—after about 50 members of the International Socialists tried, unsuccessfully, to disrupt Irving's speech—Mark Bauer and his buddies relaxed. As harried-looking hotel staff looked on, hoping that the skins would leave, Bauer and his buddies leaned against the walls of the drawing room. When the

police were a safe distance away, Bauer reached into his bomber
jacket and pulled out a copy of a small pro-Nazi magazine called
Canada Awake! Produced by Bauer and a few supporters in Montreal
and Ottawa, the 24-page publication described itself as "a pro-white
publication [that] is printed for all white nationalists. We do not produce
'hate literature,' our publication is for the advancement of the white
man. . . . We believe in peace among our own race, in an exclusively
white land. We do not hate other races, but demand segregation. . . . A
holy land of our own." In his editorial, Bauer thanked a number of
racist groups and leaders for their contributions to *Canada Awake!*—
among them Don Andrews, Terry Long, Tom Metzger's White Aryan
Resistance and the Chicago-Area Skinheads.

The first edition of Bauer's magazine featured reviews of recordings by Nazi skinhead bands Skrewdriver and No Remorse; a pro-
motional blurb for the Nationalist Party of Canada; an interview with
a member of the British Movement; a review of media coverage of
the skinhead movement; an interview with international Aryan
Nations leader Richard Butler; reviews of books about white
supremacy; and a listing of addresses for a number of neo-Nazi and
white supremacist groups. None of the articles were signed.

The second issue of *Canada Awake!* was published in June
1989 and, compared to its predecessor, was a good deal more
overt about its Nazism. Above the first article, which discussed
the need for better "white nationalist" leaders in Canada, Bauer
reproduced a large swastika alongside the words "DEATH TO RACE
MIXERS!" The article read: "There are those who are helping individuals to prepare themselves for a racial awakening. Take for
instance Don Andrews and his Nationalist Party, or Terry Long,
founder of the Canadian Aryan Nations. Already we have leaders
and an oligarchy who will accept the responsibility of guiding our
people through a race revolution."

The rest of the issue contained a three-page interview with Long;
more record reviews; an editorial by Bauer titled "Save Your Race";
an interview with the leader of the Confederate Hammerskins in

Dallas, Texas (complete with photographs of their members making Nazi salutes and fondling handguns); a brief history of the Ku Klux Klan; a profile of Thom Robb's Arkansas-based KKK; a listing of more addresses, among them David Duke's National Association for the Advancement of White People, the Aryan Nations and neo-Nazi organizations based in England, Australia and the United States; and, finally, a fawning tribute to Hitler on the occasion of his 100th birthday:

> In time, the truth will become widely known. The fairy tales will be laid to rest. We will remember a man with an incredible ambition to reunite his country and bring it out of poverty. A man who wanted the best for one of the world's greatest empires. A man who dared to envision a new white race which strove for success and new heights.
>
> Hitler's accomplishments are still unchallenged. No white society has the same socially successful programs that existed in Nazi Germany. Instead, we live in mostly money-driven, racially polluted, crime infested, dog-eat-dog societies with crooked, dishonest governments. Adolf Hitler didn't die in 1945, he became immortal. He will be remembered throughout time. ADOLF HITLER, WE SALUTE YOU!!!

Mark Bauer flips through the second issue of his magazine, then passes it to one of the other skinheads present, a short and stocky man named Dan. Bauer grins. "The idea of *Canada Awake!* is to give a true platform to organizations that don't have such a platform," says Bauer. "They have their own stuff which they put out, but the Nationalist Party, the British Movement, the Aryan Nations, the Klan, whatever other movement there is, they don't have a regular platform in Canada. We're just giving them that platform, and wider circulation.

"It doesn't mean we particularly endorse these groups, that we agree with these groups, or that we disagree. We are just giving them a platform."

Bauer explains that *Canada Awake!* is designed to reach out to young men and women who are interested in racist organizations but lack the means to find out about them. It is, in a sense, a catalogue of neo-Nazi and white supremacist groups. Readers can browse through its pages and write away for more information or, ideally, membership cards. Other such magazines are produced by ARM branches in St. Catharines and Mission, he says. All are firmly committed to Nazi doctrine. "I'm a National Socialist," Bauer says. "And I believe we have the truth. I am very happy with what I believe in. They are going to have to shoot me to change me."

When Manuel Prutschi got his hands on the first two editions of *Canada Awake!*, however, he did not necessarily want to shoot Mark Bauer. But Prutschi, who at the time was national director of community relations for the Canadian Jewish Congress, was upset. He wrote letters of complaint to the director of the Ontario Provincial Police General Investigations Branch. More than a year later, in August 1990, one of the many counsel toiling at the office of the provincial attorney-general wrote to Prutschi indicating that an OPP investigation had found "no evidence" of an "intent to promote hatred against an identifiable group on the part of the publishers and distributors of *Canada Awake!*" With its tributes to Hitler, its Holocaust-denial and its "demand" for racial segregation, it is difficult to imagine what the Ontario attorney-general had in mind when his bureaucrats determined that *Canada Awake!* was not promoting hatred against anybody. But Mark Bauer, for one, does not give the system credit for much intelligence.

"They're all idiots," he says, laughing. He points at a copy of his magazine. "You notice we don't make any threats in here. We don't threaten anybody. This is the funny thing, though: all these groups think we're the threat. I can't understand why it's a threat when white people get together and are proud of being white. The Jew thinks that's a threat, because then the white man is going to see through his lies and his deceit." He laughs again. "Idiots."

In July 1989, Mark Bauer and his friends in the Aryan Resistance Movement decided to display their "pride" in a forum that was not

nearly as anonymous as *Canada Awake!* In that month, Bauer organized security at the Save Our Canada Day Festival, a July 1 and 2
get-together for what was described as "white kinsmen and skinheads."
Posters advertising the event, circulated around Toronto, Montreal and
Ottawa, stated that the whites-only festival would be held at "Miles
North—the White Man's Mission near Minden, Ontario." Two skinhead bands, Cross and Cyclone, would be performing at the event. And
at midnight on July 1, posters read, "a 'light' will burn in honor of
Canada's birthday." Admission was $20, paid in advance.

Miles North was the name for the two-acre homestead rented by
John Beattie, former leader of the Canadian Nazi Party. The tree-lined
property was a short drive from Minden, a town of 2,000 in the heart
of Ontario's cottage country. Since 1987, Beattie had lived in a small
cottage on Bobcaygeon Road with his wife, Hazel, a nursing home
worker, and the couple's three children. Beattie was not well known in
Minden, although he occasionally demonstrated a loud fondness for
drink at the town's Legion Hall. Originally from Saint John, New
Brunswick, Beattie started to organize pro-Nazi rallies in Toronto in
1965. One rally, at Allan Gardens in that first year, ended in a riot
when 5,000 protestors mobbed Beattie and his puny band of followers.
In 1978, after his Canadian Nazi Party had fallen apart, Beattie teamed
up with former Western Guard leader John Ross Taylor. The two
aging anti-Semites formed something called the British People's
League, which opposed non-white immigration policy and idolized Sir
John A. Macdonald.

For Beattie, the 1989 Save Our Canada Day Festival was not the
first of its kind. A similar event, held in 1988, attracted only ten
skinheads. But in 1989—thanks to an avalanche of media coverage
in the days leading up to Canada Day, and thanks to the organizational efforts of Mark Bauer and other skinhead leaders—Beattie
drew three dozen uniformed Ontario Provincial Police officers, two
dozen reporters and more than 200 neo-Nazi skinheads. In the only
interview he gave before the event, Beattie said: "I'm having a party
here, that's all. I had a party here last year."

"I had a past in the sixties," Beattie added. "I was known as a white supremacist. But I have nothing to do with that now."

It was known that Beattie had been busily chatting about the good old days of the Canadian Nazi Party with John Ross Taylor and Don Andrews. In the spring of 1988, for instance, Minden's streets were littered with Nationalist Party leaflets that read: "RACE-MIXING IS GENO-CIDE FOR ARYAN RACIAL UNITY," "GOD IS A RACIST" and "RACE IS THE ISSUE." Andrews admitted that he and some of his skinhead followers had been in town to visit Beattie, and had left the leaflets behind.

After discussing the matter with Don Andrews and John Beattie, Mark Bauer agreed to provide security at the Canada Day event. On Friday, June 30, Bauer led a convoy of about a dozen Ottawa-area neo-Nazi skins to Minden. In a later interview, he admitted that he was not a John Beattie enthusiast. "He's not our leader. We are the true white men in this country. The right wing in Canada is a joke. The old men like Beattie? They've never done anything. We are the future of the movement."

In this Mark Bauer was correct. Throughout the Save Our Canada Day Festival, Beattie stalked around his property, cursing wildly and calling the media "worms." But it was clear who exercised the real control at the event: ARM's Mark Bauer, the Nationalist Party's Peter Mitrevski and Montreal KKK leader Michel Larocque. Bauer's black-shirted security patrol walked the perimeter of Beattie's acreage, brandishing knives and billy clubs. A few of them stood watch at a picnic table barricade to the driveway, ignoring media questions and shepherding away any inebriated skinheads who were looking for a fight. After dark, they shone bright lights in the faces of reporters and protestors.

A good example of one of Bauer's followers was Richard Arbic, a muscular 20-year-old skinhead who was present throughout the festival. Decked out in camouflage pants, Arbic stood watch in the northwest corner of the property, atop a big rock, an enormous buck knife on his belt and a pronounced frown on his face. "Don't fuck with him," Bauer joked when a writer asked him about Arbic. "He'd kill you as soon as look at you." Bauer may not have been exaggerating. A few weeks after the neo-Nazi rally, an Ontario District Court judge sentenced Arbic to 90 days' imprisonment for a brutal and unprovoked assault on a Carleton University student in March 1988. Evidence given in court established that Arbic had joined two other Nazi skinheads in kicking and beating Carleton student Michael Jeffries at a local bar. Jeffries was left with serious head and chest injuries; when he was arrested by police, Arbic gave a false name and was concealing a knife. A weapons charge was dropped when he agreed to plead guilty to assault.

The Save Our Canada Day Festival was attended by neo-Nazi skinheads from all over Ontario, Quebec and New York State. Two school buses were rented by Beattie to ferry the accredited skinheads from secret locations in Toronto and Montreal. First to step off the Toronto bus was a bewildered-looking John Ross Taylor. When Taylor spotted photographers recording his arrival, he scurried into Beattie's home. Throughout the weekend, tapes of Skrewdriver and various other Oi bands were played at ear-throbbing volume over a rented sound system. At the entrance to Beattie's property, meanwhile, a few skinheads taunted the media contingent, daring them to cross the property line. With few exceptions, the assembled reporters and photographers appeared remarkably unfazed by the skinhead rally, occasionally even sharing jokes with Bauer and the friendlier members of his security patrol. A bizarre mood permeated much of the neo-Nazi rally: most of the time, there was a complete absence of tension. Everyone—the skinheads, the police, the media and the passers-by—seemed blasé about the whole thing.

That all changed at midnight on Saturday. At about 11:50, Bauer approached an Ontario Provincial Police cruiser parked on Bobcaygeon Road and asked that the OPP briefly keep watch over the entrance to the property. The OPP agreed to do so. Bauer and his men then circled behind Beattie's house, where the stage and tents had been erected. A few minutes later, the music stopped; a few muffled shouts were heard.

Alan Cairns, a genial *Sun* veteran who had travelled from Toronto to cover the rally, stood with Donn Downey, a *Globe and Mail* reporter, and a staffer from *The Ottawa Citizen.* "I guess it's time for the white power weenie roast," Cairns said, and his colleagues laughed. A few more jokes were told, and then the laughter abruptly stopped.

It was precisely midnight, and the 30-foot cross had been lit. The top half could be clearly seen from the road. From a certain angle, it almost appeared as though John Beattie's cottage was afire.

And then it started. Two hundred young voices, screaming in unison "Sieg Heil! Sieg Heil! Sieg Heil! Sieg Heil!" And then, without pausing, "White Power! White Power! White Power! White Power!"

When the screaming stopped, there was complete and utter silence on the road alongside John Beattie's property. All that could be heard was the engines of a few OPP cruisers and their radios. No one spoke for a long time. "Jesus Christ," Cairns finally said. "Jesus Christ, I've never heard anything like that before."

His colleague from the *Citizen* stirred, as if waking from a trance. "I've been covering this stuff for a few years, you know, and I've never heard anything like that, either. I actually felt shivers running up and down my spine."

"Me too," said the *Globe*'s Downey.

Down the road, an unidentified woman stood beside an OPP officer, weeping.

At precisely 10:08 a.m. on September 19, 1991, an uncomfortable-looking 21-year-old skinhead named Brett Hayes shifted in a chair in a boardroom in the Canada Trust Building on 103rd Avenue, in downtown Edmonton. Hayes was in the offices of the law firm of Molstad Gilbert to be questioned, under oath, by lawyer Tom Engel. Engel had been retained by retired Edmonton broadcaster Keith Rutherford to sue six skinheads Brett Hayes knew very well. Rutherford was also suing Terry Long and Long's wife, Janice; Aryan Nations founder Richard Butler; Silent Brotherhood member Edgar Foth; Kelly Lyle, leader of the Final Solution Skinheads; and the Church of Jesus Christ Christian itself. Brett Hayes was very familiar with all of these people and organizations, too. Rutherford was suing the group for $2.5 million plus costs and interest, for "wrongfully and intentionally assaulting [Rutherford] by kicking him and striking him with a piece of wood" at his Sherwood Park home on April 15, 1990. Rutherford was left blinded in his right eye, and two skinheads had briefly served some jail time for the assault.

Brett Hayes had been subpoenaed to appear at the offices of Molstad Gilbert because, as a former neo-Nazi skinhead leader, he knew many things. He knew Terry Long and Edgar Foth. He knew that skinheads had boasted about the attack afterwards. And, most of all, he knew that Long, Foth and the others were very, very angry about Rutherford's lawsuit. That made him nervous.

In the two years leading up to his appearance at the tidy law offices, Brett Hayes's nervousness had meant moving to new living quarters no fewer than seven times. It meant, as he told *The Calgary Herald* writer who was lucky enough to track him down, two-by-four planks being installed as bar locks on his front and bedroom doors; multiple deadlocks on his front and bedroom doors; sheets of plywood to reinforce windows and entranceways; and, just in case, a baseball bat beside his bed.

From 1986 to 1990, from Winnipeg to Calgary, Hayes had been at the very centre of western Canada's white supremacist skinhead movement. Born in Winnipeg in 1970, he left home at the age of 16. He fended for himself on the streets. Unlike the Aryan Resistance Movement's Mark Bauer in Ottawa, whom he knew in passing, Brett Hayes was no leader. With a halting speaking style and a pair of big, clumsy hands, he was a foot soldier for the cause. He fought a lot. In early 1990, he says he grew tired of the fighting and the hate and the meaninglessness. He told Calgary police about two Final Solution skinheads who, one night in November 1989, had spray-painted "SIX MILLION WAS NOT ENOUGH" on the walls of a former synagogue. After that, Hayes joined Skinheads Against Racial Prejudice and he spoke out against the evils of bigotry, even taking part in a 1991 anti-racism symposium sponsored by the Canadian Jewish Congress in

Ottawa. For all of these perceived sins, it would be fair to say that the Final Solution Skinheads would like to see Brett Hayes dead.

So he sat in the gleaming boardroom of Molstad Gilbert, telling his incredible story to Tom Engel. He told how, for much of 1990, he lived at a run-down rented house at 11429 – 89th Street in Edmonton, a house called the Skin Bin. Also living there were some of the defendants in Rutherford's lawsuit: Trinity Brandon Larocque, Mark Allan Swanson and Daniel Joshua Sims. Swanson and Sims were the skinheads who beat Keith Rutherford. At various times, the Skin Bin served as a home for various skingirls—Rachelle Straiko, Pat Pittman and Janine Boerstra. The house was also the Edmonton headquarters for the Final Solution Skinheads, Hayes explained, a group of Aryan Nations supporters led by Calgary skin Kelly Lyle and his second-in-command, Scott Fuhr, who lived in Edmonton. All of the skinheads who crashed at the Skin Bin were members of the Final Solution, with the exception of Swanson, who had been briefly associated with the Aryan Resistance Movement but, most of the time, was what Hayes called "an independent skinhead."

The Final Solution Skinheads confined their movements to Alberta and British Columbia. But occasionally the boys would strike east for a field trip of sorts. On the 1990 Canada Day weekend, two members of the group, Scott Fuhr and Wayne Granfield, travelled to Metcalfe, a small town a 20-minute drive south of Ottawa. There, the Final Solution skins rallied with about 200 of their peers on the property of Ian Verner Macdonald for Aryan Fest 1990.

The Final Solution members had been invited to attend by Mark Bauer of the Aryan Resistance Movement, and, as at Minden, Bauer's followers provided security at the event. His ARM followers communicated by walkie-talkie and carried knives, truncheons and baseball bats with large nails driven through them. One masked skinhead carried a crossbow. Like Minden, there were the ritual chants of "Sieg Heil" and "White Power," along with performances by two ham-fisted Oi bands, Ottawa's Cross and Britain's fascist dance combo of the moment, No Remorse. As the Final Solution skins slam-danced, No Remorse's singer stood on a stage decked out with ARM's logo and bellowed the lyrics to "Bloodsucker":

> Traitors there in Parliament, bought off by the Jews
> Nationalist opposition is only bound to lose
> Reject their corrupt system, stand now for your race
> 'Cause when we finally win, they will have no place.

Macdonald's Aryan Fest took place over three rain-filled days. It featured a tug-of-war between the skinheads, full-contact soccer games and plenty of hate propaganda for sale. In the fall 1990 issue of their magazine, *Storm Front*, the Final Solution skins devoted the cover to the Aryan Fest. "A few members of the Final Solution have recently returned from a big rally down East. It took place on the Canada Day weekend and served as a tribute to our flag. We travelled a fair distance, but it was a worthwhile trip, all in all. . . . It was well-organized and well-funded and our highest regards go out to Mark Bauer and his wife Michelle. We salute the Ottawa branch of ARM. They did one hell of a job."

The Skin Bin in Edmonton, where the Final Solution skins lived, was a dirty place. A few ancient couches were pushed here and there, and National Socialist posters were tacked to the walls. Above the oven, someone had pasted up a sign that read "SIX MILLION SERVED." In a sense, those who lived in the Skin Bin were a family, Hayes recalled. The young people who spent time there, he says, ranged in age from 12 to 23. All were on welfare. And most, if not all, were from broken or dysfunctional families. Said Hayes to Engel: "There were parent problems, with parent abuse and stuff like that. They would talk about suicides in the family and stuff like that. There was lots of that. Lots of it." He stops for a moment. "Skinheads have problems, and the only person they can turn to is Terry Long. And Terry Long knows that."

Despite appearances, the Skin Bin was also as exclusive, in its own way, as Calgary's posh Petroleum Club. Not everyone was granted admission. Said Hayes: "To become a Final Solution member, you have to prove yourself. In order to prove yourself, you have to fulfil something. And I fulfilled myself in the duty that I was asked to fulfil. It was either beating somebody up or stabbing somebody. I don't know [which]." To gain membership in the Final Solution Skinheads, Brett Hayes put two Calgary gay men in the hospital in the spring of 1988. For that assault, he was jailed for only a month.

In October 1988, the initiation complete, Hayes, Larocque and Sims travelled to Caroline, Alberta, with two other white supremacists, Final Solution skinhead Joey Bertling, who would become infamous at the September 1990 Provost Aryan Fest, and Matt McKay, a huge member of the Canadian Armed Forces who was also a neo-Nazi. McKay occasionally travelled to Alberta from his barracks in Winnipeg to socialize with his neo-Nazi pals. The soldier would later achieve his own type of fame, in May 1993, when it was revealed that his superiors had sent him to Somalia to protect black people—with knowledge of his white supremacist beliefs.

Sims had invited Hayes to Long's acreage "just to show him who I was," Hayes testified. In the summer of 1988, Hayes had gotten to know Kelly Lyle and, through Lyle, he had secured an invitation to the Aryan Nations compound in Hayden Lake, Idaho. During his visit at the armed compound, Hayes bought an Aryan Nations patch, which he stitched onto his jean jacket. He attended various Christian Identity lectures but found them boring. "I wasn't into God and stuff like that. I was just more into the violence and the neo-Nazism and stuff like that."

Approximately 45 other skinheads were also bunking at the Aryan Nations compound during Hayes's visit. "There was lots of people there, lots of skinheads. Lots of them."

In a letter he wrote to the Aryan Nations at the time, Hayes recalled, "I used Kelly Lyle as a reference. I told them what I felt about black people and Jewish people and what I have seen, and what I have dealt with, and the people I know up in Winnipeg. I mentioned their names, people like Bill Harcus.

"I just explained that I disliked niggers, and the Jews were always taking over, and we have to stop this before it is too late. . . . I just explained how the Jews were Zionist, and they were the enemy, so we had to rid them of our city [*sic*], and to do so I needed to know more about [the Aryan Nations] organization. . . . And I wished to become a member of the Aryan Nations."

As their pick-up truck bumped over the driveway at the secluded acreage outside Caroline, Terry Long was out front, waiting for them. Hayes told Engel he was "so excited" to be there. It was as if he had come home, he recalled: "Terry Long was like a father, you know. I never told him that or anything, and none of the members tell him that. But you can feel it. You can feel it once you are in the organiza- tion. You can feel the family, you know. It is a tight-knit family. It felt really good."

Hayes recalled that he felt slightly uneasy at the time. "I was the only punk with a Mohawk," he said. "I was trying to recruit other punks to go out and hit or bash negroes. I was showing the other skin- heads that, and I thought it was about time I showed that to the highest guy of the Aryan Nations." During his visit to Caroline, Hayes and his friends joked with Long about Jews and non-whites. After dinner, they were shown one of Long's arsenals of automatic weapons. Later that evening, they returned home, to the Skin Bin.

A frequent visitor at the Skin Bin was Edgar Foth, the man who had been one of two Canadian members of the Aryan Nations terrorist offshoot, the Silent Brotherhood. Foth was "a really good guy," Hayes recalled. He met the mysterious Klansman in a fast-food restaurant at Edmonton's Eaton Centre in 1988. At first, Hayes thought Foth "was just a cowboy kind of guy." But he grew to like him. Foth would often visit the Skin Bin to show the skinheads how to find and destroy elec- tronic surveillance devices. He would explain KKK lore and history. Said Hayes: "He would suggest that if we ever saw a Jewish person or something like that, don't take it kindly, you know?" He also would talk about the Silent Brotherhood—or, as it was also known, the Order. Foth would play videotapes of news items recalling the Order's various criminal exploits, while the skinheads would look on with awe. Sometimes, he would pull out a small box of medallions. Two of the medallions, Hayes said, were those that had been forged for members of Bob Mathews's Silent Brotherhood.

In the fall of 1990, Foth escorted a group of skinheads out to the Tofield, Alberta, home of his ex-wife, Gloria, and his six-year-old son, Danny. When Gloria Foth told him that she did not want her son exposed to Edgar Foth's skinheads, he was angry. When she told him that she did not understand why he could spend money on the skinheads and was seemingly unable to pay $100 a month in court-ordered child support, Edgar Foth flew into a rage. As his son and the skinheads looked on, Foth beat his ex-wife with a boot, leaving her with a bleeding and bruised ear and nose. A friend of Foth recalls: "She told him to get the hell out and never come back. If he did, she told him she would call the police and shoot him, and not necessarily in that order." After that, Foth seldom returned to his ex-wife's home and when he did, it was never with any of the Final Solution Skinheads.

Occasionally, Hayes said, Foth would show his youthful admirers how to make bombs. "He showed us how to make a light bulb bomb . . . When the [victim] came in, there was not going to be nothing left of his face." These devices, Foth told the skinheads, were to be used on Jews.

Added Hayes: "And then there were pipe bombs, where you just fill a can full of nails, and then you would take a canister of some sort, something that you can buy in a hobby store for a little rocket car, and you put that inside the can, and you put a wick on it and you light it, and you just get the hell out of there. There would just be shrapnel everywhere. It wouldn't kill anybody." He stopped, looking uncertain. "Well, if they were close enough, it would kill somebody, maybe. Just put nails in your face, maybe. Like it would be a grenade.

"He also taught us certain points where to hit a guy if you want to kill him, really hard. If you want to kill him fast." Foth told the skinheads he could supply them with handguns, rifles and shotguns.

"You told us that you viewed Long as a kind of father figure or a grandfather figure," Engel said. "What about Foth?"

"Like an uncle, I would say," Hayes replied. "He was just always there, you know. You know, if we ever needed help, he would be there." Foth, who always seemed to have lots of money, supplied the Skin Bin's residents with cash for groceries and beer. He also told them that, if they ever got in trouble with the law, they were to "keep our mouths shut," Hayes said, "and he would have a lawyer appointed for us."

Brett Hayes's story is confirmed by Daryl Rivest, another resident of the Skin Bin. Like Hayes, Rivest was examined by Tom Engel under oath. His testimony, which took place over two days in the summer of 1991, revealed that Rivest—an enormous, tattooed skinhead with a reputation as a streetfighter—was born in May 1972 in Scarborough, Ontario. In 1986, he moved to Stony Plain, a town of about 5,000, a half-hour drive west of Edmonton, with his mother and his brother. Rivest was attending Stony Plain Memorial Composite School when he dropped out in Grade 12 to join the skinhead scene full time. Since he was about 16, Rivest had known a few of the Final Solution skins—Trinity Larocque, Wayne Granfield and Scott Fuhr— so it was somewhat inevitable that he was pulled into the hate movement. He was not a Nazi, he said. That was a slang term for what he really was: a National Socialist. All of them, Rivest told Engel, were National Socialist skinheads. They believed in what he called "one race, one nation, under God." To achieve it, they would employ "threats, intimidation, violence, whatever it took." To prove his commitment, he had himself decorated with no fewer than 13 white supremacist tattoos.

For a time, Rivest and his Final Solution pals lived in another Skin Bin, this one at the corner of 107th Street and 106th Avenue in Edmonton. It was a poorer area of town, where lots of visible minorities lived. Sometimes, Rivest would walk to the local convenience store with Edgar Foth, who was a frequent visitor. Recalled Rivest: "Every time, he always commented on how he wished he had a fully automatic gun of some sort just so he could start mowing people down and that. He wished he had his 9-mm there so he could eliminate some of this yellow scum."

Whenever the former Silent Brotherhood member showed up, "it was almost like a holiday at the Skin Bin," Rivest recalled. "It was almost as if he was some sort of a god or something."

Aryan Nations leader Terry Long was also god-like in the skinheads' view. On one occasion at Long's home, while Sims and Rivest were chopping wood for $5 an hour, the pair were given the opportunity to shake hands with former high-school teacher Jim Keegstra. On another occasion, Rivest answered the phone in Long's kitchen. Later, Long told him the caller had been Keegstra's lawyer, Doug Christie. (In 1990, Long arranged for Rivest and Sims to provide security at a Western Canada Concept meeting where Christie was scheduled to speak. Said Rivest: "The WCC was a political front for the Ku Klux Klan here in Canada.")

Rivest told Engel he had nothing but fond memories of his times at Terry Long's acreage down by the Clearwater River. "He was really nice when we stayed down there. He made sure we were well fed. He had beds made up for us before we even got there. You know, it was pretty good." He paused. "He paid for us working out on the sawmill, chopping wood for him or whatever we were doing. Then he gave us everything we needed for free. And if there was something you didn't understand, he would just sit there and talk to you about it. He wasn't the kind of person that got mad if you asked questions and whatnot, like if you didn't understand something. He would take the time to sit back and explain it to you, made sure you understood it before he kept going."

On return trips from Caroline, Rivest and Sims would ride in Edgar Foth's pick-up truck. They would read copies of the *Klansman*, the National Socialist *Vanguard*, *Thunderbolt* and other white supremacist publications. At small towns between Caroline and Edmonton, such as Devon, the trio would drive through slowly. Recalled Rivest: "As soon as we would drive into town, a bunch of kids would be running up to the truck. We just parked in front of this one place. Kids would come running over. We would hand it to them out the window of the truck and take off."

Every skinhead had a talent. Some excelled at organizing; some were known as effective creators of hate propaganda; some even distinguished themselves as talented tattoo artists. Rivest's particular skill was violence. He was one of the Final Solution Skins' enforcers. In this capacity, he was probably closer to Edgar Foth than any other skinhead, with the possible exception of Dan Sims. During his time in the hate movement—about five years in all—Rivest would do what needed to be done. "I would start getting extremely aggressive," he recalled. "And I would see a black guy or an Indian or whatever. Or I would see a white guy with a non-white girlfriend, or even members of the Anti-Fascist League or SHARP [Skinheads Against Racial Prejudice]. And I would just jump on them, hit them in the head a few times until they hit the ground and then kick them in the face until they just quit moving. And I would leave them there."

"Some of it was just thrill beating. Because those were kind of popular with us, too. If you are in a bad mood, the easiest way to deal with it when you are living with these people is just to go out and kick the shit out of someone." Some of the violence that was discussed included decapitation of an anti-racist group's leader: "So we basically had a murder planned. We were going to kill him and nail his head to his front door." Once, Rivest and his friends "carved swastikas" onto one man: "It was probably more of a humiliation thing than anything." And on one memorable occasion, Sims and Rivest plotted to murder Scott Fuhr in what he called "an execution-style thing." The reason: "He was letting this Edmonton representative of the Final Solution thing get to his head, and he was pulling a big power trip on a lot of people." The assassination did not take place, Rivest said, because he left the hate movement and because Dan Sims fled to the United States to escape further jail time for assaulting Keith Rutherford. Said Rivest: "It seems that as far as skinheads go, we have got the most violent ones in Canada here in Edmonton."

It was this willingness to be violent that made the Final Solution Skinheads so attractive to Terry Long and Edgar Foth. For them, the Final Solution provided a means by which Jews, gays and non-whites could be terrorized with little or no fear of prosecution. Said Rivest: "Oh, Terry Long thought the skinheads were the greatest thing that ever happened to him. [With us,] he didn't have to get his hands dirty. In the literature, they never actually used specifics. Like they never said 'intimidate,' they never said 'beat.' They never said anything like that, but they always used the phrase 'by whatever means necessary.' . . . [Long] thought we were the best thing that ever happened to them, because that way people would get hurt, people would get scared, people would start running, and he wouldn't even have to get his hands dirty. And he did tell us that.

"The skinheads were the modern version of the Brownshirts, just to rough people up, cause trouble. And, you know, let the older guys deal with the actual publicity problems and whatnot. [Long] said we were better with our hands and our feet than we were with our minds and our mouths."

To Rivest, violence was always easier than talking. "If I have a personal problem with someone, I would rather beat his head in than talk it out with him, any day. But, I don't know, being expected by everyone you know to kick somebody's head in at least once a week—which I did for years—kind of gets on your nerves. They treated me almost like the alcoholic hit man, you know? They would take me to the bar and get me really drunk. Then they would just pick a guy in the bar who had been, you know, causing a problem for them. And they would get me drunk and point at this guy and say: 'Well, Daryl, that guy called you a Jew.' It wasn't so much the ideology that was bothering me. It was just more the way I had chosen to go about doing things. Because, like, I . . ." His voice trailed off. "I hurt some people really bad. Like I don't even know if some of those people even got up and walked away. Like, for all I know, I might have killed people. I have no clue. And to be brutally honest, I don't want to know."

The culture of violence was not confined to beatings alone. Disturbingly, the skinheads also developed a keen interest in firearms. On occasion, Foth would bring Sims and Rivest up to his home, near—ironically enough—Bruderheim, a small town northeast of

Edmonton. There, the group would indulge in target practice. They would use 12-gauge shotguns, .303s and .30-06s. Foth also claimed to own Chinese-made AK-47s, Uzi machine guns, plastic explosive, hand grenades and even "a .50-calibre machine gun up in his attic for special occasions. He said that if CSIS [Canadian Security Intelligence Service] ever decided they were going to go out and pay him a visit, he was going to blow all their heads off."

In an isolated field near Edgar Foth's hideout, Rivest and Sims would fire at large grain sacks that had been stuffed with hay and dirt. Rivest, a former air cadet, was a good shot. "Was there any purpose for the target shooting?" Engel asked him.

"Get to be better shots."

"For what purpose?"

"In case we ever had to shoot anybody," Rivest said. "It's a pretty big waste of ammo if you can't shoot and you're trying to hit something."

"You are talking about shooting people?" Engel asked.

"Yeah, people."

In the event that any of the Final Solution Skinheads ever succeeded in killing someone, they were instructed to immediately contact Edgar Foth. "You know," Rivest recalled Foth telling him on one return trip from Caroline, "if you ever kill anybody or anything like that, don't worry about it. Just let me know. I can hook you up with a new name, new face, the whole nine yards. Then I will ship you off to South America."

Not all of the Final Solution gang were accorded such treatment. Daryl Rivest and Dan Sims seemed to have been particular favorites of Foth and Long. The two racist leaders apparently wanted the two young Identity Christians to revive the Silent Brotherhood. As Bob Mathews had done, the two men told the skins to read *The Turner Diaries*. Also recommended were Hitler's *Mein Kampf* and George Lincoln Rockwell's *White Power*. Said Rivest: "Me and Dan were basically being groomed by Terry Long to unite the Edmonton skins. He was basically going to set us up to take over basically northern Alberta."

Foth and Long's ultimate goal was plain, Rivest said. It is the same goal every far right leader in Canada now has for the growing skinhead movement.

"It is to get a bunch of people together who aren't afraid to go to jail, who aren't afraid to get killed, beaten, stabbed, anything like that. It is to arm them—and create mass destruction."

Statistics bear out what Daryl Rivest and Brett Hayes have to say. In July 1993, for example, the Anti-Defamation League of the B'nai Brith concluded that the skinhead movement had become far and away the most violent of the U.S.-based hate groups. More than 3,500 committed neo-Nazi skinheads live in all but 10 of the 50 states, the ADL reported, and have been responsible for 22 murders since 1990. Concluded the human rights watchdog: "The skinheads are today the most violent of all white supremacy groups. Not even the Ku Klux Klans, so notorious for their use of the rope and the gun, come close to the skinheads in the number and severity of crimes committed." The older hate movement leaders were "using" the skinheads, the ADL noted, as "front-line warriors."

In Canada, the picture is depressingly similar. In its yearly reports, the B'nai Brith has shown that Canadian neo-Nazi and white supremacist leaders have been phenomenally successful in attracting young people—particularly young men—to the racist cause. In recent years, the B'nai Brith notes, the number of racist skinheads has been increasing at a dramatic rate. Police confirm that most violent racist crimes committed in Canada are now linked to skinheads. And, unlike their leaders, these young men do not hesitate to use violence. Their goal, as Daryl Rivest testified, remains to "create mass destruction."

10

LE KLAN DE QUÉBEC

The young skinhead named Brent Klauser whispers conspiratorially into the telephone. "Meet us at 4:30 on Friday at the Poutinière de Laval. It's out front of the Java Bingo, okay?" says Klauser, a member of a Montreal Ku Klux Klan offshoot called White Power Canada. "Don't bring any cameras, or you will be sorry, okay?"

"Okay, fine," says the writer who has been invited to attend the weekend's festivities. "But how will I know who you are? What will you be wearing? What do you look like?"

Klauser laughs. "Don't worry about it. We already know what you look like."

"Okay, whatever. How many other reporters know about this thing?"

"Nobody," says Klauser. "You will be the only one there."

On Friday, July 31, 1992, at about 4:30 p.m., the writer from Ottawa approaches Java Bingo on Cartier West in Laval. The low-level building is surrounded by a dozen police cars. In the parking lot, a uniformed officer is directing the flow of traffic. Already, three camera crews are present. One station has even sent a live remote truck, complete with satellite dish. A few members of an anti-racism group, the World Anti-Fascist League, are maintaining an uneasy vigil at the far end of Java Bingo's property.

Word of the Aryan Fest has apparently leaked out.

Inside Java Bingo's abandoned coffee shop, two skinheads sit in a corner, drinking coffee. One is wearing a ring emblazoned with the Nazi SS symbol. The other is slouched in a black nylon bomber jacket with the words "Stride for Pride" stitched across the back, above a Celtic cross. The writer from Ottawa approaches them. "Where's Brent?"

"Don't worry," one of the skinheads says without looking up. "He'll be here soon." The skinhead pauses and grins at his colleague. "He already knows you are here."

Outside the coffee shop, the owner of Java Bingo looks frantic. When a skinhead swaggers across his parking lot from the direction of Des Laurentides Boulevard, sporting a pair of dark sunglasses and a small Confederate flag wrapped around his face, the owner yells at him: "Ce place est privée, là!" This is private property.

The skinhead ignores the owner and steps up to a cameraman who has been filming him. As the police look on, the skinhead slaps the camera's lens, yelling obscenities. The cameraman backs away.

Suddenly, from the corner, a whisper: "Hey, over here."

While the confrontation has been going on in the parking lot, Brent Klauser and a group of skinheads have crept around the back of Java Bingo, unseen. Klauser is barely out of boyhood, no more than perhaps 15. He stands about five feet tall, and his eyes are bloodshot. There is a large bruise on his forehead. He explains that he acquired it during a fight two evenings previous, when he went "undercover" to an anti-racism rally. Someone hit him on the head with a copper pipe, he says.

Brent Klauser is wearing a Ku Klux Klan baseball cap. On the upper left sleeve of his blue bomber jacket, the word "RAHOWA" can be seen. Klauser reaches inside his bomber and pulls out a map. A large swastika has been marked on La Plaine, a small community about an hour north of Montreal. "Here," he says. "Remember: no cameras."

"Okay."

As the writer starts to head back to his car, Klauser calls to him. "Hey! Don't forget—you're going to be alone up there."

"I won't."

The site of the 1992 Aryan Fest is a ramshackle white house on rue Curé Barette, just down the road from Restaurant 335, out on the Montée Mathieu. To the east of the house is a large German shepherd chained to a tree in a muddy yard; a hundred yards beyond the dog is a run-down barn where a few skinheads are waiting out the rainstorm. It is unseasonably cold. The skins are drinking beer and listening to a tape of a Steve Earle song, something about "white trash." They have paid $25 to take part in the Aryan Fest, which will feature, among other things, a burning of a large swastika and a racist concert. At the end of it, they will get a T-shirt silk-screened with a skull superimposed on a large swastika.

Out front, a large white cross stands at the entrance to the gravelled driveway. Someone has tacked a Canadian flag to it. Behind the house is a large makeshift stage and a portable generator. Later in the weekend, the stage will be the site of a concert by Rahowa. Five or six tents have been set up a few yards from the stage.

There is quiet. The downpour has turned the field behind the house into a mudpit, and the skinheads are in a foul mood. More than 200 pro-Nazi skins had been expected, but with the rain and the cold, no more than 80 will finally show up.

Alain Roy, the genial Exalted Cyclops of the Invisible Empire Knights of the Ku Klux Klan, steps out of the cab of a truck to greet his guest. He is a well-built man, with a shock of short black hair. He stands about five-nine in his running shoes. He takes a swig of beer. On the back of Roy's right hand, there is the "Triple 7" tattoo of South Africa's neo-Nazi Afrikaner Resistance Movement.

Roy squints up at the darkening sky. "This goddamn rain," he says in a thick French accent, then decides to make a joke out of it. "We can't have any pointed hats or anything."

Originally, the 1992 Aryan Fest was set to be held in Ste-Anne-de-Sorel, about 35 miles northeast of Montreal. Leaflets advertising the event had been circulated by members of White Power Canada and Roy's Invisible Empire Knights. (The Quebec-based Invisible Empire Knights of the KKK are a branch of a small incorporated klavern boasting the same name in Crawfordsville, Indiana.) Even Tom Metzger's White Aryan Resistance, based in faraway Fallbrook, California, had issued a few plugs for the event on its telephone hate line. Residents of the Ste-Anne region circulated anti-Nazi petitions, lobbied local politicians and braced themselves for the arrival of 200 neo-Nazis on the last weekend in July.

But, at the last moment, something happened: the KKK changed the site to La Plaine. Why? It is known that a plainclothes member of the Sûreté du Québec met with Roy. The two had a pleasant encounter, Roy recalls. "The Sûreté is always criticized by the left wing here in Quebec, every time something happens," he says, disapproving. "They say they are Nazis, that they are terrorists."

He pauses. "Anyway, a guy came to see me, to ask if the [Aryan Fest] party was going to happen in Sorel. He was just trying to do his job. I said to him: 'Don't worry, it's not in Sorel any more.' He said okay, that's no problem then. So I gave him some literature."

Whereas a Nazi rally in Ste-Anne-de-Sorel had been a significant concern for the Sûreté, a Nazi rally in La Plaine apparently was not. In La Plaine, the Quebec provincial police were as good as invisible, intervening only to detain leftist protestors trying to make their way to the Aryan Fest site. When asked why his Klan enjoyed such a positive relationship with the Sûreté that weekend, Alain Roy merely smiles. The Sûreté, for its part, insists it had nothing to do with the change of venue. Says Sûreté du Québec constable Richard Bourdon: "We knew they were going to have a meeting in Sorel. But the change was made all on their own initiative."

Quebec's summer of 1992 was long, hot and, as Roy correctly

notes, ripe for Ku Klux Klan agitation. It seemed that everywhere one looked in Quebec that summer, there was anger and intolerance. In the same week the Aryan Fest was to take place, for example, *Photo Police*, a garish Montreal-based tabloid newspaper with a fetish for Quebec's men in uniform, published an openly white supremacist issue titled "Les Blancs en ont assez des Noirs" (Whites Are Fed Up with Blacks). In a six-page special section, the editors offered their readers a variety of articles that could have fit quite comfortably in the pages of any one of Alain Roy's favorite hate sheets: "Gangs of Blacks Spread Terror," one article was headlined; another read, "They Endanger the Lives of Innocents"; a third screamed that blacks were responsible for "A Heritage of Crime and Death." For good measure, the tabloid also ran a photo of Dan Philip, president of the Black Coalition of Quebec, with the caption: "Asshole of the week."

A battered Ford Escort pulls into the driveway. It carries New York vanity licence plates: "ARYAN TWO." Inside are a chain-smoking woman and a long-haired man in camouflage pants wearing a T-shirt with rifle crosshairs superimposed on a photo of Martin Luther King, Jr.; below, the T-shirt reads "OUR DREAM." He is Thomas W. Cool, a self-described hate movement "organized organizer" from Auburn, New York. Alain Roy jogs over to greet Cool and his friend. As they speak, Sûreté du Québec cars slowly cruise by. At one point, a masked skinhead waving a Confederate flag gives one of the Sûreté officers a Nazi salute.

Alain Roy steps back from Cool's car and grins. For a minute, he confers briefly with occupants of the rented house, Daniel Tremblay and Brigitte Lavoie. When Roy arrived, the bearded Tremblay had been sporting a swastika armband. Roy told him to remove it. "The guy doesn't know anything about the movement," says Roy, clearly unimpressed.

Roy is holding some hate propaganda that Cool has brought across the border. He is also holding some other material that was brought to La Plaine by Quebec's Ku Klux Klan for distribution at the Aryan Fest. One popular item is a small sticker that reads "HITLER AVAIT RAISON!" (Hitler Was Right). To one side of that message is a swastika. Below it, an address: NSDAP–AO, Lincoln, Nebraska, USA.

This French-language sticker and many others containing anti-Semitic and white supremacist messages in French only have been produced by a pro-Nazi outfit in Nebraska. If it seems unusual that a hate group in the U.S. Midwest is producing hate propaganda in French, rest assured—Alain Roy agrees that it is. The group is the National Sozialistische Deutsche Arbeiter Partei–Auslands Organisation (NSDAP–AO), the National Socialist German Workers Party–Overseas Organization, and it is led by American neo-Nazi Gary Rex Lauck, a Milwaukee native who grew up in Lincoln and now speaks passable German. The NSDAP–AO, by Lauck's admission, has few supporters in Nebraska. He says: "It is a front, here. A mailing address." Out of this address, Lauck mails hundreds of thousands of pieces of National Socialist material to countries all over the world—among them Germany, England, Australia, South Africa, Belgium, Holland, Spain, Italy, Japan, Denmark, France, Finland, Sweden, Hungary and Argentina. What distinguishes Lauck's group from other neo-Nazi mailing houses is that he possesses the capability to produce hate material in the language of his target audience. (Ernst Zundel, the world's other large producer of National Socialist propaganda, mails out of Toronto and prints only in German and English.)

Says Alain Roy: "I have had contact with NSDAP–AO for a while. They make publications in different languages, and they publish in French, which is good for us. Their material has had a good impact with our members." Roy holds up a copy of NSDAP–AO's *Nouvelles NS*, which contains news about neo-Nazi groups in France, Belgium and Quebec. The quality of the French is excellent, Roy notes.

As the rain starts to clear, more cars can be seen pulling into Tremblay's driveway. The licence plates reveal the neo-Nazis to be primarily from Quebec, although a few cars carry Ontario and New York plates. Most of the Ontario skinheads are members of either the

Heritage Front or the Church of the Creator, the two largest racist groups in that province. Wolfgang Droege, leader of the Heritage Front, has travelled from Toronto but keeps away from the Aryan Fest site; Church of the Creator leader George Burdi, however, has dropped by to lead his band, Rahowa, in a few numbers. Also in attendance are members of the Aryan Resistance Movement, led by veteran Montreal skinhead Mike (Fifi) Parmiter; the Aryan Defence Network; and Ste-Foy's Aryan Youth Movement. By the time the event is over—culminating with the Saturday-night burning of a large wooden swastika, within sight of passersby on rue Curé Barette—about 100 neo-Nazis will have passed through town. Alain Roy will be pleased.

Sitting in a writer's car early on Saturday morning, waiting for the rain to stop, Alain Roy pulls on a beer and recalls how he got involved in Quebec's hate movement. Born in 1967 in Boisbriand, a town of 50,000 near St.-Eustache and 20 miles north of Montreal, Roy is proud of his roots. "I came from a town where there were no niggers," he says. "In Boisbriand, there's a small community of 5,000 Jews. They live around each other. They don't pay tax. When we were young, we would go and check out the Jews. They were strange."

Roy avoids talk of his family. But he will say that a friend's father, whom he will not name, was a prominent political activist. "[He] gave us lots of information," says Roy. "Like, he would take us into a restaurant and say: 'Watch, the Jews are going to take all of the spareribs for $3.99.' So there would be 50 Jews or something, and they would do that. This guy's father made us understand lots of things." One of the things the man taught Roy, for example, is that there is a "Kosher tax"—a hidden levy on certain foods, with the proceeds going to Israel and Jewish groups. The "tax" is apparently supported by some bureaucrats at Revenue Canada: in August 1994, the federal Minister of Revenue said a few public servants had been mistakenly permitting the tax to go through.

Among the things that Alain Roy came to understand, he says, was that Jews were conspiring to crush Quebec's nationalist movement and the French language. "Québécois here know who is anti-Quebec, anti-101, anti-French," says Roy. "It's the Jew. They are the people who make the big declarations and provoke us. I can understand why a guy is angry when the guy comes from Canada and lives in the West Island [of Montreal], and he has a business and he has to use French, when in the past his father used only English. I can understand all that.

"But the people like Mordecai Richler, Henry Morgentaler, Robert Libman of the Equality Party, the Bronfmans"—he spits out each name. "They all make these big declarations that are against the people who live here. And it is always the Jew who does this. They are very subversive. They make these big declarations against the French, and they really have no respect for us. They talk like they are landlords and we are, what is that word, tenants.

"Quebec is not their country. Their country is Israel."

Roy dropped out of school after Grade 10. He liked sports—and also liked drugs. In 1987, at the age of 20, he left home and moved to Montreal. There, he held down two jobs, delivering carpet and toiling as a mover. It was, he says, hard work. "I was tired. And I had other interests in life. So I decided to go into the army, and I made all of the applications. I was ready to go."

But on St.-Jean-Baptiste Day in June 1989, before he was to formally join Canada's Armed Forces, Roy and four friends got into a fight with what he says were "15 Arabs" at a Métro station on boulevard Lajeunesse, in Montreal's north end. Roy and his friends had been drinking beer. Angry words were exchanged; a fight broke out; the police were called. A few days later, Roy—without a lawyer to represent him, and without an understanding of how the legal system works—received a six-month sentence. "After that," he says, "I couldn't go in the army, and I lost my jobs." He pauses. "I had always had problems with blacks on the street. So, in 1988, I got my first Klan newspaper from Michel Larocque."

Michel Larocque had the distinction of being the first Quebecker to establish a Ku Klux Klan cell in the province since the 1920s. A thin man with longish hair and a penchant for berets and scarves, Larocque says he has always been a white supremacist. He was also violent. In January 1992, for example, Larocque, Roy and a member named Martin Belhumeur, along with 37 neo-Nazi skinheads, were arrested in east end Montreal. Larocque, Roy and Belhumeur were searched and found to be carrying Molotov cocktails. Charges against Larocque and Roy were dismissed; Belhumeur was sentenced on charges of conspiracy in March 1993.

In a September 1990 court action in which he was a witness, Larocque testified that he favored stringent controls on immigration. Immigrants, Larocque told the Quebec Superior Court, "should be white and Christian." Jews, meanwhile, were fine as individuals, but Larocque admitted that he objected to them "as a group." Larocque's first Klan, Roy says, was a loose alliance of young neo-Nazis in 1988, the year Roy learned of its existence. By May 1990, it had grown to become a formal branch of James Farrands's Shelton, Connecticut-based group bearing the unwieldy name The Invisible Empire Knights of the Ku Klux Klan.

Farrands, a Roman Catholic who assumed control of the Knights of the KKK in September 1986—the remnants of the organization founded, and then abandoned, by David Duke in the 1970s—is the Imperial Wizard to well over 2,000 Klansmen in virtually every American state. (The Quebeckers, along with Klansmen in Ontario and the Maritimes, were directly under the leadership of Thomas Herman, northeastern leader for the United States and a former Newfields, Maine, police officer.) With the link to Farrands came far right respectability. The members of Larocque's group now had fancy titles (Roy's was Exalted Cyclops), Klansman robes, secret code words and a command structure. It was a pile of fun, says Alain Roy.

Roy also liked his new friends, and he liked what he read in the Invisible Empire newspaper Michel Larocque had given him. Within time, he was writing to Klan factions across North America. (One such klavern was Bill Harcus's Manitoba Knights of the Ku Klux Klan. Through Harcus, Roy purchased Klansman robes for himself and his colleagues.) With Larocque, Roy learned the symbols, traditions and ideology of the KKK. They got into fights with non-whites, they painted swastikas on Montreal synagogues and they purchased hate propaganda from NSDAP–AO and other pro-Nazi groups across the United States. They were extremely active.

In a 115-page report released in June 1992, a group of Jewish and minority community leaders calling itself the Committee Against Racial Violence showed just how active Quebec-based racist groups were. The report detailed a stunning number of criminal racist acts in 1989 and 1990. Among these were the following: 57 graves were desecrated with swastikas at Shaar Hashomayim Jewish cemetery in the Montreal suburb of Côte St-Luc in August 1989; in October, more than 30 Nazi skinheads attacked spectators at a concert by an anti-racism band at the Spectrum on St. Catherine Street; skinheads attacked a group of young Jews at a party in Côte St-Luc in March 1990; in the same month, a dozen skinheads beat up a young black at the Peel Métro station; in April, more swastika spray-painting took place, this time at Jewish cemetery Baron de Hirsch; in May, at least 60 pro-Nazi skinheads attacked a group of young blacks at an amusement park called La Ronde, using hatchets, knives, clubs and machetes; later, about 125 Nazi skins battled with African-Americans in the city's Métro system; in the same month, a Native youth was gravely wounded after an attack by 20-odd armed skinheads at the Pie IX Métro station; also in May, "WHITE POWER" slogans were painted at a Jewish cemetery in Ste-Foy; later in that month, five armed skinheads attacked a black on St. Laurent Boulevard; in June, there was another battle at La Ronde between blacks and skinheads; in the same month, more anti-Semitic vandalism and graffiti occurred at both the Yeshiva Gedola School and the Chevra Thillim synagogue in Outremont and Côte-des-Neiges; also in June, three skinheads savagely beat an Arab-Canadian in Montreal, one of them yelling: "We don't like foreigners taking our jobs from us!" These incidents, police noted, were known only because someone had bothered to make an official complaint. Many more racist incidents were going unreported, they acknowledged, because the victims feared retribution.

It was at the height of this orgy of racism and anti-Semitism, in early August 1990, that Alain Roy, Michel Larocque and the Montreal Klan decided to visit Oka.

Located west of Montreal, Oka is home to about 1,500 Mohawks. Since 1987, the federal government had been negotiating a land claim settlement with the band. So, in July 1989, all the relevant levels of government—federal, provincial, municipal and Indian Act bands—hammered out an agreement that would see the creation of another reserve in the disputed area, which was adjacent to a municipal golf course. But, in January 1990, Mohawk clan mothers appointed a new chief and council for the reserve. Negotiations were scuttled. Shortly afterwards, Oka's city council lifted a moratorium on expansion of the golf course. The Mohawks, in turn, erected a barricade on a nearby recreational road. On July 11, 1990, Sûreté du Québec officers came to town to remove the Mohawk barricade. Tear gas and stun grenades were fired. In the ensuing gun battle, one police officer, Marcel Lemay, was killed.

On the evening of August 21, after enduring a Mohawk Indian roadblock at Kahnawake that had lasted more than a month, 300 angry residents of Châteauguay, Quebec, established a roadblock of their own. Using cars, branches and garbage, they blocked the northern span of the Mercier Bridge, which effectively prevented Mohawks from travelling from their reserve, Kahnawake, to a monastery where talks were being held to resolve the bloody event that came to be known as the Oka crisis.

In their excellent 1991 book, *People of the Pines: The Warriors and the Legacy of Oka*, journalists Geoffrey York and Loreen Pindera recount how the Mercier Bridge standoff attracted racists and bigots like moths to a flame. One man, host of a Montreal radio phone-in show, cheered on the Châteauguay residents and made racist remarks about the Mohawks. This man "was also an outspoken Quebec nationalist," York and Pindera wrote, "and he often reminded his listeners that the Mohawks could not speak French. In the climate of fervent Quebec nationalism that followed the failure of the Meech Lake Accord in June, any reference to the language issue was bound

344 WEB OF HATE

to evoke a passionate response, and many of the people in the mobs resented the fact that the Mohawks had sided with the English for hundreds of years."

Into this volatile mix stepped Roy and Larocque. In late August, they and other Klansmen appeared on the scene. Larocque, for one, had been observing the events at the Mercier Bridge since early August. The Klansmen distributed hate pamphlets and other propaganda to the crowds who gathered at the barricade every evening. They even paraded about carrying anti-Mohawk placards. One KKK tract advised Quebec's government to immediately cease providing any social services to the Mohawks. The Klan, the leaflet boasted, would defend "the values and the ideals of the white majority."

"Yes, I went to the barricades at Châteauguay," Roy recalls. "I demonstrated with the people who wanted a white majority."

In the afternoon of Tuesday, August 28, 100 Mohawk women, children and elderly men decided to flee the isolated Indian community. Their evacuation was organized by Alwyn Morris, a respected Mohawk leader and Olympic gold medallist. Morris had been promised by the Sûreté du Québec that the evacuees would be protected from the angry Châteauguay mob.

But when the Mohawk motorcade reached the north end of the Mercier Bridge, Larocque, Roy and 13 of their Klan followers started to shower the Mohawk vehicles with fist-sized rocks and chunks of asphalt. Some of the locals—media estimates say they numbered 300—joined the rock-throwing Klansmen. The officers of the Sûreté stood by and watched as the Mohawk women and children were attacked by the mob. In the end, six Mohawks were seriously injured, among them a 76-year-old man and a young child. The 76-year-old man's son, Kahnawake Community Services executive director Don Horne, was transporting his father in his car when the barrage began. Horne recalls: "A chunk of concrete nearly the size of a soccer ball smashed through the window behind me and landed on my father's chest. He was covered in broken glass. There was glass in his socks, in his hair. He was bleeding all over [and] he was yelling."

Alain Roy's recollection of the attack is much more positive. He claims that a media organization paid the Quebec Klansmen to pelt the Mohawks with rocks. "They paid us to throw things at the barricades. There were 15 guys there—15 of us from the Klan. We made people pay attention to us."

Among those who "paid attention" were millions of horrified Canadians watching the television news that night, most of whom had never before seen such an overt display of racist violence on Canadian soil. In a lead editorial, the Montreal *Gazette* wrote that "there is a putrid smell in this province's air. It lingers from the white thugs who gave a stomach-turning display of cowardly vengeance at the Montreal end of the Mercier Bridge." Prime Minister Brian Mulroney, for his part, was also troubled by what he had seen on television, stating: "Racism, at any time, under any circumstances, is an evil." Mulroney said he had asked for a report into the incident.

But Alain Roy says his group had already prepared a report, one for their own use. In an Oka postmortem, Larocque and Roy's Ku Klux Klan was stunned and delighted by the amount of news coverage—and new recruits—it picked up during the attack on the Mohawk women and children. "Since the Mohawk crisis, it's been better for us," Roy says. He adds that Quebec's KKK has learned that there are tremendous benefits associated with the manipulation of isolated systemic racial incidents. Most of the time, as at Oka, the incidents do not initially involve organized hate groups. But Quebec's Klan now ensures that these incidents usually end with the participation of its members. The Quebec Klan is always on stand-by, says Roy, ready to deliver hate propaganda, organizers and trouble-makers to some hot spot at a moment's notice.

Says Roy: "We are learning. We are starting to link with other groups in the other provinces, and we are learning good communications [techniques]. Me and my people, we're not going to be stopped. Money is not an object.

"We do the right things at the right time. And we wait."

* *

What comes first: white supremacist unity or Quebec nationalism? For most Quebec skinheads, it would seem, racial consciousness was far more important. As one gregarious skinhead put it at the La Plaine Aryan Fest, "For a true National Socialist, language isn't as important as skin color." Alain Roy agrees, saying: "We want to separate from our enemies. That doesn't mean I want to separate from Canada."

But for 35-year-old Michel Larocque, Exalted Cyclops of the Invisible Empire Knights of the Ku Klux Klan in Quebec, the reverse was true. Unlike most white supremacist leaders, who regard boundaries between nations, provinces and states to be meaningless scratchings on a map, Larocque appeared to be a good deal more nationalist than he was supremacist. After the Oka crisis, Larocque says he stumbled across evidence that Imperial Wizard James Farrands was favoring Eric Vachon, federalist leader of the Sherbrooke Klan chapter, over his separatist Montreal branch. "I learned Farrands was trying to favor the Sherbrooke takeover of Montreal, at my expense," Larocque later recalled. "They interfered in our affairs."

In the fall of 1990, Larocque broke with Farrands and Vachon, labelling the U.S.-based Klan leader an alcoholic and incorrigible smoker of marijuana in a newsletter. He then set up a group he called Longitude 74 KKK—Montreal being situated on the 74th longitude. That group, which published a pro-Identity Christianity newsletter called *L'Empire*, lasted a year. Then Larocque established a group called Mouvement des Revendications des Droits de la Majorité, which was associated with Thom Robb's Knights of the Ku Klux Klan faction in Harrison, Arkansas. Because he is an Identity Christian, Robb's anti-Semitism is more overt than that of many Klan leaders. As he has said in the hate sheet he edits, *The White Patriot*: "I hate Jews. I hate race-mixing Jews. We've let the anti-Christ Jews into our country and we've been cursed with abortion, inflation, homosexuality and the threat of war. Anglo-Saxon and kindred people are the true Israel." This sort of anti-Semitism was tremendously popular among nationalist Québécois racists.

But Michel Larocque had other concerns, and his KKK started to drift. While he dithered with name changes and personality conflicts, leaving a substantially sized leadership void, the Sherbrooke Klan hit the streets. Their streets of choice were the dusty backroads in and around Sherbrooke, a city in Quebec's Eastern Townships, not far from the Vermont border. In April, half a dozen rural mailboxes were stuffed with copies of the *Klansman*, a newsletter produced and edited by James Farrands. (The *Klansman*, the official organ of the Invisible Empire, made its debut in 1975, when Louisiana far right leader Bill Wilkinson bolted David Duke's Knights of the Ku Klux Klan to form his own group. Farrands later became Wilkinson's successor.) One article noted that Abraham Lincoln "had been murdered by agents of the international Jew bankers." Another article told how, following blacks' emancipation from slavery, "many beautiful white women were savagely raped, murdered or brutalized by power-hungry Negro beasts."

In July, Vachon's Klan grew bolder. Fifteen hooded Klansmen went on a membership drive. Standing on street corners in four locations in the Eastern Townships—Bury, Compton, Sawyerville and Johnville—the KKK members handed out copies of the *Klansman* to passersby. Then, in early August 1991, as part of a national organizing drive, 5,000 copies of that month's *Klansman* were said to be heading north from Connecticut to Quebec. The newsletters were to be shipped to Sherbrooke, headquarters of the Invisible Empire's Quebec branch.

Within a matter of days, the 12-page issue—which featured a hooded Klansman above the headline "EVOLUTION OF A KLAN: INVISIBLE EMPIRE EXPANDS INTO CANADA"—was being found in residential mailboxes all over Montreal's anglophone West Island. One article stated that the failure of the Meech Lake Accord was the fault of Jews who "plan to divide Canada even more." In an oblique reference to the acceptance of turban-wearing Sikhs into the ranks of the RCMP, another article stated that the federal police force "prefers clowning around with this new uniform to investigating Marxist/Jew conspiracy against the true Canadians." Copies of the *Klansman* were left at addresses in Dorval, Lachine and Pointe-Claire. Montreal Urban Community police received a half dozen complaints.

Quebec Justice Minister Gil Rémillard acted on the complaints. In mid-August, he told the press that two seized editions of the *Klansman* likely constituted hate propaganda under the terms of the Criminal Code. Then, in November, police arrested 21-year-old Vachon as well as two other Sherbrooke Klansmen: Laval residents Jean-Pierre Bergeron, 23, and Stéphane Pigeon, 21. Seized were 1,250 copies of the *Klansman*. The three men were caught by the Sûreté du Québec as they crept through a wooded area near Stanhope, trying to make it from Vermont into Quebec.

When the trio appeared for their trial in April 1992, it was revealed that their lawyers had negotiated a plea bargain with the Crown. Instead of being tried on the more serious charges of conspiracy, illegal possession and smuggling of hate literature, the three men agreed to plead guilty to simple illegal importation. They were fined $500 each and given six months to pay it. Human rights groups were outraged. "Five hundred bucks and six months to pay? It's a joke," said Jack Jedwab, a Canadian Jewish Congress spokesman. Canadian customs law, apparently, does not make any distinction between a carton of smuggled cigarettes and a fistful of vicious hate propaganda, but it does regard smuggled pornography as more serious than smuggled tracts calling for the extermination of Jews.

Eric Vachon's Klansmen would not comment on the outcome of the case, so no one knew whether the three men were pleased. But as Vachon left the Sherbrooke courtroom, a large smile on his face, he made a Nazi salute. He certainly seemed to be pleased.

By month's end, copies of the *Klansman* were being found once again in mailboxes in the Montreal suburb of Verdun.

Unlike Ontario or Alberta—where veteran hate group organizers Wolfgang Droege and Terry Long generally succeed in keeping their skinhead followers under control—Quebec is truly a distinct society. Its native hate movement is fractured and somewhat disorganized.

But its skinheads are probably the most vicious streetfighters in the country. Anglo-Canada's skinheads, for the most part, know when to cut and run. Quebec's skins, however, are renowned for their fearlessness as much as their ruthlessness. Even Heritage Front leader Droege will admit this is true. Says Droege, who started to organize a Heritage Front branch in Montreal in August 1993, "They are crazy up there, those guys. What they need is a good leader to come in and lead them."

In 1990, Michel Larocque and his second-in-command, Alain Roy, tried to control Quebec's uncontrollable young skinheads. They formed a group called White Power Canada (WPC), which was designed to act as a junior Ku Klux Klan club, Roy says. But it was also an attempt to organize a group that would do the Klan's dirty work, leaving Larocque and Roy free from messy criminal indictments and encounters with the law. (Droege has embraced a similar approach with an alliance with the Church of the Creator's "Security Legions"; the Aryan Nations' Terry Long has done the same with the Calgary-based Final Solution Skinheads.) WPC's members were younger skinheads, half anglophone, half francophone. It was headquartered in Montreal, where the group had about 60 members. Other WPC cells were set up in Quebec City and the Gatineau Hills region, north of Ottawa, with about 15 members each. Says Roy: "White Power Canada is more for young people. And they are very active against the World Anti-Fascist League and SHARP [Skinheads Against Racial Prejudice]. They're very active." He grins. "They fight for us."

Brent Klauser, who is a member of White Power Canada, describes one such fight that took place at a community centre on Pie IX Boulevard, in Montreal, two nights before the Aryan Fest. Inside the community centre, the World Anti-Fascist League was sponsoring a discussion on hate groups, when skinheads appeared outside the building. Klauser was one of them. "As far as neo-Nazis go, there were only seven skinheads there, if you include me, and I don't consider myself a skinhead," says Klauser. "There were about 50 of us. All of the other people were normal. All we were doing was standing in front of the building chanting 'White power!' And we were saluting, too. Later on, I personally, with about four other guys, got chased by about 15 SHARP skins and about ten police. The police saw the SHARP guys hit me over the head with a metal pipe, and they did absolutely nothing."

The most startling aspect of Brent Klauser's story is confirmed by reporters who rushed to the scene: while anti-racist activists barricaded themselves inside the community centre, locking doors and windows and making frantic calls to 911, a mob of local residents showered the building with rocks and smashed windows. Despite repeated calls, police took well over 30 minutes to arrive. When they finally did, *The Montreal Gazette* reported the next day, dozens of area residents were among those chanting "White power!"

As front-line racists, like the teenaged drummer boys who led charges in the Napoleonic battles of old, the members of White Power Canada appeared to be doing their job well. Larocque, Roy and other senior Klansmen were not being directly linked to any racist crime while urban Quebec's non-whites, minorities and Jews were being subjected to an ever-increasing campaign of terror. As hate campaigns go, it was an effective one. But, in late 1992, WPC went too far.

On November 29, four young skinheads linked to White Power Canada—aged 15 to 17—beat to death a man they incorrectly believed was gay. As he was jogging through a wooded area in Angrignon Park, a well-known hang-out for gay men, 51-year-old Yves Lalonde was attacked and savagely beaten with tree branches and a baseball bat, police said, and robbed of $92. On December 3, acting on anonymous tips, police arrested the four neo-Nazi youths and charged them with first-degree murder.

The murder provoked shock waves of disbelief across Quebec and Canada. Michael Crelinsten, president of the Canadian Jewish Congress of Quebec, told *The Globe and Mail*: "If the reported facts are accurate, this has to be viewed as one of the most serious incidents of its kind ever in Canada." But it was not over yet. Two weeks later, a 37-year-old schoolteacher was found beaten to death at a rest stop in Joliette—a rest stop reputed to be a popular meeting place for gay men. The high-school teacher, Daniel Lacombe, was beaten on the head until he suffered a fatally ruptured aneurysm. Five young men aged 16 to 19—again linked to White Power Canada—were arrested and charged with manslaughter, aggravated assault and conspiracy to commit a criminal act.

Brent Klauser, who says his organization fell apart after the two murders, insists that the youths involved were what he calls "independent skinheads." "I knew them to say 'hi,' but that was it. They were okay guys. They weren't members, though, and I don't care what the cops say. I was a member of White Power Canada, and those guys weren't at any of our meetings."

Klauser now regrets his involvement with White Power Canada, saying that it has attracted far too much official scrutiny. In recent months, he says, agents from the Canadian Security Intelligence Service (CSIS) have visited his parents' Montreal home to ask him questions and called his friends to ask them about him. Says the young skinhead: "I'm having a lot of problems with CSIS. Try being 16 years old and telling your parents why CSIS is coming by to ask you questions. It's not a lot of fun." But Klauser has not abandoned his white supremacist creed. Through his considerable contacts in Canada's racist network—his cousin, police say, is a senior member of the Heritage Front in Toronto—Klauser has kept active in the Montreal skinhead scene. In mid-August 1993, in fact, he was one of a group of neo-Nazis who organized a "racialist concert" in Terrasse Vaudreuil. More than 200 skinheads attended.

By April 1993, most of the boys charged in the Lalonde slaying had pleaded guilty to second-degree murder. Contrary to what Klauser says, two of them had, in fact, been active members of White Power Canada. Police say these two youths had boasted about "doing faggots." All of the boys were completely sober at the time of the murder. They received the maximum possible sentence under the Young Offenders Act: three years in a reformatory and two years' probation. "The rest got three years in 'juvie'—juvenile detention," Klauser says.

The boy who had wielded the baseball bat was 15 years old. He told police he wanted to "rid the park of faggots so children could play there again."

Asked if he has ever read anything about Adrian Arcand, Lionel Groulx, André Laurendeau or any of the other colorful anti-Semitic personalities who have played substantial roles in the history of modern Quebec, Ku Klux Klan Exalted Cyclops Alain Roy shrugs. "Yes," he says, appearing uncertain. "But our people don't know a lot about that stuff any more."

Perhaps they should, if for no other reason than to realize that the writings of Arcand, Groulx et al. would provide a ready supply of anti-Semitic filler for Roy's French-language Ku Klux Klan publications. No discussion of Quebec's modern hate movement is complete without a discussion of the men who served as its spiritual grandfathers half a century ago. In the case of Adrian Arcand, for example, his influence continues to be felt in far right circles, even though he has been dead for almost two decades. And Père Lionel Groulx, unbeknownst to many of his admirers, remains a beacon of nationalist inspiration—notwithstanding the fact that he was an unashamed propagandist.

Arcand was born in Quebec City in October 1899, the son of a carpentry union organizer. Like all Quebec children of his era, he studied in Catholic Church–run institutions. In 1919, at the age of 20, he decided he wanted to be a journalist. A passable reporter, Arcand plied his trade for a time at the Montreal daily *La Patrie*, then at *The Montreal Star*. From there, he joined the staff at *La Presse*, where he would remain for the next decade. During this period, he married a French-Canadian girl named Yvonne, fathered three sons, pursued his hobby of astronomy and was commissioned a lieutenant in Châteauguay's militia. But then, in 1929, he was fired from *La Presse* for trying to organize a union drive.

Unable to find work at any of Montreal's dailies, Arcand hooked up with a Montreal printer named Joseph Ménard. Within a short time, the two men—Arcand with his trim figure and military bearing; Ménard, a squat, jowly little man with access to his father's printing presses—had launched no fewer than three weekly papers. With the help of a few well-appointed Quebec businessmen and politicians, among them Montreal Mayor Camillien Houde, the pair churned out *Le Patriote*, *Le Goglu* and *Le Chameau,* among others. No longer bound by mainstream journalism's concerns about neutrality, accuracy or good taste, Arcand unburdened himself of a number of prejudices within the pages of these papers. Arcand and Ménard took aim at American industrialists, Liberal politicians and, most of all, Jews. Jews, Jews and more Jews. The 1.5 per cent of the national population who were Jewish were "responsible for all of the evils of the world today," Arcand declared. Through the three weeklies, Arcand and his portly sidekick were able to continue an unrelenting anti-Semitic barrage, ranting about the powers of secretive "Jewish syndicates," how Jews were "sneaky and fraudulent," and pillorying the likes of "Jew-lover" Mackenzie King. (Nothing could have been further from the truth, of course; King was quietly anti-Semitic.) Between advertisements by well-to-do French-Canadian professionals, they also published grotesque anti-Semitic cartoons and caricatures, complete with horns, claws and fangs.

No issue was safe from Arcand and Ménard's anti-Jewish manipulations. The Lindbergh baby had been kidnapped by Jews, the two wrote, and its blood had been drained for use in their "rituals." The Baron de Rothschild was none other than Bolshevik Leon Trotsky. Vladimir Ilich Lenin was the son of a Jewish mother and he spoke fluent Yiddish. Jews were the killers of Christ. They caused plagues and famines. They were Satan-worshippers. They murdered children in furtherance of Talmudic decree. They were a "race" responsible for the twin evils of capitalism and modernism (when that was insufficient, they were to blame for communism, too). Their thirst for anti-Semitism seemingly unquenchable, Arcand and Ménard even peddled reprints of the infamous czarist hoax, "The Protocols of the Learned Elders of Zion," for a few extra pennies.

Laboring "to free the white race from its Jewish chains," Arcand made contact with a startling number of professional anti-Semites around the globe. Among these were the British Imperial Fascist League, Australia's National Guard, the National Social Christian Party of South Africa, the Fascist Party of Rhodesia and, last but not least, Hitler's NSDAP in Germany. Although he was for many years an enthusiastic supporter of R.B. Bennett's Conservatives, Arcand did not believe that party was sufficiently to the right on the political spectrum. So, in November 1929, he founded the Patriotic Order of the Goglus, a group of anti-Semitic nationalists named for a colorful bird seen in Quebec's wheat fields. Like the bird from which they took their name, the Goglus were noisy and determined—and dedicated to "exterminating dangerous vermin," as Arcand put it.

Following his 1930 electoral victory in Germany, Hitler was hailed by Arcand and his Goglus legion as no less than the savior of Christian civilization. "We salute with great enthusiasm the supreme triumph of this great hero," Arcand wrote of Hitler in *Le Goglu*. In the same vein, he was contemptuous of liberal democracy, calling it "an internationalist-minded Jewish invention which was imposed on France in 1789 and spread by Napoleon throughout France." Hitler's violent campaign against the Jews—state-sanctioned boycotts; the anti-Semitic 1935 Nuremberg Laws, which forbade Gentile and Jewish intermarriage; the mounting cycle of pogroms—was hailed by Arcand and Ménard. "What is being accomplished in Germany at the moment can also be accomplished in the province of Quebec, where live the vast majority of Canadian Jews," Arcand opined in *Le Miroir* in June 1932.

Father Lionel Groulx was fishing the same stream at about the same time, albeit with considerably less notoriety. Born in January 1878, Groulx was taught in a classical college in Ste-Thérèse, in rural Quebec, and was propelled into the priesthood while still in his teens. From 1915 to 1949, he taught history at the University of Montreal, founded in 1920 the Action Française, a nationalistic movement, and wrote a number of books of French-Canadian history. He was a favorite writer of Quebec premier René Lévesque and he was called "the spiritual father of modern Quebec" by former Quebec Liberal Party leader Claude Ryan. He was admired—even adored. But Groulx is less known for his many contributions to Quebec's impressive body of anti-Semitic and white supremacist literature.

That Groulx was an anti-Semite and a white supremacist there can be no doubt. In her controversial 1992 doctoral thesis, Quebec writer Esther Délisle calmly lays waste to Groulx and his contemporaries, and the result is devastating. Under his own name—or under pseudonyms he favored, such as Lambert Clossé, Jacques Brassier, XXX, L. Adolphe and nine others—Groulx wrote that the French-Canadian "race" was under attack by "traitors in our midst," that is, the Jews. Groulx believed that French Canadians were a race apart: "God put on our foreheads the mark of the chosen." For this reason, he decreed, francophones must resist the "calumny" of interbreeding with the "inferior element[s]" and "cancerous growths" of blacks, aboriginals and other ethnic groupings. "The French-Canadian nation," he wrote, "is a pure race without a trace of crossbreeding."

Although as much a white supremacist as Alain Roy, Lionel Groulx reserved his harshest criticisms for the Jew. "The Jew is interested in one thing, and one thing alone," he wrote under the name Lambert Clossé. "That is why he can be found wherever business is being transacted. It is the source of his internationalism." This is not nearly as benign as it sounds, writes Groulx under the Brassier name in September 1933: "Jewish internationalism is one of the most dangerous forces of moral and social decay on the planet."

Many years later, Ernst Zundel, Jim Keegstra and others would deny that the Holocaust had taken place. Yet Groulx achieved the distinction of denying it while it was taking place. To this man of God, the Nazis' extermination of Jews was "persecution occurring at the end of the world, which may or may not be true." His lack of concern seemingly related to his belief that "Jewish influence is present in every conspiracy and at the base of all revolutions which always have the same goal: the obliteration of Christianity." To make this point clear, Groulx, who often quoted approvingly from "The Protocols of the Learned Elders of Zion," dwelt at great length on "Jewish commercial tyranny" in Montreal; on the fact that Canada's economic system was an "unjust, anti-social, unpatriotic Jewish creation of international scope [that was] anti-Christian and murderous"; and on Jews, who were "an ethnic minority of no particular significance."

But who would erase the stain of Judaism from Groulx's longed-for French-Canadian utopia? Who would banish the Jewish and non-white hordes from what he called "our miserable little democracies?" Groulx asked. The beloved priest had no answer, but he had one or two candidates in mind as a role model: Adolf Hitler and Benito Mussolini. Of Hitler he wrote: "Happy Austria, to have found its leader and, with him, the road to resurrection! How we too need a National Front and a man who is like the young and captivating [Hitler]!" Of Mussolini Groulx said: "The Duce, who is a former teacher, understands how to mold the dough of human minds. . . . Fortunate country whose schools are possessed of a soul! Fortunate countries to whom fate has delivered a leader!"

In all of this unblushing Nazi sloganeering, Groulx was not alone. As Délisle dryly notes, there were others, like André Laurendeau, *Le Devoir* and Action Française. They were, she writes, "a small group of intellectuals, well-informed and educated, spewing their endless and hate-filled madness upon the imaginary Jew—for the anti-Semite's Jew is always a symbolic construct—and seeking desperately to convince the ignorant masses that this delirium is real, while all the while, the very same masses just don't seem to get it."

Laurendeau, a Groulx follower who became editor-in-chief of *Le Devoir*, was an unashamed pro-Nazi propagandist for a goodly part of his life. Jews, he noted, "do not allow themselves to be assimilated anywhere. No race has successfully absorbed the occult rites of this Eastern civilization." As a consequence, French Canadians "will give them the boot," Laurendeau wrote, adding elsewhere: "Throw them out. Too bad for them if they do not manage to emerge unscathed." Writing directly to Jews who have the temerity to complain about such Nazi-style exterminations of their families and friends, Laurendeau stated: "You insinuate yourselves among us myopically; your obnoxious lack of tact, your presumption when you are strong, and your spinelessness when you wax eloquent will get you into trouble. If you could only feel the exasperation your presence everywhere provokes."

Le Devoir, sadly, was no better during this period. Founded in 1910 to, as Délisle puts it, defend Roman Catholicism and francophone nationalism, the award-winning newspaper was, for a time, as anti-Semitic as Groulx, Laurendeau and even Arcand. "The Jewish house of commerce," the paper editorialized in August 1934, was "the streetwalker-in-chief of Israel." The Jews were the authors of something *Le Devoir* called "Judeo-American Finance with Bolshevik sympathies" who "aspire—as everyone knows—to the happy day when their race will dominate the world." They were a "crooked-nosed people milling about whose fingers are heavily, or at least visibly, covered with rings." They "give off a strong, alliaceous Jewish stench"; they "absolutely reek of garlic."

Adrian Arcand, it would seem, was no lonely fascist voice in Quebec's political wilderness. With Lionel Groulx, André Laurendeau and *Le Devoir*, he had plenty of high-profile company. As a consequence, when he wrote in this period that Jews were the products of "filthy ghettos" and that they were "the flotsam and jetsam of the Red Sea," not many people noticed. Nor did many eyebrows arch at his conclusion that Jews were, in fact, the "left-over[s] from the justifiable furnaces of Nebuchadnezzar." The Jewish community, however, was understandably concerned about the culture of anti-Semitism sweeping Quebec in the 1930s; in particular, Canadian Jews were concerned about Adrian Arcand. When petitioned to do something about him by Quebec's Jewish community, the response of Premier Louis-Alexandre Taschereau was sympathetic but ineffective. With few exceptions, the province's Roman Catholic ruling class did nothing.

Quebec's Jews were not deterred. Accounts of a Nazi-led holocaust against Jews in Europe were shaking the foundations of the

Canadian Jewish establishment; as a result, it would be an understatement to say that Canadian Jews were alarmed by Arcand's unbridled anti-Semitism and growing influence with many Quebeckers. Many were, in fact, terrified. Montreal lawyer Samuel W. Jacobs, one of the first Jews to be elected to the House of Commons, declared in 1933 that the "language used by American Jew-baiters [was] mild to that compared to that here"—and he was probably right. A few decided it was time to take action against the growing domestic fascist menace.

Liberal politician Peter Bercovitch—the first Jew to be elected to Quebec's National Assembly—led the charge against Arcand and his ilk. Bercovitch, a respected Montrealer who had been an effective representative of the city's Jewish community on issues related to schooling, rents and labor relations, wanted to spur Taschereau's government into action against the Goglus. For this, Bercovitch earned the considerable antipathy of Arcand and his fascist followers. To them, he was "a false prince." (In fact, Bercovitch was the Jew Arcand had in mind when he penned the "left-over from the justifiable furnaces of Nebuchadnezzar" slander.) *Le Devoir* editorialized that "the role [Bercovitch] has accepted . . . makes him odious." Noted the newspaper: "He is Jewish—Jewish to the depths of his soul and in every fibre of his body. . . . This Jew [is] trying to cover up the truth . . . in an era in which his people are hated more universally than they have ever been before."

Undeterred by the threats and the name-calling, in January 1932 Bercovitch introduced a bill in the provincial legislature that would outlaw "the publication and distribution of outrageous subject matter against any religious sect, creed, class, denomination, race or nationality."

Some still believe the Bercovitch bill was a legal stroke of genius. Whereas individuals could sue for defamation, groups of individuals traditionally could not. As one Jewish leader put it at the time: "If one were to call me a thief or a murderer or a seducer of women, I could go to court and obtain justice. But if one says that all Jews are murderers, thieves and seducers, there is no redress." (It is interesting to note that a number of U.S. states—and one Canadian province, Manitoba—have since followed Bercovitch's lead. In some states, aggrieved citizens who make recourse to group libel statutes have been able to sue hate groups out of existence—and all without making recourse to the sometimes messy criminal prosecution route.)

As expected, Arcand's legions whipped themselves into a frenzy over the bill. In an editorial that seemed to be a textbook-perfect example of the sort of viciousness that Bercovitch had hoped to prevent, *Le Miroir* screamed that Taschereau's government was ready to "permit the residue of Yiddish immigrants from Poland and Russia to hinder the rightful claims of an honest and upright race which does not want to submit any longer to the exploitation, thievery, perfidy, immorality, filth and corruption and Bolshevik propaganda of the Sons of Judas." The fascists and *Le Devoir* were not alone in their opposition. Much of the mainstream press opposed the bill. Displaying the sort of journalistic knee-jerk utilitarianism that persists to this day, *The Montreal Gazette* called the bill "a huge steam-driven crusher deployed to crush tiny kernels of fanaticism." *Le Devoir* declared that newspapers would be forced to endure committees of Jewish censors that would, "like the Kosher butcher shops," allow nothing to be printed "which is not approved according to Talmudic prescriptions."

Despite a number of stirring speeches in support of the Bercovitch bill in the National Assembly, the legislation was doomed. After much public hand-wringing, Premier Taschereau concluded in February 1932 that public opinion "was not ready for such a radical measure." The bill was allowed to die on the parliamentary order paper.

Arcand, Ménard and the Goglus were overcome with glee, but it was to be a short-lived celebration. In July 1932, E. Abugov, a Jewish merchant from Lachine, sought an injunction against Joseph Ménard, publisher of *Le Goglu*, *Le Chameau* and *Le Miroir* to prevent the distribution of further "articles libellous of the Jews in general." Quebec Superior Court judge Gonzalve Désaulniers reflected on Abugov's petition over the summer of 1932 and, in September, delivered his decision. "The Jewish race is one marvellously gifted," Désaulniers wrote in his seven-page judgment. "They offer for our reflection the prodigious and outstanding example in history of a people surviving the empires which enslaved it." But Désaulniers concluded, with obvious reluctance, that he lacked the judicial authority to issue the requested injunctive relief.

Quebec's Jews were not surprised by the outcome of the case. Nor, surprisingly, were they displeased. While Arcand et al. had won the legal battle—barely—they had lost something else: resources. Never particularly solvent to start with, the three anti-Semitic weeklies were subjected to a number of organized advertising boycotts and, in 1931, an arson that destroyed Ménard's presses. By 1933, the three newspapers were bankrupt.

But Adrian Arcand was not to be hindered by such minor setbacks. Inspired by the Third Reich, and having grown somewhat tired of the role of journalistic rabble-rouser, he more or less abandoned the Patriotic Order of the Goglus in 1934 and, in the same year, created another political vehicle. This one was openly and proudly fascist; it was called the Parti national social chrétien, the National Socialist Christian Party (NSCP). Arcand—who had taken to carrying a nickel-plated revolver to protect himself—was its natural leader. Despite his megalomania and paranoia, Arcand was an impressive public speaker. As he told an enraptured *Life* magazine correspondent in July 1938, "In mass meetings, I speak like a man in the streets speaks and thinks." Three years later, Arcand boasted a membership of 80,000—but the true figure was probably closer to no more than 2,000. His influence should not be measured in membership cards alone, however. In 1934, he remained a close associate of R.B. Bennett and a paid publicist working for Bennett's Conservative Party. The following year, he was paid to edit a Quebec government publication called *L'illustration Nouvelle*, and he was well known to Premier Maurice Duplessis.

Among other things, the National Socialist Christian Party called for the forced resettlement of Jews to a concentration camp near Hudson Bay. Under Arcand's leadership, citizenship would be restricted to "the two great races that have made up Canada's population since the beginning, and the other Aryan members of the population who agreed to identify with the two founding races." Jews would be shipped to Madagascar, Arcand declared in a February 1938 interview with *The Nation*, where they would be "all together and happy." All "books, publications of all sorts, theatrical representations and cinema . . . works of a corrupting art, etc. . . . which have a pernicious influence on morality, the national character and accepted traditions" would be summarily banned.

Membership in the NSCP was restricted to "all the French Canadians and Aryans resident in Canada [who] wish to identify themselves as French Canadian." An anglophone branch was established as well. Members were expected to distribute hate propaganda, recruit members and attend rallies. These events typically ended with rousing chants, in French: "Long live the King! Long live Canada! Long live the Party! Long live Arcand!" In exchange for their efforts and their enthusiasm, members were permitted to wear the dark blue military-style uniform of the NSCP. Its emblem, found on every member's shirtsleeve, was a swastika surrounded by maple leaves and topped by a beaver.

In its first electoral effort, in April 1934, the NSCP backed the losing campaign of Salluste Lavery for Montreal mayor. Lavery went on about the "Jewish menace" and picked up 12,740 votes. The mayoralty race's victor, Camillien Houde—who had taken to condemning anti-Semitism and racism—won almost 90,000 votes. On the federal scene, Arcand could not quite bring himself to abandon the side of his good friend Conservative Party leader R.B. Bennett. As he wrote in March 1933, in one of the final editions of *Le Goglu*, Bennett was a "great patriot and a great Christian. . . . Our Prime Minister intends to defend our regime with the utmost national and Christian energy. . . . His public declarations on what our public regime ought to be are in perfect harmony with those of Mussolini and Hitler."

In this period, Arcand also played ideological footsie with the rabid anti-Semites in the Social Credit Party, then the government in Alberta under William Aberhart. Overtures were also made by the NSCP to Quebec's Union Nationale. In both cases, Arcand felt that the leadership of the Alberta Social Credit Party and the Union Nationale lacked sufficient moral commitment to the NSCP's Hitlerite struggle.

So the NSCP followed its own agenda. Its members—some 2,500 at the NSCP's height of popularity—were drilled in military style by Arcand acolyte Maj. Joseph M. Scott. This private fascist militia was trained in judo, marching and hand-to-hand combat. The NSCP founded a number of mysterious front organizations, with such names as the Women's Anti-Communist League and the Canadian Anti-Jewish Front. As young members of Quebec's White Power Canada would do a half century later, it would affix swastika stickers to the windows of Jewish businesses and hand out hate tracts on buses, streetcars and wherever people congregated. The NSCP's headquarters was on St. Lawrence Boulevard, across from the *La Presse* building. It was decorated with huge red swastika banners, anti-Semitic cartoons and charts detailing the plans of the international Jewish conspiracy.

Here and there, Adrian Arcand and his National Socialist Christian Party enjoyed some degree of popular support. In Sorel, for example, the mayor joined Arcand onstage at a rally where he received a gift of a mirror engraved with the swastika. The Sorel mayor promised to display it in his office, Lita-Rose Betcherman recounts in her seminal work, *The Swastika and the Maple Leaf*. Another rally, this time in Quebec City in May 1939, drew 3,500 people; once there, the crowd gave a few fascist salutes, recited the Lord's Prayer and pledged allegiance to the monarch. In the press, Arcand also acquired a modest amount of success. In December 1937, *The Globe and Mail* called him "the brilliant young French Canadian." The *New York Post* claimed that no fewer than 100,000 Quebec fascists could be found in the Great White North—and the *New York Times* questioned, in January 1938, whether Quebec was turning into a fascist bastion as a result of Adrian Arcand's efforts. In July 1938, Arcand attempted to capitalize on this fawning media attention with the creation of a Canada-wide fascist alliance called the National Unity Party, but the NUP was neither national nor unified. It did not get off the drawing board.

It was around this time—in the summer of 1939, when Hitler's growing strength was finally alarming Jews and non-Jews alike in North America—that Canadian Gentiles also started to regard Adrian Arcand with concern. Before, the quirky French-Canadian fascist had been easy to dismiss as a harmless lunatic. But now, with Arcand making contacts with the likes of British fascist Sir Oswald Mosley and receiving funding from fascist governments in Europe, he was not so laughable. Quebec Premier Maurice Duplessis, who had previously been sanguine about Arcand working as a paid contributor to one of his own Union Nationale newsletters, now intoned that "those who raise racial issues are the worst enemies of this Canada of ours, and of the Province of Quebec."

In September 1939, Britain and France declared war on Germany. Ten days later, the Allies were joined by Canada. That summer, the RCMP hurriedly interned hundreds of fascists and Nazis "considered dangerous." Dozens of Germans and German-Canadians were bundled off to camps at Petawawa, Ontario, and Kananaskis, Alberta. Adrian Arcand, meanwhile, chose discretion over valor; he went to ground for a few months.

But it was to no avail. In May 1940, the RCMP swooped down on Canada's fascist glitterati and confiscated their propaganda and membership lists. Adrian Arcand himself was arrested at his summer home in the Laurentian mountains. In the following month, the attorneys-general of Quebec and Canada agreed that a fascist conspiracy existed in a number of provinces and that Adrian Arcand was one of the men who led the conspiracy. Criminal proceedings were to be held in abeyance, but Arcand would spend the remainder of the war in the internment camp at Petawawa.

Arcand was released in July 1945, a broken man. He returned to his cottage north of Montreal, where he indulged himself in some oil painting and classical music. He wrote the odd anti-Semitic pamphlet, but it was nothing like the old days.

Then, in 1961, he was approached by 22-year-old Ernst Zundel, a commercial artist who had arrived in Canada from Germany three years before. The two spent many hours together at Arcand's humble cottage, discussing the conspiracy and what should be done about it. Zundel would later remark that Arcand changed his life, for when the aging anti-Semite took him under his wing, he passed on most of his pro-Nazi library—and the names of hundreds of his far right contacts in Europe and North America—to his young German follower. In turn, Zundel would go on to become one of the world's largest producers of neo-Nazi propaganda and one of the most enthusiastic financiers of the international hate movement. The legacy of Arcand continues to be felt today, many years after his death in 1967.

And what does Ernst Zundel have to say about Adrian Arcand? "It was a French Canadian," he says, "who turned me into a German."

When the swastika-lighting was over, and the Aryan Fest T-shirts had been handed out, and the band Rahowa was packing up its instruments for the return trip to Toronto, Alain Roy, Exalted Cyclops of the Invisible Empire Knights of the Ku Klux Klan, allowed himself a few moments' reflection. Sitting on the roof of a car, he fingers some leftover French-language hate propaganda, produced by NSDAP–AO. "It's not hate propaganda," he says, unconcerned that a journalist has described it as such. "Everything we do is legal. It's in French for the territory of Quebec."

Roy agrees that Quebec's neo-Nazi movement is in transition, that it is looking for a leader who can unite the various factions and warring hate groups. Asked whether the Ku Klux Klan is capable of providing that leadership, he shrugs. "The Klan is a good tool, and it has provided some good contacts for us," he says. "But I think, in the future, we're not going to use the name of the Ku Klux Klan. I know our group is always going to survive here. We have a good organization now."

What does his "organization" want?

"To start, we want some land for ourselves, a place for ourselves. It will just be a start. We also want to unite everybody [in the hate movement in Quebec], because, in terms of philosophy, we are already all together."

Everyone? French-speaking and English-speaking racists?

"It's not a question of language," says Roy. "It's more a question of protection. If we can do something to protect white culture, we have to do it, you know? I don't want to separate white Canada from white Quebec. We don't have to make a new country, we have to make a real country.

"Our country, you know?"

11

THE ENCOURAGEMENT OF MALCOLM ROSS

As far right leaders go, Maritimer Malcolm Ross is not particularly noteworthy. He does not call for the extermination of the Jews, as does the Aryan Nations' Terry Long. He does not insist upon the forcible repatriation of non-whites, as does the Heritage Front's Wolfgang Droege. He does not openly advocate stockpiling restricted weapons, or guerrilla training at white supremacist survivalist camps—although, some of his admirers say, he *does* possess a black belt in karate.

His books—he has written four to date and is at work on another—are undeniably anti-Jewish. He denies, for example, that the Holocaust took place; he believes that abortion is a largely Jewish plot to destroy white Christian civilization. In his speeches to ultra-rightist organizations—some members of which assert that he has "a delightful sense of humor"—he does not hesitate to make racist jokes. But, at the end of the day, when the works and words of Malcolm Ross are contrasted with the ruminations of Canadian neo-Nazi and white supremacist leaders with whom he has more than a passing acquaintance, Ross is not particularly noteworthy. In the far right universe, it is even safe to say that he is decidedly average.

What makes Malcolm Ross important—apart from the singular distinction of being the best-known anti-Semite in the Atlantic provinces—is his huge circle of friends and admirers. From pro-apartheid South Africa to the Confederate southern States to the farthest corners of racist Canada, Malcolm Ross is well known and well admired. Over the course of a decade, he has forged an impressive network that encompasses every shade of opinion, and every geographic region, known to the far right. He is, in fact, a case study in the way Canadian neo-Nazis and white suprema-cists come together to support one of their own.

"My address is in the phone book," says Malcolm Ross, when asked to explain how a man so quiet has been able to acquire so much support. "People can contact me. If they get one of my books somewhere, and they enjoy them, they might write me, and they might tell their friends. It's, as they say, a grass-roots thing. It's not well planned or well orchestrated in my case."

In one sense, the Moncton, New Brunswick, junior high school remedial schoolteacher may be right. The Ross network is by no means as large or as organized as that of, say, human rights or envi-ronmental organizations such as Amnesty International or Greenpeace. But it is powerful and it is active.

At the centre of the network is the son of a Presbyterian minister, born in May 1946 in a Winnipeg hospital. Ross's father taught his sons Malcolm and William a healthy appreciation of the Gospels and a respectful fear of God. From an early age, Malcolm Ross was devoted to his father; at the time of the elder man's death in September 1987, Ross called him "a faithful servant of our Lord Jesus Christ, and a wise man whose counsel I sorely miss. . . . He steadfastly supported my efforts." For the early part of his life, Ross's family was nomadic, moving wherever there was a need for a preacher and what Ross calls "traditionalist Christianity." When Malcolm was still a child, the Rosses moved to the Miramichi region of New Brunswick, near

Newcastle. He received all of his elementary and secondary schooling in the North Shore and Miramichi area. There, young Malcolm applied himself to his studies—he favored history—and whiled away the summers fishing for salmon. "The region is famous for salmon fishing," he recalls. "Everybody up there likes to fish."

Malcolm Ross was a quiet youth, and he would grow up to be a quiet man. In person, he stands slightly over six feet and is lean with an athletic build. Above his neatly trimmed mustache, his eyes are perhaps his most distinctive feature; dark and heavy-lidded, they reveal nothing, but they do not appear to miss much. In conversation—which is done only rarely with reporters, and usually at the Tim Horton's on Mountain Road, on Moncton's outskirts—Ross speaks in a measured and controlled voice, resorting occasionally to sarcasm to describe his adversaries, whom he calls "those who hate freedom." Like Jim Keegstra, whom he greatly admires, Ross oozes conviction and sincerity from every pore: he genuinely *believes* there is a con- spiracy at work, one led by "a powerful anti-God force which hates and fears our race, our civilization and, most of all, the religion of Christ." He *believes* that "this conspiracy has been too well docu- mented to be seriously denied."

In 1968, at the age of 22, Ross graduated from the University of New Brunswick with a degree in education and a burning commit- ment to the religion of Christ. For the next ten years, he labored in obscurity as a teacher employed by school districts in rural New Brunswick—from September 1971 to June 1976, at Birchmount School in the Number 15 School District; from September 1976 onwards, he worked as what is called a modified resource teacher at Magnetic Hill School, teaching about 13 students every day. In the evenings, he would scrutinize hard-to-get revisionist tracts and ques- tionable translations of the Talmud. (One Talmudic interpretation used over and over by Ross was actually the work of a notoriously anti- Semitic Roman Catholic priest, I.B. Pranaitis, who twisted words and phrases to give them an anti-Christian flavor.) Alone with his dusty old books, Ross researched; he pondered.

Then, in 1978, while toiling as a math and English teacher, he wrote and published *Web of Deceit*. Later, he would recall what motivated him to write that book, which went on to become one of the most notorious English-language anti-Semitic works produced by a Canadian in this century. "I knew I was dealing with a very controversial subject, and that many others had been silenced because of these revelations," Ross wrote. "[But] I believed I had no choice but to share what I had researched. It was an honest, although perhaps overly ambitious, effort to have Christians look at the present state of our society, and see if anything could be done to restore our Christian values."

Web of Deceit was not nearly so benign as that. It declared that both Anne Frank's diary and the Holocaust were hoaxes and that an international conspiracy existed to wipe Christianity off the face of the Earth. The principal players in this conspiracy, Ross wrote, were international Communists, international financiers and international Zionists. In his short but virulent book, Ross likens Jews to "a deadly poison" and asks: "Cannot blacks and whites live separately and at peace? Why are we being forced to mix against the wishes of both groups?" On the Holocaust, Ross wrote: "From the evidence, suppressed as it may be, I believe we should be able to see that the Jewish casualties should be numbered in the thousands, not the millions."

As anti-Jewish polemics go, *Web of Deceit* did not break any new ground; its hoary sentiments and historical revisionism stretched back at least as far as the "Protocols of the Learned Elders of Zion" (which, incidentally, Ross in his book calls "both true and authentic").

But in Atlantic Canada, where the "Protocols" and similar hate propaganda are as scarce as prairie wheat fields, Malcolm Ross's private obsession generated considerable public debate. "Almost immediately," he later wrote in *Spectre of Power*, "the media moved into action and commenced making inflammatory statements about me and the book, which showed they either knew nothing about the subject with which I was dealing, or else they were simply following the prescribed course of action laid out for them by those who fear exposure above anything else."

One of Ross's early critics was Gary McCauley, a courageous Anglican minister and later a Liberal member of Parliament. In a May 1978 community television broadcast, McCauley ripped into *Web of Deceit*: "I have just finished reading a dirty book. Words cannot describe the filth, the obscenity, the pornography, the profanity. . . . What is even more astonishing is that one is allowed to pursue his nefarious purpose as a teacher. How many impressionable youngsters has he poisoned with his filthy mind?"

And that, with differing degrees of emphasis, was a question that would continue to be asked in relation to the controversy swirling around Malcolm Ross. Had Ross—like Jim Keegstra did for so long in a classroom in Eckville, Alberta—passed on to his students his views about a Jewish conspiracy? Had he taught hate? In *Web of Deceit*, Ross himself may answer this question. In the chapter titled "Education," he writes that he would dearly love to tell his students what he thinks about Jews: "What would happen if teachers began teaching the Conspiracy theory of history as well as the theories of the anti-Christian historians? The students of Canada deserve a chance to hear the other side of the story, a side so suppressed that those who promote it are subjected to official censure. . . . The students of Canada are being denied their Christian heritage."

Across the Atlantic provinces, where men like Malcolm Ross are very rare, the debate raged around water coolers and in letters-to-the-editor columns. "No doubt Ross's book is hate literature," the North Shore *Leader* editorialized; another newspaper opined that the book was "an obscenity, worse than pornography." One University of Toronto professor who had been following the case from afar, meanwhile, wrote to the New Brunswick Human Rights Commission to request that Ross be prosecuted for publishing hate literature. David Attis led a campaign to prevent *Web of Deceit* from being sold in New Brunswick bookstores. Attis lobbied book merchants to keep the book off their shelves. Although the campaign was, for the most part, a success, Ross was equally successful in peddling thousands of copies to fellow travellers across North America, and even to a few hundred supporters in Europe and South Africa. The book sold out two editions and remains out-of-print.

Interestingly, in 1979, Ross sent a letter to a Toronto-based far right newspaper, *Speak Up*, to provide his central Canadian followers with an update on *Web of Deceit*. In the letter, Ross notes that the John Birch Society had approached him for two copies of the controversial book. "I certainly agree [the Birchers] put out a lot of excellent material," enthused Ross.

In the same period, the New Brunswick Human Rights Commission issued a report stating that "it was not possible to prosecute [Ross] under the Criminal Code sections on hate literature because sufficient evidence could not be found to enter prosecutions." However, the commission suggested to the superintendent of the School District 15 board to keep an eye on Malcolm Ross.

For a time, at least, there was no need to be vigilant about the schoolteacher. In 1979, Ross says, he became "seriously physically ill" and was hospitalized. He was unable to work for months. By 1982, though, he had made a full recovery—and, along the way, in 1980, he wed a fiery French Acadian woman who would become one of his most ardent defenders. In 1981, Malcolm and Nicole Ross became parents. They now have four children, ranging in age from 12 to four. The family lives in a large house in the quiet Moncton residential neighborhood of Boundary Creek. The schoolteacher will say little about his family. "I'm a private person," he says. "I keep my family life as separate as reasonably possible." He pauses, then adds with a smile: "But I've got a great family."

In 1983, Ross decided to write another book. "The abortion issue touched my heart and, even though I knew I was a marked man, I felt I had to write about this terrible evil," he recalls. "Like many Canadians, I was getting fed up with all the movies and stories surrounding the Holocaust of World War Two. Therefore, I decided to write a book on the abortion question comparing the Holocaust of European Jews, as portrayed by Hollywood, with the Holocaust of unborn Christians, as verified by government statistics."

372 WEB OF HATE

The resulting 45-page mini-book, *The Real Holocaust: The Attack on Unborn Children and Life Itself*, was in many respects more anti-Semitic than *Web of Deceit*. The cover depicts a grotesque caricature of a bearded Jewish man throwing tiny coffins, presumably containing aborted fetuses, into a hole in the ground. Beside the man, a sign reads: "WELCOME TO DR. HEROD'S ABORTION CLINIC." In the introduction, Ross states that his focus will be "abortions performed in our White Christian Nations." The white race is his concern, he explains, because "it is the white race, especially the British and Northern European segment, which God has permitted to receive and spread the Gospel of Jesus Christ, and which has remained relatively free of the Conspiracy's absolute control."

Abortion, Ross states, is a creation of secular humanism, an "anti-Christ religion" that is "the power behind movements supporting World Government, complete sexual freedom, abortion, euthanasia, homosexuality, suicide, legalization of drugs and pornography." The people who make up this very busy movement, he notes, are "smut pedlars, atheists, perverts and seducers of children." These people, he says, are forces behind rock music, modern art and the drug trade.

In conversation, Ross attempts to dismiss the avalanche of criticism that has greeted each of his various publications, saying: "I'm a fairly secure person." But, to anyone reading *The Real Holocaust*, it becomes rapidly obvious that Ross has been stung by the many attacks. In one passage, for example, he states that white Christians "have been conditioned by Humanists to accept their economic theories, their moral perversions and their historical fairy tales by their careful conditioning processes and their famous reinforcing buzzwords, such as 'bigot,' 'fascist,' 'racist' and 'anti-Semite.'"

To Ross, one such historical fairy tale, of course, is the mass extermination of millions of Jews by Nazi Germany. Calling the Holocaust an "imaginary mass slaughter" that "has been used to create a false sense of guilt in Christian nations," Ross contrasts the Nazis' final solution with the prevalence of abortion in Canada. In one passage that betrays more than a hint of white supremacy and anti-Semitism, he writes: "Never has our Race had such a challenge as today. Faced with massive conditioning designed to make you hate your Western Christian Heritage through such movies as 'Holocaust' and 'Roots,' and through textbooks that attempt to portray our ancestors as fools and liars, you must be prepared to break through this wall of fabrications to find the truth. . . . [Past generations have] succumbed to the Humanists' lies and allowed two World Wars to destroy the flower of our Race. Now, through abortion, they are willing to sacrifice the BUDS of our Race. They have opened the floodgates of immigration, diluting our blood while slaughtering those of our Race by the millions. In fact, the White Race's proportion of the world's population is steadily declining."

With *The Real Holocaust*—as with *Web of Deceit*—Malcolm Ross again touched off a massive controversy in Atlantic Canada. By early April 1984, his second book was being roundly condemned on newspaper editorial pages and from the pulpit. And, once again revealing a rather thin skin, Ross expressed his annoyance with certain Roman Catholic clergy who had criticized him. These same priests, he wrote, had been "sitting down and negotiating a deal with these overbearing and presumptuous [Jews]." Concerned that Christian churches were doing nothing to point out what to him was obvious—namely, a worldwide Jewish conspiracy at work undermining Christianity, the white race, etc., etc.—Ross took pen in hand and published a prepared lecture in booklet form, titled "Christianity vs. Judeo-Christianity: the Battle for Truth." Like *The Real Holocaust*, the new treatise was published by the Stronghold Publishing Company, a firm owned and operated by Ross himself and run through a Moncton post office box number.

In the booklet, Ross writes that the instigators of the Russian Revolution and international communism, and hate laws, and child pornography, and Marxism, and the "so-called Jewish Holocaust" were what he calls "these people we know as Jews." With their allies in the Jewish community, liberal Christian churches were promoting a "web of deceit known as Judeo-Christianity" that was undermining the "Celto-Saxon and related peoples of the Earth." The content is nothing new. What is most significant about the booklet, instead, is a small notation on its title page. There, Ross identifies himself as "Executive Director of the Maritime Branch of the Christian Defence League of Canada." This tiny revelation was the first confirmation of Ross's growing links to viciously anti-Semitic groups that favored the rhetoric of violence and terror. (Ross also referred to himself as CDL Maritime Director in letters to *The Times-Transcript* in Moncton in June 1984 and July 1985.)

The Christian Defence League had been formed in the fall of 1983 in Alberta to raise funds for Jim Keegstra's legal defence fund. It was led, in the early days, by well-known Albertan anti-Semites Jim Green, Tom Erhart and, significantly, Terry Long. Long, who was the CDL's first president, of course, would go on to infamy as the High Aryan Warrior Priest of the Church of Jesus Christ Christian Aryan Nations. Ross now clearly regrets making public his connection to the CDL, which at the time was the most extreme anti-Jewish organization active in Canada. Asked about his involvement with the league, he is extremely evasive. "I was involved with it, a bit," he says, sounding uncomfortable. "Do you think this is only for Keegstra, or what?"

After receiving his guest's assurances that the Christian Defence League went on to act as a lobby group for other Holocaust-deniers—people like him—Ross appears mollified. "I suppose if they were looking for someone in the Maritimes, I would be their natural choice, since I had written my book in 1978. I was known, somewhat, out [in Alberta] at that time."

Pressed for further detail about the CDL connection, Ross balks. "I really don't know," he says. "I don't remember. . . . It's a lot of water under the bridge."

Is he still involved with the CDL?

"Well, at least not . . . no," he says, his frustration clear and his facts not quite straight. "I don't know what's going on. To a great extent, I suppose something is needed [like the CDL in Atlantic Canada]. Basically, we all attempt to, as the name suggests, defend our Christian faith and heritage. I don't think it's anything terribly formal. I think it's people working, each in his own way, to advance what he believes is the truth."

The protestations aside, Malcolm Ross's discovery of the Christian Defence League in 1983 was an epiphany of sorts. Previously restricted to the support of a small number of anti-Semites and conspiracy theorists in Atlantic Canada, he found that the CDL opened many doors, behind which could be found an organized neo-Nazi network that stretched from one end of Canada to the next. In the months that followed the publication of *The Real Holocaust* and "Christianity vs. Judeo-Christianity," Ross would need the network.

In July 1984, a Miramichi resident and retired chemist named Dr. Julius Israeli complained to the New Brunswick attorney-general, David Clark, about *Web of Deceit* and *The Real Holocaust*. For the next 13 months, Ross would remain under police investigation as New Brunswick authorities pored through the two books. For much of the fall of 1985, Ross's file shuttled between various desks in government offices in the provincial capital. In time, it became clear that Clark and his Justice Department officials were uncomfortable with the conclusions reached by the police. Finally, in August 1985, while Ross was on holidays, Clark confirmed that no charges would be laid against the schoolteacher. *Web of Deceit*, he noted, undoubtedly met the Criminal Code definition of hate propaganda, but it was also out-of-print. Said Clark: "There has been an exhaustive examination of the case. This affair has been, without question, the most troublesome decision I've been faced with as a minister. I've labored over it and lost sleep over it. I've consulted widely and found it to be the single most difficult thing I've been called on to do."

Ross's reaction to the decision: "Obviously, that should have been the end of the matter, and I should have been allowed to enjoy the rest of my holidays in peace. However, such was not the case. Some clever sleuth found there were two copies of *Web of Deceit* in the regional libraries, and also one in the library of the University of New Brunswick, and perhaps a few more somewhere else in the province."

After Clark announced that he would "rethink" his decision not to prosecute, another Justice Department investigation was launched. In September 1986, Clark confirmed his decision not to proceed.

For a few weeks, the Malcolm Ross issue was once again confined to newspaper editorial pages and lunchroom chatter. Then, in October, Julius Israeli laid another complaint—and, once again, Clark initiated another investigation into alleged hate promotion. This, too, concluded in a decision not to charge.

Then, following a January 1987 CBC national radio broadcast in which two anonymous former students stated that Ross was "very prejudiced" and talked "about Jewish [sic] and communism and that" in the classroom, another investigation was launched. This three-person probe was initiated by the District 15 school board and was made up of representatives from the district administration, the Department of Education and the board itself. In late February, after interviewing 59 witnesses over four days, the panel wrote a report titled *The Possible Educational Implications of the Alleged Private Actions of Mr. Malcolm Ross*. The report was not released publicly, but the panel unanimously concluded that Ross's private beliefs had no influence whatsoever on his pupils, even the ones who read newspaper accounts about a proud anti-Semite being employed by an institution of learning. The board's chairman noted that there was "strong support for Mr. Ross" in the school system, among both students and colleagues. Says Ross: "At this time, the man on the street was overwhelmingly supportive. I think people could sense that this is an attack on their faith, or on freedom of speech, and they were concerned."

In April 1987, after three copies of *Web of Deceit* were found gathering dust in a New Brunswick grocery store, another investigation, the fourth, was launched by the provincial attorney-general. Later in that month, Clark announced that a criterion for any criminal prosecution was some likelihood for success. "That test is not met in this case," he told reporters. Jewish groups were understandably upset with Clark's fourth unsuccessful attempt at some kind of action. In an interview with the *Telegraph-Journal*, for example, Dr. Israeli said that

Clark's decision would leave "a dark blot on the government and people of New Brunswick, a blot that will be hard to erase." David Attis, then national secretary to the Canadian Jewish Congress, agreed, saying, "This is a grave injustice to the people of New Brunswick."

For his part, Malcolm Ross was seething at the response of the Jewish community. After contemplating a civil action for defamation—and after concluding that it would be unsuccessful—he wrote: "One can understand the reluctance on the part of our ancestors to permit a massive influx of Jewish refugees when one hears these vicious attacks against men who are bending over backwards to satisfy them." What Ross was saying, in a sense, was that Nazi-style anti-Jewish immigration policies made sense, because Jews sometimes express their disapproval of their elected leaders.

School Board District Number 15, which had been virtually silent throughout most of this period, finally decided to take some action. On March 11, 1988, a lawyer representing the province's legal services branch told the school district's administrators that they were eminently entitled to take action against Ross. "In my view," Clyde Spinney wrote, "Mr. Ross's publication of his views has limited his usefulness and effectiveness as an employee of the board, and some form of discipline can be justified." The following month, Ross's employers sent him a letter. In it, they told him to refrain from further public pronouncements, or else. (In September 1989, after the school district drafted a so-called tolerance policy, the "gag order," as Ross called it, was lifted. Ross promptly went on a cable television program in November and waxed on about the Jewish conspiracy. This led to a formal warning in December that he had violated board policy, but no other discipline.)

Whether the school board liked it or not, Ross was meanwhile quietly writing a new book, *Spectre of Power*. He was also receiving expressions of support from anti-Semites and white supremacists across North America. The third book was released in 1988 and reprinted at least once, in 1989. At 160 pages, it was Ross's largest project since *Web of Deceit*. In it, Ross devotes a few chapters to a rehash of his dealings with the New Brunswick government and various human rights activists. In the remainder of the book, he states that his purpose is to demonstrate that powerful forces are working to "betray Jesus Christ in our society" and, along the way, to convince his reader that "I am not a hatemonger, but simply a watchman on the wall, calling out and warning you to take steps to preserve your safety and that of your children from those who would destroy your souls."

It was at this point, in the spring of 1987, that the Malcolm Ross network first sprang into action. Word had gone out that there was a strong possibility, in this New Brunswick election year, that the schoolteacher could lose his job; Frank McKenna's rejuvenated Liberal Party, in fact, had been most unambiguous about its desire to remove Ross from his position. But the ultra-conservatives were not about to let that happen. Simultaneously, from virtually every region of Canada, far right activists flooded New Brunswick school and government officials with expressions of support for Ross. In April 1987, for example, Keltie Zubko—common-law wife to Doug Christie—issued a call for Canadian ultra-conservatives to rally to Ross's side and write letters to the superintendent of School District Number 15, the provincial minister of education, the attorney-general and a number of local newspapers. Wrote Zubko in her *Friends of Freedom* newsletter, published in Victoria, B.C.: "Various pressure groups seem intent upon intimidating the province's attorney-general and the local school board long enough to at least endanger Mr. Ross's job."

In the same month, and thousands of miles to the east, Paul Fromm's Canadian Association for Free Expression (CAFE) issued a summation of the Ross case in its quarterly newsletter. (Ross and Fromm first met at one of CAFE's Alternative Forum meetings in Toronto in 1982.) Fromm ridiculed Julius Israeli, who had expressed concern about the safety of minorities in the light of the provincial government's puzzling inability to take a firm stand on Ross. Wrote Fromm: "Israel's [sic] comments are ludicrous and inflammatory. To say that because a schoolteacher/author isn't locked up that Jews will be beaten and synagogues burned in New Brunswick is silly."

In the summer 1988 issue of the CAFE newsletter, Fromm returned to the Ross case, ridiculing the efforts of the Atlantic Jewish Council to prevent the publication of further anti-Semitic tracts by Ross. He wrote: "It is frightening to learn that this group had as its top priority for two years its attempt to get this family man fired from his job. To the best of our knowledge, Ross, whatever his controversial religious views, has not attempted to have others fired for merely expressing their beliefs. The activities of the Atlantic Jewish Council may well give Jews a bad name." The following spring, Fromm was back at it with a vengeance. In an article headlined "Malcolm Ross Under Attack Again," he wrote: "The enemies of freedom of speech in this country usually conduct a trial by media prior to actually dragging the intellectual dissident before a court of law. This was the process in the Zundel, Keegstra and Andrews/Smith cases. Malcolm Ross, a Moncton schoolteacher, has found himself under repeated media attack over the past few years for several books he's authored. His enemies are especially interested in removing him from his job and adding yet another family to New Brunswick's already-heavy welfare rolls." After recounting anti-Ross statements by the dreaded Frank McKenna, Fromm urged his followers to write to the New Brunswick premier and provided the relevant address and postal code.

Perhaps encouraged by Fromm, Christian Defence League founder Jim Green wrote to *The Times-Transcript* in Moncton in May 1988 to decry the treatment his Atlantic Canada executive director was receiving at the hands of the news media. Lambasting "the crude attempts to discredit Malcolm Ross," Green—a committed Holocaust denier and opponent of Jews, whom he calls the "power boys" of international finance—urged "everyone [to] get the book *Spectre of Power*, read it, check the references. Try and refute this book of facts."

Jim Green's entreaties, and those of Paul Fromm, Keltie Zubko and others, had the desired effect. Across the country, neo-Nazis and white supremacists and Holocaust deniers sat down at their typewriters and tapped out critical letters to McKenna. In Ottawa, for instance, the pro-Ross crusade was led by Ian Verner Macdonald and his Society for Free Expression.

Macdonald, who had met Ross once before, in Ottawa, was a fascinating figure. Born in Ottawa in 1925, he was a senior and respected member of the Canadian diplomatic corps for much of the 1950s and 1960s. Significantly, from 1965 until 1969, he was the most powerful Canadian trade official in the entire Middle East region. He was also, however, a committed white supremacist and anti-Semite who prospered despite—or perhaps because of—his extremist views. Macdonald's views were well known within the elite foreign service. In a classified October 1963 memorandum, for example, he stated that blacks are inferior to whites because they evolved much later: "The inequality theory is given a further element of respectability through the support of Professor Carleton S. Coon, the prominent anthropologist, who demonstrates fairly convincingly from fossil evidence that the human races evolved more or less independently in five different areas."

In 1987, after having been dismissed from the foreign service, Macdonald and a group of like-minded Ottawa residents formed an ad hoc group known, sometimes, as the Society for Free Expression. The group, which was made up of perhaps 20 members, met weekly at a restaurant on Bank Street, where they discussed ways to combat liberalism, government and Jews. "Jews are a separate group, leeching on our society, not really regarding themselves as part of it," says group member Phillip Belgrave, a retired Department of National Defence employee who admits to being an anti-Semite. "The Jewish people will lie and cheat and kill for the sake of their ethnicity, and for the sense of power."

Other members of the group were Ingrid Beisner, a Kemptville, Ontario, housewife who raised funds for Ernst Zundel; John Murchison, a retired Justice Department lawyer; Norman Van Cleaf, a follower of British Israelism who believed that Jews were "sent by Satan"; Leo Gallien, a convenience-store owner who wanted to name the group the Canadian National Rights Movement; John Kroeker, a two-time Ottawa mayoralty race candidate who falsely passed himself off as a member of various Canadian actuarial groups; and Jean Harris, a New Brunswick native and retired federal public servant. "The Society for Free Expression," Macdonald says, "has a certain communal interest in the preservation of the traditional Canadian values, the most important of which is free expression. I have met with roughly 40 people around Ottawa. They are people who will write letters to the editor, or go see David Irving, for example, when he comes to town. Some members are already liaising with people in other provinces, like Malcolm Ross in New Brunswick."

Macdonald pauses. "It is a real shame Malcolm Ross has been persecuted as he has been. He has been telling the substantial truth."

For much of 1987 and 1988, Malcolm Ross was at the centre of the Society for Free Expression's efforts on behalf of "free speech." Jean Harris, a kindly, soft-spoken woman who has met with Ross to discuss his case, agrees with Macdonald, saying, "I just think he's not getting very good treatment down there, because of lack of freedom of speech. He should be allowed to say what he wants to say."

Macdonald, Harris and the others wrote letters to officials in New Brunswick to plead the case of Malcolm Ross. In a letter to McKenna dated March 27, 1988, Macdonald discusses the "countless abominations" Jews have perpetrated against Christians, adding: "Many of the observations made by Malcolm Ross and described as exaggerations by his critics are, if anything, understatements. For example, in his most recent book, *Spectre of Power*, he writes of Jewish disrespect for the Christian religion. Jewish antipathy to Christianity in fact far transcends mere criticism and ridicule. . . . Malcolm Ross has demonstrated insight, scholarship, patriotism and, not least of all, courage in publicly warning his fellow Canadians of the threat to their spiritual well-being and has correctly identified the source. He deserves commendation, not condemnation."

In another pro-Ross letter, written in May 1988, Macdonald tells the school district chairman that "until now, virtually all of the criticism of Malcolm Ross has consisted of invective and misrepresentation. Significantly, little or no attempt has been made to disprove his statements on the inordinate and dangerous influence exercised by Zionists in both national and international affairs." Ross should be given "the freedom to criticize Jews," Macdonald concludes.

Jean Harris, for her part, describes herself as a "friend of Malcolm Ross"—but Ross insists that he has met with Harris only once. Whatever the truth of the matter, Harris says: "It is a great concern to me that one of our own Christian Canadian citizens, a hard-working family man, is not allowed to express his views. . . . He has never forced his beliefs on anyone, and he has been vilified and harassed for a number of years to an unbelievable extent." Harris, who worked on occasion with Terrence Leblanc, director of the pro-Ross New Brunswick Free Speech League in Fredericton, wrote a March 15, 1988, letter to the school district board of trustees on Ross's behalf. "I have read Mr. Ross's new book, *Spectre of Power*, and think he has done an excellent job of telling his side of the story of how a well-financed and dedicated minority are using fear, guilt and greed to undermine our Christian heritage and faith. We have very few people who are as brave as he is to stand up and give us the truth of how our society is being de-Christianized."

Tellingly, Harris goes on to outline the extent of the Ross network: "Malcolm Ross is not alone in his beliefs. There are many of us in Canada, the United States, the United Kingdom, Australia, New Zealand and the rest of the Western world. And as one is silenced, another will spring up, and eventually more and more." Copies of the letter were published in the Fredericton *Daily Gleaner* and the *Telegraph-Journal*.

As Jean Harris had inadvertently pointed out, the Ross network extended far beyond Ontario and the Society for Free Expression. Take, for example, Ron Gostick. Gostick is an Alberta-born man who founded the anti-Jewish Canadian League of Rights in 1968. He is an ardent Ross supporter. By the early 1980s, his league was believed to have upwards of 10,000 supporters across Canada. It opposed foreign aid, sexual permissiveness, abortion, gun control, the Anti-Defamation League of the B'nai Brith, the United Church, pro-Communist Jews, race-mixing and fluoridation. It was inevitable that Gostick became a vocal supporter of Ross and a key component of his network.

In the April 1988 issue of the *Canadian Intelligence Service*, a regular publication of the Canadian League of Rights, Gostick wrote: "Malcolm Ross is a highly respected junior high school teacher. . . . Even his critics do not deny his teaching skills and the fact that he does not bring his political or religious views into the classroom." After briefly detailing the campaign that nameless "pressure groups" had brought to bear on Malcolm Ross, Gostick asked: "What can you do about it? Spread the truth. Get an extra copy of *Spectre of Power* to loan around. It's too hot for the regular trade to handle, but we can supply copies: $12 each, two for $20. It's the battle for freedom! Over to you!"

Asked about his connections to the Canadian League of Rights, Canada's largest anti-Semitic organization on the fringe right, Ross sounds reluctant. He confirms that Gostick's group has sold many of his books and that the league has mounted letter-writing campaigns on his behalf. But that is all, says Ross, adding: "I'm attempting to defend our Christian heritage, and they're attempting to defend the same thing. We've got common grounds and common aims. On certain things, anyway."

Farther west, in British Columbia, another chartered member of the Malcolm Ross network is the Council on Public Affairs, the far right group run by Eileen and Claus Pressler in Salmon Arm. Eileen Pressler wrote to McKenna in March 1988 to pronounce on Ross's case. In her letter, written on the letterhead of the British Columbia Free Speech League, Pressler ripped into McKenna: "The Zionists who you serve so diligently will not stop until they destroy the object of their vengeful hatred—Malcolm Ross. . . . Quite frankly, Mr. McKenna, Canadians are quickly tiring of the incessant wailing of Jews about their alleged holocaust, their war crimes witch-hunts, and their vicious attacks upon Christianity. . . . It is the duty of your government, sir, to assure the welfare of all Canadians by not capitulating to pressures from a small Jewish minority which already exerts far more influence and control than its numbers warrant. Already, our governments, our courts and the media are used by the Zionists for their own personal interests. . . . Please tread very carefully, Mr. McKenna, when you begin to tread on our God-given rights." For reasons known only to herself, Pressler sent a copy of her letter to Julius Israeli. (Later, in May 1992, Pressler invited Ross to attend her group's Leadership '92 Conference in Vernon, B.C. There, Ross was to be honored at the Council on Public Affairs awards banquet. Also slated to receive a tribute was Jim Keegstra.)

Pressler was not the only far right type to harass Israeli on Ross's behalf. Leonard R. Saunders, a Penticton, B.C., resident and associate editor of the Council on Public Affairs's *Digest*, has written to Israeli on a number of occasions. In November 1988, he sent Israeli (and, significantly, Malcolm Ross) a photocopy of a November 1, 1988, *Globe and Mail* obituary. The subject of the article was Bernard Vigod, a respected Fredericton historian, author and national vice-president of the B'nai Brith. Driving to a meeting of the Atlantic Jewish Council's biannual conference in Moncton, Vigod was struck by a transport truck on the Trans-Canada Highway, and he was killed. He was survived by his wife and two young daughters. Beside the obituary, Saunders typed: "Like Saul of Tarsus, this Jew was on his way to stone Malcolm Ross, but he was stricken by a large transport put on the highway by the Almighty. He and his car were squashed and there was Jew juice all over the tarmac!! PRAISE THE LORD!" On other occasions in 1988, under the letterhead of his own neo-Nazi group, the Canadian Resistance Movement, Saunders wrote again to Israeli. In August, he sent a photo of one of the ovens at the Birkenau death camp. In September, he told Israeli he would like to provide him with a copy of "The Protocols of the Learned Elders of Zion." And, in December, he wrote to tell Israeli that he could not tell whether the New Brunswick minister of education was "Jew or human." "So-called Jews," Saunders wrote, "are determined to destroy the very fabric of our country through the same willful destruction they have exacted in Palestine."

Malcolm Ross attempts, whenever possible, to distance himself from supporters who embrace extremist measures and vicious language. In order for him to maintain the support of the ordinary people of New Brunswick—support that is crucial if he is to keep his teaching post—Ross must be careful not to sound too extreme or to be seen consorting too often with neo-Nazis. So, when asked about Pressler and Saunders, he is understandably vague. "I don't attack other people for the way they're attempting to defend me," he says, refusing to be drawn into a discussion of the B.C. residents' tactics. But in *Spectre of Power*, he makes very clear his views on Saunders's hateful letter-writing campaigns, he calls the elderly B.C. man a "tireless defender of freedom and superb letter writer." However, he does not explain how someone who could find humor in the death of a young father of two children—or dream up an obscenity like the "Jew juice" remark—is a tireless defender of freedom.

In September 1988, after receiving hundreds of letters defending Malcolm Ross from neo-Nazis and white supremacists around the globe, the New Brunswick government decided enough was enough. Instead of trying to find yet another way to prosecute Ross, the McKenna government elected to hold a public inquiry into the case. Reacting to more than a hundred formal complaints from New Brunswickers, the government established a one-man commission of inquiry into the matter of Malcolm Ross. The inquiry would be conducted by New Brunswick law professor Brian Bruce. The focus of the probe would be an April 21, 1988, complaint filed with the provincial Human Rights Commission by David Attis, a Jewish community leader and parent who lived in Moncton. In his complaint, Attis alleged that the school board of District 15—to which his children belonged—was fostering anti-Semitism by continuing to employ Ross as a teacher: "By its own statements and its inaction over Malcolm Ross's statements in class and in public, the school board has condoned his views, has thus fostered a climate where students feel more at ease expressing anti-Jewish views." In June 1988, the Human Rights Commission appointed one of its officers to arrive at a "settlement" in the case, but was unsuccessful.

On September 1, the McKenna government accepted the recommendation of the Human Rights Commission to inquire into Attis's complaint. Ross immediately retained Doug Christie, whom he had met some years before. "I think Mr. Christie is the battling barrister for freedom of speech," says Ross. "And I think, certainly, he was taken by the case." After some unsuccessful preliminary skirmishing, which saw Christie attempt to have the board of inquiry ruled unconstitutional, and after more than a year of delay and an October 1989 trip to the Supreme Court of Canada by Ross, the inquiry went ahead in December 1990.

(In June, Ross's entire body of writings were critiqued by James A. Beverley, a professor of theology and ethics from Mount Allison University. In *Spectre of Power*, Ross states: "No one has ever tried to point out my errors to me." In an essay titled *Web of Error*, Beverley takes up that challenge and performs a line-by-line analysis of Ross's musings. The result, in the end, is simply devastating for the Moncton schoolteacher. With meticulous analysis, Beverley destroys the bizarre theories around which Malcolm Ross has built a second career. Beverley and Ross met twice, in July and October 1987. Beverley told Ross, to his face, that he had been able to document literally hundreds of "serious" errors of fact that called into question all of his writings. Ross was unmoved. Says Beverley: "[His] ideas are eccentric, mistaken and harmful. . . . On virtually any topic, he will trust anti-Semitic and racist literature and simply ignore other sources. . . . I have never doubted his sincerity, but I will not allow his buzz words about wanting only the 'Kingship of Christ' in society to blind me to the dangerous and false views he advocates.")

The Human Rights Commission hearings were scheduled to run for eight days, commencing on December 5, the same week a Holocaust exhibit was on display at the Moncton Public Library. The week before, a 16-year-old pro-Nazi skinhead decorated a Moncton synagogue with swastikas. When he was apprehended, the youth, a member of the Aryan Resistance Movement, told police, "Hitler should have shot all the Jews." The atmosphere in Moncton was charged as the inquiry got under way at the Crystal Palace—an amusement centre where Malcolm Ross fundraising events were known to take place.

The first witness to be called was the complainant, David Attis. The father of four children, Attis testified that Ross's books—he had first read *Web of Deceit* in 1978—were the "height of obscenity." Attis stated that, because of the school board's willingness to continue to employ an anti-Semitic propagandist, his 14-year-old daughter, Yona, wanted to go to high school outside New Brunswick: "She can't put up with the harassment she receives while attending school, because she is different, because she is a Jew." Not surprisingly, Christie, as is his wont, mocked and ridiculed the Jewish man at every opportunity. But Christie was not alone. The school district's lawyer, as well as the teachers' association lawyer, busied themselves with attempts to discredit the source of the complaint. In one exchange with Attis, Jim Letcher, the school board's counsel, stated: "You know, Mr. Attis, we could keep going and what you're going to be left with is a small group of people who hold no opinions about anything and who, in your opinion, would qualify as schoolteachers."

For many, the atmosphere in the inquiry was poisonous. On December 7, Christie called Attis "the most intolerant man in existence." On December 10, Christie called Attis—in open court—"an evasive liar." On the following day, Christie made what many regarded as a controversial statement when he said: "That the Germans did intern many Jews in their concentration camps is true. The Canadian government did the same thing with the Japanese on the West Coast, and probably with less reason." (This statement, interestingly, is a word-for-word quotation taken from the chapter titled "Zionism in History" in *Web of Deceit*.) Christie and the other lawyers—the *Daily Gleaner* called them "a bizarre alliance"—likened the inquiry to the 1925 John Scopes trial, in which the Tennessee teacher was fined for teaching the theory of evolution to his students.

Often, when a child was called to the stand, Christie succeeded in reducing the youthful witness to tears. One such witness was Grade 9 student Yona Attis, daughter of the complainant. At one point during Christie's cross-examination, when the 14-year-old broke down in tears, chairman Brian Bruce called for a brief adjournment. An unidentified man yelled, "Is he human?" This man then approached Christie and angrily demanded, "If I hit you, would you say I was provoked?" The man strode away without striking Christie, who looked decidedly uncomfortable.

Asked about criticisms that Christie was a bully with children, Ross is unconcerned. "I thought he was extremely fair. As long as they were answering the questions truthfully, there were no problems. When he found inconsistencies, they often got . . . frustrated. But it wasn't because he was a bully, certainly. He was very gracious. He was defending me, and that was his job."

The hearing, which was often delayed by line-by-line reviews of Ross's writings, was taking longer than Brian Bruce had thought it would. After ten days of testimony and argument, he decided to reconvene the hearing in April 1991. The second phase of the human rights inquiry ran from late April until early May.

The second round began with testimony by Ernest Hodgson, an expert in educational administration who was called to testify on behalf of Attis. Hodgson, a retired University of Alberta professor, stated that the school board's attempts to deal with Ross had "failed miserably." In his cross-examination, Christie repeatedly ridiculed the 68-year-old man. At one point, after not receiving the answer he was seeking, Christie asked Hodgson whether he understood the English language. The older man exploded, saying to Bruce, "I object very strongly to the sarcasm of this man. You are out of line!"

As the hearing wound down, Christie called a number of witnesses to testify on Ross's behalf. One, a guidance counsellor at Magnetic Hill School, told the inquiry that she was "amazed" by the positive effect the teacher had on his students. "Mr. Ross's class has an atmosphere of acceptance," Elizabeth Doucet testified. "He is empathetic, understanding and caring about the kids. . . . From my observation, I think Malcolm Ross teaches all students equally, regardless of race or background." Ross MacCallum, the superintendent of schools, called Ross "a very positive role model."

The glowing sentiment notwithstanding, in late August 1991, Brian Bruce ordered the school board to place Malcolm Ross on "a leave of absence without pay for 18 months." During that time, the board was told to find Ross a non-teaching position. If none could be found, Bruce ruled, Malcolm Ross could be fired. He could also be immediately fired if he "publishes or writes for the purpose of publication, anything that mentions a Jewish or Zionist conspiracy, or attacks followers of the Jewish religion"—or if he sold any of his previously published books or pamphlets. In his decision, Bruce wrote: "It would be an impossible task to list every prejudicial view or discriminatory comment contained in his writings as they are innumerable and permeate his writings. . . . Malcolm Ross's primary purpose is clearly to attack the truthfulness, integrity, dignity and motives of Jewish persons rather than the presentation of scholarly research. . . . By his writings and his continued attacks, [he] has impaired his ability as a teacher and cannot be allowed to remain in that position if a discrimination-free environment is to exist."

Doug Christie announced that he would appeal to the New Brunswick Court of Queen's Bench. Malcolm Ross, meanwhile, got back to the business he loved: promoting anti-Semitism.

As he awaited the court's ruling, Malcolm Ross continued to spread his message. In March 1991, Paul Fromm's Canadian Association for Free Expression invited Ross to a well-attended get-together at the Latvian Hall in Toronto. In his fiery introduction, Fromm said: "Even his worst opponents will agree that Malcolm Ross does what the Board of Education down in Moncton, New Brunswick, pays him to do: namely, to instruct students in math and English. He's not there running a political indoctrination show nor a religious revival show. He teaches them math and English. Nonetheless, he has been under constant attack for the past 12 years because of the books he has written.

"We have followed his career, and CAFE has been among his strongest supporters, if we can consider writing letters to the editor and harassing various public officials, if you can consider that support. And I think we do. Our voices must be raised in the defence of anyone whose right to freedom of speech is challenged."

In his speech, during which he was a good deal more animated than he is during interviews with the media, Ross cracked jokes about Jews observing the Sabbath as well as the number of Chinese living in Toronto. He lambasted the Liberal government of New Brunswick premier Frank McKenna; he reviewed the various inconclusive police and government investigations; he ridiculed Julius Israeli and David Attis. Said Ross, to wild applause: "When fighting this battle, it's important to know your enemies, and to know that they know you and your weaknesses. It's important to pace yourself, otherwise you'll burn out very quickly. These masters of mind control know how to frustrate and intimidate and manipulate you into making statements, or committing acts, that they will then use against you."

After the speech, which Fromm said concerned "the forces of darkness," the CAFE leader urged his followers to dig deep for Malcolm Ross. "I'd like you to give Malcolm Ross money," Fromm said. "I want you to give it to him directly. . . . If you want to help Malcolm Ross to continue this fight, one of the ways you can do it is to give him some money. Give whatever you possibly can to Malcolm Ross this evening, whether it's in the form of a cheque or post-dated, I'm sure he trusts you as we do. If you cannot manage that, perhaps you can send him something later. . . . It's our task to help people like Malcolm Ross, who are fighting for our rights to freedom of speech and freedom of expression."

Later that year, on September 6, Ross gave a speech at the Crystal Palace, ironically the site of the human rights commission inquiry. There, he railed, *comme toujours*, against the Jews: "Today the enemies of freedom are holding us in bondage to evil philosophies and the fear of being branded a bigot. They fear the huge bubble of lies they have blown up might be pricked by the sharp pin of truth."

The fall of 1991 was filled with similar speech-making about "the enemies of freedom," and then Malcolm Ross won a partial victory. New Brunswick Court of Queen's Bench judge Paul Creaghan ruled in January that it was appropriate to keep Ross out of the classroom (the school board had hired him as a curriculum planner). But, in his 20-page judgment, Creaghan struck down the ban on further anti-Semitic publications, on the grounds that the order had violated Ross's constitutional rights.

Not satisfied with partial victories, Christie and Ross took their case to the New Brunswick Court of Appeal in September 1992.

It was in this period that one letter revealed what some say may be the true character of the men and women who make the Ross network and, perhaps, the true character of Malcolm Ross himself. In an April 27, 1992, letter to a Halifax newspaper, "Brig.-Gen." Gordon (Jack) Mohr passed on his views about the trials and tribulations of Malcolm Ross. In the letter, presented on the letterhead of the Crusade for Christ and Country, Mohr wrote: "Instead of castigating Ross for [his] statements, why is it the media does not look into what international Judaism has openly taught for centuries? The plans are all there to see for anyone who is honest enough to search for it. . . . You can castigate Ross and myself until you are blue in the face, but it will not change the truth."

This letter, more than any other that has been sent by members of the Malcolm Ross network, was significant because of whose neat signature concluded it: Jack Mohr. As Ross knows—and as those few who follow the escapades of the radical right in Canada and the United States know—Jack Mohr is no Paul Fromm, or Leonard Saunders, or Eileen Pressler, or Keltie Zubko, or Ron Gostick, or Jean Harris, or Jim Green, or Ian Macdonald. He is the real article.

A former leader of the John Birch Society, Mohr regularly conducts seminars in Identity Christianity and urban warfare. At the July 1984 Aryan Nations World Congress attended by Terry Long, Carney Milton Nerland, Edgar Foth and many other Canadians, for example, Mohr and former Texas KKK Grand Dragon Louis Beam,

Jr., instructed more than a hundred neo-Nazis and white supremacists on how to build effective pipe bombs and how to convert semi-
automatic assault rifles to full automatic. In one of Mohr's booklets,
"What Jews Say About Communism," he writes: "Hitler understood
the plans of international Jewry and what they were trying to do to
Western Christian civilization." And at a November 1987 meeting of
the Southwest Kingdom Christian Fellowship, Mohr declared:
"There is a false Israel in the world today. . . . Those that say they
are Jews are not, but are of the synagogue of Satan."

When he is asked about Jack Mohr, Malcolm Ross grows agitated. When asked if he knows who, exactly, Jack Mohr is and what,
exactly, Jack Mohr advocates, Ross is vague. He listens as his guest
explains that Mohr is a proud promoter of Adolf Hitler, virulent anti-
Semitism and guerrilla warfare. Finally, he says: "I just don't get
involved in things like that. . . ."

"But, Mr. Ross, Jack Mohr advocates race war," Ross's guest says.
"He teaches people how to make bombs and use weapons so that they
can kill Jews and non-whites. He calls Jews the spawn of Satan.
When a Denver talkshow host ridiculed Mohr on a radio program, he
was murdered by neo-Nazi extremists. Don't you think receiving support from someone like Jack Mohr may hurt your cause more than it
will help it?"

Malcolm Ross pauses one last time. "Many people have encouraged me. There are many people who are very articulate and courageous, but I don't know them all that well personally.

"We all need encouragement, I guess."

On December 20, 1993, the New Brunswick Court of Appeal
released its decision on Malcolm Ross. In a 2-1 ruling, it stated that
since Ross never expressed his views in the classroom there was no
"pressing and substantial" reason to stop him teaching or expressing
his views outside the classroom. Ross said he was delighted by the
decision.

12

MATT McKAY'S YOUTHFUL FOLLY

In 1993, millions of Canadians indirectly experienced the reality of organized hate for the first time when, as they viewed the nightly television newscasts, they learned that a group of violent neo-Nazis and Klansmen had been accepted into the ranks of the Canadian Armed Forces. For many Canadians, the notion of a few Hitler freaks congregating at the margins of society was not particularly disconcerting. But the notion that neo-Nazis were being given uniforms and guns by our country's military went, for many, beyond the pale.

Matt McKay's name first became public on September 13, 1992, when *The Winnipeg Sun* published a lengthy exposé about white supremacist activity in Manitoba's capital. Alongside a story by Joanne Faryon and Dawna Dingwall headlined "Neo-Nazis Open Doors to Soldiers," a large photograph of McKay was published. The photo is dramatic; McKay is giving a fascist salute with one tattoo-covered arm. Instead of a uniform, he is wearing Doc Marten boots with red laces, jeans, suspenders and a Hitler T-shirt. Hanging above his head is a large swastika banner.

Faryon says an anonymous source gave the *Sun* the photograph along with a number of other photos, most of which featured Manitoba Knights of the Ku Klux Klan leader Bill Harcus posing with some of his supporters. The photo of McKay, apparently, had been taken in 1990, when the soldier was stationed in Winnipeg. In the resulting news story, McKay was reached by Faryon and Dingwall at Canadian Armed Forces Base Petawawa, just west of Ottawa. McKay confirmed that he had been involved with neo-Nazi groups in western Canada, but added: "I've totally left that thing . . . early in '91. My military career is more important to me than some little organization like that. It was a stupid mistake." He then slammed down the phone. (Much later, he would tell an Ottawa *Citizen* reporter: "I woke up one day and saw what was going on and said no way, I'm out.")

Even more startling than what McKay had to say, perhaps, was the reaction of some of his superiors. "As long as they don't do anything illegal," said Capt. Daniel Lachance, "they can do anything they want. This is a free country." A National Defence spokesperson in Ottawa, Lieut. Karen Mair, took a similar line: "We don't have a policy. It's not illegal."

That was incorrect. Sections 93 and 129 of the National Defence Act make it an offence for a soldier to engage in "disgraceful conduct" or to do anything that prejudices "good order or discipline." Section 19.44 of the Canadian Forces' Administrative Orders makes clear that "no officer or non-commissioned member of the regular forces shall take an active part in the affairs of a political organization." And other regulations, enacted in 1991 to deal with peacekeeping missions, are also quite clear: "For some missions, cultural, religious or other sensitivities of the parties or host country may have to be respected for the mission to be accomplished safely and effectively." But for Matt McKay, the rules were apparently different. There was to be no disciplinary action. In fact, McKay was transferred out of Winnipeg—and promoted to corporal.

Outside Winnipeg, and outside of the Department of National Defence, few people knew about the *Sun*'s story. For a few months,

Matt McKay was forgotten. Then, in late January 1993, an aide in the office of Liberal leader Jean Chrétien was sent a copy of the *Sun* story by Faryon. The aide telephoned Matt McKay's superiors in Petawawa, who confirmed that McKay was, in fact, still a member of the Canadian Airborne Regiment—and that he had been shipped to Somalia as part of a United Nations peacekeeping mission. To the aide, it seemed incredible that senior officials in National Defence, after learning about the presence of a committed neo-Nazi within the Airborne Regiment, would promote that individual, then send him to Somalia, where, presumably, he would be called upon to protect non-whites.

With Jean Chrétien's approval, the aide started to investigate further. He learned that in August 1991, Daryl Rivest, the former Final Solution skinhead from Edmonton who had been subpoenaed to testify as a witness to the assault on retired broadcaster Keith Rutherford, had told Rutherford's lawyer, Tom Engel, that McKay had been very active in Harcus's Manitoba-based KKK and that he had been close to Canadian Aryan Nations leader Terry Long as well. Under oath, Rivest testified that McKay was "a skinhead from Winnipeg that comes out [to Edmonton] from time to time to pay a visit." Rivest, who was on the large side himself, described McKay as a "big, scary guy." McKay wore red laces in his boots, Rivest said, because he was a "hardcore National Socialist with extremely violent tendencies." When in Edmonton, McKay would stay at the Skin Bin, the house on 107th Street frequented by Final Solution Skinheads. For kicks, McKay, Rivest and other skinheads would frequent a run-down park within walking distance of the Skin Bin. There, they would look for Natives to beat up. (Police sources say that McKay used the Canadian Armed Forces "cheap flight" privilege to jet around the country, organizing white supremacists. Police add that Department of National Defence officials should have been aware that McKay was using the privilege in this way.)

On one occasion in 1990, Rivest recalls that a few of the skinheads decided to beat up one of their own, a young man named Rob, who happened to be a cousin of Final Solution member Scott Fuhr. The skinheads were mad at Rob because he had borrowed a pair of cherry red Doc Martens and scuffed them up. The Docs belonged to Dan Sims, one of the two skinheads who had assaulted Rutherford. One night, Sims and Rob started to fight about the boots; very quickly, it became clear that Sims was losing the battle. At that point, Rivest recalls, Matt McKay came "flying" out of the Skin Bin's kitchen. McKay punched Rob in the face, and he fell to the ground. Says Rivest: "The boots Matt wore then, they weren't Doc Martens. They were what is called Commandos. . . . They have big solid steel in the toes. It's 12-gauge steel. Like, you can drop a chunk of I-beam off a roof and have it land on your toe, and it won't even scratch. And they have studs in the bottom so you can walk on ice and not slip. Big, scary boots. And [McKay] started kicking Rob in the face with these things and busted his head wide open. There was blood all over the walls and all over Matt and all over everyone standing around watching. And then, well, after that we decided we needed some beer." Rivest does not recall what happened to Rob.

Brett Hayes, the former skinhead called as a witness in Rutherford's civil action against his assailants and Aryan Nations leaders, confirmed Rivest's recollections about McKay. At one time the leader of the Calgary chapter of Skinheads Against Racial Prejudice, and now once again a neo-Nazi, Hayes testified that he travelled to Terry Long's acreage in Caroline, Alberta, with McKay in October 1988. Also present were Final Solution skins Sims, Trinity Larocque and Joey Bertling. The Aryan Nations leader focussed most of his attention on McKay during the visit. Under examination by Engel, Hayes stated: "Terry Long was really interested in Matt, because Matt was a full-blown white supremacist. And I guess Terry Long liked that because he is so big and can stomp people. And a lot of people looked up to Matt, too, because he was bigger and stronger and stuff. And Terry Long and Matt, they chatted for a while. I don't know what they were talking about."

"You say he used to stomp people?" Engel asked.

"Oh, yeah. For sure."

"So [he was] a very violent individual?" Engel asked.

"Oh, yes, yes," Hayes said, adding that the younger skinheads idolized the Armed Forces member. "We would *never* talk down to him. The younger guys, they talked to him like, 'So Matt, so Matt, what are you going to do when we get back [to Edmonton]? Are we going to fight? Are we going to fight or something?' . . . And they would talk like that right in front of Terry Long about that stuff, and Matt would just go, 'Stomp some niggers or something.'"

There was a lot of talk about "niggers" at Long's home, Hayes recalled. As the group sat in Long's living room, a bust of Adolf Hitler looking down on them, they would joke about it. Added Hayes: "We would all say that. You know, we would all chuckle and laugh at it, and the kids would even join in. The little girl and the little guy would jokingly say things about niggers before the dinner table."

Engel stirred. "*At* the dinner table, you mean?"

"Well, before it," Hayes said. "They couldn't say it at the table."

"Why couldn't they say it at the table, do you know?"

Hayes shrugged. "Well, I guess it was out of respect for the wife that was cooking the meal."

"Did she look like she was upset about negroes being talked about in this way?" Engel asked.

"No way," Hayes said. "She was chuckling. They were all laughing. It was like such a normal house, you know, except for them talking about niggers and Jews and kikes and stuff like that."

Hayes told Engel that, at Long's home, it was considered generally impolite to discuss Jews in mixed company—as if Jews were some sort of a social disease. Said Hayes: "We wouldn't talk about Jewish people in the house. They were . . . they were like the lowest form of. . . " He paused to find the right words. "Like, with negroes, it wasn't their fault, you know. But the Jews, they were the biggest problem. We talked a little about Jews outside, before we left. As we were going to our truck, Terry Long said the real problem is the kikes. That is what the real problem is. It's not the niggers and Pakistanis and stuff like that. The real problem is the kikes, because they own so much and are the media and all this crap."

Long instructed McKay and his skinhead buddies to determine the names of the leaders of the Jewish community in Edmonton, Calgary and elsewhere. "Find the leaders of the Jewish Defence League," Long said, "and do something about it." Hayes said he took this remark to mean commit some act of violence.

Long led McKay and his group to an outhouse near his sawmill. The Aryan Nations leader opened the door, revealing a toilet positioned on a wooden floor. Grinning, Long pulled up a few boards, and the skinheads saw a flight of crude stairs. In the subterranean cellar, which was approximately eight feet square and tall enough for a man to stand in, there were dozens of weapons. Said Hayes: "I saw a lot of guns. I guess they were AK-47s. They looked like automatic weapons. Like, you put the clip on the bottom. I didn't see any Uzis or anything like that, but he had a lot of guns, 20 or 25 of them. He had a lot of tin ammo boxes, too."

As they left, Hayes recalled, all of the skinheads were upbeat and laughing. "I felt pretty good. I felt stronger. I felt more prepared," said Hayes.

"To do what?" Engel asked.

"To do stuff for the cause."

"What kind of stuff?"

"Well," Hayes said, "my stuff would have been violence. I would get more people. To go out and commit acts against non-whites, against Jewish people, against the synagogues."

Engel leaned forward. This was the sort of information that he was hoping for when he subpoenaed Brett Hayes. "Violent acts?" he asked.

Hayes nodded. "Violent acts."

"And in this group, was it discussed whether it was felt that this was something Terry Long wanted you to do?"

"Very much so, yes," Hayes said.

"Can you elaborate on that a little bit?"

Hayes reflected for a moment. "He wouldn't say, 'Go out and kill somebody,' you know. He wouldn't have to say it. We knew it. He

would hand us literature, and we would read it, and in that literature
it would say to commit acts against negroes and kikes and stuff
like that. . . . It would be saying, 'To support and help your cause, you
shouldn't be out here sitting and talking about it. You should be out
doing it,' you know? These organizations didn't want people to sit
around and drink coffee." The white supremacist bonhomie subsided
when an RCMP cruiser pulled over the truck a short distance from
Long's property. All of the skinheads, McKay included, were checked
for identification; none were concerned. This, Hayes said, was routine.
(Unbeknownst to McKay and his chums, the hulking Canadian Forces
members had been under CSIS surveillance as early as July 1989.)

The Liberal aide's investigation into Matt McKay's neo-Nazi
activity continued for several weeks. Meanwhile, the Conservative
government was conducting an investigation of its own. On April
26, 1993, minister of defence Kim Campbell sent notices to the
Liberal and New Democrat defence critics, advising them that she
planned to make "a statement" in the House of Commons later that
day. The statement concerned a series of scandals that had plagued
the Canadian peacekeeping mission in Somalia. Several members of
the Canadian Airborne Regiment's Battle Group—Matt McKay's
regiment—had already been detained in connection with the beating
death of a Somali man on March 16. Three other Somali civilians
had died while in Canadian custody, and police investigations were
under way.

In her short speech in the House, Campbell provided brief sum-
maries of the circumstances surrounding each of the four deaths.
After admitting there were "problems" related to the way in which
her department initially handled these incidents, Campbell said:
"Broad concerns have been voiced. . . . There is a concern about the
Canadian forces and the units sent to Somalia. There have been press
comments about violence and racism exhibited by Canadian troops in
Somalia." She concluded by stating that she had decided to establish
an inquiry into the way the Canadian Airborne Regiment had conducted itself in Somalia. Part of the seven-person panel's mandate

would be an examination of "the extent, if any, to which cultural differences affected the conduct of operations."

"Cultural differences," of course, was a polite way of saying racism. Campbell's abbreviated speech was the closest she or her department had ever come to admitting that there was, in fact, a problem associated with racism in Matt McKay's regiment. A few days later, two senior Liberal MPs, House Leader David Dingwall and external affairs critic Lloyd Axworthy, decided to go public with what had been learned about the Matt McKay story. After some discussion, the Liberals concluded that Kim Campbell should be questioned about McKay. Because she was touring the country campaigning for the Conservative Party leadership, she was rarely in the House of Commons. The Liberals therefore waited to question Campbell on Wednesday, May 5, when she was to appear before the House of Commons Standing Committee on National Defence.

Near the end of that hearing, which was primarily occupied with Campbell's defence of the government's decision to purchase attack helicopters, a Liberal assistant, Frank Schiller, quietly distributed copies of *The Winnipeg Sun* story to select reporters. As he did so, Liberal MP Christine Stewart asked Campbell why McKay had been permitted to remain in the Armed Forces. The minister, however, did not answer—and not a single reporter filed a story about the exchange.

The next night, CBC's "Prime Time News" broadcast a report about the presence of McKay in the Canadian Airborne Regiment as well as the presence of other neo-Nazis in the armed forces. Where the Liberals had failed in attracting attention to the issue, CBC was wildly successful. In the report, CBC interviewed Heritage Front leader Wolfgang Droege, who stated, "The military is a good recruiting ground for organizations such as the Heritage Front. I don't think there is any question, because many of their views coincide with those of ours."

In the House of Commons on Friday, with news stories circulating that as many as two dozen members of the armed forces were members of the Heritage Front, Axworthy and associate Liberal defence critic

Fred Mifflin raised the issue with Conservative House Leader Harvie Andre. (Campbell was not in the House.) Said Mifflin: "It is apparent that the Department of National Defence has had knowledge for some time now that serving uniformed members are involved with recognized racist organizations. I want to ask, because of the sensitivity of the issue, precisely what was known, when it was known and what was done about it."

Replied Andre: "I am disappointed the honorable member would make the accusation that the military has known for a long time of significant white supremacy and so on. That is not true. . . . I do not think the Liberal Party distinguishes itself in leaking to the press gallery this accusation and applying that suggestion. In terms of what the government has done about it, it has adopted a policy of zero incidents in respect of all aspects of harassment. That includes any racism that may be involved."

Mifflin, a former navy rear admiral, pressed on. "On the one hand, the government says only yesterday as a fundamental principle that the army will not tolerate racism. On the other hand, we are told by the military it is not against regulations. They cannot have it both ways. On the policy of military association with racist organizations, what is it? Is it allowed or not?"

Said Andre: "It is not permissible for Canadian Armed Forces personnel to be actively associated. I do not think that accusation is out there, even with respect to the individual [McKay] whose dossier was circulated by the Liberal Party. I think that is from the past. I do not think the Canadian Armed Forces has the capability, and I think people would be very upset if we tried to institute a scheme of inquiring into people's minds. We can only deal with their behavior."

Questioned further by NDP House Leader Nelson Riis, Andre, looking very annoyed, called the Opposition's questions "McCarthyism." He acknowledged that regulations did not permit McKay to join any political organization. "But they can go to meetings and they can think," Andre said. "Under the Charter of Rights, you are allowed to do that in Canada, even if you are in uniform."

Like Andre, the Department of National Defence was not the least bit contrite about the revelations. In fact, the department called the media reports, and the Opposition's questions, baseless. Said spokesperson Karen Mair: "The [CBC] report revealed no concrete evidence to support their claims that there are currently members of the Canadian Airborne Regiment affiliated with extremist groups or activities."

Not surprisingly, the government's apparent indifference stirred up a storm of controversy. The Conservatives' case was not helped, perhaps, when Campbell revealed to reporters in Edmonton that she had known about the presence of white supremacists in the armed forces "for ages." Minority activists were shocked; the Jewish community, in particular, was outraged. Irving Abella, president of the Canadian Jewish Congress, told reporters that McKay should be removed from active service. He said: "The very idea of neo-Nazis within the Canadian Armed Forces should send a chill down the spine of every decent Canadian. At the very minimum, an immediate government inquiry is needed to determine the extent of this infiltration and reasons why the Department of National Defence has taken no action."

In the United States, anti-racist groups noted, members of white supremacist and neo-Nazi organizations are not tolerated on military bases or in barracks. In 1979, after a group of U.S. soldiers stood guard at a rally in Euless, Texas, attended by KKK leader David Duke and Louis Beam, Jr., the military cracked down. In that same year, the navy transferred and disciplined several men based on the USS *Concord* who had been involved with the Ku Klux Klan. Other soldiers were disciplined in other branches of the military. In September 1986, the Defense Department gave field commanders authority to prevent military personnel from engaging in activities sponsored by racist groups, including fund-raising, public demonstrations and recruiting and training members. But in Canada, where tough hate laws had been enacted, no such action had ever been taken.

On Monday, May 10, the Opposition returned to the issue. Liberal and New Democrat MPs wanted to know why Campbell and her department, unlike their U.S. counterparts, had not moved quickly to stamp out white supremacy in the military. The Liberals' Dingwall asked Andre why armed forces personnel were not permitted to participate in the activities of mainstream political parties, "but it is fine, as the government House leader and the minister responsible said last week, for a person to be a member of the Ku Klux Klan and the armed forces at the same time." Andre was unmoved, persisting in his freedom-of-thought argument. The Constitution of Canada permitted McKay to attend KKK and Aryan Nations meetings, Andre suggested. "What is not against the law in this country, and I hope the honorable member recognizes and supports it, is to attend meetings or to think."

The controversy continued unabated. Campbell, making a rare appearance in the House of Commons the next day, told Mifflin that "racism or racist attitudes are completely unacceptable to members of the Canadian Armed Forces."

But Dingwall was not satisfied. "I ask the minister of national defence, why does the minister prevent Jews, Muslims and women from serving Canada in the Middle East, but permits a known white supremacist to serve in Somalia?"

Campbell replied: "I have never permitted a known white supremacist to serve in Somalia. I am in the process of ensuring that members of the Canadian forces who wear this country's uniform do not have those kinds of attitudes."

Earlier, during a campaign swing through Winnipeg, Campbell had been shown a photograph of Matt McKay by a *Sun* reporter. She told the reporter that McKay's neo-Nazi involvement was "youthful folly." When news of that remark reached Ottawa, Liberal MPs were astounded. And when they learned that the photograph had been taken in McKay's barracks, where the Airborne corporal often hung his swastika banner for all to see, the Grits were apoplectic. With Campbell again absent, Newfoundland MP Brian Tobin was assigned to question Harvie Andre. "A few days ago in Winnipeg the minister of defence dismissed a photograph of a Canadian forces corporal making a fascist salute, wearing a Hitler T-shirt, standing below a swastika banner, and I quote her, as mere 'youthful folly'. I want to say to the minister that photograph was taken in the corporal's barracks! I want the minister to be aware that the swastika was hanging on the property of the Canadian Armed Forces! . . . I want to ask the minister if he regards that kind of incident, that kind of abuse of Canadian forces property, as mere youthful folly."

Andre, looking ill at ease for the first time, replied: "I wish the honorable member would allow due process and accept the statement by the minister of national defence to the House that in fact there is no tolerance for racist behavior on the part of Canadian Armed Forces personnel." Outside the House of Commons, in a massive scrum of reporters, Andre made matters worse for himself when he described McKay's activity as a "boyish prank." That statement infuriated the Jewish community; Liberal finance critic Herb Gray, for one, said: "A boyish prank? I wonder what Harvie Andre would call the Holocaust." When questioned by Tobin about the remark the next day, Andre replied: "[Tobin] cannot know that in fact the swastika was hanging up there. He cannot know that perhaps it was not a boyish prank. Apparently it was in a private room of the barracks. I just ask the honorable member to think for half a minute that there is the possibility it was a prank."

With the media's attention fixed on the approaching Progressive Conservative Party leadership convention, Matt McKay's name briefly slipped from the national political agenda. But the issue of racists in the military would not go away. In June, the Department of National Defence confirmed that personnel at Canadian Forces Base Esquimalt, in Victoria, had been investigated in August 1992 for their links to the Aryan Nations. The department confirmed that a group of naval trainees had attempted to copy Aryan Nations hate propaganda at a suburban Victoria print shop. And some members had tried to recruit young people in the city's downtown. Despite Opposition demands, however, Kim Campbell and her department refused to make public the report into the allegations. Later that same month, Harvie Andre, answering for Campbell, confirmed in the House that five CFB Esquimalt personnel had been investigated.

Two were subsequently dismissed from the Armed Forces for their involvement with the Aryan Nations.

Throughout the summer, the special inquiry into the activities of the Canadian Airborne Regiment in Somalia continued behind closed doors. Then, on the last day of August, the first "phase" of the board's report was released at a packed press conference in Ottawa. For the Canadian military, the news was not good: Matt McKay, the inquiry found, was not the only committed white supremacist wearing a Canadian Armed Forces uniform. There were others, many others.

The sub-unit of the regiment to which McKay belonged, called 2 Commando, had been assigned the task of providing security for the Somalian town of Belet Huen and its surrounding area. Because 2 Commando patrolled continuously—day and night— Somali citizens, unaware of the irony, gave them a nickname: The Clan Who Never Sleep.

The Clan Who Never Sleep were also, the inquiry discovered, The Clan Who Tolerated Racist Members. In the early 1980s—no one is sure of the precise date—2 Commando adopted a unit banner: the Confederate flag. According to 2 Commando lore, the flag, which many U.S. white supremacists and neo-Nazis regularly display at their rallies and cross-burnings, was presented to the unit after its members participated in a particularly demanding joint exercise. At the time, the 2 Commando soldiers were told they possessed a "rebel" attitude. The Confederate flag, and the rebel name, were quickly adopted by the unit. "[This] seemed to have had official sanction, indeed, encouragement," the report stated. "The flag was waved at various competitions to rally support. . . . Later, the leadership saw a linkage between an internal discipline problem and this symbol. The rebel flag was apparently flown on occasions when the authorities had done something with which the soldiers disagreed." As a result, the flag was banned but the unit stubbornly refused to obey.

The report went on to concede that, while the Confederate flag "has been associated by some with racism . . . the Board discovered no evidence that this connotation was ever intended or adopted within the Canadian Airborne Regiment." That said, the board's report is somewhat contradictory when it discusses the problems created by members of Matt McKay's unit. On the one hand, the report's authors seem dismissive of these problems: "They are young and dynamic and, from time to time, get into trouble. They live in quarters together and, in a relatively isolated base like Petawawa, tend to spend their weekends and holidays together, relaxing with those with whom they share common interests and values." Elsewhere, however, the board admits that "problems" arise when those same interests and values run counter to accepted norms. In this section of the report, which had been heavily censored, with entire paragraphs blacked out, the rebels are actually referred to as a "cabal."

One whole section of the report was given over to "cultural differences" and racism. "The Board discovered that a range of nicknames had been adopted by some Canadians to depict certain Somalis, especially 'the enemy' Somalis. These nicknames include gimmes, niggers, smufties and nig-nogs." The report's authors state that the use of such epithets by a peacekeeping operation was "most inappropriate and unprofessional" and must be stopped.

The report then went on: "The Board did find some evidence that there may have been one or two individuals in the Battle Group who were believed to hold views that might be classed as white supremacist in nature. However, after extensive questioning, the Board concludes that this problem was, at worst, confined to a tiny minority." All of the remaining text had been removed by censors.

At a press conference called to respond to the report, senior military officials—including the Chief of the Defence Staff, Admiral John Anderson—declined to provide further details about the presence of white supremacists in the rebel unit. But, on the same day the report was made public, hundreds of pages of testimony by board witnesses was released at only one place: the Department of National Defence library in Ottawa. Although heavily censored, the testimony provided intriguing details about the Canadian Armed Forces' white supremacists.

One unidentified member of McKay's regiment testified, under oath, that a colleague openly boasted that he was going to Somalia to "shoot me a nigger." The soldier's testimony seems to suggest that the man who made the statement was an officer. The soldier also testified that "eleven or twelve" current or former members of the Airborne carried white supremacist tattoos on their arms. The soldier, identified only as the sixty-third witness, said he was "shocked" by the large number of white supremacist and neo-Nazi soldiers, adding that members often discussed "beating up niggers" at drinking parties. In 2 Commando, the soldier testified, white supremacists were "all around. Everywhere you look."

Needless to say, many Canadians found this revelation disconcerting. So did minority rights activists. On May 7, July 23 and September 15, for example, the Canadian Jewish Congress wrote to Kim Campbell and her successor as defence minister, Tom Siddon, to call for action on the issue of white supremacists in the Canadian Armed Forces. For months, the congress received no reply from either. Finally, at the end of September, Siddon's scheduling secretary wrote to declare that the minister of defence would be unable to meet with Jewish community representatives.

On October 5, the CJC's national president and its national chair of community relations wrote a toughly worded fourth letter to the government. In it, Irving Abella and Hal Joffe stated that Campbell's and Siddon's inaction had "tarnished the good name of the Canadian Armed Forces." They went on: "If Matt McKay can remain active in the Canadian Armed Forces, how many other neo-Nazis are on active duty? Your own report, recently released, indicates that McKay is not the only one. Clearly a full and public inquiry is urgently required."

Others were gravely concerned about the presence of McKay and other neo-Nazis in the Canadian forces. In late September, the Dominion secretary of the Royal Canadian Legion informed the government that his group had passed this resolution at its Pacific Command Convention: "Be it resolved that we, as members of the

Royal Canadian Legion, in memory of our comrades who laid down their lives, and of those who are still suffering from honorable wounds received in war against the Nazis, send a very strong message of our feeling of disgust and betrayal, to the government of Canada, for allowing this movement to operate within the Constitution of Canada."

After receiving letters from the Legionnaires and the CJC, the Conservative government, then in the middle of a national election campaign, went into damage-control mode. In interviews with reporters, Siddon stated that his department had a "zero tolerance" policy with respect to organized racism. He added that he would now be happy to meet with representatives from the Canadian Jewish Congress. When asked why he had not dealt with the issue sooner, Siddon blamed his own employees: "I have no difficulty meeting with [CJC]. I just regret it wasn't brought to my attention sooner." He was kept in the dark, he said, by "some well-meaning staff who probably didn't understand the seriousness of their concern."

On October 14, CJC officials finally met with Siddon in Vancouver. At the meeting, sources say, the former defence minister lambasted the CJC for having the temerity to bring up such an explosive issue during an election campaign. That done, Siddon informed the delegation—led by community relations chair Joffe—that his department had enacted tough new policies to deal with the problem of racists in the military. The regulations, which were promulgated with no public notice on August 19, declared that "racist attitudes are totally incompatible with the military ethos and with effective military service, and any behavior or conduct which promote such attitudes cannot be tolerated." A new Canadian Armed Forces administrative order would give commanding officers the power to discipline and release personnel who associate with white supremacist or neo-Nazi groups.

Said Joffe, "I was pleased with the new regulations that were promulgated. That's a positive step. But the jury is still out on [how well the government] will enforce the policy." Joffe added that he was concerned that a known neo-Nazi—Matt McKay—was still wearing a Canadian Armed Forces uniform.

And what of Matt McKay? After his tour of duty in Somalia, McKay moved to Canadian Forces Base Calgary, where he lives with his wife and three children. (Later, he was transferred out of the Airborne.) In early October, he broke his self-imposed silence for the first time since *The Winnipeg Sun* broke his story. McKay slammed the media for victimizing him. (At least one media star agreed with him—in an October 1994 column, *Sun* writer Peter Worthington called criticisms of McKay "McCarthyism.") McKay told *The Ottawa Citizen* that Siddon's investigation into racist armed forces members was "stupid." In an expletive-filled interview with reporter April Lindgren, McKay said: "I'm a professional soldier and that's what I want to do. And I have a family and I don't want to lose that. If I lose my job, I don't have nothing because I ain't got no education to get a job on civilian street."

Reached a few days after the *Citizen* interview, and sounding bitter, McKay seemed to regret his moment of candor. "I can't tell you anything," he said, his voice thick with anger. "I don't want to talk about nothing, and I don't know anything." He referred all further questions to the deputy commanding officer of CFB and hung up.

In January 1995, an amateur video of McKay and his Airborne pals in Belet Huen was released to the media. In it, McKay can be seen sitting bare-chested in his tent, a large Celtic Cross tattoo plainly visible. Asked what he thought about the Somalia mission, McKay said: "It sucks cock, man! We ain't killed enough niggers yet!" Following the release of a second video a few days later—in which a black Airborne recruit is seen with the words "I LOVE KKK" scrawled in feces on his back—Defence Minister David Collenette ordered the Airborne Regiment disbanded.

Matt McKay was not the first of his kind, and he will not be the last. There are other examples of neo-Nazis and white supremacists recruiting on Canadian Armed Forces bases. Eric Fischer, the head of security for both the Heritage Front and the Church of the Creator, is a former Airborne Regiment officer. So too is Roy McKnight, the

Saskatchewan man who is a close associate of that province's imprisoned Aryan Nations leader, Carney Nerland. And as recently as April 1994, James Russel Lisik, a member of Canada's newest and fastest-growing racist group, the Northern Hammerskins, joined the armed forces reserves—despite the fact that the army knew that Lisik had been charged in connection with a vicious gay-bashing in Winnipeg. (Lisik missed a March 30 court date because he was training with the reserves outside Winnipeg.) A former armed forces major, who spoke on the condition that he not be identified, scoffed at government claims that very few forces personnel are members of organized hate groups. "In virtually every regiment, across the country, you will find these kinds of guys," said this officer. "They disgust most of us, but they are also tolerated by the brass. I don't know why."

For the millions of Canadians who followed the strange tale of Cpl. Matt McKay in the spring and summer of 1993, the answer was also elusive. Never in recent memory had the rise in organized white supremacy and neo-Nazism attracted so much attention. The controversy had rocked the Conservative government and, most importantly, cast a cloud over the excellent reputation enjoyed by the Canadian Armed Forces. As millions of Canadians took notice for the first time of the spreading web of hate, politicians and community leaders were asked: what can be done to stamp out the forces of intolerance?

13

CONCLUSION

Across Canada, in every region, in almost every town and city, the web of hate continues to spread. White supremacist and neo-Nazi leaders continue to print pamphlets that deny the Holocaust and slander minorities. They continue to send out their skinhead disciples to assault innocent people. They continue to grow and organize. When they suffer setbacks or legal challenges, they go underground or form support networks across the country. Sometimes, they turn to foreign governments—or foreign neo-Nazi groups—for funding and support. And they grow.

They are aided, in part, by history. While Canadians traditionally regard themselves as members of a society that is kinder and gentler than that of our neighbor to the south, it cannot be denied that deep seams of bigotry run throughout our past. Our treatment of aboriginal peoples—and, at different times, French-Canadians, Japanese-Canadians, Chinese-Canadians, Jews and many others—have muddied our collective reputation as a nation of tolerance and goodwill. Those who belong to the racist right know that in yesterday walks tomorrow; they know that if a head tax was applied against Chinese immigrants in the past, or that Jews fleeing the Holocaust were denied entry to Canada, or that refugees from South American dictatorships are being turned away, there is always the hope that equally discriminatory measures may be applied against other victims in the future.

Many other Canadians, however, have shown themselves prepared to own up to sins of intolerance. In a short time, they have built a nation that is multicultural, generous and respected throughout the world. They have done so, in part, by manifesting a willingness to confront racism and hatred and stamp them out in whatever form they appear.

Stamping out white supremacy, anti-Semitism, homophobia and their variants unfortunately will not be easy. At this stage in Canada's history, a number of forces are conspiring to assist racist leaders. Memories, for one, are fading: the horrors of World War Two become increasingly remote with the death of each Holocaust survivor, and Holocaust deniers are attempting to promote a more benign view of past events. In addition, harsh economic realities are crushing the hopes and dreams of a generation—and pushing some of these young people towards the simplistic siren song of hate. Finally, with changing immigration patterns, Canadians are being forced to come to grips with the presence of growing numbers of visible minorities—and they are being asked to accommodate lifestyles and cultural differences that, at first blush, seem strange. The pollsters tell us that all of these things, rightly or wrongly, have left many Canadians feeling insecure, threatened and under siege. And onto the stage have stepped the Klansmen and the neo-Nazis, with their calls for a return to the so-called status quo—and to a time when things were supposedly better for "white" Canadians.

That is not all: racist leaders are aided ironically by advances in technology. With the investment of only a few hundred dollars, they can spread their hateful messages with impunity. They can do so across national and international borders, far from the eyes of police agencies, using computer bulletin boards, fax machines and the like. Increasingly, too, the Canadian ultra-rightists are co-operating with each other. At rallies, conferences and on telephone lines, they are coming together as never before to recruit, attack minorities and propagandize. A good example of the effectiveness of their networking is found in the case of schoolteacher Malcolm Ross. The Moncton resident claims to be a lone dissenting voice in the proverbial wilderness. In fact, he is the beneficiary of the attentions of hundreds of neo-Nazis across Canada, the United States and Europe.

Who is susceptible to the recruitment techniques of these hate-mongers? Their numbers include the unemployed, the disenfranchised and, most significantly, the young people who have been marginalized by chronic unemployment and society's increasing selfishness. Among these newcomers to racism we see, for example, the skinheads, who bring a fondness for violence that defies comprehension. Also joining the ranks of haters are a few members of ostensibly mainstream political organizations such as the Reform Party, some of whose activists are increasingly associated with extreme expressions of bigotry and intolerance. To his credit, Reform Party leader Preston Manning expels these individuals whenever the media bring their existence to his attention. But the question Manning has yet to answer, of course, is this: if his party is not racist, why are so many racists attracted to it?

At the end of the day, the message is simple: Canadians can no longer afford to look the other way. Our far right can no longer be dismissed as a mere lunatic fringe.

Every citizen of this country must work—and work hard—at maintaining the multicultural society that is Canada. Using the law, using the education system, we must remain vigilant. Canadian racist leaders are better organized, better funded and better united than they have been at any time in our history. If we do not fight organized racism for ourselves, then we must do it for our children—because it is the hearts and minds of our children, after all, that the racist leaders are determined to keep.

To date, Canadian law—and Canadian lawmakers—have experienced mixed results as they confront the messengers of hate. In some instances, such as the recent prosecutions of Wolfgang Droege and members of his Heritage Front, there has been a good deal of success. But in many more cases, such as the prosecutions of Ernst Zundel, Bill Harcus, Carney Nerland and various skinheads, the law's effect has been minimal, if not non-existent. In Zundel's case, in fact, the application of the law seemed to have had precisely the opposite effect of what was intended.

This is not to say, of course, that those who oppose organized racism should abandon legal remedies. However imperfect it may be, the law remains our best instrument in restricting—and eventually stopping—the dramatic growth in racist ideologies in Canada. We must continue to apply the law to what is, when stripped to its core, a criminal movement. And, where necessary, we must continue to shape the law to counter the growing sophistication of the far right—and restrict the dissemination of their hateful messages.

Like anyone else who has anything to say, Canadian white supremacists and neo-Nazis communicate their "ideas" with words. In books, in pamphlets, in broadcasts, on telephone answering machines, on computer bulletin boards and on synagogue walls, they use words to defend their creed or attack their opponents. But, unlike just about anyone else, they also communicate using their fists.

Canadian law has a good deal to say about the communication of hatred through both spoken word and clenched fist. It goes without saying, of course, that when the chosen vehicle of expression is violence, mainstream Canadian opinion is unanimous and supportive of criminal sanctions. In recent years, white supremacists and neo-Nazis have been charged with offences ranging from assault to murder. Although racism has been regarded as a factor in no more than about four dozen criminal cases in Canada—traditionally, Crown attorneys have been reluctant to introduce evidence of bias, fearing it will jeopardize a prosecution—this is changing. More and more, police and Crown attorneys are seeking tougher sentences when the accused is involved in the hate movement. "We're educating ourselves about bias crime," says Det.-Sgt. Dan Dunlop, of Ottawa's anti-hate police unit. "And it's making a difference."

Meanwhile, non-violent communication of hate is also considered socially undesirable and is punishable by a variety of sanctions. But despite that, a debate persists—involving, for the most part, conscientious citizens with bona fide opinions on the subject—about the desirability of restricting the communication of hate through the medium of words.

Followers of Jeremy Bentham and John Stuart Mill assert, in good faith, that it is wrong to suppress the communication of ideas, no matter how pernicious those ideas may be. Mill, in his seminal book *On Liberty*, asks: "Who can compute what the world loses in the multitude of promising intellects . . . who dare not follow out any bold, vigorous, independent train of thought, lest it should land them in something which would admit of being considered irreligious or immoral?" This attractive notion finds currency in this century in one of the most important judgments ever issued by a Canadian court, the Alberta Press Act Reference. In that 1938 judgment, written in the main by Supreme Court of Canada Chief Justice Lyman P. Duff, an attempt by Alberta's Social Credit government to control the province's press is found to be unconstitutional. In one memorable section of his decision, Duff writes: "There can be no controversy that [public] institutions derive their efficacy from the free public discussion of affairs, from criticism and answer and counter-criticism, from attack upon policy and administration and defence and counter-attack; from the freest and fullest analysis and examination from every point of view of political proposals."

In Canada, regrettably, some of the most stirring defences of unbridled free expression come, ironically, not from civil libertarians or utilitarians but from this country's far right. The names of their various groups reflect their professed fondness for free speech. Ottawa's Ian Verner Macdonald, the former policy adviser to the Grand Wizard of the Canadian Knights of the Ku Klux Klan, briefly led a group known as the Society for Free Expression. Victoria's Doug Christie, the barrister the Law Society of Upper Canada says has made "common cause" with the forces of anti-Semitism, leads a group called the Canadian

Free Speech League. High River's Ron Gostick, who has rallied to the side of virtually every single white supremacist and neo-Nazi this country has produced in the past 30 years, leads an innocuous-sounding group known as the Canadian League of Rights. Toronto's Paul Fromm leads a group called the Canadian Association for Free Expression. These are groups with names that suggest lofty principle and devotion to some noble cause, names that do not sound particularly racist— which, one supposes, might be the intended impression.

Christie, for one, seems quite genuine about the subject of free expression. In one small book he published through Fromm's Citizens for Foreign Aid Reform, *Free Speech Is the Issue!*, the controversial lawyer writes: "An artificial silence or an artificial expression of people who are endeavoring to speak the truth is more damaging to society than any of the temporary hurts that words may carry. . . . We cannot abolish the freedom to express the truth because, in some cases, there might be lies told. That argument would abolish the right to tell the truth in any circumstance. It would make an a priori judgment, making it illegal to shout 'fire' in a crowded theatre, even though there might be a fire, even though the accused might have a reason to believe there was a fire. It is far better to allow the right to say it, for the value it might have on a few occasions when it is true, than—by abolishing that right—to prohibit the means of society rectifying a legitimate and actual wrong."

If it is Christie's argument that there are dangers associated with the suppression or inhibition of the free circulation of truth—of ideas—he is undoubtedly right. History is littered with examples of the folly of suppressing ideas. But the question that remains is one that Christie and his ilk are not usually eager to answer: namely, is it an "idea" to stand in a field in Provost, Alberta, and chant "Death to the Jews"? Is it an "idea" to spray-paint the words "Hitler was right" on the side of a synagogue? Is it an "idea" to stand before a survivor of Auschwitz, as Carney Nerland did in September 1990, and say, "You're one of the ones they didn't work to death, you parasite! You fucking weren't able to work in the camps good enough to feed the

Nazi war machine"? Are these "ideas" that in any way assist the development of a vibrant, multicultural state? Are these words representative of "ideas" at all? To any fair-minded person, the answer should be obvious. The answer to both questions should be no.

In recent years, opinions on this point have been far from unanimous. Legislators, police officers, lawyers and minority activists continually debate the utility and necessity of prosecuting racists for verbal and written expressions of white supremacy and anti-Semitism.

Nowhere was this debate seen more dramatically than in the 1990 case of *R. v. Keegstra*, when the Supreme Court of Canada decided, by a slim vote—four to three—that the law under which Keegstra had been charged was a reasonable limitation on constitutionally protected guarantees of free speech. In the majority judgment, written by then-chief justice Brian Dickson, the court stated: "Hate propaganda contributes little to the aspirations of Canadians or Canada in either the quest for truth, the promotion of individual self-development or the protection and fostering of a vibrant democracy where the participation of all individuals is accepted and encouraged." It found that, although the law under which the former Alberta schoolteacher had been charged—that is, willfully promoting hatred against an identifiable group, Jews—was contrary to the Canadian Charter of Rights and Freedoms, it was reasonable. The law was kept on the books.

But three of the Supreme Court justices felt otherwise. They felt the law should be thrown out and that Jim Keegstra should be free to preach hatred to children. In her dissenting opinion, Justice Beverley McLachlin wrote: "While many may find Mr. Keegstra's ideas unsettling, it is not suggested that they are made with the intention or have the effect of compelling Jewish people or anyone else to do one thing or another." As in the later case of *R. v. Zundel*, this appeared to have missed the point. It is certainly true that there is no evidence that Keegstra encouraged children to go out and murder Jews. But what he did—beyond a reasonable doubt—was create an environment in which acts of violence against Jews were not only understandable, they were commendable. He created an environment that absolved Nazi murderers of their sins against humanity. Jews, Keegstra told young children, were "treacherous," "subversive," "power hungry" and "child killers." He also told them blacks were inferior to whites and that Catholics were in league with Jewish Communists. As law professor Richard Moon noted in the *University of British Columbia Law Review* in 1992: "Much of what is labelled hate propaganda is meant to threaten and intimidate members of a victim group. The Nazi march in the Jewish suburb or the swastikas painted on walls are not meant to engage the audience in dialogue or to stimulate their thinking" (emphasis added). In 1991, after the Supreme court made its decision, the Alberta Court of Appeal again quashed Keegstra's conviction and ordered a new trial. In 1992, the new trial found Keegstra guilty for the second time; he was fined $3,000. In September 1994, the Alberta Court of Appeal overturned that conviction. A few days later, the Alberta government decided to appeal again to the Supreme Court of Canada.

The Supreme Court took a different approach in the other major case on free speech and bigotry, *R. v. Zundel*. The Toronto anti-Semitic publisher had been charged under a different Criminal Code section from the one under which Keegstra had been tried. For the application of Keegstra's section of the code to "kick in," law enforcement must first obtain the permission of the attorney-general of the province in which the hate crime took place. But when then-Ontario attorney-general Roy McMurtry's permission was sought by a group of Jews, the Ontario minister of justice—like so many of his colleagues in the intervening years—refused to give it. As a result, the Jewish community in Toronto was faced with an unappealing choice. Either initiate a private prosecution under a different section of the code, one that did not require McMurtry's assent, or forget about the whole matter. In December 1973, Holocaust Remembrance Association member Sabina Citron opted for the former and swore a private complaint against Zundel on the grounds that he had published false news about the Holocaust—namely, that it did not happen.

It took precisely eight years for the case to wind its way through the courts to the Supreme Court of Canada. The issue, phrased simply, was this: was the false news law constitutional? Writing for the majority— two judges dissented from her opinion—McLachlin concluded that it was not. In a judgment that was issued in late August 1992 and, sadly, threw Canada's far right into an orgy of celebration, McLachlin stated: "I cannot accede to the argument that those who deliberately publish falsehoods are for that reason alone precluded from claiming the bene- fit of the constitutional guarantees of free speech." To reach that con- clusion, the high court majority seemed reluctant to subject the words in issue to any type of functional analysis, meaning that they did not consider the effect of those words upon Zundel's victims. By failing to analyze the nature of the "speech" in question—speech that is hateful and without a single grain of truth, by any reasonable standard—the Supreme Court, critics say, failed to observe that such "speech" has been repeatedly used, in recent years, to terrorize minorities and legit- imize violence with great effectiveness.

In their dissent, Justices Peter Cory and Frank Iacobucci did take note of the nature of the words. Not confined by the analysis favored by the majority, the two justices highlight what the majority missed: that lies in the style of Zundel and Keegstra are not ideas. "[Zundel's hate propaganda] do not merely operate to foment discord and hatred, but they do so in an extraordinarily duplicitous manner. By couching their propaganda as the banal product of disinterested research, the purveyors of these works seek to circumvent rather than appeal to the critical faculties of their audience. The harm wreaked by this genre of material can be best illustrated with reference to the sort of Holocaust denial literature at issue in this appeal. . . . Holocaust denial has perni- cious effects upon Canadians who suffered, fought and died as a result of the Nazis' campaign of racial bigotry and upon Canadian society as a whole. For Holocaust survivors, it is a deep and grievous denial of the significance of the harm done to them and thus belittles their enormous pain and loss. It deprives others of the opportunity to learn from the lessons of history. To deliberately lie about the indescribable suffering and death inflicted upon the Jews by Hitler is the foulest of falsehoods and the essence of cruelty. . . . The facts reveal with dreadful clarity that racism is a current and present evil in our country. It is a cancerous growth that is still alive, growing and thriving on ignorance, suspicion, fear and jealousy."

With the Supreme Court of Canada's Zundel judgment safely tucked away in their arsenal—and with the added bonus of the narrow split decision in the Keegstra case, signalling that the court could easily go their way the next time—the leaders of Canada's racist right are confident that legal victory is not very far off. They may well be right. With the false news section of the Criminal Code now gone, and with the "willful promotion of hatred" section continuing in a legal limbo of sorts, neo-Nazis and white supremacists look forward to the day when a U.S.-style situation prevails—one in which they can say and write almost anything, no matter what the consequences for Jews, gays and non-whites.

As a result, some Canadian human rights activists have turned their attention to another section of the code, one that makes the promotion of genocide an offence. This section has been used only once, in the unsuccessful attempt to prosecute Bill Harcus and his Knights of the Ku Klux Klan followers. Groups such as the Canadian Jewish Congress prefer this section because it is less problematic, legally, than the willful promotion section. But the fact is that this section also requires the prior approval of a provincial attorney-general. And the fact is that provincial attorneys-general have been notoriously reluctant to grant that permission. Says the CJC's Bernie Farber: "In terms of the legislation to fight hate, we have the legal technology. What we appear to lack is the moral will to apply that technology."

In Ontario, in its nearly quarter-century of existence, the willful promotion of hatred section has been used only four times. This is surprising when one recalls that the B'nai Brith, for one, estimates that there are thousands of reported and unreported incidents of anti-Semitic crime across Canada every year. Farber disagrees with minority activists who call for the removal of the section that requires an attorney-general's approval before a hate charge can be laid. He says, "If we remove one comma from that law, we may end up throwing out the baby with the bath water. Remember that the Keegstra decision was only a four–three split. My fear is, if we remove the attorney-general permission section, we may see the Supreme Court throw the law out next time." Farber adds that "the sacred right of free speech" must continue to be protected, and says that the Criminal Code hate laws, which are designed to prevent "vilification of minorities," should be used sparingly and with great care.

But as Farber and others note, the Criminal Code of Canada is not the only source of anti-hate remedies. Other tools have been used very effectively against neo-Nazis and white supremacists in the past. The Canadian Human Rights Act, for example, prohibits discrimination on the basis of race, ethnicity, color, religion and so on through the vehicle of telephone hate messages. This act has been used effectively against the Western Guard, the Aryan Nations, the Ku Klux Klan, the Canadian Liberty Net and, most recently, the Heritage Front. Another tool has been provincial human rights statutes. In Alberta, for example, the province's Individual Rights Protection Act was relied upon to prohibit the public exhibition of the swastika, Klan symbols, burning crosses and white power insignia by members of Terry Long's Aryan Nations. And the federal government has given authority—an authority that seems to be infrequently exercised—to Customs and Excise officers to seize any and all material crossing the border that "constitute hate propaganda" under the definition given in the Criminal Code. (Industrious racist leaders, such as Terry Long, have been circumventing these laws for more than a decade with computers and modems. There is little anyone can do to monitor—or restrict—the practice.)

Leaving aside the sort of argument favored by the Supreme Court of Canada in the Zundel appeal—that is, make or publish any hateful statement one wishes, even statements that incite others to violence—there is one compelling argument against hate prosecutions. And that is the argument best articulated by that most inarticulate of men, Ernst

Zundel. In March 1985, after he was convicted in his first trial, Zundel stated that he had in a sense won, because the trial had given him "one million dollars' worth of publicity." Although Carleton University professor Conrad Winn also produced a survey to show that the trial had sensitized many Canadians to the issues of anti-Semitism and Holocaust denial, the fact remains: Zundel did receive a million dollars of publicity during the course of his trial. The prosecution transformed him from a little-known hatemonger into a household name, and not just in Canada. In his 1993 book, *The Fourth Reich*, German writer Michael Schmidt states that Zundel has made a fortune out of selling hate propaganda to German neo-Nazi groups. Canadian police sources confirm that the trial helped to transform Zundel into a millionaire; the notoriety given to the German immigrant by the prosecution led to thousands of requests for hate propaganda—at a fee—from all over the world.

How, then, to deal with hate? The mass media have a role to play. In many cases, nothing is more damaging to racist groups than dispassionate, well-researched journalism. When mainstream media organizations subject Klansmen and neo-Nazis to scrutiny, these same Klansmen and neo-Nazis inevitably scatter. Conversely, sensationalistic Geraldo-type "exposés" tend to do little more than boost the fortunes of organized racists. Some Canadian school boards, meanwhile, have addressed the issue head-on, with admirable success. The Ottawa Board of Education, for example, introduced a Holocaust studies program to its curriculum in 1987, after a noisy battle with local white supremacists. And in 1993, the same board held a series of seminars for teachers and administrators on the subject of hate crime. The board's employees were taught how to recognize hate groups and what to do about them. Other boards across Canada have expressed an interest in confronting hate activity.

As the Zundel and Keegstra trials have shown, the Criminal Code has been somewhat less than effective in stamping out hate. Provincial human rights codes are occasionally helpful but, most of the time, these statutes are limited to very narrow types of activity. However, in the

United States, anti-racist activists have recently tried a new approach, and with resounding success: they have hit the neo-Nazis and white supremacists in their wallets.

On the evening of November 12, 1988, three skinheads and their girl-friends went out for a ride around Portland, Oregon. Earlier that night, one of the skinheads, Ken (Death) Mieske, had been given some hate propaganda by his roommate, Dave Mazzella. Mazzella, who had been sent to Portland from California in September by his leader, White Aryan Resistance (WAR) leader Tom Metzger, was told to organize Mieske and the East Side White Pride skinheads into a WAR chapter. Along with the hate propaganda, Mazzella brought with him a few baseball bats. One of the pamphlets he brought with him featured a cartoon of a skinhead carrying a knife in one hand and a baseball bat in the other. "THE WHITE STUDENT ISN'T FIGHTING FOR JUST HIMSELF, BUT FOR THE FUTURE OF HIS RACE," the caption read.

That night, after Mieske and his pals Steven Strasser and Kyle Brewster passed out some of the pamphlets to people on the street, the group went cruising. Just after midnight, the skinheads drove past a car containing several black men. One of the men, Mulugeta Seraw, was standing outside the car, saying goodnight to his friends. Shouts were exchanged and a few obscene gestures; Mieske jumped out of the car and smashed the other vehicle's windows with a base-ball bat. Strasser, meanwhile, started to beat one of the men. The man escaped further harm by crawling under the car. Mieske then turned his attention to Seraw. He beat the Ethiopian student with the baseball bat, and Strasser joined in. Later in court, Strasser testified: "[Seraw] looked like he was pretty delirious and he started yelling. It was a real freaky kind of yelling . . . it was like cryin' death. It's something you'd never forget." Then, the final blow: "It sounded really gory, like taking a bag of chips or something and crunching them all up. It was loud. He looked dead and there was blood com-ing out of his head." The skinheads escaped and had a few beers to celebrate. "We really fucked that guy up!" Mieske said, laughing.

Six days later, Mieske was arrested. At the police station, he called Tom Metzger in Fallbrook, California, collect. Metzger advised him not to talk to police. In a WAR telephone hate message he later recorded, Metzger praised Mieske, Strasser and Brewster for doing their "civic duty." Less than a year after the murder, all three skinheads were serving lengthy prison terms; Mieske was given a life sentence.

But Tom Metzger and his son John—leader of the Aryan Youth Movement—had not escaped punishment. In October 1989, Mulugeta Seraw's family, with the assistance of an anti-racist group called the Southern Poverty Law Center, filed a civil suit against the Metzgers, along with their organization, Mieske and Brewster. Mazzella acted as the plaintiff's chief witness. The former skinhead testified that the entire WAR organization was focussed upon committing acts of violence against non-whites and other minorities. In October 1990, the jury reached a decision: $12.5 million in damages was to be paid to the Seraw family by the Metzgers, their organization and their followers.

Since the decision was handed down, the White Aryan Resistance has been crippled. The Metzgers are broke, and their organization is far less effective than it was. As a result, they have turned their attentions to recruitment and fund-raising in Canada, where they are not affected by the terms of the civil lawsuit.

Many believe that it is time to emulate the Seraw precedent in Canada. In Manitoba, the provincial Defamation Act permits persons who have been libelled by hate propaganda—that is, material "likely to expose persons belonging to [a] race or . . . religious creed to hatred, contempt or ridicule" and that tends "to raise unrest or disorder among the people"—to sue for damages. But no other province has a similar statute.

In Alberta, following the Seraw family's lead, retired broadcaster Keith Rutherford continues to sue the Aryan Nations organization for $2.5 million for assault and the loss of his eye. In pre-trial hearings, skinheads who have left the Nazi fold have confirmed that Long and his followers are terrified that Rutherford may succeed in "doing a Metzger," as one skinhead put it. Asked if he is concerned that he may never recover a cent in his civil action, Rutherford says: "I want to put them out of business. I want justice."

Despite all of the evidence of a growing violent far right movement, it is important to remember that all is not lost. For many racist leaders, it is not a good time. Police agencies are becoming increasingly tough with racist groups. In Ottawa and Toronto, for example, hate crimes units have been recently established and have become models for police forces across the country. The Ottawa officers, Det.-Sgts. Dan Dunlop and Gerry Doucette, have become experts in dealing with hate groups and in preventing organized racism from taking root. They have investigated dozens upon dozens of bias incidents and, in many cases, laid charges. Community groups, too, are becoming more sophisticated and knowledgeable about the purveyors of hate. After the Aryan Nations training camp controversy in August 1986, for example, dozens of Calgary groups and individuals banded together to form an ad hoc group to educate Albertans about hate crime and hate groups. And in November 1992, close to 200 people representing police, minority and community groups convened in Vancouver for discussions on the growing far right menace; the forum's participants have called for a national registry on hate crime and hate criminals. People are fighting back.

In British Columbia, the Canadian Liberty Net's Tony McAleer has been jailed for breaching court orders to shut down his hate line. Doug Christie is representing an increasing number of far right types, but with only a few exceptions—Ernst Zundel and Manitoba's Ku Klux Klan—he usually loses. In Alberta and B.C., Terry Long is still organizing skinheads, but he has been struck mute by the provincial human rights inquiry. His partner, Silent Brotherhood member Edgar Foth, has recently been charged with possession of a restricted weapon—a semi-automatic 9-mm pistol—and on September 8, 1993, pled guilty. Teàrlach Dunsford Mac a'Phearsoin has been jailed. In Saskatchewan, Long's lieutenant, Carney Nerland, was released into the RCMP witness protection program in December '93 after agreeing to inform on his Aryan brothers; there, he awaits the outcome of another provincial inquiry, this one called to determine if his case had been mishandled. In Manitoba, Ku Klux Klan leader Bill Harcus remains in hiding. In Ontario, Heritage Front leader Wolfgang Droege was sentenced in June 1994 to three months in prison for refusing to obey a court order to shut down the Heritage Front hate line (Gary Schipper and Heritage Front member Kenneth Barker were also imprisoned); and George Burdi is also facing jail terms for assault and obstruction of justice. (His Church of the Creator has fallen apart following Ben Klassen's suicide; Burdi says he has given up on the group.) In Quebec, young White Power Canada members remain behind bars for the murder of two Montreal men in late 1992.

Canada's racist leaders may face some legal difficulties, but no one believes that the threat has disappeared for good. In the past, the forces of intolerance have encountered similar inconveniences, and they have always come back. New leaders take the places of the old. They persevere, and they learn from their mistakes. Above all, they do not go away.

One hot and sunny afternoon not so long ago, a few weeks before he is to become a national celebrity, Terry Long strolls around his acreage, talking to a reporter. Leaning against his sawmill, a "WHITE PRIDE" trucker's cap on his head, Long looks off into the distance, into the future. "It has already started," he says. "If you are waiting for the big shot that is going to be heard around the world, I don't think you are going to hear it. The prime motivating factor will be the economic situation. Very, very few people can, with an open mind, arrive at an all-encompassing, reasoned perspective, as I have, without first being hit in the pocketbook. You saw it in the thirties. It took 15 years of people starving to death and having their faces rubbed in the dirt before they finally saw the truth, as represented by Adolf Hitler."

His words hang in the air for a few moments, and then he continues. "All the time, more people are waking up. People are becoming more reasonable to talk to—whereas a few years ago, when they had good-paying jobs, they wouldn't even discuss it with you. Now, people are more open. People are even approaching me. They are waking up to what I believe in."

From his house, as if on cue, there is a sound. It is the sound of his telephone ringing.

"There," Terry Long says, laughing. "There's another one calling me right now."

CHAPTER NOTES

Very few books have been published exclusively on the subject of Canada's racist right. Many materials, however, have proved invaluable in my research, among them examples of hate propaganda that, although distasteful, must be read before one can obtain a full understanding of this subject. Important sources include:

Abella, Irving, and Harold Troper, *None Is Too Many*, Lester & Orpen Dennys, Toronto, 1983

Anti-Defamation League of B'nai Brith, *Extremism on the Right*, B'nai Brith, New York, 1988

Anti-Defamation League of B'nai Brith, *Hate Groups in America*, B'nai Brith, New York, 1988

Barrett, Stanley R., *Is God a Racist? The Right Wing in Canada*, University of Toronto Press, Toronto, 1987

Beam, Louis R., Jr., *Essays of a Klansman*, Akia Publications, Hayden Lake, Id., 1983

Bennett, David H., *The Party of Fear*, Vintage Books, New York, 1990

Bercuson, David, and Douglas Wertheimer, *A Trust Betrayed: The Keegstra Affair*, Seal Books, Toronto, 1987

Beverley, James A., *Web of Error: An Analysis of the Views of Malcolm Ross*, Mount Allison University, Sackville, N.B., 1990

Brake, Mike, *The Sociology of Youth Culture and Youth Subcultures*, Routledge, London, 1980

Coates, James, *Armed and Dangerous: The Rise of the Survivalist Right*, Noonday Press, New York, 1987

Cyllorn, Jud, *Stop Apologizing!* Procult Institute, Vancouver, 1991

Davies, Alan (ed.), *Anti-Semitism in Canada*, Wilfrid Laurier University Press, Waterloo, Ont., 1992

Delisle, Esther, *The Traitor and the Jew*, Robert Davies Publishing, Montreal, 1993

Dolan, Edward F., Jr., *Anti-Semitism*, Franklin Watts, New York, 1985

Findley, Paul, *They Dare to Speak Out*, Lawrence Hill, Westport, Conn., 1985

Flynn, Kevin, and Gary Gerhardt, *The Silent Brotherhood*, Signet Books, New York, 1989

Government of Canada, *Senate Special Committee on Terrorism and Public Safety Report*, Supply and Services Canada, Ottawa, 1987

Hebdige, Dick, *Subculture: The Meaning of Style*, Routledge, London, 1979

Hill, Ray, *The Other Face of Terror: Inside Europe's Neo-Nazi Network*, Grafton Books, London, 1988

Hoffman, Michael A., *The Great Holocaust Trial*, Institute for Historical Review, Torrance, Cal., 1985

Kane et al. v. Church of Jesus Christ Christian—Aryan Nations, et al., board of inquiry decision, Queen's Printer, Edmonton, 1992

The Klanwatch Project, *Hate, Violence and White Supremacy*, Southern Poverty Law Center, Montgomery, Ala., 1989

The Klanwatch Project, *The Ku Klux Klan: A History of Racism and Violence*, Southern Poverty Law Center, Montgomery, Ala., 1991

Knight, Nick, *Skinhead*, Omnibus Press, London, 1982

Klassen, Ben, *The White Man's Bible*, Church of the Creator Press, 1981

Lethbridge, David, *This Is Racism*, Salmon Arm Coalition Against Racism, 1992

Levitt, Cyril H., and William Shaffir, *The Riot at Christie Pits*, Lester & Orpen Dennys, Toronto, 1987

Lutz, Chris, *They Don't All Wear Sheets: A Chronology of Racist and Far Right Violence*, Center for Democratic Renewal, Atlanta, Ga., 1987

Martinez, Thomas, *Brotherhood of Murder*, McGraw-Hill, New York, 1988

Mertl, Steve and John Ward, *Keegstra: The Trial, the Issues, the Consequences*, Western Producer Prairie Books, Saskatoon, 1985.

Putnam, Carleton, *Race and Reason: A Yankee View*, Public Affairs Press, Washington, D.C., 1961

Quinley, Harrold E., *Anti-Semitism in America*, Transaction Books, New Brunswick, N.J., 1979

Ridgeway, James, *Blood in the Face*, Thunder's Mouth Press, New York, 1990

Robin, Martin, *Shades of Right: Nativist and Fascist Politics in Canada, 1920 to 1940*, University of Toronto Press, Toronto, 1992

Ross, Malcolm, *Christianity vs. Judeo-Christianity: The Battle for Truth*, Stronghold Publishing, Moncton, N.B., 1987

Ross, Malcolm, *The Real Holocaust: The Attack on Unborn Children and Life Itself*, Stronghold Publishing, Moncton, N.B., 1983

Ross, Malcolm, *Spectre of Power*, Stronghold Publishing, Moncton, N.B., 1989

Schmidt, Michael, *The New Reich: Violent Extremism in Unified Germany and Beyond*, Pantheon Books, New York, 1993

Sher, Julian, *White Hoods: Canada's Ku Klux Klan*, New Star Books, Vancouver, 1983

Troper, Harold, and Morton Weinfeld, *Old Wounds*, Penguin Books Canada, Toronto, 1988

2: CANADA'S WESTERN KLAN

Interviews conducted for this chapter took place between the summer of 1986 and late 1993. Those interviewed include Teàrlach Dunsford Mac a'Phearsoin, Larry Ryckman, Tom Erhart, Terry Long, Jim Keegstra, Robert Scoggin, Det. Loren J. Shields, A. Webster Macdonald Sr. and other sources who did not wish to be identified. For the Winnipeg Klan section, I interviewed various Harcus family members, Inspector Conrad Gislason, Brett Hayes, Don Andrews, Helmut-Harry Loewen, Sgt. Doug Zaporzan, assorted neighbors and police sources. Particularly helpful were transcripts of Bill Harcus's court appearances.

On Teàrlach Dunsford Mac a'Phearsoin, little has been written in the mainstream media. Some of the helpful stories include "Alberta Klan head seen with gun in daze after slaying, court told," in *The Globe and Mail* of December 9, 1975; "Alberta Klan head led policeman to body, trial told" by Suzanne Zwarun, in *The Globe and Mail* of December 10, 1975; "The Klan is alive in Alberta" by Dan Powers, in *The Edmonton Journal* of

430 WEB OF HATE

August 9, 1980; "Crosses burn at Red Deer," in the Red Deer *Advocate* of August 12, 1980; "Bylaws may douse Klan plans," and "Klan rally to include cross-burning, hoods" by Debbie Weismiller, in *The Edmonton Journal* of September 5, 1980; "Two held in anti-Jewish bomb plot," in *The Calgary Herald* of June 5, 1988; "JDL links Yank to conspiracy" by Mike Hayes, in *The Calgary Sun* of June 6, 1988; "Bomb plot against Jews linked to KKK," in *The Ottawa Citizen* of June 6, 1988; "Klan supporters face charges in Alberta plot to slay Jewish leader" by Drew Fagan, in *The Globe and Mail* of June 6, 1988; "The plot to bomb the Jews" by Paula Simons and others, in *Alberta Report* of June 13, 1988; "Predator used bomb plot pair" by Monica Zurowski, in *The Calgary Herald* of February 28, 1989; and"Intolerant KKK plotters jailed for five years" by Monica Zurowski, in *The Calgary Herald* of March 1, 1989.

On the Manitoba Klan: News stories include "Police infiltrate local Klan cells, net ring leaders" by Paul Wiecek, in *The Winnipeg Free Press* of December 20, 1991; "Cops crush Klan" by Joanne Faryon, and other stories, in *The Winnipeg Sun* of December 20, 1991; "Local Klan facing federal probe" by Stevens Wild, in *The Winnipeg Free Press* of March 6, 1992; "Hate crime lawyer will defend Klan" by Dawna Dingwall, in *The Winnipeg Sun* of March 25, 1992; "Undercover in the Klan" by Dawna Dingwall and Joanne Faryon, in *The Winnipeg Sun* of June 23, 1992; "Flyer promotes violence: expert" by Kevin Rollason, in *The Winnipeg Free Press* of June 24, 1992; "Ku Klux Klan focusses on activities of group in U.S." by Paul Samyn, in *The Winnipeg Free Press* of June 26, 1992; "Officer put out Klan flyers" by Kevin Rollason, in *The Winnipeg Free Press* of June 23, 1992; "Police infiltrated KKK, court told" by Brian Pardoe, in *The Ottawa Citizen* of June 23, 1992; "Lawyer seeks mistrial in Klan case" by Dawna Dingwall, in *The Winnipeg Sun* of June 24, 1992; "Christie accuses KKK infiltrator of faking notes" by Kevin Rollason, in *The Winnipeg Free Press* of September 3, 1992; "Police bungling kills KKK trial" and other stories by Dawna Dingwall, and other stories, in *The Winnipeg Sun* of September 9, 1992; "Officers under the gun" and other stories by Kevin Rollason and others, in *The Winnipeg Free Press* of September 9, 1992; "White hate" an excellent in-depth look at Manitoba's Ku Klux Klan by Dawna Dingwall and Joanne Faryon, in *The Winnipeg Sun* of September 11, 12 and 13, 1992; "McRae holds off action on racists" by Joanne Faryon, in *The Winnipeg Sun* of November 7, 1992; "Penner urges cutting KKK phone line" by Dan Lett, in *The Winnipeg Free Press* of November 13, 1992; "Cops look at hate-crime unit" by Richard Cloutier, in *The Winnipeg Sun* of November 30, 1992; and "Tribunal orders KKK to stop using phone to spread hatred" by Leonard Stern, in *The Winnipeg Free Press* s of December 17, 1992.

3: DIAL 88 FOR HEIL HITLER

I interviewed many people for this chapter, among them Ernie Britskie, Tony McAleer, Eileen Pressler and Doug Christie. The interviews were conducted primarily in 1992.

Documentary material includes an excellent exposé of the B.C. far right scene, written by Terry Gould, in *Vancouver* magazine of May 1989. Other news stories: "Racist wooing students" by Harold Munro, in *The Vancouver Sun* of December 8, 1992; "School staff ordered to investigate penetration of white supremacists" by Harold Munro, in *The Vancouver Sun* of December 9, 1992; "Racists come out of the closet to spread message of hate," by Kathleen Kenna, in *The Toronto Star* of March 6, 1990; "Hate groups surface in B.C." by Kevin Griffin, in *The Vancouver Sun* of November 21, 1991.

On Jud Cyllorn: "No side gives podium to B.C.'s racist fringe" by Tim Harper, in *The Toronto Star* of October 21, 1992; "White, male and proud of it, writer of hate book says" by Kevin Griffin, in *The Vancouver Sun* of November 26, 1991; "Death camps pictures called evidence" by Charlie Anderson, in *The Vancouver Province* of October 30, 1992; "Too many extremists on No side," by Brian Schecter, in *The Ottawa Citizen* of October 27, 1992; and "Federal probe sought into mailing of book," by Don Murray, in *The London Free Press* of November 25, 1991.

On the Canadian Liberty Net and the Presslers: "Injuction bans telephone hate messages" by Paul Lungen, in the *Canadian Jewish News* of March 12, 1992; "Hot line and hate letter linked, committee told" by Doug Ward, in *The Vancouver Sun* of May 26, 1992; "Racist's end run try violates order: judge," in *The Winnipeg Free Press* of July 11, 1992; "Network owner jailed for two months" by William Boei, in *The Vancouver Sun* of August 2, 1992;

"Neo-Nazi scared off by anti-racist rally" by William Boei, in *The Vancouver Sun* of January 2, 1993; and "Their own spot to call home" by Peter Stockland, in *The Ottawa Sun* of January 11, 1993.

4: COUNSEL FOR THE DAMNED

I have interviewed Doug Christie on several occasions between September 1988 and August 1993. For the purposes of this book, he refused to be interviewed. I was, however, assisted by members of his family, including his father, and by former professional colleagues, members of the Western Canada Concept, Terry Long, Gary Botting, Ernst Zundel, Kirk Lyons, Jim Keegstra, and many others, including a number of police officers.

Helpful opinion pieces include "Free Speech is the Issue" by Doug Christie, 1990; information from the files of the Center for Democratic Renewal, in Atlanta, Georgia; the 1980 *Canadian Annual Review of Politics and Public Affairs*; the 1993 decision of the Law Society of Upper Canada investigation into the professional conduct of Christie; "Counsel for the damned" by Paula Kulig, in *Canadian Lawyer*, November 1990. News stories include: "Christie lawsuit opens" by Kevin Stevenson, in *The Edmonton Sun* of October 25, 1984; "WCC wants no link with Christie" by Mike Sadava, in *The Edmonton Journal* of February 26, 1988; "CoR denies party on deathbed in Manitoba," in *The Winnipeg Free Press* of March 23, 1990; "Westerners' support of Reform a tragic mistake, Christie says" by Rick McConnell, in *The Edmonton Journal* of November 15, 1990; "Christie flogging dead horse of separatism: Reform Party now holding the reins of western discontent" by Ashley Geddes, in *The Vancouver Sun* of November 29, 1990; "N.B. win thrusts Knutson to centre stage: Confederation of Regions party back in political stream" by Ed Struzik, in *The Edmonton Journal* of September 30, 1991; "Knutson blasts Reform Party's language plans" by Don Richardson, in the *New Brunswick Telegraph-Journal* of November 27, 1991; a letter by Douglas Christie to *The Ottawa Citizen*, November 13, 1991; "Klan victory sparks action" by Frank Goldspink, in *Manitoba Report* of September 21, 1992; "Rights issues drive lawyer" by Richard Cloutier, in *The Winnipeg Sun* of September 9, 1992; "Lawyer for Zundel, Finta won't face professional-misconduct charges" by Stephen Bindman, in *The Montreal Gazette* of February 24, 1993; "Watchdog won't charge lawyer: Defender of Holocaust deniers 'engaged in bad advocacy,'" by the Canadian Press in *The Globe and Mail* of February 24, 1993; "Lawyer says accused war criminal just confiscating Jewish property," in *The Ottawa Citizen* of June 4, 1993.

5 AND 6: THE RELIGION OF HATE AND CANADA'S HIGH ARYAN WARRIOR PRIEST

These two chapters were many years in the making. Interviewed for chapter 4 were Richard Butler, Carl Franklin, Norman Van Cleaf, Larry Ryckman, Daniel Bauer, Tom Martinez, Kevin Flynn, Gary Yarbrough, Edgar Foth (very briefly), Wagner Saende, Colin Kelly, Tom Erhart, Jim Keegstra, Gary Botting, Larry F. Moore, Norm Stephenson, Wayne Manis, Alan Whitaker, Peter Mueller, Gene Wilson, Harvey Kane, Keith Rutherford, Terry Long and others. These interviews were conducted between July 1986 and September 1993.

Interviewed for chapter 5 were Long himself, his wife Janice, his mother Beatrice, and many members of his family, including Marjorie McNeill. Also interviewed were Cliff Stalwick, Doug Christie, Ray Paradis, Will Paradis, Bill Paradis Sr., Frank Cottingham, David Bercuson, Jim Martin, Teàrlach Mac a'Phearsoin, Meir Halevi, David Strauss, Irv Rubin, John Ross Taylor, Keith Rutherford and some of those interviewed for the previous chapter: Butler, Franklin, Ryckman, Bauer, Erhart, Keegstra, Botting and many sources with CSIS, the RCMP and other police agencies.

Useful discussions of the theological foundations of the Aryan Nations, Christian Identity and British Israel are found in "The Identity Churches: A Theology of Hate," a publication of the Anti-Defamation League of the B'nai Brith, 1983, and various issues of the *Kingdom Digest* and *The Prophetic Expositor*, published in Dallas and Toronto, respectively, by the British Israel World Federation and the Kingdom Bible Institute.

There exist hundreds of news articles about Terry Long. Some of the more significant ones include "Aryan leader returns" by Mike Lamb, in *The Calgary Herald* of April 28, 1993; "Skinhead shooting," Canadian Press, March 16, 1993. An excellent profile of Terry Long, by Edmonton *Journal* reporter David Staples, ran in *The Ottawa Citizen* of August 29, 1987.

Articles on the Aryan Nations include "Group dodges anti-Semitic label" by David Rooney, in *The Calgary Herald* of November 1, 1983; "Hating by computer" by Anita Elash and Shawn McCarthy, in *Alberta Report* of September 17, 1984; "Idaho church part of network set on genocide" by Ben Tierney, in *The Calgary Herald* of May 10, 1985; "House burns after battle with fugitive," in *The Calgary Herald* of December 9, 1984; "Neo-Nazis in U.S. launch crime wave," in *The Calgary Herald* of December 27, 1984; "The right to hate" by Kenneth Whyte, in *Alberta Report* of January 7, 1985; "Militancy comes to fore in far right sect" by Robert L. Jackson, in *The Calgary Herald* of January 28, 1985; "Phone computer link circumvents hate legislation" by Trevor Rowe, in *The Calgary Herald* of January 28, 1985; "Tracking the hate mongers" by Tom Fennell, in *Alberta Report* of July 15, 1985; "Storm trooper for Christ" by Stephen Lequire, in *The Calgary Sun* of August 25, 1985; "White supremacists guilty of racketeering," in *The Calgary Herald* of December 31, 1985; "White supremacists get long sentences," in *The Calgary Herald* of February 7, 1986; "Child soldiers honored at white racist assembly," in *The Calgary Herald* of July 14, 1986; "White racists' numbers stable despite arrests," an Associated Press story in *The Calgary Herald* of July 21, 1986; "White supremacists declare new Aryan nation in U.S.," in *The Globe and Mail* of July 21, 1986; "Ballad of an American terrorist" by L.J. Davis, in *Harper's* of July 1986; stories by the author in *The Calgary Herald* August 5, 6, 7, 9, 12, 15, 16, 19, 21, 22, 23, 25 and 29, September 7, 14 and 22, October 5, 12 and 19, November 23, December 21, 1986, January 26 and 28 and March 15, 1987.

Other articles concerning Alberta's "Aryan summer" include: "Campaigning against hate" by Marcus Gee, in *Maclean's* of September 1, 1986; "The Aryan conquest of the media" by Fay Orr, in *Alberta Report* of August 25, 1986; "Tall tales" by David Bercuson, in *Saturday Night* of October 1987; "The dial-a-racist flap" by Tom Philip, in *Alberta Report* of March 9, 1987; "No more dial-a-diatribe" by Bruce Hutchinson, in *Alberta Report* of August 14, 1989; "Line goes dead for Aryan Nations hate tape," in the *B'nai Brith Covenant* of September 1989; and numerous stories concerning the Aryan Nations in *The Ottawa Citizen* of July 12, August 7, 11, 20, 23, 25, 26, 27 and 28, September 8 and 22, October 2 and 25, December 22, 1986, January 26, 1987, April 20 and October 28 and 31, 1988.

On the Rutherford incident: "War crime tales confirm man's suspicions since '50s" by Richard Watts, in *The Edmonton Journal* of May 9, 1985; "Canadian justice should rise above Soviet propaganda" a letter by Douglas Christie to *The Edmonton Journal*, May 16, 1985; "The belated Nazi hunt," in the *Alberta Report* of March 30, 1987; "Jews targeted" by Tony Blais, in *The Edmonton Sun* of February 20, 1990; "Skinheads' victim defiant" by Jamie Wilson and Roberta Staley, in *The Edmonton Sun* of April 17, 1990; "Beaten man not cowed by intimidation" by Rick McConnell, in *The Edmonton Journal* of April 17, 1990; "Skinheads sentenced today" by David Bray, in *The Edmonton Sun* of August 10, 1990; "Assault victim says sentence not enough" by Megan Parker, in the Sherwood Park *News*, date unknown; "Sentences increased for skinheads convicted in Rutherford case" by Carol Ritch, in *The Edmonton Jewish Times & Record* of November 21, 1990; "Long under new cloud" by Tom Olsen, in the Edmonton *Sun*, date unknown; "Battling the dark side: A Calgary skinhead speaks out for tolerance" by Anne Georg, in *The Calgary Herald Sunday Magazine* of June 16, 1991; "Ex-Aryan discloses death plot" by Bill Morlin, in the *Spokesman-Review/Spokane Chronicle* of February 16, 1992; "A skinhead's adventures in America" by Brad Clark, in *Western Report* of March 12, 1992.

7: PROVOST, AND TWO MEN WHO WERE THERE
Carney Nerland refused requests for an interview. Useful news sources included the September 12, 1990, and March 4, 1992, issues of the Provost *News*; "Betrayed: Racist group riles Provost" by Sheldon Alberts, in *The Calgary Herald* of September 16, 1990; "The supremacists' picnic" by Brad Clark, in *Alberta Report* of September 24, 1990; "Censuring supremacism" by Greg Heaton, in *Alberta Report* of February 11, 1991; "Shooting moves native to attend Aryan inquiry" by Sheldon Alberts, in *The Calgary*

Herald of August 11, 1991; "Convicted racist remains at large" by Jane Armstrong, in *The Toronto Star* of August 15, 1991; "Aryan rites and wrongs" by Rick Bell, in *Alberta Report* of September 16, 1991;"Arrest warrant issued for Aryan Nations leader" by Gordon Kent, in *The Calgary Herald* of September 17, 1991; "No haven for Long in U.S." by Tom Olsen, in *The Calgary Sun* of September 18, 1991; "Alberta's most wanted" by Rick Bell, in *Alberta Report* of September 30, 1991; "The cost of doing justice" by George Takache, in *Alberta Report* of November 18, 1991; "JDL leader calls inquiry a sham" by Andy Marshall, in *The Calgary Herald* of December 24, 1991; "The racist underground" by Rick Mofina, in *The Calgary Herald* of February 9, 1992; "Aryan Nations leader not expected to show up for release of report" by Gordon Kent, in *The Edmonton Journal* of February 27, 1992; "Albertans warned of specter of evil" by Miro Cernetig, in *The Globe and Mail* of February 29, 1992; "Hunt for Long called off" by David Bray, in *The Edmonton Sun* of March 3, 1992; "Confronting swastikas," an editorial in *The Edmonton Journal* of March 4, 1992; "Journey through the cold-eyed world of hate" by Gordon Kent, in *The Edmonton Journal* of March 8, 1992; and "Free speech versus fear" by Lorne Gunter, in *Alberta Report* of March 16, 1992.

Also helpful were "Manslaughter suspect linked to Aryan Nations" by Connie Sampson, in *The Prince Albert Daily Herald* of February 1, 1991; "Supremacist charged in shooting" by Amy Santoro, in the *Windspeaker* of February 15, 1991; "The life and death of Leo LaChance" by Dana Wagg, in the *Windspeaker* of March 1, 1991; "Jewish Defence League in P.A. for Nerland case" and "White supremacist admits killing Indian" by Connie Sampson, in *The Prince Albert Daily Herald* of April 12, 1991; "Convicted neo-Nazi gets four years in day care" by Donella Hoffman, in *The Saskatoon Star Phoenix* of April 13, 1991; "Nerland plea bargaining protested" by Connie Sampson, in *The Prince Albert Daily Herald* of April 20, 1991; "Jailing a racist" by Greg Heaton, in *Alberta Report* of April 22, 1991; "Supremacist gets four years" and other stories by Dana Wagg, in the *Windspeaker* of April 26, 1991; "Justice department probes fatal P.A. shooting" by Randy Burton, in *The Saskatoon Star Phoenix* of December 10, 1991; "Provincial justice system focus of Hughes inquiry" by Dave Yenko, in *The Saskatoon Star Phoenix* of June 3, 1992; "Cloak of hatred" by Chris Varcoe, in *The Regina Leader Post* of March 28, 1992; "Depth of inquiry concerns RCMP" by David Roberts, in *The Globe and Mail* of May 28, 1992; "RCMP sensitive about subject matter at inquiry" by Dave Yenko, in *The Saskatoon Star Phoenix* of May 28, 1992; "Racist attitude exists on force, P.A. officer says" by Dave Yenko, in *The Saskatoon Star Phoenix* of May 30, 1992; "How did men not notice dying victim?" by Connie Sampson, in *The Prince Albert Daily Herald* of June 18, 1992; "Impartiality of Hughes commission questioned" by Donella Hoffman, in *The Saskatoon Star Phoenix* of June 18, 1992; "RCMP appeal stalls probe" by Connie Sampson, in *The Prince Albert Daily Herald* of June 26, 1992; "Inquiry stalled over RCMP informant's identity" by David Roberts, in *The Globe and Mail* of June 27, 1992; "Allegation Nerland an informer doesn't surprise Police chief" by Dave Yenko, in *The Saskatoon Star Phoenix* of June 29, 1992; "Lawyers say ruling hampers probe into trapper's death" by David Roberts, in *The Globe and Mail* of August 24, 1992; "Shooting not racially motivated, white supremacist says," in *The Globe and Mail* of March 18, 1993; "Nerland ignores inquiry, goes public" by Donella Hoffman, in *The Saskatoon Star Phoenix* of March 18, 1993; "Report supports Nerland charge," in *The Regina Leader Post* of March 20, 1993; "Manslaughter case supported" by Connie Sampson, in *The Prince Albert Daily Herald* of March 23, 1993; "Officer says informant gave RCMP information," in *The Regina Leader Post* of March 24, 1993; and "Aryan sympathizers suspected in RCMP ranks" by Connie Sampson, in *The Prince Albert Daily Herald* of March 24, 1993. One excellent account of the Nerland case, by Lisa Kowal (a pseudonym), is "Führer of Saskatchewan," in *Saturday Night* of April 1993.

8: THE WOLFIE AND GEORGE SHOW

This chapter is based on interviews with Wolfgang Droege, George Burdi, some of Burdi's family members, Don Andrews, Robert Smith, Paul Fromm, John Ross Taylor, John Beattie, Ernst Zundel, Anne Ladas, Peter Mitrevski, Jacob Prins, David Irving, Leigh Smith, Eric Hartmann, Steve Dumas, Ian Verner Macdonald and many lesser-known members of the Heritage Front, the Nationalist Party, the Western Guard and the Canadian Knights of the

Ku Klux Klan. Also interviewed were Bernie Farber, Manuel Prutschi, Karen Mock, Warren Bass, Lorne Shipman, Tony Davy, Amy Go, Dan Dunlop, Bill Dunphy, Scot Magnish and a number of police officers who asked that they not be named. Interviews were conducted between May 1988 and October 1993. Documentary material was culled from newspaper reports, court transcripts, files of the Canadian Jewish Congress and publications and newsletters published by the groups being studied.

On Paul Fromm, newspaper stories include "Edmund Burke Society founder: Tory official backs idea of supreme race" by Christie McLaren, in *The Globe and Mail* of April 28, 1981; "Right-wing or racist?" by Lindsay Scotton, in *The Toronto Star* of October 8, 1983; "Guelph protesters call speaker 'racist'" by Greg Crone, in the *Kitchener-Waterloo Record* of March 1, 1990; an opinion piece by Fromm in *The Ottawa Citizen* of August 14, 1990; and "A stalking horse for the ultra-right? Anti-French alliance has kept ties with extremist organizations" by Gerald Caplan, in *The Toronto Star* of March 18, 1990. "Board reprimands teacher who spoke at neo-Nazi rally," in *The Toronto Star* of April 30, 1992; "Lawyer to report on teacher's activities," in *The Globe and Mail* of November 5, 1992; "Teacher probed for racist links" by Paul Lungen, in the *Canadian Jewish News* of April 23, 1992; "Reading, 'riting, and repression," an editorial in *The Globe and Mail* of June 23, 1993; "Teacher fingered at rally of racists," in *The Calgary Herald* of April 13, 1992; From the files of the Canadian Jewish Congress came a very useful profile of Fromm dated April 1992.

Newsletters and articles published by the groups in question: Doug Collins in the March 28, 1988, edition of *On Target*, published by Canadian Intelligence Publications; "Demjanjuk Trial—An obscene travesty" in *On Target* of May 2, 1988; various articles in the July/August 1990 and the January/February 1992 editions of the *Free Speech Monitor*, published by the Canadian Association for Free Expression (CAFE); "Political Terrorism and the Peace Movement in Canada" by Paul Fromm; the Citizens for Foreign Aid Reform (C-FAR) newsletters of August 1, 1986, December 14, 1986, and August 1, 1987; the Spring 1986, Spring 1987, August 1987 and Winter 1988 editions of the *CAFE Quarterly*, a newsletter of the Canadian Association for Free Expression; the June 1978 edition of *The Truth About China Newsletter*, published by the Canadian Friends of Free China Association (Patrick Walsh, editor); the September 1991 edition of the Alliance for the Preservation of English in Canada (APEC) *Newsletter*; *SusPop News*, the newsletter of the Sustainable Population Society, October 1992; and a letter from the Reverend Kenneth Campbell, national leader of the Christian Freedom (Social Credit) Party of Canada, dated January 25, 1993.

On the Northern Foundation and its president, Anne Hartmann: the Winter 1992, Summer 1992 and Fall 1992 editions of *Northern Voice*, the newsletter of the Northern Foundation; a letter by Hartmann to *The Ottawa Citizen*, January 23, 1993; a Northern Foundation brochure entitled "Speaking Up for Canada's Silent Majority"; "Reform Party ousts Ottawa member" by Scot Magnish, in *The Ottawa Sun* of December 1, 1992; "Revoked" by Tim Naumetz, in *The Ottawa Sun* of December 8, 1992; "Billboard Classified" from the Spring 1992, Summer 1992, and Fall 1992 editions of *Northern Voice*; the Fall 1990 edition of *The Continuing Crisis*, a propaganda arm of the Northern Foundation; an advertisement for the Northern Foundation in the National Personals section of *The Globe and Mail* of October 17, 1992; a pamphlet entitled "Women and the Charter of Rights," published by REAL Women of Canada; a letter by Hartmann (this time as a director of REAL Women of Canada) to *The Ottawa Citizen*, February 25, 1990, headlined "Simplistic diatribe against REAL WOMEN"; "Reality up-date" and other related material published by REAL Women of Canada in 1989; and numerous letters to *The Ottawa Sun* in response to the Tim Naumetz exposé of the Northern Foundation (these mostly appeared during December 1992).

On David Irving: "No place for Holocaust deniers in Canada" by Ian Kagedan, in *The Ottawa Citizen* of November 6, 1992; "The case of David Irving: Why muzzle the wackos?" by Pierre Berton, in *The Toronto Star* of November 14, 1992; "Campus snubs Irving," in *The Ottawa Sun* of November 11, 1992; "Holocaust-denier ordered deported," in *The Globe and Mail* of November 14, 1992; "Victim calls blaze 'intimidation'" by Sarah Cabott, in *The Toronto Sun* of November 9, 1992; "Author Irving deported to England" by Phil Novak and Gail Swainson, in *The Toronto Star* of November 14, 1992; "Defiant Irving to speak twice in Ottawa" by David Gamble, in *The Ottawa Sun* of November 10, 1992; "Revisionist historian denied bail" by Bill Dunphy, in *The Ottawa Sun* of November 3, 1992; "B'nai Brith critical of management of Irving case, calls for enhanced co-ordination among agencies responsible," a press release issued by the League for Human Rights of B'nai Brith Canada on November 2, 1992.

On the Ku Klux Klan and Wolfgang Droege in Ontario: "Ottawa office next? Racism wears a shy smile in the Klan" by Kerra Lockhart, in *The Ottawa Citizen* of July 8, 1980; "Klan visits school to talk to students" by Julia Turner, in *The Globe and Mail* of March 11, 1981; "Ku Klux Klan chief denies bigotry: 'We are just pro-white'" by Chisholm MacDonald, in *The Montreal Gazette* of December 6, 1980; "Cross burned by Klan" by Mike Tenszen, in *The Toronto Sun* of November 9, 1980; "KKK: How they nearly found me out" and "The racists who run the KKK in Metro" by Neil Louttit, in *The Toronto Star* of July 9, 1981; "Police hunt for rifle," in *The Ottawa Sun* of April 15, 1993; "Residents baffled after Klan shows up in Halton Region" by Peter Small, in *The Toronto Star* of January 18, 1993; "Upscale London-area enclave is site of cross-burning rally" by Gail Swainson, in *The Toronto Star* of May 16, 1993; and "Vehicles covered with hate literature" by John Duncanson, in *The Toronto Star* of March 16, 1993.

On John Ross Taylor and the Western Guard: various articles, and a transcript of the human rights tribunal hearing into the Western Guard Party and John Ross Taylor, which ran from June 12 to 15, 1979.

On the Nationalist Party of Canada: the "constitution" of the failed Carleton University branch of the Nationalist Party of Canada; "Toronto pair jailed for racist articles," in *The Ottawa Citizen* of December 14, 1985; "Toronto men found guilty of promoting hatred against non-whites,"in *The Ottawa Citizen* of December 10, 1985; "Candidates on the fringe lament lack of funds" by Susan Reid, in *The Toronto Star* of October 18, 1991; "Racial problems resurface at school" by Philip Mascoll, in *The Toronto Star* of October 3, 1991; and "Hate laws necessary for society, court says" by David Vienneau, in *The Toronto Star* of December 14, 1990.

With regard to the Heritage Front, there have been hundreds of articles in the past few years. Some of the most useful were "Scenes from the far right" by Kirk Makin, in *The Globe and Mail* of February 8, 1993; "Toronto recording company banks on furore hate music creates," in *The Ottawa Citizen* of August 21, 1993; "Heritage hearing," Canadian Press, August 19, 1993; "Racism hearings," Canadian Press, August 18, 1993; "Racism protest" Canadian Press, August 17, 1993; "De l'inquiétude chez l'antigang: Heritage Front trouve preneur" by Julie Vaillancourt, and "Gagnon-Tremblay condamme le Heritage Front" in *Journal de Montréal* of August 17, 1993; "Anti-racism rally to condemn supremacists" by Alexander Morris, in *The Montreal Gazette* of August 14, 1993; "Hundreds join rally against neo-Nazis" by Ann McLaughlin and Paul Wells, in *The Montreal Gazette* of August 15, 1993; "Don't ignore white supremacists: Saturday's anti-racist march was a fitting rebuke," an editorial in *The Montreal Gazette* of August 17, 1993; "Heritage Front," Canadian Press, August 13, 1993; "Teen spread hate: police" by Bill Dunphy, in *The Toronto Sun* of August 10, 1993; "When white makes right: Skinheads carve out their niche in America's violent culture of hate" by David Van Biema, in *Time* of August 9, 1993; "Police admit they erred in comment on hate law" by Gail Swainson, in *The Toronto Star* of August 7, 1993; "Le groupe d'extrême droite Heritage Front s'apprête a fonder une cellule a Montréal" by Pascal Corbusier, in *The Montreal La Presse* of August 6, 1993; "NDP vows action on hate crimes" by Peter Small, and "Hate crimes on rise, police say" by Gail Swainson, in *The Toronto Star* of June 16, 1993; "Manifestation antiracist à Toronto," in The Montreal *La Presse* of June 13, 1993; "Three arrested in abduction" by Bill Dunphy, in *The Toronto Sun* of June 10, 1993; "Free speech key to freedom" by Stephen Elliott, in *The Ottawa Citizen* of June 8, 1993; "Cop bashing" by Scot Magnish, in *The Ottawa Sun* of June 8, 1993; "'Keep out, Ottawa chief tells hate groups" by Jacquie Miller and Charles Lewis, in *The Ottawa Citizen* of June 1, 1993; "Group criticizes police for role in riot" by Mike Shahin, in *The Ottawa Citizen* of May 31, 1993; "Ottawa clash sparks call to toughen anti-hate laws," in *The Globe and Mail*, June 1, 1993; "Bloody clash marks neo-Nazi concert" by Scot Magnish, in *The Ottawa Sun* of May 30, 1993; "600 anti-racist protesters battle police" by Mike Shahin and Peter Hum, in *The Ottawa Citizen* of May 30, 1993; "Neo-Nazis et anti-racistes s'affrontent à Ottawa," in The Montreal *La Presse* of May 31, 1993; "Hearing on neo-Nazi hot line to begin" by Mark Palmer, in *The Globe and Mail*, date unknown; "Reform expulsion," in *The Globe and Mail* of July 15, 1993; "Racist group sets up hate hotline" by Scot Magnish, in *The Ottawa Sun* of

May 13, 1993; "Neo-Nazis to sign up teens" by Scot Magnish, in *The Ottawa Sun* of April 29, 1993; "Racist groups won't take root in area, say experts" by Charles Lewis, and "Recruiting for 'holy racial war': Toronto white supremacist leaders pose as 'love-mongers' while courting local youth" by Peter Hum, in *The Ottawa Citizen* of May 1, 1993; "Toronto journal: To battle bigots, help from south of the border" by Clyde Farnsworth, in *The New York Times* of February 12, 1993; "Non-violence best in trying to deal with today's Nazis" by Davis Lewis Stein, and "White supremacist being deported today" by Allan Thompson, in *The Toronto Star* of January 27, 1993; "Group aiming to shut hateline" by Bill Dunphy, in *The Toronto Sun* of June 26, 1993; "Why does Reform draw racists like moths to a porch light?" by David Trigueiro, in *The Montreal Gazette* of January 26, 1993; "Two arrested as racism protest turns ugly" by Moira Welsh, and "Protesters, police clash," in *The Toronto Star* of January 26, 1993; "Racism clash" by Kay Fisher, January 25, 1993; "Hearing on neo-Nazi hotline to begin" by Mark Palmer, in *The Globe and Mail* of January 25, 1993; "Anti-racism rally bars white supremacists" by Michael Tenszen, in *The Toronto Star* of January 20, 1993; "Immigration officials detain supremacist from the U.S." by Allan Thompson, in *The Toronto Star* of January 23, 1993.

On the Reform Party: "Reform boots 5 from party" by Michael Allan, in *The Ottawa Sun* of March 11, 1992; "Reform searches for racists: Ontario problem could be worse than first feared" by Jim Cunningham, in *The Calgary Herald* of February 29, 1992; "Manning fears plot behind racist infiltration" by Hugh Winsor, in *The Globe and Mail* of February 29, 1992; "Racists infiltrate Reform Party" and "Reformers warn the racists in their ranks: We'll squash 'em" by Bill Dunphy, in *The Toronto Sun* of February 28, 1992; "Reform Party member turfed: Calgary man supports anti-Holocaust stand" by Bill Kaufmann, in *The Calgary Sun* of July 14, 1992; "Jews honored," in *The Calgary Herald* of July 15, 1992.

General sources include "White supremacist activity on the upswing in Canada," in the December 1992 *Klanwatch: Intelligence Report* published by the Southern Poverty Law Center; and "A whiter shade of hate: White supremacists are recruiting our children," in *eye weekly* of July 15, 1993. Also relied upon were all issues of *Up Front* the official publication of the Heritage Front—issued between December 1991 and August 1993.

On Ernst Zundel: "Newspapers debate free speech" by Paul Lungen, in the *Canadian Jewish News* of September 10, 1992; "Zundel guilty on hate charges" by Stephen Bindman, in *The Ottawa Citizen* of May 12, 1988; "Supreme court ruling will only encourage Canadian racists" by Warren Kinsella, in *The Ottawa Citizen* of August 31, 1992; "New charges for Zundel up to Ministry" by Cal Millar, in *The Toronto Star* of September 1, 1992; "To prosecute or ignore?" by Valerie Lawton, in *The Ottawa Citizen* of September 3, 1992; "No victory for hate," an editorial, and "Law struck down in Zundel case" by David Vienneau, in *The Toronto Star* of August 28, 1992; "The right ruling on false news," an editorial, and "Top court quashes Zundel's conviction" by Sean Fine, in *The Globe and Mail* of August 28, 1992; "Victory for free speech," an editorial, and "False news not a crime" by Stephen Bindman, in *The Ottawa Citizen* of August 28, 1992; "Supreme court hears challenge to criminal code by Nazi sympathizer" by Stephen Bindman, in *The Ottawa Citizen* of December 10, 1991; "A right to lie?" by Randal Marlin, in the Canadian Bar Association *National* of November 1992; "Zundel triumphant after Supreme court acquittal" by John Ward, in *The Winnipeg Free Press* of August 28, 1992; and "Why is Zundel not charged?," an editorial in *The Montreal Gazette* of March 12, 1993. Also relied upon were various accounts of Zundel's trials, including those found in his own publications as well as in *Insight* from New Westminster, B.C.

On the Church of the Creator and George Burdi, I made use of "Armed and dangerous" by Bill Dunphy, in *The Toronto Sun* of November 30, 1992; "U.S. rock group stopped at border" by Paul Lungen, in the *Canadian Jewish News* of September 10, 1992; "Dancing to the tribal rhythms of Racial Holy War" by Enzo Di Matteo, in *Now* magazine of September 3, 1992; "Nazi rally touts white power" by Scot Magnish, in *The Ottawa Sun* of August 2, 1992; "Hate campaign probed in Metro" by Michael Tenszen, in *The Toronto Star* of March 17, 1992; "Church of the Creator puts race above the law" in *Klanwatch: Intelligence Report* of April 1991; "It's a long way from 'Let it Be'" by Gail Swainson, in *The Toronto Star* of August 15, 1993. Also helpful were various issues of *Racial Loyalty*, the official publication of the Church of the Creator.

On Ian Verner Macdonald: "Extreme right courts the left" by Howard Goldenthal, in *Now* magazine of November 5, 1987; "Ultra-right-wingers organize to fight Holocaust teachings" and "The Zundel fringe" by Warren Kinsella, in *The Ottawa Citizen* of July 23, 1988; "The somewhat right of centre views of Ian Verner Macdonald" by Warren Kinsella, in *Ottawa Magazine* of September 1989. Dozens of letters, memoranda and classified reports written by Macdonald between 1963 and 1988 were provided to the author.

On Ottawa rightists generally: "Danger of banning books," letter by Jean Harris to *The Ottawa Citizen*, February 11, 1988; "Not alone in his beliefs," letter by Jean Harris to the Fredericton *Daily Gleaner*, April 6, 1988; and various other letters by Harris sent to the author. Also useful were letters to *The Ottawa Citizen* and the author by Norman Van Cleaf; letters to *The Ottawa Citizen* by John T. Murchison; letters to *The Ottawa Citizen* and the author by Ingrid Beisner, as well as issues of Beisner's hate sheet, "Canada Endeavour"; and letters to *The Ottawa Citizen* and to the author by Phillip Belgrave, as well as issues of Belgrave's hate magazine, *Rally on Centre*.

Also helpful were stories concerning plans by The Ottawa Board of Education to establish a Holocaust studies program, printed between October 1986 and March 1988; "Ottawa group raises ire of Metro Jews" by Elaine Moyle, in *The Toronto Sun* of July 24, 1988; "Neo-Nazi vandals strike in market" by Scot Magnish, in *The Ottawa Sun* of December 3, 1992; "Swastikas on the streets of Ottawa" by Aharon Mayne, in *The Globe and Mail* of December 18, 1992; "Racism spreads its arms" by Scot Magnish, in *The Ottawa Sun* of December 13, 1992; "Hate mail campaign targets Jewish groups" by Charles Lewis, in *The Ottawa Citizen* of December 3, 1992; and "Hate groups on rise in area schools" by Victor Gomez, in *The Ottawa Sun* of March 22, 1993.

9: SKINHEADS

This chapter is based on dozens of interviews with many skinheads since the fall of 1988, among them Peter Mitrevski, Brett Hayes, Mark Bauer and Liam McCarthy. Other interviews were conducted with Ingrid Beisner, Terry Long, Paul Fromm, Don Andrews, Ernst Zundel, Ian Verner Macdonald, Tony McAleer, Richard Butler, Carl Franklin, Tom Metzger, John Metzger and many others. Also helpful were Manuel Prutschi, Scott Bristow and the Brett Hayes and Daryl Rivest court transcripts in the Rutherford lawsuit. The police and anti-racism activists mentioned earlier also provided invaluable help.

Articles include "Skinheads: Aimless violence sparks a police crackdown" by Dawn King, in *The Globe and Mail* of April 9, 1988; "Action urged to control 'racist' teens: But police say hands are tied against skinhead gangs" by Laurie Monsebraaten, in *The Toronto Star* of March 14, 1989; "Police forming unit to fight 'swarming'" by Don Dutton and Tracey Tyler, in *The Toronto Star* of March 14, 1989; "Street gangs: Why they're getting worse" by Rosie DiManno, in *The Toronto Star* of March 11, 1989; "Veteran of Canada's extreme right recruiting alienated youths" by Deborah Wilson, in *The Globe and Mail* of March 23, 1989; "The Skinhead reich," a ground-breaking piece by Jeff Coplon, in *Rolling Stone* of May/June 1989; "America's youthful bigots" by Art Levine, in *U.S. News & World Report* of May 7, 1990; "The long shadow" by Tom Mathews, Rod Nordland and Carroll Bogert, in *Newsweek* of May 7, 1990; "Skinheads invited to whites-only weekend" by Mike Blanchfield, in *The Ottawa Citizen* of June 17, 1989; "Town outraged by neo-Nazis' rally on Canada Day," in *The Globe and Mail* of July 3, 1989; "Ottawa skinheads help publish pro-Nazi magazine" by Warren Kinsella, in *The Ottawa Citizen* of August 10, 1989; "Irate pickets fail to stop fascist speech" by Robert Sibley, in *The Ottawa Citizen* of March 7, 1989; "Ottawa: Mobilizing against neo-nazi lies" by Brian McDougall, in the *Socialist Worker* of April 1989; "The colleges: Fear, loathing, and suppression" by Nat Hentoff, in the *Village Voice* of May 8, 1990; "Vengeance is theirs: Ex-skinhead lives in fear" by Linda Slobodian, in *The Edmonton Sun* of September 23, 1990; "Halifax skinhead group's tolerance a sharp contrast to Nazi counterparts'" by Cathy Krawchuk, in *The Halifax Chronicle-Herald* of November 29, 1990; "Former neo-Nazi skinhead admits reality of racism" by Randy Fisher, in the *Canadian Jewish News* of October 24, 1991; "The Nazi-skinhead konnection" by John Schrag, in *The Montreal Mirror* of November 22, 1990; "Racism hits Edmonton schools" by George Oake, in *The Toronto Star* of December 12, 1991.

Additional references are "The music of hate rocks in Germany" and "2 Germans admit arson attack that killed 3 Turkish nationals," in *The New York Times* of December 2, 1992;

"Racist hate groups look to the young to swell their ranks" by Bernie Farber, in *The Toronto Star* of May 25, 1993; "Rising hatred: Neo-Nazis prey on youth in bad times" by Les Whittington, in *The Montreal Gazette* of June 2, 1993; press package issued by B'nai Brith Canada on August 10, 1989, entitled "League of Human Rights—Update on Skinhead Activity"; a booklet entitled "Knowledge," published by Ken Stoddard of the Aryan Identity Fellowship in March 1990; "Skinheads in Canada," published by the League for Human Rights of B'nai Brith Canada in November 1990; "Battling the dark side" by Anne Georg, in *The Calgary Herald Sunday Magazine* of June 16, 1991; "Shaved for battle: Skinheads target America's youth," published by the Anti-Defamation League of B'nai Brith/Civil Rights Division in 1987; "Long day's journey into white" by Kathy Dobie, in the *Village Voice* of April 28, 1992; correspondence from the Ontario Ministry of the Attorney General to Manuel Prutschi of the Canadian Jewish Congress, dating to July 1990; "Neo-Nazi Skinheads and Youth Information Packet," published by the Center for Democratic Renewal, in Atlanta, Georgia; an issue of *Storm Front*, a newsletter of the National Socialist Skinheads.

On John Beattie: "I spied on the Nazis," cover story, by John Garrity, in *Maclean's* of October 1, 1966; "Skinheads: A new generation to carry racism's banner" and "Jews protest skinheads' rally" by Warren Kinsella, in *The Ottawa Citizen* of July 3, 1989; numerous articles in the Minden *Times* of June 26, 1989; "Race forum planned to counter Nazi rally" by Jack Lakey, in *The Toronto Star* of July 6, 1989; "White power rally near Minden attracts 100 neo-Nazi skinheads" by Warren Kinsella, in *The Ottawa Citizen* of July 2, 1989; "From Allan Gardens to Minden: The career of John Beattie" by Ben Kayfetz, in the *B'nai Brith Covenant* of September 1989.

10: LE KLAN DE QUÉBEC

For this chapter, I interviewed Alain Roy, Brent Klauser, Michel Larocque and a number of lesser-known lights in Quebec's racist spectrum. Others interviewed were Thomas W. Cool, Gary Lauck, Geoffrey York, Wolfgang Droege and members of the Sûreté du Québec. Documentary evidence relied upon included "Il n'y en a pas eu, d'émeute!" by Benoit Aubin, in *L'Actualité* of August 1993; a report, "Violence et racisme au Québec," published by the Comité d'intervention contre la violence raciste in June 1992; "CDR helps build international network: Counters growing links among white supremacists" and "Robb's Knights of the KKK stage small comeback: Seek to imitate David Duke" in the May 1992 edition of *The Monitor*, published by the Center for Democratic Renewal, in Atlanta, Georgia; "Soixante familles mohawks evacuées sous des volées de roches et de briques" by Caroline Montpetit, in The Montreal *Le Devoir* of August 29, 1990; "Police promised protection before rock attacks: Mohawk" by Michael Orsini and Jeff Heinrich; "Police turn blind eye to mob violence: No excuse possible for attack by whites" by Don MacPherson, and "No amnesty for stone-throwers: Stain of racism must be erased," an editorial, in *The Montreal Gazette* of August 30, 1990; "Enquête de la SQ sur le bombardement des autos remplies de Mohawks à LaSalle" by Isabelle Paré, in The Montreal *Le Devoir* of August 30, 1990; "KKK mag denounced as hate literature" by Mary Lamey, in *The Montreal Gazette* of August 2, 1991; "Ku Klux Klan delivers newspaper to residents on West Island" by Mary Lamey, in *The Montreal Gazette* of August 4, 1991; "Ku Klux Klan denounced in Sherbrooke" by Dan Hawaleshka, in *The Montreal Gazette* of August 6, 1991; "Rights groups hail Quebec move against Ku Klux Klan" by Irwin Block, in *The Montreal Gazette* of August 10, 1991; "White-only immigration a KKK goal, leader tells court" by René Laurent, in *The Montreal Gazette* of September 5, 1991; "Police lay precedent-setting charges against Klan" by Judy Fostey-Owen, in the Canadian Bar Association *National* of February 1992; "Hate law under debate" by Janice Arnold, in the *Canadian Jewish News* of April 16, 1992; "KKK hate literature left in mailboxes of Verdun homes" by Ann McLaughlin, in *The Montreal Gazette* of April 20, 1992; "Racism on rise, Quebec report says" by André Picard, in *The Globe and Mail* of July 8, 1992; "KKK recruitment fliers raise emotions in Point" by Bart Kasowski, in *The Montreal Gazette* of June 14, 1992; "Fascist 'festival' called off," in *The Ottawa Citizen* of July 7, 1992; "Neo-nazis from Canada and U.S. hold rally at Quebec farm," Reuters, August 2, 1992; "Le 'festival nazi' de la Plaine attire peu de gens" by Marie-France Leger, in The Montreal *La Presse* of August 2,

1992; "Le festival nazi a eu lieu!" by Michel Larose, in *Le Journal de Montréal* of August 2, 1992; "Outnumbered" by Paul Waldie, in *The Montreal Gazette* of Saturday, August 1, 1992; "Il faut interdire le festival aryen," a letter by Christiane Haegal to *Le Journal de Montréal* of August 1, 1992; "Les militants néo-nazis passent de Sorel à Saint-Lin" by Marie-France Leger, in The Montreal *La Presse* of August 1, 1992; "Deux néo-nazis arrêtes" by Michel Larose, in *Le Journal de Montréal* of August 3, 1992; "Anger swells in La Plaine" by Mike King, in *The Montreal Gazette* of August 3, 1992; "Klan rally," in *The Globe and Mail* of August 3, 1992. "Synagogues, a church, a mosque" in *The Montreal Gazette* of January 6, 1993; "Handling murder with kid gloves" by André Picard, in *The Globe and Mail* of April 13, 1993; "Jews shaken by new wave of vandalism" by Eddie Collister, in *The Montreal Gazette* of January 28, 1993.

Other sources include a 1992 edition of the newsletter *Nouvelles NS*, published by the National Socialists; the *New Order* of September/October 1992 published by the National Socialists; *L'aut'journal* of October 1991; "An Introduction to the Invisible Empire Knights of the Ku Klux Klan," date and author unknown; *The Organized Organizer* of 1991 and April 1992, published by Thomas Cool; "Why did Mathias Rust fly to Moscow?" and "The religious and historical background of the October 8, 1990, Haram al-Sharif (Temple Mount) massacre" by Jack Wikoff, reprinted from *Remarks* newsletter, published by Jack Wikoff; *A Collective Shock: Report of the Commission des droits de la personne du Québec*, prepared by Monique Rochon and Pierre Lepage of the Commission des droits de la personne du Québec in April 1991; "Soldiers show their Iron," from *One Nation Under the Gun: Inside the Mohawk Civil War* by Rick Hornung (Stoddart Publishing, 1991); an excerpt from *People of the Pines: the Warriors and the Legacy of Oka* by Geoffrey York and Loreen Pindera (Little Brown Canada, 1991); excerpts from *The Legacy of Oka*, a report by Maurice Tugwell and John Thompson issued by the Mackenzie Institute in 1991; and excerpts from "The Land Claim Dispute at Oka," a background paper by Patricia Begin, Wendy Moss and Peter Niemczak, issued in 1990 by the research branch of the Library of Parliament.

11: THE ENCOURAGEMENT OF MALCOLM ROSS

Malcolm Ross consented to interviews in the summer of 1993. Others interviewed between October 1988 and fall 1993 include Doug Christie, Terry Long, Ernst Zundel, Jim Keegstra, Paul Fromm, Gary McCauley, Ian Verner Macdonald, Philip Belgrave, Norman Van Cleaf, Leo Gallien, John Murchison, Ingrid Beisner, Jean Harris, John Kroeker and various police officers and anti-racism activists. Media and print sources include "Ross will keep writing, distributing his books," a letter by Ross to *The Miramichi Leader*, October 22, 1986; letters by Ross to *The Moncton Times-Transcript*, June 1984 and July 10, 1985; "Malcolm Ross responds to accusations," a two-part interview in the Northumberland *News* of October 15 and 22, 1986; *Web of Deceit* by Ross (Stronghold Publishing, 1978); the decision of the board of inquiry appointed to investigate the complaint of David Attis in 1990; the decision of the Court of Queen's Bench of New Brunswick in the hearing of Ross with regard to the complaint lodged by David Attis in 1991; "Ross antithesis of school board's policy" by Manuel Prutschi, in the *Canadian Jewish News* of February 17, 1992; "Lockyer rejects request to charge Ross" and "School board official: Ross knew he was taking risk," in *The Fredericton Daily Gleaner* of May 3, 1991; "Summations made at rights inquiry," in *The Fredericton Daily Gleaner* of May 18, 1991; "Malcolm Ross human rights inquiry: Board chairman describes handling case" by Chris Morris, in *The Fredericton Daily Gleaner* of April 30, 1991; the July 29, 1992, edition of *On Target*, published by Canadian Intelligence Publications; "New complaints delay Malcolm Ross decision" by Tom McKegney, in *The Moncton Times-Transcript* of May 21, 1991; "Trustee wary of N.B. ruling: Ross decision raises questions about monitoring teachers outside classroom" by Kevin Cox, in *The Globe and Mail* of August 31, 1991; "Ross ordered to stop teaching," and "N.B. could learn from mayor's prompt action on Ross books" by Don Hoyt, in the *New Brunswick Telegraph-Journal* of August 30, 1991; "Ross decision needs appeal," an editorial in *The Montreal Gazette* of January 5, 1992; "Defending the indefensible," an editorial in *The Globe and Mail* of January 4, 1992; "N.B. judge upholds removal of teacher over anti-Semitism" by Rudy Platiel, in *The Globe and Mail* of January 3, 1992; "Ross ne peut plus enseigner" by

Daniel Chrétien, in *L'Acadie Nouvelle* of January 3, 1992; "L'affaire Ross en appel" by Philippe Gagnon, in *L'Acadie Nouvelle* of September 18, 1992; "Les tribunaux devront décider si les sanctions prises contre Malcolm Ross etaient légales" by Philippe Gagnon, in *L'Acadie Nouvelle* of September 2, 1992; "Malcolm Ross wants apology," Canadian Press, 1993; "First Report: This Is Racism" by the Salmon Arm Coalition Against Racism; "Spinney: Inquiry decision must balance human rights" by Liz MacQuade, in the *New Brunswick Telegraph-Journal* of May 10, 1991; and "Lawyer defends Nazi internment of Jews," in the Fredericton *Daily Gleaner* of December 12, 1990.

Also useful were the Spring 1987, Summer 1987 and Spring 1988 editions of the *Cafe Quarterly*, the newsletter of the Canadian Association for Free Expression; "Censored News: Re. Zundel's Trial and Ross's Persecution," a publication of the Canadian Intelligence Service, April 1988; "The Malcolm Ross 'human rights' hearing" by Ron Gostick, in *On Target* of January 7, 1991; and several editions of *Insight*, a hate newsletter, published in New Westminster, B.C.

12: MATT McKAY'S YOUTHFUL FOLLY

For this chapter, I interviewed Matt McKay as well as various members of the Armed Forces who did not wish to be identified. Also interviewed were Joanne Faryon, Dawna Dingwall, Hal Joffe and Bernie Farber. The interviews were conducted between the fall of 1992 and the fall of 1993.

For documentary evidence, I relied upon sworn evidence taken from transcripts in Keith Rutherford's civil action against the Aryan Nations organization; *Hansard*, May 7, 10, 11, 12 and 13, 1993; a transcript of a story by CBC "Prime Time News," May 6, 1993; and various Department of National Defence reports obtained under access to information legislation and reports and testimony issued by the Board of Inquiry into the Canadian Airborne Regiment Battle Group.

Helpful news stories: "How far can military go in getting rid of racists?" by Jacquie Miller, in *The Ottawa Citizen* of June 19, 1993; "Neo-Nazis open doors to soldiers" by Dawna Dingwall and Joanne Faryon, in *The Winnipeg Sun* of September 13, 1992; "Military watching white racist activity in its ranks," in *The Ottawa Citizen* of May 7, 1993; "Elite forces members linked to racist group" by Gail Swainson, in *The Toronto Star* of May 7, 1993; "Military's hands tied, House Leader declares" by Geoffrey York, in *The Globe and Mail* of May 8, 1993; "Campbell's department suffers yet another blow" by Tim Harper, in *The Toronto Star* of May 8, 1993; "Military feels heat for racism" by Brian Laghi, in *The Edmonton Journal* of May 8, 1993; "Racists have no place in the forces" by Andrew Cardozo, in *The Ottawa Citizen* of May 11, 1993; "Forces broke own rules, Liberal MP charges" by Geoffrey York, in *The Globe and Mail* of May 11, 1993; "Screen troops" by Dave Rider, in *The Winnipeg Sun* of May 11, 1993; "Racists in military not acceptable" by Geoffrey York, in *The Globe and Mail* of May 12, 1993; "Two dismissed from Armed Forces for racist views" by Gord McIntosh, in *The Ottawa Citizen* of June 17, 1993; "Canada can't ignore neo-Nazis in the Armed Forces" by Alan Borovoy, in *The Toronto Star* of June 21, 1993; "Getting racists out of the forces," an editorial in *The Halifax Chronicle-Herald* of June 21, 1993; "Siddon: No tolerance in Forces for racism," in *The Victoria Times Colonist* of October 7, 1993; "Fire those with racist past, Jewish group tells Forces" by April Lindgren, in *The Ottawa Citizen* of October 7, 1993; "Too few good men" by Bruce Wallace, in *Maclean's* of September 13, 1993; "Canadian Forces ignored racism edict, papers hint" by Tim Harper, in *The Toronto Star* of September 2, 1993; and "Soldier planned to 'shoot me a nigger'" by Geoffrey York, in *The Globe and Mail* of September 2, 1993.

13: CONCLUSION

For this chapter I interviewed Bernie Farber, Dan Dunlop, Ian Kagedan and many other anti-racism activists, as well as lawyers expert in hate promotion.

Useful articles on racism's victims included: Mab Segrest's *Quarantines and Death: The Far Rights Homophobic Agenda*, published by the Center for Democratic Renewal, in

Atlanta, Georgia, 1991; "Violent backdrop for anti-gay measure" by Timothy Egan, in *The New York Times* of November 1, 1992; "All minorities targets of racial violence, experts say" by Jack Kapica, in *The Globe and Mail* of January 4, 1993; and "Montreal police face rising wave of violence against gays" by Ingrid Peritz, in *The Ottawa Citizen* of December 20, 1992.

On anti-racist groups: editions of *The Monitor*, published by the Center for Democratic Renewal, in Atlanta, Georgia; annual audits of anti-Semitic incidents by the League for Human Rights of B'nai Brith Canada; *Hate Groups in Canada: Impact and Challenges*, by Martin Thériault with the Ministry of the Solicitor General of Canada, 1993; "Anti-Semitism is ominous: report" by Aaron Derfel, in *The Montreal Gazette* of March 3, 1993; "Ottawa racist attacks up 67%" by Andrew Philips, in *The Ottawa Sun* of March 3, 1993; "Jewish leaders play down report on anti-semitism" by Charles Lewis, in *The Ottawa Citizen* of March 4, 1993; "Racial bigotry growing," in *The Toronto Star* of August 12, 1993; and "Poll finds one in three hostile to minorities" by Roger Gillespie, in *The Ottawa Citizen* of April 10, 1993.

On hate groups in the U.S.: annual audits of anti-Semitic incidents by the Anti-Defamation League of B'nai Brith; *Propaganda of the Deed: The Far Right's Desperate Revolution*, a publication of the Anti-Defamation League of B'nai Brith, 1985; *The Pace Amendment* a report by the Anti-Defamation League of B'nai Brith, 1987; and *Racist and Far Right Organizing in the Pacific Northwest*, a report by the Center for Democratic Renewal, 1988.

INDEX

A

Abella, Irving, 402, 407, 428
Abells, R.S., 229
Aberhart, William, 362
Abugov, E., 359
Action Française, 354, 356
Adrian (ARA member), 291-292, 352, 357, 360, 362-364
Afrikaner Resistance Movement, 335
Aikenhead, Sherri, 224
Alberta Human Rights Commission, 11, 23, 171, 177, 201, 218, 220, 224
Alberta Press Act Reference, 415
Alberts, Sheldon, 195, 224, 432
Alexander, Carl, 273
Alliance for the Preservation of English in Canada, 260, 434
American Nazi Party, 59, 64, 106, 114, 203, 241
Anderson, J.T.M., 21
Anderson, John, 21, 406
Andre, Harvie, 401, 403-404
Andrews, Donald Clarke, 41, 242
Anti-Defamation League, 140, 155, 203, 332, 382, 428, 431, 438, 441-442; see also B'nai Brith
Anti-Racist Action, 283, 286-287, 290-291
Arbic, Richard, 318
Arcand, Adrian, 318
Armstrong, Dan
Arthur, Dwight, 97
Aryan Brotherhood, 257
Aryan Defence Network, 339
Aryan Fest, 186, 190-194, 196-198, 200-202, 218, 223-228, 235, 322-324, 334-339, 346, 349, 364-441
Aryan National State Platform, 229
Aryan Nations,1, 11, 24, 30, 32-33, 35, 40, 42-43, 46, 48-49, 51, 56, 58, 61-66, 89, 98, 101-105, 107, 111-114, 121-122, 124-126, 128-131, 134-135, 138-139, 144-145, 147, 150-152, 154, 159-171, 173-174, 177-179, 182, 184-186, 188-189, 191-194, 196-197, 201, 203-204, 206, 216, 218-222, 225, 230-231, 233-235, 256-257, 260, 263, 274-275, 297-298, 307-308, 314-315, 320, ·322, 324-325, 328, 349, 366, 374, 391, 395-396, 398, 403-405, 410, 421, 424-425, 429, 431-433, 440-441; see also Aryan Fest; Church of Jesus Christ Christian Aryan Nations; Silent Brotherhood
Aryan Nations Liberty Net, 65

Aryan Resistance Movement (ARM), 40, 58, 60-65, 69-71, 79, 105, 112, 151, 164, 172, 178, 214, 233, 267, 311, 316, 318, 322-323, 332, 383, 393, 429, 434, 440
Aryan Youth Movement, 339, 424
Atlantic Jewish Council, 379, 384
Attis, David, 370, 377, 385, 387, 390, 439
Attis, Yona, 387-388
Australian League of Rights, 154, 400
Axworthy, Lloyd, 400

B

B.C. Association for the Preservation of Canadian Values, 58
B'nai Brith, 140, 155, 171, 203, 281, 309, 332, 382, 384, 420, 428, 431-432, 434-435, 438, 441
Baldrey, Keith, 73
Barr, John, 54
Barrett, Stanley, 252, 428
Bauer, Daniel, 92, 122, 431
Bauer, Mark, 310, 312-313, 315-318, 321-323, 437
Bauer, Michelle, 323
Beam, Louis Ray, Jr., 11
Bear, Darwin Alvin, 208-210
Beattie, Hazel, 317
Beattie, John, 191, 243, 317-320, 433, 438
Beck, John, 2
Beisner, Ingrid, 313, 380, 437, 439
Belgrave, Phillip, 261, 380, 437
Belhumeur, Martin, 341
Bellamy, James R., 14
Bennett, R.B., 20, 354-355
Bennett, W.A.C. (Bill), 76
Benson, Ivor, 154
Bentham, Jeremy, 415
Bercovitch, Peter, 358
Berg, Alan, 123, 128, 135, 155, 160
Bergeron, Jean Pierre, 348
Bertling, Michael Joseph, 199
Betcherman, Lita Rose, 362
Beverley, James A., 386, 428
Bird, Alphonse, 218
Bishop, Maurice, 254
Black, Don, 203
Bobiwash, Rodney, 278
Boerstra, Janine, 322
Boguski, Rick, 199
Botting, Gary, 92, 95, 431
Botting, Heather, 95
Bourdon, Richard, 336
Bradley, Janet, 188, 220
Bradley, Ray, Jr., 188
Bradley, Raymond Maxwell, 188
Bradley, Wade, 188
Brewster, Kyle, 423

Bristow, Grant, 2, 235, 258-259, 273-274, 281, 293, 296, 298, 300
Bristow, Scott, 312, 437
British/European Immigration Aid Foundation, 58
British Imperial Fascist League, 354
British Israel, 108-109, 431
British League of Rights, 154
British Movement, 64, 304-307, 314-315
British People's League, 317
Britskie, Ernie, 57-60, 430
Bronfman family, 340
Brotherhood of Regular People/Brotherhood of Racial Purity (BHORP), 188, 191, 225, 227
Brothers, Richard, 108-109
Brownbridge, Gar Wallace, 213
Brownlee, J.E., 17
Bruce, Brian, 385, 388-389
Bryant, J.F., 21
Burdi, Andrew, 267
Burdi, George, 261-262, 264-265, 267-268, 270-271, 274-275, 283, 289-293, 339, 426, 433, 436
Burwell, L.E., 27
Butler, Betty, 106, 107
Butler, Clarence, 105
Butler, Eric, 153
Butler, Richard Girnt, 101-107, 110-114, 116, 118, 119, 121-123, 125, 127, 129, 135, 151, 153, 154, 159, 160, 161, 165, 172, 174, 185, 196, 203, 229, 231, 307, 311, 320, 431, 437, 442-443
Butz, Arthur R., 150, 158

C

Cairns, Alan, 319
California Committee to Combat Communism, 106
California Rangers, 107
Campbell, Kim, 77, 399-400, 404, 407
Canadian Airborne Regiment, 2, 291, 395, 399-400, 402, 405-406, 440
Canadian Anti-Jewish Front, 362
Canadian Armed Forces, 160, 178
Canadian Association for Free Expression, 310, 378, 389, 416, 434, 440
Canadian Association of Journalists, 221
Canadian Charter of Rights and Freedoms, 417
Canadian Congress of Black Women, 223
Canadian Forces' Administrative Order, 394
Canadian Free Speech League, 68, 83, 98
Canadian Human Rights Act, 421
Canadian Human Rights Commission, 66, 102, 170-171, 244, 277, 279, 283

Canadian Jewish Congress, 2, 66, 83, 93, 155, 221, 229, 272, 275, 281, 297-298, 316, 321, 348, 350, 377, 402, 407-408, 420, 434, 438
Canadian League of Rights, 32, 58, 69, 71, 154, 382-383, 416
Canadian Liberty Net, 1, 60, 64-68, 83, 98, 235, 275, 421, 425, 430
Canadian Nazi Party, 191, 243, 317-318
Canadian Resistance Movement, 384
Canadian Security Intelligence Service (CSIS), 2, 258-259, 285, 291, 293-300, 331, 351, 399, 431
Carlyle, Daniel C., 14
CAUSE (Canada, Australia, United States, South Africa and Europe), 40, 48, 56, 82, 92, 99-100, 133-134, 143, 160, 163, 171, 176, 178, 183, 185, 193, 243-244, 247, 271, 275, 302, 321, 323, 330, 332, 392, 398-399, 415-416
Center for Democratic Renewal and Education, 54
Charles, Mary Eugenia, 238
Charlottetown Accord, 79
Chicago-Area Skinheads, 307, 314
Chinese Immigration Act, 15
Christian, Tim, 221-222, 231-232
Christian Defence League of Canada, 32, 70, 90, 151, 157, 161, 185, 374-375, 379, 443-444, 446
Christian Defense League (Louisiana), 110, 152
Christian Defense League (Rev. Swift's), 151
Christian Identity, 38, 42, 48, 58, 64, 69, 107, 109, 122, 158, 185, 324, 431
Christian Nationalist Crusade, 107
Christian Patriots Defense League, 130, 155
Christie, Douglas, Sr., 431
Christie, Douglas Hewson, Jr., 53, 82-85
Chrétien, Jean, 395
Chumir, Sheldon, 201
Church of the Creator, 1, 261-263, 268-271, 274-276, 282, 284-287, 291, 293, 339, 349, 409, 426, 429, 436
Church of Jesus Christ Christian Aryan Nations, 42, 48, 101, 113, 121, 161, 170, 178, 185-186, 189, 191, 218-219, 225, 231, 234, 307, 374, 429-441
Church of the Living Faith, 146, 157
Citizens for Foreign Aid Reform, 266, 310, 416, 434
Citron, Sabina, 418
Clark, Brad, 197, 432
Clark, David, 375, 377
Clark, Joe, 87
Clarke, Edward Y., 12